PENGUI
BOLLYWOC

Ganesh Anantharaman spent the first thirty-two years of his life in Mumbai, where he acquired both his love for film music and an MPhil in political science. He taught that subject at the undergraduate level for six years, before moving on to training and development as his vocation after becoming professional member of the Indian Society for Applied Behavioural Sciences (ISABS) in 1998. He is currently an organization development consultant based in Bangalore, living there with his wife and five-year-old son.

Bollywood Melodies
A History of the Hindi Film Song

GANESH ANANTHARAMAN

Foreword by
MAHESH BHATT

PENGUIN BOOKS

PENGUIN BOOKS
Published by the Penguin Group
Penguin Books India Pvt. Ltd, 11 Community Centre, Panchsheel Park, New Delhi 110 017, India
Penguin Group (USA) Inc., 375 Hudson Street, New York, New York 10014, USA
Penguin Group (Canada), 90 Eglinton Avenue East, Suite 700, Toronto, Ontario, M4P 2Y3, Canada (a division of Pearson Penguin Canada Inc.)
Penguin Books Ltd, 80 Strand, London WC2R 0RL, England
Penguin Ireland, 25 St Stephen's Green, Dublin 2, Ireland (a division of Penguin Books Ltd)
Penguin Group (Australia), 250 Camberwell Road, Camberwell, Victoria 3124, Australia (a division of Pearson Australia Group Pty Ltd)
Penguin Group (NZ), 67 Apollo Drive, Rosedale, North Shore 0632, New Zealand (a division of Pearson New Zealand Ltd)
Penguin Group (South Africa) (Pty) Ltd, 24 Sturdee Avenue, Rosebank, Johannesburg 2196, South Africa

Penguin Books Ltd, Registered Offices: 80 Strand, London WC2R 0RL, England

First published by Penguin Books India 2008

Copyright © Ganesh Anantharaman 2008

All rights reserved

10 9 8 7 6 5 4 3

The views and opinions expressed in this book are the author's own and the facts are as reported by him which have been verified to the extent possible, and the publishers are not in any way liable for the same.

ISBN 9780143063407

Typeset in Goudy Old Style by SŪRYA, New Delhi
Printed at Repro India Ltd., Navi Mumbai

This book is sold subject to the condition that it shall not, by way of trade or otherwise, be lent, resold, hired out, or otherwise circulated without the publisher's prior written consent in any form of binding or cover other than that in which it is published and without a similar condition including this condition being imposed on the subsequent purchaser and without limiting the rights under copyright reserved above, no part of this publication may be reproduced, stored in or introduced into a retrieval system, or transmitted in any form or by any means (electronic, mechanical, photocopying, recording or otherwise), without the prior written permission of both the copyright owner and the above-mentioned publisher of this book.

For my parents
T.M. Anantharaman and Lalitha,
for gifting me the love of music

Acknowledgements

I would like to express my gratitude to the following people for their support at various points of time in writing this book:

My wife Kavitha who encouraged me to pursue my dream of writing this book, managing everything else uncomplainingly during all the months I was completely immersed in it; my son Ananth for gamely putting up with my kind of music being played round the clock; my journalist dad T.M. Anantharaman from whom I drew inspiration to write on music; my mother Lalitha and mother-in-law Padma for their loving understanding of my moods as writer; my colleague and friend Chitra for putting me in touch with Penguin early on; my commissioning editor Udayan Mitra for always being enthusiastic about whatever I wrote; copy editor Shantanu Ray Chaudhuri for his painstaking editing and invaluable suggestions; friends Hersh Kohli and T. Surendar for very patiently finding the contacts of all the Bollywood celebrities featured here; friend Rusi Engineer for giving me a home in Mumbai when I needed it for this book; and film-maker Mahesh Bhatt for generously agreeing to write a foreword.

Contents

Foreword: Mahesh Bhatt	xiii
Author's Note	xvii
The Journey of the Hindi Film Song	1

PART I: THE MELODY MAKERS

First-generation Composers: The Pioneers — 23
    Pankaj Mullick 23
    Khemchand Prakash 25
    Anil Biswas 26
    Naushad Ali 29

Second-generation Composers: The Masters — 35
    C. Ramchandra 35
    Shanker–Jaikishan 38
    S.D. Burman 42
    Madan Mohan 47
    O.P. Nayyar 50
    Salil Choudhury 54
    Roshan 58
    Hemant Kumar 58
    Ravi 60
    Jaidev 60
    Vasant Desai 62

Third-generation Composers: The Bravehearts   63
    Kalyanji–Anandji   63
    R.D. Burman   66
    Laxmikant–Pyarelal   70
    Khayyam   75
    Ravindra Jain   77

Fourth-generation Composers: The Followers   78
    Bappi Lahiri   78
    Rajesh Roshan   80
    A.R. Rahman   81
    Anand–Milind   82
    Nadeem–Shravan   83
    Annu Malik   84
    Jatin–Lalit   84
    Twenty-first-century Composers   85

Dev Anand Remembers S.D. Burman   86

Down Memory Lane with Pyarelal   89

PART II: THE SONGWRITERS

First-generation Lyricists   101
    Kidar Sharma   101
    D.N. Madhok   103
    Pradeep   104

Second-generation Lyricists   107
    Majrooh Sultanpuri   107
    Shakeel Badayuni   110
    Sahir Ludhianvi   112
    Shailendra   115
    Kaifi Azmi   118

Third-generation Lyricists   121
    Gulzar   121
    Anand Bakshi   124
    Javed Akhtar   127

Gulzar on the Poets of Hindi Film Music   130

PART III: THE PLAYBACK SINGERS

First-generation Singers 141
    K.L. Saigal 141
    Noorjehan 144
    Suraiya 146
    Shamshad Begum 148

Second-generation Singers 151
    Lata Mangeshkar 151
    Geeta Dutt 158
    Asha Bhonsle 162
    Mukesh 168
    Talat Mehmood 175
    Mohammed Rafi 178
    Kishore Kumar 187

Third-generation Singers 194
    Udit Narayan 194
    Kumar Sanu 195
    Anuradha Paudwal 196
    Kavita Krishnamurthy 197
    Sonu Nigam 198
    Alka Yagnik 198

Manna Dey: An Echo from the 200
    Golden Era of Hindi Film Music

Lata Mangeshkar on Other Playback Singers 206

Index of Songs 214
General Index 253

Foreword

Music surrounds us. And we Indians wouldn't have it any other way, would we? If you are an Indian and have been exposed to Hindi film music, just pause and look back through the mists of time, and you will discover that there is a tune buried somewhere in your consciousness which kick-started your first love affair. Without Bollywood melodies how would you have coped with those exhilarating and restless nights and days when you felt the first stirrings of attraction and passion? How would you have dealt with your achy breaky heart without the haunting melodies of love and betrayal sung by the icons of yesteryears like Mukesh, Rafi and the inimitable Kishore Kumar?

Don't you think it's time for you to raise a toast to a Sahir Ludhianvi or a Kaifi Azmi for giving you those life-altering insights that helped you grow from a boy to a young man? To acknowledge that the edge of the intense loneliness you felt was blunted by the soul-stirring melodies of Shanker–Jaikishan, Naushad, Madan Mohan and Laxmikant–Pyarelal? Whether you have lived through the 1940s, 1950s, 1960s or are a new millennium youngster, there is no getting away from the inescapable fact that without Bollywood music, your life would have been so much more parched and colourless. So, for those who want to revisit those times in their lives, this book by Ganesh Anantharaman, *Bollywood Melodies: A History of the Hindi Film Song*, is a true gem.

As I flipped through the first few pages of this work of love and nostalgia that this young writer has put together, it hurled me back into the pages of history where I was thrown into intimate contact with the works of icons of every age, who have pulled out jewels from their hearts and scattered them through the sands of time. It was akin to taking a sepia-tinted journey through those glorious watershed years of Hindi film music.

It was whilst reading about the 1930s, which was the era when the studios ruled, that I not only discovered that the first Hindi film song to be recorded in Indian cinema was from *Alam Ara* in the year 1931, but also something about my own genesis. The 1930s was the era when the talkies began and that in turn gave birth to the film song. And it was in the 1930s that my father came to Bombay, became a sound engineer and met my mother, who was an actress, which resulted in my birth nineteen years later in free India!

In my growing years, the highbrows who prescribed what is culturally correct looked down on Bollywood melodies. Those were the days when only classical music played on All India Radio and one had to tune into Radio Ceylon to listen to Ameen Sayani who would give us a sample of the Bollywood chartbusters every week in *Binaca Geetmala*. Those were the days when I would play huge LPs for my mother on a hand-operated old-fashioned gramophone, which you may find in Chor Bazaar's antique shops now. So much has changed since then! Today, my maid listens to music on her cellphone while washing the dishes, and FM Radio and TV programmes are making a killing selling Bollywood melodies.

But alas, as Ganesh laments, somewhere in the mid-1980s the Hindi film song started to lose its 'Indianness', and it was only in the early 1990s with movies such as *Aashiqui, Dil Hain Ki Maanta Nahin* and *Saajan*, and the arrival of Nadeem–Shravan, that there was a return to the intrinsic Indian melody. It's amazing that, in spite of being an outsider, and an organization development consultant to boot, Ganesh has been able to view the spectrum of the music industry's journey with such clarity and insight.

One of the most fascinating chapters of this book is his interview with Lata Mangeshkar, in which she talks about her childhood days when she was exposed to the music of Saigal. Noorjehan was her favourite among the female singing stars, and it was from her that she learnt the significance of Urdu diction. It is fascinating to read the nightingale of India emphasizing how critical it is for a singer to be able to articulate the words of a song in order for it to leave its true impact. And then in closing, she goes to the heart of the problem of our times when she says that it is the need for instant success today that has resulted in the disintegration of music. She minces no words when she states that it is because the Indian landscape today is bereft of mentors of the likes of Ghulam Haider, Anil Biswas and Naushad, under whom she had the privilege to study, that music has become so soulless and mindless. She clearly says it is not because the singers are less talented but because of the lack of composers today that we don't have music that endures. Ganesh needs to be applauded for getting the gentle and generous Lata to make such definitive and insightful comments and suggest ways to the practitioners of Indian film music to bail them out of this sterile phase that they are stuck in.

Remembering the past may seem like a mindless indulgence in nostalgia to many. There is no denying that the past is a collection of shadowed memories. Nonetheless these memories can help many of us connect with our lost heritage and help us shape our future. At times it is necessary for one to go back if one wants to go forward. The past chronicled in Ganesh's book can provide us with material for creating new tunes and weaving new myths. There is a magical 'there' yonder that will reveal itself if you look hard enough in the rear-view mirror of the past. Ganesh's book plays the part of that rear-view mirror. Come gaze into it.

October 2007   MAHESH BHATT

Author's Note

*T*he idea of writing a book on Hindi film music took hold of me way back in 1989, when I had just stepped into my twenties. It took me fifteen years to get down to writing it. But I guess, the book was taking shape in my mind during all the intervening years, as I kept listening to and thinking about the music of the 1950s and 1960s, firmly holding on to my belief that those were the most creative years for Hindi film music. Even if it amounted to a prejudice, I am glad to have nurtured it for so long, because it is on the strength of that conviction that I got started with this book.

Though I wasn't enthusiastic at the start, I agreed to my editor's suggestion that this book have a wider span, covering the origin, growth and decline of Hindi film music during the period 1935–2005. In retrospect, I am thankful to him, because in the course of writing this book, I have had the joy of discovering the music of the 1930s and 1940s, and the pleasure of rediscovering the music of the 1970s and 1990s. I don't know if I have substantially changed my belief that the 1950s and 1960s were the best years, but today I am more objective, less dismissive of the music of the later decades, and the people who made it.

This book is meant to be a history of the Hindi film song, but a selective one, through an account of the work of some of the most prominent musical personalities. The effort is not so much to provide complete or objective information to the reader, as much as convey my own subjective experience of the music all these people made. The opinions are mine; the choices on the personalities included in this book and those left out are mine too. Therefore, I take complete responsibility for the shortcomings of the book.

I am aware of many of them: factual errors being the first. For many films, there is no conclusive authority on the year of their release. The same confusion exists about the years of birth of some personalities. Perhaps it is the consequence of so little documentation being available on this genre. Secondly, this book does not talk much about the music of the twenty-first century. Partly because I don't find it very appealing, having always equated music with melody, but also because I think we are too close in time to be objective about the music of the present. Third, many musical personalities get only a passing mention; some not even that. The only defence I offer is that I have written about people who, in my opinion, mattered most to film music, and not about people who, despite talent, were insignificant in the overall scheme of things.

The Journey of the Hindi Film Song

In a nation with a rich tradition of folk music and two well-defined systems of classical music handed down over generations, it didn't take long for film music to emerge as the most popular. In a matter of decades, film songs have pervaded many aspects of Indian life—weddings, funerals, religious festivals, get-togethers or political conventions. Hindi film music is such an integral part of the musical consciousness of so many Indians that it merits the status of a separate genre: '*Hindustani Cine Sangeet*' as film music critic Raju Bharatan named it.

Music has always been integral to art forms in India, particularly drama and theatre. Be it the golden age of Sanskrit theatre in ancient India, Jatra in Bengali theatre, Kathakali of Kerala, or the Jashn of Kashmir, the use of song and music in drama has been a strong indigenous tradition over centuries. Thus, when music arrived in films in the early twentieth century, it inherited a rich legacy of song and dance.

Each decade since the 1930s saw Hindi film music grow from strength to strength, in the process absorbing the best of almost every other form of music that existed or emerged in India. If the 1930s were about the influence of Rabindra Sangeet from Bengal and Marathi Bhavgeet, the 1940s absorbed the best of folk music of north India. The 1950s saw the taming of Hindustani classical music and the 1960s Indianized pop and jazz. Though the next three decades were not remarkable for their innovativeness or for attempts to enlarge the scope of this genre, they have nevertheless given us a steady fare of hummable tunes.

THE 1930s: THE STUDIO ERA

Ardeshir Irani's *Alam Ara* (1931), India's first sound film, has gone down in history as the film that featured the first-ever song in Indian cinema. *'De de Khuda ke naam pe pyaare'* sang Wazir Mohammed Khan, and Indians have not stopped asking for more ever since.

The rudimentary recording facilities of those years meant that the songs had to be recorded even as the scene was being filmed, with the actors singing live. The musicians stayed outside the frame, sometimes atop trees! For all these constraints, *Alam Ara*, which had seven songs, spurred in its wake a spate of musicals in the early 1930s. *Indrasabha* (1932) reportedly had as many as sixty-nine songs while *Jawani Ki Hawa* and *Dhoop Chaon* (both 1935) boasted of at least a dozen each.

With the advent of talkies, the Hindi film song gave birth to a whole new industry of song-writing and composing. Thus began the studio era, where each of the major film studios had their own composers, lyricists and actors who originally hailed from Marathi, Parsi or Bengali theatre. Bombay Talkies, owned by producer Himanshu Rai, discovered Saraswati Devi, India's first woman composer. Her real name was Khursheed Minocher-Homji and she had learnt music from the well-known musician Pandit Vishnu Narayan Bhatkhande. Though she composed many songs with a classical base in the 1930s, her songs at Bombay Talkies, mainly in the voices of Devika Rani and Ashok Kumar with simple, nursery rhyme-like tunes such as in *'Main ban ki chidiya'* (*Achhut Kanya*, 1936), proved to be extremely popular.

Two other major studios that left their mark on Indian cinema in the 1930s and early 1940s were the Prabhat Film Company from Pune and New Theatres from Calcutta. The former's musical repertoire was shaped mainly by Bal Gandharva's Gandharva Natak Mandali which provided its two most famous music composers: Govindrao Tembe, who composed and sang *'Chhod aakash ko sitaare'* for *Maya Machhindra* (1932), and Master Krishnarao. Prabhat's musical output, as seen in films such as *Amritmanthan* (1934) and *Amar Jyoti* (1936), was rooted in the traditions of the Marathi Bhavgeet and Lavani, but composers were to soon move beyond Marathi roots and influence. Keshavrao Bhole at Prabhat was the first to use musical instruments such as the piano, the Hawaiian guitar and the violin in his compositions, banking on his experience of playing live for Western orchestras in theatres during the silent era. In *Duniya Na Maane* (1937), he even got lead actress Shanta Apte to sing an entire song in English! Prabhat's *Aadmi* (1939) was the first film with a multilingual song.

New Theatres was one of the most elite film banners of pre-independence India. The studio, with its highly educated personnel, gave films a respectability on par with literature. With stalwart composers like R.C. Boral, Pankaj Mullick and Timir Baran within its fold, New Theatres was instrumental in adapting Rabindra Sangeet to film music, creating many musical hits in the 1930s.

The 1930s were years of singing stars. New Theatres created the two most popular, Kundan Lal Saigal and Kanan Devi, while Shanta Apte reigned supreme at Prabhat. With the massively popular songs of *Chandidas* (1934) and *Devdas* (1935), Saigal became an icon. His reputation as singer far exceeded his popularity as film star. Kanan Devi came with the brooding sweetness of the Bengali voice, and was the number one female singing star at New Theatres, on par with Saigal after *Vidyapati* (1937). Her popularity in the initial stages was more due to her acting prowess, and it was only with songs like 'Aye chand chhup na jaana' and the racy 'Toofan mail' in *Jawaab* (1942) that she achieved glory as a singer.

Shanta Apte had pleasing looks, acting talent and a classically trained voice that made her the most popular singing star of Prabhat in the 1930s. When she sang, she managed to convey a zest for life through her mellifluous voice. Her songs 'Kamsini mein dil pe gham Ka' (*Amritmanthan*) and 'Suno suno, ban ke prani' (*Amar Jyoti*) were big hits. The contrast between the zest of Shanta Apte's voice and the melancholic strains of Saigal's and Kanan Devi's could also be attributed to the difference in the themes that Prabhat and New Theatres tackled in their films. The latter had an atmosphere of doom to many of its films (*Devdas, Street Singer*) while Prabhat's V. Shantaram focussed on redemption and hope (*Amar Jyoti, Duniya Na Maane, Aadmi*).

In terms of sheer popularity, Saigal towered over everyone else in the 1930s. For the connoisseur of Hindi film music, this era is all about Saigal. K.C. Dey and Pankaj Mullick sang well, but they could never match the Saigal magic. With his free-flowing, largely untrained voice, it was Saigal who defined melody in the male voice for all times to come. His ability to convey pathos in the shades of Raag Des in *'Dukh ke ab din'* (*Devdas*) and Raag Bhairavi in *'Babul mora'* (*Street Singer*, 1938), remains unmatched till date.

The year 1935 saw the biggest revolution in the development of the Hindi film song. At New Theatres, Nitin Bose, along with his younger brother Mukul Bose and music director R.C. Boral introduced pre-recorded singing. The song was first recorded and then played back and picturized, thus freeing the artiste and the camera from the bondage of the microphone. This was for the film *Dhoop Chaon*. Initially, even as songs were recorded and picturized in this manner, artistes continued to sing their own songs. However, this process paved the way for trained musicians and singers to enter the film industry. Now songs could be recorded in the voice of a playback singer, and shot on a different actor. The advent of playback freed composers from the limitations of the actors' voices, and was to inspire awesome creativity in the 1940s.

THE 1940s: THE FOLK INFLUENCE

The 1940s saw the integration of folk songs of Punjab and other parts of north India into Hindi film music, giving it a more robust and less melancholic feel than the 1930s. A host of new composers aided by new playback singers were responsible for this shift. Lahore-born Ghulam Haider introduced the folk music of Punjab to the beats of the dholak in the film *Khazanchi* (1941). The film also saw the debut of singer Shamshad Begum, who was noticed for her nasal yet hearty voice in the song *'Ek kali naazon se pali'*. By 1946, Shamshad was to overtake all other female playback singers. Ghulam Haider had an uncanny knack for spotting singing sensations. It was he who gave Noorjehan her Hindi break in *Khandan* (1942) and Lata Mangeshkar her first big hit in *Majboor* (1948).

Anil Biswas, who had started composing in 1937, was to emerge as a force to reckon with when he joined Bombay Talkies. His *Kismet* (1943) was one of the biggest hits of the decade, with the Ameerbai Karnataki–Aroon Kumar duet *'Dheere dheere aare badal'* and the patriotic *'Door hato aye duniyawalon'* capturing the imagination of the nation. Anil Biswas went on to create a string of melodies through the 1940s and 1950s. Lucknow-born Naushad

Ali started composing in 1940 with *Prem Nagar* and created a sensation with his folk-based tunes in *Rattan* (1944). The song '*Akhiyan milake*' sung by Zohrabai Ambalewali was to give a new fillip to the folk wave of the 1940s, furthered by Naushad in films like *Anmol Ghadi* (1946), *Dard* (1947) and *Dillagi* (1949).

By the mid-1940s, Naushad, Ghulam Haider and Anil Biswas had surged far ahead of all the composers of the 1930s in terms of the sheer popularity of their songs. Other composers like Shyam Sunder, Sajjad Hussain, Khemchand Prakash and Husnlal–Bhagatram were also making their mark. Punjabi folk had replaced Marathi Bhavgeet and Bengali Rabindra Sangeet as the new flavour in Hindi film music.

With the songs of *Shahjehan* in 1946, Shamshad had emerged as the lead female playback singer. Naushad preferred the 'transparency' in Shamshad's voice to Zohra and Ameerbai's more melodious and rounded voices, helping Shamshad inch past the two formidable singers. Mohammed Rafi made a tepid entry with the song '*Hindustan ke hum hain Hindustan hain hamara*' for Naushad in *Pehle Aap* (1944). Mukesh was luckier, getting noticed for Anil Biswas's '*Dil jalta hain toh jalne de*' in *Pehli Nazar* (1945), which he sang in a style strongly reminiscent of Saigal.

The strides playback singers made in the 1940s notwithstanding, the nation was most in love with the voice of a new singing star— Noorjehan. Over a span of just six years (1942–47) and barely a dozen films, Noorjehan acquired a reputation that equalled Saigal's. Like Saigal, she had something more than every other singer of that time: the sheer melody of her voice. She also had the uncanny ability to be in touch with the feeling of the song, and used her classical training to embellish every song unobtrusively. Her songs in *Anmol Ghadi*, '*Awaaz de kahaan hain*' and '*Jawan hain mohabbat*', bear testimony to this ability, and represent the best work of the decade. Much like Saigal's influence on every male singer, Noorjehan was to become the role model for all female playback singers of the era.

1947: A WATERSHED YEAR

The year 1947 was a significant one in the history of Hindi film music. K.L. Saigal died early that year, succumbing to alcoholism, ironically leaving his fans with the strains of '*Jab dil hi toot gaya, hum jeeke kya karenge*', his last hit from *Shahjehan*. Lata Mangeshkar made her debut in the Hindi film *Aap Ki Sewa Mein*, Geeta Dutt gained stardom with the songs of *Do Bhai*, and Suraiya had her first big hit in *Dard*. Mohammed Rafi had his first hit in the duet '*Yahan badla wafa ka*' with Noorjehan in *Jugnu*. Perhaps the biggest surprise was that films continued to be made and film music remained ever popular, despite the trauma of partition.

The biggest blow of partition to the world of Indian film music was Noorjehan's move to Pakistan. Like Saigal, it was almost as though she had a foreboding of the future: her last solo in the film *Jugnu* was the melancholic '*Hamein toh shaam-e-gham mein kaatni hai zindagi apni*'. Noorjehan's exit was to pave the way for Lata to take over as the custodian of her musical legacy. It also helped Suraiya occupy the number one position as the singing star in the years 1947 to 1950.

The year was critical for Hindi film music also because of the people who decided to stay back in India. Naushad made that choice, thereby going on to create all the hits in the late 1940s through to the 1960s. There would have been no *Daastan* (1950), *Baiju Bawra* (1952) or *Mughal-e-Azam* (1960) if Naushad had moved to Pakistan. Mohammed Rafi had come from Lahore in 1944, and though he was still struggling in 1947, decided to stay. To think that we could have been denied Naushad or Rafi in 1947! The soul of Hindi film music would have been lost.

1947–50: THE SECOND GENERATION TAKES OVER

The impact of the partition continued to be felt even after 1947. Ghulam Haider saw many of his musicians migrate to Pakistan, and after a period of indecision, he too quit India in 1949, after his last hit *Shaheed* (1948). With recent hits like *Majboor* (1948) and *Shaheed* to his credit, Ghulam Haider could have posed a threat to Naushad's ascent had he stayed on. At the same time, Partition also saw the coming of new talent from across the border, which would infuse the Hindi film music scene with vigour and creativity. Sahir Ludhianvi decided to move from Lahore to Delhi in 1948, finding Lahore stifling his freedom. He went on to become one of the most respected lyricists ever in Hindi cinema.

Another composer who was Bombay's gain post partition was Omkar Prasad Nayyar who moved from Lahore in the late 1940s to try his luck with films in Bombay. A decade later, O.P. Nayyar had become the highest paid composer.

The late 1940s saw a sudden infusion of new talent into film music. The new playback singers, Mukesh, Mohammed Rafi, Lata Mangeshkar and Geeta Dutt, were well on their way to displacing the earlier lot of singers by 1949. With her sweet if rather uncertain voice finding instant acceptance, Suraiya had become the newest singing star sensation after a string of hits under the baton of Naushad. Second-generation composers such as C. Ramchandra, Shanker–Jaikishan and S.D. Burman also had their breakthroughs in the late 1940s. Those years also saw new lyricists emerge. Majrooh Sultanpuri, Shailendra and Sahir Ludhianvi were to play a significant role in giving poetry in Hindi films the status of serious art.

C. Ramchandra, much to the dismay of his mentor Anil Biswas, created the next revolution by legitimizing fun and frolic in film music with his snazzy tune of '*Aana meri jaan Sunday ke Sunday*' in *Shehnai* (1947). If the decade began with the freshness of Punjabi folk, it ended with the freewheeling lyrics of '*Mere piya gaye Rangoon, wahan se kiya hain telephone*' (*Patanga*, 1949), again composed by C. Ramchandra.

With her songs in *Andaaz* (1949), Lata had moved firmly into the Naushad camp, displacing Shamshad Begum. What helped Lata were also the songs from *Barsaat*, composed by the new duo Shanker–Jaikishan. From *Barsaat* began the Raj Kapoor-Shanker-Jaikishan-Lata-Mukesh-Shailendra musical journey that went on to create many more hits well into the 1960s.

Naushad also groomed Rafi as his lead playback singer with the songs in *Andaaz* and *Dulaari* (1949). The latter film had Rafi's career-defining song '*Suhaani raat dhal chuki*', on the strength of which Rafi was to rule filmdom for two decades.

THE 1950s: WHEN CLASSICAL REIGNED SUPREME

If Lata seamlessly replaced Shamshad as Naushad's lead singer, she also obliterated other seniors like Ameerbai, Zohrabai and Rajkumari. Pitted against her formidable talent, the fledgling careers of others like Uma Devi (who later became famous as comedienne Tuntun) didn't stand a chance. The only competition she really faced was from Geeta Dutt. By 1950, Lata and Geeta were neck to neck in the race to the top. With the release of *Mahal* (1950) and her bewitching '*Aayega aanewala*', Lata emerged as a clear winner. Geeta moved on to the sexy, sultry numbers that Lata would not sing. Thus, the best in the music of the 1950s and 1960s came to be created with the help of Lata's vocals.

While film music in the 1940s was basically folk-based, the 1950s saw the arrival of classical music with a bang. It was Naushad who spearheaded this wave, supported by other composers like Anil Biswas, Roshan and Madan Mohan, all of whom made Hindustani classical music accessible to the layperson in the voices of Lata and Rafi. By the mid-1950s, the ability to sing classical songs had become essential to a playback singer. Those who couldn't, like Shamshad Begum, were banished from the scene.

With *Baiju Bawra*, Naushad started a trend of classical music in films, composing every song to a different raag. He was perhaps biding his time, and found the inspiration for classical compositions once he had playback singers of the calibre of Lata and Rafi. Lata's '*Mohe bhool gaye sanwariya*' in Raag Bhairav and Rafi's '*Man tarpat Hari darshan ko*' in Raag Malkauns gave film music a new respectability that did not exist earlier. *Baiju Bawra* also brought classical music closer to the ordinary filmgoer, who loved the songs, even if he didn't know the raags in which they were composed!

Like most success stories, *Baiju Bawra* spawned a classical revolution in Hindi films. Every composer, old and new, had to prove his mettle with a classical score. C. Ramchandra created the immortal songs of *Anarkali* (1953) in Lata's voice; Shanker–Jaikishan had old-timer Anil Biswas gasping with their awesome classical score of *Basant Bahar* (1956); Vasant Desai moved out of the Marathi Bhavgeet and Lavani constraints by composing for *Jhanak Jhanak Payal Baaje* (1955) and *Goonj Uthi Shehnai* (1959), the latter having no less a maestro than Ustad Bismillah Khan playing the shehnai! The trend of a predominantly classical score continued into the 1960s with Roshan's *Taj Mahal* (1963) and S.D. Burman's *Guide* (1965).

Alongside the classical, the ghazal acquired a musical identity through Hindi films in the 1950s. Ghulam Mohammed's score for

Mirza Ghalib (1954), where Suraiya sang 'Nukta cheen hain' and Talat Mehmood rendered 'Dil-e-naadan tujhe hua kya hain', was as significant a happening as the classical revolution that started with Baiju Bawra. Though less spectacular, the ghazal wave continued right through the 1950s and 1960s. Madan Mohan, more than any other composer, ensured that the filmi ghazal was an enduring musical form. His ghazals in Adalat (1958), 'Unko yeh shikayat hain' and 'Yun hasraton ki daagh', both rendered by Lata, and in Dekh Kabira Roya (1957), Talat's 'Humse aaya na gaya', are a case in point. Talat Mehmood was the primary male vocalist of the filmi ghazal. Lata, of course, was the favourite female playback for ghazals.

WESTWARD HO!

On the lighter side, the 1950s also saw Western influence on film music like never before. The influence of pop and rock music in Hindi films began in the 1950s, in the form of rock 'n' roll numbers. C. Ramchandra was the first to dare to westernize film songs, though Punkaj Mullick had, a decade earlier, westernized interlude music. Heavily influenced by Benny Goodman, C. Ramchandra introduced the use of Western instruments in a big way, using the alto sax in combination with the guitar, harmonica and also whistling. Throughout his career, Ramchandra continued working with Western sounds; even assimilating scat singing and rock rhythms as he brought a freewheeling hip approach to the Hindi film song. 'Aana meri jaan Sunday ke Sunday', 'Gore gore, o baanke chore' (Samadhi, 1950) and the path-breaking duet with Lata, 'Shola jo bhadke' in Albela (1951), set a new trend of fast-paced, jazzy numbers. S.D. Burman followed suit by turning Sahir's lyrics of 'Tadbeer se bigdi hui' in Baazi (1951) into a racy Western tune, shocking Sahir who intended it to be a ghazal! O.P. Nayyar created perhaps the biggest hit of the decade with the rock 'n' roll number 'Mera naam Chin Chin Choo' (Howrah Bridge, 1958), making it mandatory thereafter for even seasoned composers like Naushad and Anil Biswas to give in to the trend of including a cabaret or rock 'n' roll number in their films. Geeta Dutt survived the Lata onslaught by effortlessly going Western. The fledgling careers of Asha Bhonsle and Kishore Kumar too benefited from the rock 'n' roll invasion.

BIG BANNERS AND MUSIC

The third dimension to the growth of film music in the 1950s, apart from composers and singers, was the establishment of independent production banners by the film-maker trio of Raj Kapoor, Dev Anand and Guru Dutt. Each banner came to be identified with a particular kind of music. RK with the simple yearnings of the common man, so effectively penned by Shailendra and articulated by the unpretentious voice of Mukesh in songs like *'Awara hoon'* (*Awara*, 1951) and *'Mera joota hain Japani'* (*Shri 420*, 1955); Dev Anand's carefree approach to life conveyed through Kishore Kumar's voice in *'Hum hain raahi pyaar ke'* (*Nau Do Gyarah*, 1957); Guru Dutt's despair and cynicism evidenced in *'Yeh duniya agar mil bhi jaaye toh kya hain'* (*Pyaasa*, 1957) or *'Bichde sabi baari baari'* (*Kaagaz Ke Phool*, 1959) in Rafi's voice, all constitute an important part of the music of the decade.

Apart from the new musical frontiers conquered, the decade was also significant for putting playback singers at the centre of film music. In the preceding decades it was the composer who reigned supreme. Barring Saigal, it did not matter who sang the song. The 1950s changed all that. Lata, Rafi, Talat, Hemant Kumar, Mukesh, Geeta Dutt and Manna Dey became household names. It became difficult to say if Lata and Rafi created Naushad's success or vice versa.

In terms of setting standards in film music, the 1950s were a benchmark of sorts—the best in filmi classical, ghazal, rock 'n' roll or waltz happened then. It was the most 'original' decade in film music, influencing, like no other, everything that happened subsequently in film music.

THE 1960s: RHYTHM TRIUMPHS OVER MELODY

FROM CLASSICAL TO GHAZAL

The filmi ghazal which originated in the 1950s truly came into its own in the early 1960s. Roshan's *Barsaat Ki Raat* (1960) that had Rafi singing *'Zindagi bhar nahin bhoolegi woh barsaat ki raat'* inaugurated the ghazal wave. Madan Mohan, Roshan and Naushad outdid each other in composing ghazals to the lyrics of Sahir, Majrooh and Shakeel Badayuni. The result was a plethora of ghazals in films like *Sanjog* (1961), *Mere Mehboob* (1963), *Taj Mahal* (1963), *Woh Kaun Thi* (1964), *Mamta* (1966) and *Dil Diya Dard Liya* (1966). Madan Mohan steered the ghazal wave brilliantly with songs like '*Lag jaa gale*' (*Woh Kaun Thi*), '*Tu jahaan jahaan chalega*' (*Mera Saaya*, 1966) and '*Naghma-o-sher ki saugaat kise pesh karoon*' (*Ghazal*, 1964) all in his favourite singer Lata's voice. What is arguably Rafi's best ghazal was composed by S.D. Burman's assistant Jaidev in Navketan's *Hum Dono* (1961). '*Kabhi khud pe kabhi haalaat pe rona aaya*' could well have been Jaidev's own lament, as this talented composer had to remain content with B-grade movies despite being so erudite. Increasingly aware that his days in films were numbered, Talat too put his heart and soul into '*Phir wohi shaam wohi gham*' in *Jahan Ara* (1964), tuned yet again by Madan Mohan.

The Swinging 60s

The ghazal wave of the early 1960s was short-lived. Mainstream cinema during the decade was bursting with the suppressed sexuality of youth, and this needed a more forceful expression than what the ghazal would allow. To appreciate how music changed in the 1960s, we have to understand the social context of the music in the previous decade. For all its creativity, music in the 1950s rarely challenged the existing social conventions, except for a socialist outlook in a few films and songs ('*Jinhe naaz hain Hind par*' in *Pyaasa*; '*Woh subah kabhi toh aayegi*' in *Phir Subah Hogi* [1958] for instance). The hero was usually a gentleman and the heroine the girl next door, who only shyly responded to his overtures. Only the vamp in the nightclub sang the 'naughty' songs. In the few films where the hero was a smuggler or a gangster, the heroine reformed him in the end. There was a very black and white view of morality in the films that got reflected in the kind of music made.

One man changed all that. Shammi Kapoor started out as a gentleman lover in *Laila Majnu* (1954). But by the time of *Tumsa Nahin Dekha* (1958), he had acquired the image of the happy-go-lucky hero, which was further developed in films like *China Town* (1962) where he could brazenly sing '*Baar baar dekho*' to his heroine in the club. But it was with *Junglee* (1963) that Shammi broke the final chain of restraint and proclaimed to the world that he did not care what the world thought of him—'*Chahe koi mujhe junglee kahe, kehne do ji kehta rahe*'. After *Junglee*, the time for gentle romance and therefore ghazals was over. The hero who would tease the heroine had arrived. It was time for celebrating all the wildness of youth. Other films like *Jaanwar* (1965), *Teesri Manzil* (1966) and *Brahmachari* (1969) further developed this image of Shammi Kapoor, and by extension the 1960s hero. Between Shanker–Jaikishan, Rafi and Shammi Kapoor, a new kind of wild music was born which resonated with joie de vivre. In fact, it was Shammi Kapoor who started the trend of music in the film being determined by the hero.

If the hero was brazen in his declaration of love, the heroine was not far behind. The 1960s also saw the heroines becoming bolder, making their attraction to the hero very plain. Asha Parekh singing '*Aaja aaja main hoon pyar tera*' in *Teesri Manzil* would have been unthinkable for a heroine a few years ago. The heroines of the era—Asha Parekh, Sharmila Tagore and Mumtaz—were all game for the new image of the carefree heroine. Even Vyjayanthimala gave in to this trend in *Sangam* (1964) with the song '*Main kaa karun Ram, mujhe buddha mil gaya*' in the oh-so-careful Lata's vocals.

Film music certainly became louder as the jazz–pop wave overtook the classical–ghazal surge. The latter half of the 1960s were years of fusion music, heavily influenced by the West. It was almost as though the coming of age of rock and pop in the West had its impact on Hindi film music too. Films like *Teesri Manzil*, *Jewel Thief* (1967) and *Brahmachari* typified this trend. Purists like Naushad and Anil Biswas decided to retire, whereas Shanker–Jaikishan and S.D. Burman moved with the times. But the senior Burman's failing health and the split between Shanker and Jaikishan left the field open for the third-generation composers Kalyanji–Anandji, R.D. Burman and Laxmikant–Pyarelal to take over.

Lata zealously guarded her top position from any competition, even agreeing to her first cabaret number '*Aa jaan-e-jaan*' in *Inteqam* (1969). Rafi juggled, with some effort, '*Kisko pyar karoon*' for Shammi Kapoor in *Tumse Achcha Kaun Hai* (1967) and '*Teri aankhon ke siva*' for Sunil Dutt in *Chirag* (1969). Asha Bhonsle came into her own after years of obscurity, occupying the slot vacated by Geeta with songs like '*Jaayiye aap kahaan jaayenge*' in

Mere Sanam (1964) and 'Aage bhi jaane na tu' in Waqt (1964). Talat, Hemant and Manna Dey struggled to stay in the race but did not quite succeed. The most significant event of the late 1960s was Kishore Kumar zooming to the top with his songs in Aradhana (1969), ending two decades of Rafi dominance. The RD–Kishore team would define the contours of film music for the whole of the next decade and a half.

THE 1970s: MUSIC BECOMES SECONDARY

With the classical wave of the 1950s and the ghazal wave of the 1960s having retreated, music in the 1970s was struggling for a distinct identity. The pop–jazz revolution that began in the latter half of the 1960s continued to gain momentum under the baton of R.D. Burman who experimented like never before with the synthesiser and electronic instruments. With the help of Kishore Kumar and Asha Bhonsle's vocals, RD created mega hits like Kati Patang (1970), Yaadon Ki Baraat (1973) and Hum Kisi Se Kum Nahin (1977). The latter two are landmark films, in the sense that they ushered in the disco trend in Hindi films.

The 1970s were the years of R.D. Burman. No other composer mattered. RD could, much like his father, effortlessly straddle the pop and the classical world. He got Asha to sing her sexiest number 'Mera naam hain Shabnam' in Kati Patang, and Lata to emote the classical 'Raina beeti jaaye' in Amar Prem (1971) just a year later. Right through the decade, RD continued to deliver one musical hit after another.

He could not have done that but for Kishore Kumar. After twenty years of relative obscurity, Kishore came into his own as the voice of Rajesh Khanna in Aradhana (1969), singing 'Mere sapnon ki rani kab aayegi tu' and 'Roop tera mastana'. He was responsible in no small measure for Rajesh Khanna's superstardom. Both Kishore and Khanna scaled new heights with songs like 'Yeh jo mohabbat hain' (Kati Patang), 'Kuch toh log kahenge' (Amar Prem), 'Diwana leke aaya hain' (Mere Jeevan Saathi, 1972) and 'Main shayar badnaam' (Namak Haram, 1973), all composed by RD. With his ability to convey all shades of love and longing with a simple directness, Kishore ousted Rafi as the lead male playback singer in 1970, and ruled filmdom till his death in 1987. Much like Rafi in the 1960s, Kishore was the voice of every hero—Rajesh Khanna, Amitabh Bachchan, Dharmendra, Rishi Kapoor and others.

Despite Kishore and R.D. Burman, music became less critical to films in the 1970s. They were years when action became more important than romance in cinema, with revenge replacing love as the reason for existing. Amitabh Bachchan was the new superstar, and music was not important in his films like *Zanjeer*, *Sholay* and *Deewar*. His films were a rage because of his charisma, his fights and dialogues. Though there were other superstars too—Rajesh Khanna, Dharmendra, Hema Malini and Rekha to name a few—people came to films to see and hear their favourite stars and not quite for the music.

If mainstream cinema concentrated on action and dialogues, the decade also saw a steady stream of small-budget films that had good music. Much of the nostalgia for that decade is for the music of films like *Parichay* (1972), *Aandhi* (1975), *Chhoti Si Baat* (1975), *Chitchor* (1976), *Kinara* (1977) and *Ghar* (1978). Every composer—from RD to Laxmikant–Pyarelal to Kalyanji–Anandji—tried to fulfil their creative urges by composing for these films. The RD–Gulzar team in particular came up with some beautiful music in the films directed by Gulzar. The songs from these films continued to have their own quiet appeal, along with mega musical hits like *Yaadon Ki Baarat* and *Hum Kisi Se Kum Nahin*. Lyricist Anand Bakshi rose to prominence in the 1970s, working consistently with RD and Laxmikant–Pyarelal to produce hits.

Looking back, the 1970s were years when film music declined in quality and importance. The first-generation composers, singers and lyricists were long gone, many of the second generation had all but retired. With Rafi's death in 1980, the best articulator of melody was gone.

THE 1980s: AN ALL-TIME LOW

A decade music lovers dread to look back on, the 1980s were years when mainstream film music hit an all-time low. Things had started deteriorating by the late 1970s, but the 1980s confirmed that melody had lost irrevocably. The decade began promisingly enough with RD's mega-hit score for *Love Story* (1980) that had Amit Kumar and Lata emoting 'Yaad aa rahi hain', and new composer duo Shiv–Hari's refreshing music for *Silsila* (1981) where

Lata beautifully rendered 'Yeh kahan aa gaye hum', but the hope was to be short-lived. Whether it was the big-budget movies with Big B (*Namak Halal, Sharaabi*), the low-budget Mithun Chakravarty starrers (*Disco Dancer, Suraksha*) or the crass Jeetendra–Sridevi movies from the south (*Himmatwala, Mawali*), with composer Bappi Lahiri ruling the roost, what passed for music were songs such as 'Nainon mein sapna' (*Himmatwala*, 1981), 'I am a disco dancer' (*Disco Dancer*, 1982) and 'Aaj rapat jaaye' (*Namak Halal*, 1982). Old-timers Kalyanji–Anandji and Laxmikant–Pyarelal succumbed to the Bappi phenomenon, churning out banalities like 'Saat saheliyan khadi khadi' and 'Udi baba udi baba' in *Vidhaata* (1982) and 'Tu mera hero hain' in *Hero* (1983) respectively. The first half of the decade was the bleakest for the Hindi film song. It looked like music had lost its relevance to films.

Raj Kapoor's *Ram Teri Ganga Maili* (1985) was a notable exception, where Lata got her equation right with composer Ravindra Jain and sang the title song and 'Sun sahiba sun' with melody and spirit. Unfortunately for the music lover, Raj Kapoor's fascination with actress Mandakini's figure overshadowed the beauty of the score. The music of the film had a dignity that the film itself lacked. But it remained a flash in the pan; the trend of listless music continued unimpeded into the latter half of the 1980s, with box office hits *Karma* ('Mera karma tu, mera dharma tu', 1986), *Mr. India* ('Hawa Hawaii', 1987), *Tezaab* ('Ek do teen', 1988), *Ram Lakhan* ('One two ka four', 1989), and *Tridev* ('Oye, Oye', 1989) rubbishing poetry and music further. Composer Khayyam's lonely attempts to keep melody and poetry alive with his scores of *Umrao Jaan* ('Dil cheez kya hain', 1981), *Bazaar* ('Dikhayee diye yun', 1982), and *Razia Sultan* ('Aye dil-e-naadan', 1983) found little support, except from RD in *Masoom* ('Do naina aur ek kahani', 1982), *Sunny* ('Jaane kya baat hain', 1984) and *Saagar* ('Saagar kinare', 1985). Jagjit and Chitra Singh's score for *Arth* (1982), which remains their best ever, provided respite with songs like 'Tum itna jo muskura rahe ho' and 'Jhuki jhuki si nazar', as did their rendering of Kuldeep Singh's heartfelt compositions in *Saath Saath* ('Tumko dekha toh yeh khayal aaya*, 1982).

Poetry and melody which had moved out of Hindi films sought refuge in ghazals, as seen in the rapid rise to stardom of the premier ghazal couple Jagjit and Chitra Singh in the 1980s. It was not a coincidence that the bleakest decade in film music was also the best one for the non-film ghazal in India. Besides Jagjit and Chitra, other ghazal artistes like Talat Aziz and Pankaj Udhas also had their moment of glory during this period.

Just when obituaries were being written for film music, two films, both teenage love stories, both releasing in the late 1980s, resurrected the Hindi film song. Both had unknown composers. The Aamir Khan–Juhi Chawla love story *Qayamat Se Qayamat Tak* had debutant composer duo Anand–Milind create hits in newcomer Udit Narayan's voice with songs like '*Papa kahte hain*' and '*Aye mere hamsafar*'. Ram Laxman's easy-on-the-ear score in the Salman Khan debut *Maine Pyar Kiya* ('*Dil deewana bin sajna ke maane naa*') was such a rage that it single-handedly turned HMV around. The music in both films was catchy and clean, remarkable in itself given the general milieu of the 1980s. They revived the era of teenage love stories and musicals.

Lata's flagging career received a new lease of life with the songs of *Maine Pyar Kiya* and was further consolidated the next year with *Lekin* (1990), where composer Hridaynath Mangeshkar and lyricist–director Gulzar came up with a breathtaking score. *Qayamat Se Qayamat Tak* brought Alka Yagnik and Udit Narayan into the limelight. Lata, Alka and Udit were to be significant to the music of the next decade.

THE 1990s: RETURN OF THE MUSICALS

Predictably enough, the success of *Qayamat Se Qayamat Tak* and *Maine Pyar Kiya* set a new trend for the 1990s, leading to a complete overhaul in film music. A spate of romantic musicals, all with new actors and actresses, new composers, new lyricists and new singers were released. The power of music in film was rediscovered, particularly for love stories.

Aashiqui (1990), *Dil* (1990) and *Dil Hain Ki Maanta Nahin* (1991) were all musical hits. *Aashiqui* deserves special mention as it was a rare case where all six songs from a film became popular, a feat achieved earlier only by S.D. Burman with the songs of *Guide* in the 1960s and *Abhimaan* in the 1970s. New composer duo Nadeem–Shravan hit stardom right away. The film also turned the fortunes of Kumar Sanu, who brought back memories of Kishore with his style of singing ('*Saason ki zaroorat hain jaise*',

'*Ab tere bin jee lenge hum*') and was to reign as the top male singer of the decade. *Aashiqui* also saw Anuradha Paudwal get her due with duets like '*Main duniya bhula doongi*' and '*Tu meri zindagi hain*', after languishing for two decades. When Nadeem–Shravan, Kumar Sanu and Anuradha Paudwal achieved the same magic with the songs of *Dil Hain Ki Maanta Nahin*, it was clear that the fourth generation had taken over.

With these two films, a new revolution in the music industry occurred. Little known Gulshan Kumar's music company T-Series managed to break the monopoly of HMV in the audio industry with *Aashiqui* and *Dil Hain Ki Maanta Nahin*. The company and its founder were accused of murky deals that resulted in the murder of Gulshan Kumar in 1996, but the contribution of T-Series to promoting new talent in film music was significant. In their initial phase, composers Nadeem–Shravan, Anand–Milind and Annu Malik; singers Anuradha Paudwal, Alka Yagnik and Kumar Sanu and also lyricist Sameer gained a lot from the company. The T-Series success story also spawned other recording companies like Tips and Magnasound in its wake.

Film music lost the genius of R.D. Burman in 1994, when he succumbed to a heart attack. But not before letting the world know that he still had it in him, with the songs of *1942–A Love Story*. '*Ek ladki ko dekha to aisa laga*' and the heart-stopper '*Kuch na kaho*' represent Kumar Sanu's peak as a singer, and made RD's passing away all the more poignant. In his last years, RD chose to remain without work rather than compose something as crass as '*Choli ke peeche kya hain*' (*Khalnayak*, 1993) that his contemporaries Laxmikant–Pyarelal, in their desperate bid to remain popular, composed. Hearteningly for music lovers, the RD legacy was to be carried forward by composer duo Jatin–Lalit, who were arrangers for RD and who had inherited his talent for an uncanny combination of melody and rhythm. With the song '*Tujhe dekha toh ye jaana sanam*' in the blockbuster *Dilwale Dulhaniya Le Jaayenge* (1995), Jatin–Lalit zoomed to the top.

The industry's most successful composer duo Laxmikant–Pyarelal remained a formidable presence in the early 1990s, with their popular, even if unmusical, scores for *Hum* ('*Jumma chumma de de*', 1991) and *Khalnayak* ('*Choli ke peeche*', 1993). By the mid-1990s, Nadeem–Shravan, Anand–Milind and Annu Malik, all influenced by the LP style, had raced ahead. Laxmikant's death in

1997 brought to an end a thirty-five-year-old partnership that had earned them the nickname 'long-playing'.

The biggest phenomenon in music of the decade happened without any fanfare whatsoever. When Mani Ratnam dubbed his *Roja* (1993) in Hindi, little did he know he was creating history. Newcomer A.R. Rahman's refreshingly different score with a strong dose of melody ('*Dil hain chhota sa*', '*Roja jaaneman*') made him the most sought after composer of the 1990s and the new millennium. Never before had the Hindi film industry been so desperate for a composer from the south, who did not even know the language. With mega hits *Dil Se* and *Taal* in the late 1990s, Rahman brought back the composer as the person who mattered most for the success of the film.

The 1990s also brought Javed Akhtar into prominence, his outstanding lyrics for *1942—A Love Story* becoming a turning point in his career as lyricist. Javed Akhtar's songs in films such as *Border* ('*Sandese aate hain*', 1997) and *Yes Boss* ('*Chaand taare tod laoon*', 1997) were instrumental in bringing poetry back into film music.

On the whole, the 1990s were significant in the way music occupied centre stage in films once again. From *Saajan* (1991) to *Kaho Naa Pyaar Hain* (1999) it was music that made or unmade a movie at the box office. Blockbusters in the new millennium like Rahman's *Lagaan* (2001), Jatin–Lalit's *Kabhi Khushi Kabhi Gham* (2002) and the industry's first composer trio Shankar–Ehsaan–Loy's *Dil Chahta Hai* (2001) and *Kal Ho Na Ho* (2003) all banked in no small measure on music for their success. Film music today may have only a momentary appeal, but it is as firmly entrenched in films as in its heyday in the 1950s and 1960s.

PART I
The Melody Makers

Composers: The Heart and Soul of a Song

In many ways, the Hindi film song is a product of the heads and hearts of the composers. True, lyricists often inspire them to create even better tunes, and playback singers take their compositions to new heights with their voices and often their souls. But the genesis of the song is always in the mind of the composer. Without the creative genius of the composer, there simply wouldn't be a song.

The role that composers have played in Hindi film music goes much beyond the songs they created. They were instrumental in charting the course of film music, creating a separate genre of music in the process. Pankaj Mullick brought Rabindra Sangeet into films, Naushad, Hindustani classical, Madan Mohan, ghazals, and R.D. Burman, pop and jazz. Also, they were the godfathers who often gave breaks to struggling singers and lyricists. If Ghulam Haider had not trusted the genius in Lata, we could have been denied her. If Anil Biswas had not put his faith in Talat Mehmood's voice and Sahir's pen, we may have lost the ghazal king and the greatest lyricist in Hindi films. And these are just two instances. As Dev Anand shares in the interview at the end of this section, S.D. Burman was not just the preferred composer of his banner Navketan. Burman-da was a father figure whose opinion mattered in all aspects of Navketan films. It is not without reason that for a good part of the seventy-five years of film music, composers have had a stature far greater than that accorded to lyricists and playback singers.

So, aptly, the book begins with this section featuring twenty-seven composers, hopefully giving the reader an overview of not just their work, but also an insight into their individual personalities. It must also be mentioned that this is by no means an exhaustive list of all composers who contributed to making the Hindi film song what it is. Some are not featured at all, some mentioned only in passing. The author's preferences are one reason. Equally important, the book features only those personalities whose work is accessible to the music lover. Hence, a genius such as R.C. Boral doesn't get a separate mention, as so much of his work is unavailable to the listener. Nevertheless, it is the author's hope that a good part of the history of the Hindi film song is captured for the reader through the people featured here. The section also includes an interview with ace composer Pyarelal (of Laxmikant-Pyarelal) who reminisces about the work of many of his composer colleagues.

For the sake of structure, the composers have been categorized as belonging to four generations. However, the following pages make it evident that the influence of many composers in Bollywood extended far beyond the time-spans during which they were active.

FIRST-GENERATION COMPOSERS: THE PIONEERS

The four composers featured in this section were truly pioneers of the Hindi film song. Between themselves, Pankaj Mullick, Khemchand Prakash, Anil Biswas and Naushad gave the film song, still in its infancy, a distinct identity. It is all the more creditable that they achieved this feat in an era when techniques of recording were rudimentary and playback singing had not quite come into vogue. In their very different ways, each of them influenced the history of the Hindi film song. Pankaj Mullick dared to adapt Rabindra Sangeet to Hindi films, Khemchand Prakash introduced classical music into film songs, Anil Biswas blended Rabindra Sangeet and classical music expertly and Naushad unleashed the folk wave in the 1940s. As we shall see in the following pages, the sobriquet 'composers' composer' that Biswas earned is applicable to all four of them for a variety of reasons.

PANKAJ MULLICK: A LIFE LIVED FOR RABINDRA SANGEET

Though Pankaj Mullick was immensely popular as a singer, I believe his true contribution to film music lay in what he composed. Sweet and pleasant as he sounds in '*Piya milan ko jaana*' and '*Aaj aayi bahaar*', it is when you hear Saigal sing Mullick's songs that the composer's talent reveals itself. Mullick did give us the most authentic adaptation of Rabindra Sangeet in films in his own voice, but it is for his innovations in westernizing the orchestra and the awesome classical compositions that he got Saigal to render that he is most revered, at least by a late 1960s born, non-Bengali film music buff.

It was with an effort that I went back to the music of the 1930s and 1940s, having lived far too many years with the belief that the best in Hindi films happened in the 1950s and 1960s. Saigal and Pankaj Mullick were mere names to me, one who believed that playback began with Lata, Rafi, Mukesh, Geeta Dutt and Talat Mehmood. It was a joyous, yet humbling moment when I recently heard Ghalib's ghazal '*Nukta cheen hain*' in the film *Yahudi Ki Ladki*, released way back in 1933. I am still not sure what astounded me more: Mullick's ability to conceive the first authentic Raag Bhimpalasi composition ever in films, or Saigal's effortless grip over classical music. With just a harmonium and tabla in the background, can a song bowl you over like this?

Mullick needed Saigal's voice to inspire him to ever-newer heights. We don't know what role he played as R.C. Boral's assistant in the Saigal classic *'Dukh ke ab din'* in *Devdas*, but we can guess that it must have been significant, going by the fact that two years earlier he had already given us the first Saigal classic with *'Nukta cheen hain.'* Banking on Saigal's vocals, Mullick made memorable music in the 1930s with songs such as *'Ab main kaah karoon kit jaoon'* (*Dhartimata*, 1938), *'Karoon kya aas niras bhayee'* (*Dushman*, 1939) and *'Main kya janoon kya jaadoo hain'* (*Zindagi*, 1940). In the latter song, set to the effervescent notes of Raag Kalyan, Mullick could well have been paying tribute to his favourite singer, who was to quit New Theatres and move to Bombay soon after.

Not that his own reputation as a singer was any less formidable. Mullick was able to find his niche with the mega hit *'Piya milan ko jaana'* in *Kapal Kundala* (1939). The song was overtly Western, the first of its kind, the piano and accordion replacing the harmonium in the background, with *tonga* beats that O.P. Nayyar borrowed and used so successfully in the 1950s. Other solos like *'Madbhari rut jawan hain'* (*Nartaki*, 1940), *'Aaj aayi bahar'* and *'Chale pawan ki chaal'* (*Doctor*, 1941) saw Mullick achieve mass appeal as singer. Even as he was discovering this facet to his singing, the serious student of Rabindra Sangeet in him continued to find expression in songs such as *'Yeh kaun aaj aaya savere savere'* (*Nartaki*). Saigal's move to Bombay in 1941 affected the composer in Mullick, though he banked on old-timer K.C. Dey to put over the strains of Raag Jaunpuri in *'Man moorakh kehna maan'* (*Meenakshi*, 1943).

However, his best score was yet to come. And it happened in none other than Saigal's voice, for the film *My Sister* (1944). It was Saigal's last film with New Theatres for which he came down to Calcutta from Bombay. When Mullick set *'Aye kaatib-e-taqdeer'* to the notes of Raag Bhairavi, he equalled mentor R.C. Boral's thumri *'Babul mora'* in the same raag. Ironically, despite this gem, the world remembers Saigal more for Naushad's *'Jab dil hi toot gaya'* set to Bhairavi once again. Perhaps the ascendance of Bombay over Calcutta as the fountainhead of all talent by the mid-1940s had something to do with 'Aye kaatib-e-taqdeer' being passed over. My Sister also had another delightful Saigal solo 'Do naina matwaare tihaare'.

I wonder now whether Mullick's grip on classical music was overshadowed by his obsession for Rabindra Sangeet. It is undeniable that he, more than anyone else, made Rabindra Sangeet accessible to the layperson, using the harmonium, that Tagore was so much against, to enhance its impact, and in the process transforming it from being *Diwan-e-Khas* to becoming *Diwan-e-Aam*. This preoccupation with Tagore's music was a double-edged sword though. If he made a mark with Rabindra Sangeet in films, his complete devotion to it was also his undoing as composer, as his music got stuck with an overly Bengali flavour. His popularity plummeted in the 1950s, though he continued to score for many Hindi films in that decade.

Mullick himself never regretted that choice, confessing that Rabindra Sangeet was his life, and his redemption. He stayed with the music that he cared for most, and took a bow gracefully from active composing when the times changed, leaving listeners to mull over his solo 'Guzar gaya woh zamana kaisa'.

KHEMCHAND PRAKASH: A GRANDEUR ALL HIS OWN

If there was ever a man whose contribution to Hindi film music was far greater than just the songs he composed, it was Khemchand Prakash. His career lasted just a decade, with death snatching him away at the peak of his popularity in 1950, the movie *Mahal* having just been released, and the nation mesmerized by the strains of Lata's 'Aayega aanewala'. To Khemchand Prakash belongs the honour of composing a song that showcased Lata's musical virtuosity best. 'Aayega aanewala', like all his other hits, had a grandeur that was Prakash's trademark.

Earlier in 1948, he had already tested Lata's ability with his complex song 'Chanda re jaa re jaa re' in *Ziddi*. Possibly the first composition in Raag Chaya Nat in films, it had a long *mukhda* that, in Lata's own words, required a genius to handle. In the same film, Prakash also gave Kishore Kumar a break with the song 'Marne ki duayen kyon mangoon'. Little did he know that with his faith in Lata and Kishore he was influencing the history of film music itself.

Prakash had created a history of sorts in the early 1940s with the purely classical songs of *Tansen* (1943), where Saigal sang a most authentic Raag Gaara in 'Kaahe gumaan kare', besides the equally erudite 'Baag laga doon sajani' in Raag Megh Malhar and 'Diya jalao' in Raag Deepak. No wonder Naushad, who composed *Baiju Bawra* a full decade later, considered Khemchand Prakash his guru! To the discerning ear, Naushad's '*Mohe panghat pe nandlaal ched gayo re*' in *Mughal-e-Azam* (1960) is clearly influenced by 'Kaahe gumaan kare'. Prakash was able to bring to the songs of *Tansen* a melodic grandeur that was clearly the result of his years as the court singer of the maharaja of Bikaner. That he used the piano in a period film like *Tansen* was but a minor flaw.

Lata's 'Chanda re jaa re jaa re' was preceded four years earlier by Ameerbai's 'Chanda des piya ke jaa' (*Bhartruhari*, 1944) in Raag Hemant, where Prakash did full justice to Ameerbai's classical training. Even as he gave Lata 'Aayega aanewala' in *Mahal*, he inspired singer Rajkumari to rise to extraordinary heights in the same film with 'Ghabra ke jo hum sar ko'. The song remains Rajkumari's best solo, though *Mahal* is deservedly remembered most for 'Aayega aanewala'.

In the 1940s, Khemchand Prakash's songs had a dignity that most composers, barring Anil Biswas, could not conceive of. This dignity permeated even his lighter compositions such as Ameerbai's 'Mora dheere se ghoonghat uthaye piya' (*Bhartrahari*), the Zohrabai–Rajkumari duet 'Chun chun ghoongarwa' (*Mahal*) or the Talat–Geeta Roy stunner 'Armaan bhare dil ki lagan' (*Jaan Pehchan*, 1950). His music gave each of these songs a stature far beyond what the lyrics convey.

In a career spanning just eleven years, Khemchand Prakash composed for thirty-four films. He passed away in his early forties without seeing the big-time fame that was his due. Fifty years after his death, he was in the news when there was talk of royalty to the tune of fifty lakhs that the industry owed him for the music of *Mahal*!

ANIL BISWAS: UNCOMPROMISING MELODY

The first time I recognized the genius of the man was in 1984, as I stood mesmerized listening to 'Kuch aur zamana kehta hain' on Vividh Bharati's *Bhoole Bisre Geet* programme. Admittedly, what held my attention then was my mistaken notion that Geeta Dutt (my favourite) had sung the ghazal. I felt but a passing twinge of regret when Meena Kapoor was announced as the singer, the beauty of the composition having overwhelmed me. It was with this song that I began to know the work of Anil Biswas. What an irony that it turned out to be the last song he composed in a career spanning three decades!

That, I think, is the tragedy of Anil Biswas. His songs are recognized as classics, but the man himself is relatively unknown. He produced bewitching music in the 1940s and 1950s, always outclassing the movies they featured in. Thus, he was denied the dizzying heights of fame that Naushad, Shanker–Jaikishan and O.P. Nayyar achieved in that era. But Anil-da, as he was fondly referred to, remained unfazed, having decided early in life not to succumb to the demands of commercial success. He composed only what he wanted to, and retired in the mid-1960s when he recognized that his kind of music was not what popular taste wanted.

Growing up amidst the strains of Bhatiyali, traditional folk songs sung by boatmen in erstwhile East Bengal, and his mother's classical music in Barisal, Biswas was a child prodigy, learning to sing at the age of four, playing the tabla at six, and acting in plays at ten! His teens and early twenties were spent in participating in the freedom movement. He took to composing music in the early 1930s, having spent his revolutionary fervour serving many terms in jail. He moved to Bombay in 1935, and composed for a dozen films before tasting stardom with the songs of *Kismet* (1943).

The revolutionary in him had dared to compose '*Door hato aye duniyawalon Hindustan hamara hain*' for *Kismet*, using Ameerbai's feeling-laden voice to convey a yearning for freedom at a time when the British were extra careful in chopping all lyrics that fuelled patriotism. It was under Anil-da's baton that Ameerbai, like many a singer after her, discovered her full range. '*Dard mandon ka jahaan mein*' (*Veena*, 1948) is Ameerbai at her soulful best. Since he cared for melody more than popularity, Anil-da stuck to Ameerbai in the mid-1940s, though Shamshad Begum had become immensely popular by then.

Post retirement, Anil-da disclosed that he was really frustrated in the late 1930s and early 1940s, before the playback era really took off, because he had to depend on non-singers like actress Leela Chitnis to put over the songs. But the genius in him found ways of overcoming limitations of the singer by making the background score in songs remarkably melodious. In the use of the flute and piano to enhance the melodic effect of the tune, Biswas had no parallel. Take for instance the Surendra–Wahidan Bai duet *'Hum aur tum aur yeh khushi'* (*Alibaba*, 1940). The tune is simple, but the orchestration beautiful. It was an overjoyed Anil Biswas who used Lata's voice bravely for the solos in *Anokha Pyar* (1948), when Lata's 'tinny' vocals had still not gained acceptance with many producers and composers. Lata dazzled us with her sweetness in *'Jeevan sapna toot gaya'* and *'Mere liye woh gham-e-intezaar chhod gaye'*.

The Lata–Biswas combine produced over a hundred solos and at least as many duets in the 1950s. Right from *'Tumhaare bulaane ko jee chahta hain'* (*Laadli*, 1949) through *'Kathti hain ab toh zindagi'* (*Naaz*, 1955) to *'Intezaar aur abhi aur abhi'* (*Char Dil Char Raahein*, 1959), Lata sounded extra-sweet when singing for Biswas. It is unfortunate that Lata chose to ignore Biswas when she picked her ten best in 1967, with even rank newcomers Laxmikant–Pyarelal figuring in that coveted list. Biswas had not found a place in that list because he piqued Lata no end with his fascination for Meena Kapoor's voice, and the way he blatantly promoted her for his songs. *Anokha Pyar* has all the female solos in Lata's voice on the record, but in Meena's voice in the film! The talented Meena Kapoor achieved her brief moment of glory with the songs she sang for Biswas, but did not quite succeed as a singer, with her voice sounding too close to that of Geeta Dutt's. The 1950s were years when you had to be original to succeed.

Biswas's real contribution to music can also be gauged by considering the role he played in finding and honing talent. Zohrabai Ambalewali sang her first song for him in *Gramophone Singer* (1938). Mukesh's *'Dil jalta hain toh jalne de'* (*Pehli Nazar*, 1945) was the beginning of his rise to stardom. It was again Biswas who gave Talat Mehmood a break with *'Aye dil mujhe aisi jagah le chal'* in *Aarzoo* (1950), convincing a nervous Talat that the quiver in his voice was an asset to a composer! To Biswas also goes the credit of introducing Sahir Ludhianvi with the song *'Mohabbat turk ki maine'*, sung by Talat in *Do Raha* (1952), though *Baazi* was released earlier. In the 1950s, Talat, Mukesh and Lata were the three pillars on which Biswas built his awesome musical edifice, earning him the title 'Composers' Composer'.

Consider a sampling of the duets the man composed: '*Zamaane ka dastoor hain yeh purana*' (Mukesh–Lata, *Laajawab*, 1951); '*Seene mein sulagte hain armaan*' (Lata–Talat, *Tarana*, 1951); '*Pee bin soona ri*' (Manna Dey–Lata, *Hamdard*, 1953); '*Raahi matwaale*' (Talat–Suraiya, *Waris*, 1954); and '*Zindagi ka ajab fasaana hain*' (Mukesh–Lata, *Chhoti Chhoti Baatein*, 1965). Each dulcet duet is a testimony to Anil-da's mastery over music and, more importantly, to his integrity as composer. If one also takes into account solos such as Mukesh's '*Aye jaan-e-jigar*' (*Aaraam*, 1951), Talat's '*Jeevan hain madhuban*' (*Jasoos*, 1955) and Meena Kapoor's '*Rasiya re man basiya re*' (*Pardesi*, 1957), one understands why the man was fondly referred to as the 'uncle'. In '*Rasiya re man basiya re*', Biswas creates magic by using the muted notes of the sarod and the flute to accentuate the yearning in Meena's voice. Like peer Khemchand Prakash, Biswas did not care for the popular trend of Punjabi folk music in the 1940s with its emphasis on beats. For him, music was melody and nothing else.

In the last years of his life before his death in 2003, Anil-da used to appear on the panel of judges for the popular TV programme *SaReGaMa*. Watching him, I couldn't help wondering what it was like for the man to hear the present generation sing every other composer's song of his era, except his own. Perhaps Anil-da found solace from the lines of the song in his last film *Choti Choti Baatein*: '*Zindagi ka ajab fasaana hain, rote rote bhi muskurana hain...*'

NAUSHAD ALI: THE MAN WITH THE MIDAS TOUCH

Twice in the course of writing this book I have been overwhelmed by the extent of my ignorance about the best in Hindi film music. Both instances, in retrospect, are unforgivable. I had very little knowledge of Saigal's greatness and no understanding whatsoever of Naushad's brilliance. I was too young to appreciate Saigal and had unconsciously harboured a grouse against Naushad for rarely using Geeta Dutt's voice!

The first time I faced up to my prejudice was when, sorting through my 300-odd tapes collected over twenty years, I realized I hadn't a single Naushad film or compilation, except a combination of *Baiju Bawra* and *Mughal-e-Azam*. It was thus with a huge sense of guilt that I started paying serious attention to his music, beginning with the songs of *Rattan*. By the time I reached his *Aadmi* (1968), I had realized many times over what I had lost out on all these years. Today I believe he is the only composer whose impact went beyond the films he composed for. Naushad saab's real contribution is to be understood in terms of keeping alive a part of Indian culture itself.

Naushad took to music early, spending time as a boy listening to the live music that accompanied the movies during the silent era. A showdown with his disapproving father saw Naushad leave home and join a theatre company that toured north and west India extensively. This experience would stand him in good stead as he picked up the nuances of the folk music of the areas he toured. When the company folded up, Naushad came to Bombay in search of work in films. It was many months of living on the streets before D.N. Madhok and Khemchand Prakash helped him find work. He got his first assignment as composer for the film *Prem Nagar*, released in 1940.

In the 1940s, he, following the Ghulam Haider tradition, took to tapping the folk music of north India for his inspired compositions in film after film. After eleven average scores in the years 1940–44, Naushad hit gold with the songs of *Rattan*. Zohrabai's zesty rendering of '*Akhiyan milake*' and Ameerbai's wistful '*Milke bicchad gayee akhiyan*' compete favourably for our ear, undoubtedly the most popular solos of each singer. The tunes were simple, and Zohra and Ameerbai had never sounded as charming, but there was something special about the way Naushad used the accordion and clarinet.

It was in 1946 that he attained superstar status. In two films that year, Naushad proved early enough that his grasp of music was as good as his grip on rhythm. Tapping the gold in Noorjehan's throat in *Anmol Ghadi*, Naushad immortalized her with just this film. The simple melody of '*Jawan hain mohabbat*' is juxtaposed with the sheer brilliance of the Noorjehan–Surendra duet '*Awaaz de kahaan hain*'. Was there ever a better Raag Pahadi in films, or a better duet of yearning? The song stands tall as the best duet of that decade.

Shahjehan in the same year saw the coming together of two giants—Saigal and Naushad. Naushad knew Saigal's forte was classical, and he composed three solos set to three different raags, persuading an alcohol-dependent Saigal to record them when sober. '*Jab dil hi toot gaya*' in Raag Bhairavi, '*Aye dil-e-bekraar jhoom*' in Raag Behag and '*Chah barbaad karegi*' in Raag Bageshri all attest as much to Naushad's composing skill as to Saigal's virtuosity. With *Shahjehan*, Naushad was preparing the ground for his tribute to Hindustani classical music, *Baiju Bawra*, which came six years later. Shamshad Begum took over from Zohrabai as Naushad's lead playback singer in *Shahjehan*, with a magic all her own in '*Baadal aaya jhoom ke*'.

Naushad extracted the best out of Shamshad in *Mela* (1948), where he moderated the sharp edge to her voice beautifully in solos such as '*Mohan ki muraliya baaje*' and '*Dharti ko aakaash pukaare*'. Mukesh too was his sweetest in the duets with Shamshad, '*Main bhawara tu hain phool*' and '*Mera dil todnewaale*'. Who would have thought then that Naushad was already contemplating replacing Shamshad with Lata, and Mukesh with Rafi, as his lead singers?

He could ruthlessly put the cause of music over personal loyalties. He wanted the best for his songs and the best, you realize when you hear '*Yeh zindagi ke mele*' (*Mela*), was Rafi. Similarly, any awe you feel at how far Shamshad had come in Naushad's custody in '*Taqdeer bani bankar bigdi*' (*Mela*) disappears the minute you hear Lata caress the notes of Raag Kedar in '*Uthaye jaa unke sitam*' (*Andaaz*, 1949). *Andaaz* had three solos by Lata and four by Mukesh. '*Toote naa dil toote naa*' sang Mukesh with his characteristic honesty, knowing well his days with Naushad were coming to a close as Naushad mounted another Raag Pahadi stunner '*Suhaani raat dhal chuki*' in Rafi's voice for *Dulaari*. A brilliant composition with a slightly Western lilt to the tune and orchestration, it proved that Rafi's voice was richer, his technique superior. The song was the turning point in Rafi's career.

And what music the Naushad–Lata–Rafi trio created in *Deedar* (1951)! Rafi's best Bhairavi came under Naushad's baton in '*Huye hum jinke liye barbaad*' with its haunting harmonium strains. In conviction and treatment, the song was superior to even '*Tu Ganga ki mauj*' in *Baiju Bawra*, though the latter is more popular. As Dilip Kumar's voice in *Deedar*, Rafi shed whatever diffidence he carried with him till then. In the duet '*Dekh liya maine*', it is Lata who sounds a trifle uncertain of matching Rafi's emotion-charged voice. It was clear by 1951 that Naushad's brilliance had shifted to composing songs based on classical raags, and that it needed a Rafi to find full expression.

Baiju Bawra happened a year later. Having tested Lata in *Andaaz* and Rafi in *Deedar*, Naushad could now go to town with his mastery over classical music. He also sensed that the folk influence had run its course over ten years and people were thirsting for a change. The story of Baiju, a court musician for Emperor Akbar who had many musical duels with Tansen, came as a godsend to Naushad. And did the man give it his best!

With '*Tu Ganga ki mauj*' in Raag Bhairavi, '*Man tarpat Hari darshan ko*' in Raag Malkauns, '*O duniya ke rakhwale*' in Raag Darbari, and '*Insaan bano*' in Raag Todi, Naushad grips your mind with the way in which he distilled the essence of each raag, even as Rafi stirs your heart with his pathos. Though Naushad also created waves by getting classical maestros Ustad Amir Khan and D.V. Paluskar to sing the bandish '*Aaj gawat man mero jhoomke*' (Raag Desi) and Amir Khan again for '*Tori jai jai kar*' (Raag Marwa), the real treasure in the film are the Rafi solos. Lata's '*Mohe bhool gaye sanwariya*' (Raag Bhairav) and '*Bachpan ki mohabbat ko*' (Raag Maand) are marvellous, but fall a bit short of the Rafi impact. What the music did to people of that era can be gauged from the fact that one of my grand uncles, an orthodox Carnatic musician living in Matunga then, saw the movie twenty times, and is said to have wept each time. If ever music could melt prejudices, *Baiju Bawra* proved the point in more ways than one. '*Man tarpat Hari darshan ko aaj*' was a bhajan written by Shakeel Badayuni, tuned by Naushad and sung by Mohammed Rafi!

If the folk-based tunes in the late 1940s made Naushad zoom to the top, *Baiju Bawra* gave him something more—respectability. The score suddenly made classical musicians and the layperson brothers in arms. When the movie celebrated its silver jubilee at the Broadway Theatre in Bombay, it was a visibly moved Naushad who told producer Vijay Bhatt: 'I used to sleep on the pavement opposite the theatre when I first came to Bombay. It took me sixteen years to cross the road and get here.'

After *Baiju Bawra*, Naushad jettisoned folk music and banished the clarinet and accordion from his recording room in favour of the jaltarang, violin, sitar and tabla. The result was many more classical gems like '*Man ki been matwari baaje*' (*Shabab*, 1954, Rafi-Lata, Raagmaalika), '*Insaaf ka mandir hain yeh*' (*Amar*, 1954, Rafi, Raag Bhairavi), '*Hamare dil se na jaana*' (*Udan Khatola*, 1955, Lata, Raag Behag), and '*Madhuban mein Radhika naache re*' (*Kohinoor*,

1960, Rafi, Raag Hameer). By the end of the decade, Naushad's music had come to be associated with Dilip Kumar films.

His second truly classical score was for the Dilip Kumar–Madhubala magnum opus *Mughal-e-Azam*. If *Baiju Bawra* was a Rafi feast, *Mughal-e-Azam* was an out-and-out Lata affair. Naushad now had to compete with C. Ramchandra's ultra-melodious compositions for *Anarkali*, which was based on the same story. He was unfazed, and lavishly mounted '*Pyar kiya to darna kya*' and '*Mohabbat ki jhooti kahaani pe roye*' (both Raag Darbari), '*Bekas pe karam kijiye*' (Raag Kedar), '*Khuda nigehbaan ho tumhara*' (Raag Yaman) and '*Mohe panghat pe Nandlal ched gayo*'(Raag Gaara), all in Lata's vocals. Lata gave her best to each song, reaching her pinnacle as playback singer.

There was a grandeur that permeated all the songs in the film, yet something was missing. C. Ramchandra's score for *Anarkali* had a freshness and innocence that was absent in *Mughal-e-Azam*. Naushad had probably, by 1960, exhausted his creativity. He had got too caught up in classicism and his inability to move beyond Lata and Rafi for his songs cramped his style insidiously. It is curious that the maestro rarely got Manna Dey to sing a classical song for him, despite the latter's reputation after Shanker–Jaikishan's score in *Basant Bahar*.

Naushad's songs of the 1960s are a pale shadow of the glory he achieved in the previous decade. There was melody of course, but also a sameness to them that took away their lustre. The Naushad of yore is glimpsed in '*Mere mehboob tujhe meri mohabbat ki kasam*' (*Mere Mehboob*, solo by both Rafi and Lata) and '*Koi saagar dil ko behlata nahin*' (*Dil Diya Dard Liya*, Rafi), but his songs in many Dilip Kumar films such as *Ganga Jumna* ('*Do hanson ka joda*', Lata, 1961), *Son Of India* ('*Zindagi aaj mere naam se*', Rafi, 1962), *Leader* ('*Ik shahenshah ne banwa ke haseen Taj Mahal*', Rafi–Lata, 1964) and *Aadmi* ('*Aaj puraani raahon se*', Rafi) all sound laboured. Having become too closely identified with the success of the thespian, Naushad was at a loss when Dilip Kumar went out of fashion in the 1960s. Perhaps he also found composing in the era of Shammi Kapoor's *Yahoo* a strain. He was astute enough to realize that his time was over, and cut down assignments drastically. Though he continued to score for an odd film or two right till 2005, the music was insignificant.

It speaks for the integrity of the man that he averaged just three films a year, composing for only sixty-two films in the twenty-eight years of his prime (1940–68). His tendency to agonize over every aspect of his music for days on end is legendary, and he never worked on more than one film at a time. Forty-three years after his last hit *Mere Mehboob*, if Naushad had the privilege of being considered the Koh-i-Noor of film music right till his death in May 2006, it is because he brought to films both the music (Hindustani classical) and the voice (Rafi) that could articulate its spirit best.

SECOND-GENERATION COMPOSERS:
THE MASTERS

The eleven composers featured in this part were all geniuses. With their prodigious creativity they contributed to making this period (1947–67) the golden era of Hindi film music. Whether they made this era what it was, or whether they were products of the era is a moot point, but what is clear is that without them, melody and creativity in film music would just not have materialized. Taken together, these composers gave Hindi film music the status of a popular and respectable art. Indeed, it will be no exaggeration to say that everything that has happened subsequently in film music is an extension of what these eleven maestros created, over half a century ago.

C. Ramchandra: Melodies at the Drop of a Hat

If Naushad's agonizing over tunes and recording for days on end represent one kind of genius, quite the opposite kind is C. Ramchandra's. Here was a man who could produce sparkling melodies at the drop of a hat. Peer Salil Choudhury has spoken about how amazed he was when he saw Ramchandra in action, producing a complex thumri for Lata to sing in a matter of a few minutes. It was this spontaneity that gave Ramchandra's tunes vividness, a sparkle that is truly special.

I was quite familiar with the big hits of C. Ramchandra in *Albela* and *Anarkali*, yet totally unprepared for the simple melody of 'Dard jagake thes lagake chale gaye' (*Sipahiya*, 1949) in HMV's record *Great Maestro, Great Melodies*, released way back in 1984. Painstakingly put together, the record showcases the special tuning that existed between Ramchandra and Lata Mangeshkar that inspired both to ever greater melodic heights in the years 1949–58. Lata was as critical to Ramchandra's music as Asha was to O.P. Nayyar's. When their relationship ended, he lost not just the diary in which he had jotted down all his future tunes for Lata, but the very urge to make music.

But not before bequeathing to us a treasure trove of heart-tugging melodies. It was not without reason that the posters of *Nirala* (1950) promised money back to people who left the movie without hearing Lata's *'Mehfil mein jal uthi shama parwane ke liye'* or seeing Madhubala enact the song. Ramchandra had created a Raag Bhairavi number that was simple in tune and orchestration, but searing in impact. He surprised us again with the pathos-soaked *'Kathte hain dukh mein yeh din'* (*Parchayin*, 1952) where the single violin enhances the mood already articulated so well by Lata. Add to that his Raag Jaunpuri composition *'Jab dil ko satave gham tu ched sakhi sargam'* in *Sargam* (1950) and the thumri *'Tum kya jaano tumhaari yaad mein hum kitna roye'* (*Shin Shinaki Babla Bu*, 1952), and you are convinced that this *'Aana meri jaan Sunday ke Sunday'* man reserved his best for semi-classical numbers rendered by Lata, even before she became the rage that she did in the 1950s.

C. Ramchandra is best remembered for his unforgettable score in *Anarkali* (1953). Producer S. Mukherjee wanted Geeta Dutt to sing the songs, but Ramchandra would have none but his Lata. *'Mujh se mat pooch mere ishq mein kya rakha hain'* sang Lata with rare feeling, probably believing then that she had found her soul mate in Ramchandra. What more could Madan Mohan do for the ghazal or for Lata, you wonder as you hear this number. *Anarkali* was a veritable Lata show, with the happy and sad versions of *'Yeh zindagi usi ki hain'* etched in the memory of anyone who has ever heard it even just once. Ramchandra was honest enough to admit later that he borrowed a Marathi Bhavgeet tune for this song. *'Mohabbat aisi dhadkan hain'* and *'Aaja ab toh aaja'* evoke the tragedy of Salim and Anarkali for you even today.

Two instances of his legendary speed in composing are worth recounting. The lyrics for the *lorie* in *Albela*, *'Dheere se aaja ri akhiyan mein'*, reached Ramchandra at 4 p.m. on the day when the recording was scheduled for 6 p.m. He composed the tune in his car on the way to the recording studio! When you hear the song, there is nothing hurried about it, and it remains one of the most popular filmi lullabies ever. In 1955, Producer S.M. Naidu from the south wanted Naushad to score for his *Azaad*. Since shooting was already on in Coimbatore, he asked Naushad if he could compose all the songs in fourteen days. Naushad retorted that he was not a factory, and he couldn't even promise one song in that short a time. Naidu then approached C. Ramchandra, who gamely took on the challenge and composed all ten songs in two weeks! Here was a man who could deliver quality with amazing speed.

Lata's Bageshri strains in '*Radha na bole na bole na bole re*' are haunting, while '*Kitna haseen hain mausam*' is easy on the ear, with Ramchandra himself stepping in for Talat, who couldn't find time for the recording.

Talat Mehmood was initially Ramchandra's favourite male playback, lending his velvet touch to '*Mohabbat hi na jo samjhe woh zaalim pyar kya jaane*' (*Parchayin*) and '*Bechain nazar betaab jigar*' in *Yasmeen* (1956). He used Rafi and Manna Dey too, but the songs were not popular. His identity as a composer of class was achieved solely with Lata's vocal support. So much so that when Lata stopped singing for him in the late 1950s, his music suffered a serious setback. He did try valiantly to recreate the magic of yore with the help of Asha's voice. But a diffident Asha in those years could shine only with Nayyar. Ramchandra's score for *Navrang* (1959), *Paigham* (1959) and *Aanchal* (1960) are utterly lacking in melody, with Mahendra Kapoor and Asha proving no match for the magic of Lata and Talat. The only notable song that Asha sang for him in the 1960s was '*Dil laga kar hum yeh samjhe*' in *Zindagi Aur Maut* (1964), also sung separately by Mahendra Kapoor. Ramchandra revived himself only when Lata briefly came back to his recording room for the songs of *Stree* ('*O nirdayee preetam*', 1961) and *Bahurani* (1963), where he cast Bade Ghulam Ali Khan's Raag Hemant thumri '*Yaad piya ki aave*' as Lata's '*Balma anari man bhaaye*'. There was not much originality left in the composer by then.

There was another facet to Ramchandra, one that helped his popularity no end. He was fine with composing all kinds of music—classical, ghazal, or even pop. Inspired greatly by Bing Cosby, he created some foot-tapping numbers such as '*Aana meri jaan Sunday ke Sunday*' and the even more popular '*Mere piya gaye Rangoon*' (*Patanga*, 1949) that had lyrics going '*lungi baandh ke karte guzaara bhool gaye patloon*', shocking mentor Anil Biswas into reprimanding him. Ramchandra was undeterred, going on to compose other such songs in *Samadhi* ('*Gore gore o baanke chore*') and *Albela* ('*Bholi soorat dil ke khote*'). Kishore Kumar's popular '*Eena meena deeka*' (*Aasha*, 1957) was only an extension of the trend that began a decade earlier in *Shehnai*. In a very real sense, he was the trendsetter who legitimized fun and frolic in film songs, inspiring Shanker–Jaikishan to create the 'Yahoo' wave in the 1960s, and R.D. Burman to unleash rock music a decade later.

Nostalgia for Ramchandra's music is based on the scores of *Nirala, Sargam* and *Anarkali* though. The man was acutely conscious of this. 'I know how much I have slipped over the years,' confessed the maestro to a film music critic in the late 1960s, as he gazed at a faded poster of *Anarkali*.

SHANKER-JAIKISHAN: MEN AT THE TOP

How does one account for the SJ mania in the 1950s and 1960s? Popularity? Versatility? Flexibility? But that era also had other composers who had all these and more. Yet Shanker-Jaikishan inspire an awe that has always been larger than life. A part of it can be attributed to their unparalleled success. But a larger part is perhaps because the real trend they set was in institutionalizing the composer duo in Hindi films. Indeed, after SJ, no solo composer, barring R.D. Burman, tasted such sustained success. Even RD ruefully admitted that he lost out in the 1980s because he was up against competition from duos everywhere.

That they were trailblazers in music was evident in their very first film *Barsaat* (1949), where Raj Kapoor, keen to equal Naushad's impact in *Andaaz*, gave them a break. Kapoor understood the idiom of film music instinctively, though he lacked the creativity to compose. Shanker-Jaikishan had assisted Ram Ganguly for RK's earlier film *Aag* (1948) and therefore he knew the duo's creative ability. Equally important, he also knew they would be pliable to his own ideas about tunes. The result was pure honey as Lata came through ultra-sweetly in *'Bichde huye pardesi'*, *'Barsaat mein hum se mile tum sajan'* and *'O mujhe kisi se pyar ho gaya'*. Mukesh was as alluring in *'Chod gaye baalam'*, the lone duet in the film. Rafi made a brief impact with *'Main zindagi mein hardam rota hi raha hoon'*. It is in sheer wonder you recognize that all these songs were in the same raag, Bhairavi. Each couldn't have sounded more distinct. RK's role notwithstanding, Shanker-Jaikishan proved that they had it in them to make great music as early as *Barsaat*.

RK's instinct proved right when all songs in *Barsaat* clicked. Naturally, Shanker-Jaikishan became his favourite composers. When they repeated the magic in *Awara* the next year, a new school of music was born. The Raj Kapoor-Shanker-Jaikishan-Lata Mangeshkar-Mukesh-Shailendra-Hasrat Jaipuri team defined popular film music in the first half of the 1950s. Shanker–Jaikishan became the counterpoint to Naushad's classicism. They composed tunes that were hummed by the nation. *Awara* was less of a Lata show than *Barsaat*, with Mukesh getting entrenched as Raj Kapoor's voice with two solos. Between the popular '*Awara hoon*' on the one hand and the melodic '*Hum tujh se mohabbat karke sanam*' on the other, SJ left no one in doubt about their range. Lata continued to remain critical to SJ, putting over '*Ab raat guzarne wali hain*' with confidence and ease. The blossoming romance between Raj Kapoor and Nargis off-screen gave them an electrifying screen presence that added sheen to all tunes of SJ. When you consider the music by itself, you realize that *Awara*'s score, though more modern, lacked the melody and innocence of *Barsaat*. *Aah* (1953) had Lata and Mukesh in superb form, with the duets '*Jaane na nazar pehchane jigar*' and '*Aaja re ab mera dil pukara*' lingering as much in your mind as the Lata solos '*Yeh shaam ki tanhaiyan*' and '*Raja ki aayegi baraat*'. Musically superior to *Awara*, *Aah* was however a box office failure.

By the time *Shri 420* happened in 1955, Shanker–Jaikishan were probably tiring of RK's control over what they composed. Having scored successfully for Dilip Kumar in *Daag* (Talat's '*Aye mere dil kahin aur chal*', 1952) and for Dev Anand in *Patita* (Talat again in '*Hain sab se madhur woh geet*', 1953), they were coming out of the RK shadow. Sure, they proved their versatility again in *Shri 420* by casting Manna Dey as RK's voice in the charming duet '*Pyar hua ikraar hua*' (with Lata) and the intoxicating '*Mudh mudh ke na dekh*' (with Asha). The by-now-famous 'simpleton' image of RK was reinforced in Mukesh's '*Mera joota hain japani*' and '*Ramaiyya vastavaiyya*'. Yet there was something missing. Perhaps erudition, which RK would not allow. Shanker has gone on record to say how RK was most excited by something as mundane as '*Mera joota hain japani*'. It must have been this yearning that made them compose a hauntingly beautiful '*O jaanewale mudh ke zara dekhte jaana*' in Raag Yaman, their most classically erudite number for an RK film, typically in Lata's vocals. How they managed to slip it past the looming control of Raj Kapoor is anyone's guess. *Shri 420* represented the end of the RK-dominated first phase of SJ's career.

The second phase began with *Seema*, released the same year as *Shri 420*. Shanker's bandish '*Man mohana bade jhoote*' in Raag

Jaijaiwanti was a landmark, the most difficult classical composition any playback singer has ever rendered in Hindi films. Lata came closest to her desire to sing pure classical with this song. Jaikishan was inspired enough to compose a superb Raag Bhairavi number '*Suno choti si gudiya ki lambi kahaani*' in two versions, using the sarod expertly to accentuate the anguish in Lata's voice in the sad version, and the jaltarang to convey the budding happiness in the other. *Seema* proved once and for all that in terms of training and technique, Lata was way ahead of all other playback singers. Rafi gave his heart to '*Kahaan jaa raha hain*' and Manna Dey his soul to '*Tu pyaar ka sagar hain*', making *Seema* SJ's most moving score, despite the classical rigour.

It was with *Basant Bahar* that SJ gained a new respectability, from peers and people alike. The distributors clamoured for Shanker–Jaikishan, and old-timers Anil Biswas and Naushad were passed over. SJ bagged the chance of a lifetime to score pure classical music. They had to work extra hard, as they knew they would be compared to not only Naushad's *Baiju Bawra*, but also to Vasant Desai's score for *Jhanak Jhanak Paayal Baaje* (1955), which had released only the previous year and was still fresh. Shanker delved into his early classical training and composed '*Sur na saje kya gaoon main*' (Raag Maalika) and '*Ketaki gulab juhi champak ban phoole*' (Raag Basant) for Manna Dey, the latter song with Bhimsen Joshi who loathed the idea of losing to Manna Dey in the song, but was attracted enough by the glamour of film music to agree to sing. Jaikishan banked on his favourite Lata to render yet another Bhairavi stunner, '*Main piya teri tu maane ya na maane*', leaving listeners to make up their minds on what they are mesmerized by—Lata's vocals or the accompanying notes of Pannalal Ghosh's flute. The coup d'état was of course Rafi's bhajan in Raag Todi '*Duniya na bhaaye mohe*', where SJ masterfully restrained Rafi from getting overly emotional as he had in '*O duniya ke rakhwaale*' four years earlier.

There was a subtle classicism in much of their later work in the 1950s: '*Aaye bahaar ban ke lubha kar chale gaye*' (Rafi, *Raj Hath*, 1956); '*Rasik balma*' (Lata, *Chori Chori*, 1956); '*Aaja ke intezaar mein*' (Rafi–Lata, *Halaku*, 1956) and '*Sajan sang kaahe neha lagaye*' (Lata, *Main Nashe Mein Hoon*, 1959) are representative of this phase. They resolutely refused to get slotted though, giving C. Ramchandra a run for his money with the westernized tune of

'*Nakhrewaali*' (Kishore Kumar, *Shararat*, 1959) while resurrecting Mukesh's teetering career as a vocalist with something so apt as '*Sab kuch seekha humne na seekhi hoshiyari*' (*Anari*, 1959), thus proving their versatility all over again. The years 1955-60 saw SJ at their creative best, though their most popular phase was yet to come.

Yaaahooo, screamed Shammi Kapoor on-screen in *Junglee* (1963), bidding goodbye to melody in Hindi films for good measure. It is under SJ's baton and in Rafi's voice that the 'uninhibited youth' in the form of Shammi Kapoor came of age, proclaiming he couldn't care less if the world called him '*Junglee*'. Their ears tuned to what will sell, the market-savvy SJ composed '*Chahe koi mujhe junglee kahe*'. Ironically, they became the highest paid composers in the 1960s when their music reached its nadir in popular, if loud and unmusical numbers for Shammi Kapoor in films such as *Junglee, Jaanwar, Professor, Budtameez, Tumse Achcha Kaun Hain* and *Brahmachari*, where music was merely a pretext to heighten Shammi Kapoor's sexuality. Contrary to popular myth, it is not Amitabh Bachchan in the 1970s, but Shammi Kapoor a full decade earlier who made melody redundant in films.

SJ tried to undo the damage of the Shammi kind of music they belted out by composing melodies such as '*Tujhe jeevan ki dor se baandh liya hain*' in Raag Behag (*Asli Naqli*, Rafi–Lata, 1962); '*Yaad na jaaye beete dinon ki*' in Keervani (*Dil Ek Mandir*, Rafi, 1963); '*Yeh hariyali aur yeh raasta*' in Bhairavi (*Hariyali Aur Raasta*, Lata, 1962); '*Jao jao nand ke lala*' in Bageshri (*Rangoli*, Lata, 1962); '*O mere sanam o mere sanam*' in Shivranjani (*Sangam*, Mukesh–Lata, 1964); '*Koi matwala aaya mere dwaare*' in Darbari (*Love in Tokyo*, Lata, 1966); and '*Tadap yeh din raat ki*' in Bhimpalasi (*Amrapali*, Lata, 1966). But unlike in the 1950s there was not a single movie that had a great score in totality. Even their music for Raj Kapoor's *Sangam*, despite its popularity at that time, seems unremarkable forty years on.

There was a soulless quality to their music during the 1960s that was possibly the result of Shanker and Jaikishan having grown steadily apart. Shanker was envious of Jaikishan's tunes clicking more at the box office, and started making public who among them composed which tune. There came a point when they composed different songs for the same film without interacting with one another, though officially they appeared as Shanker–

Jaikishan on the marquee. It was the growing tension between the two that made them trade charges of engineering votes in *Binaca Geetmala*, the radio countdown show that was the true test of popularity in those years. Shanker's fascination for singer Sharda that made him fantasize she could replace Lata did not help matters either.

The closest they came to the SJ magic of yore was in lyricist Shailendra's film *Teesri Kasam* (1966). It was too intense a movie for the box office, but SJ succeeded in getting Mukesh to breathe life yet again into Shailendra's lyrics in the songs *'Duniya bananewale'*, *'Sajanwa bairi ho gaye hamaar'* and *'Sajan re jhoot mat bolo'*.

Perhaps success came too early for them in their very first film *Barsaat*, depriving them of the bond that comes from having struggled together, which might have kept competition between them at bay. Their public image too contributed to the rift. Jaikishan was savvier, always more in the public eye than Shanker, whose grasp on music was deeper. After a point, Shanker became resentful of Jaikishan's popularity as a person too. Except the ones starring Shammi Kapoor, most movies they composed for in the 1960s failed at the box office. They had become estranged from each other, and other composer duos—Laxmikant-Pyarelal and Kalyanji-Anandji—were mounting a stiff challenge.

Jaikishan was luckier. He died just as Kishore Kumar's *'Zindagi ek safar hain suhana'* in *Andaaz* was making waves. Succumbing to liver cirrhosis before he saw the failure of RK's *Mera Naam Joker* in 1971, he was spared the fate of Shanker, who had to see RK desert him in favour of Laxmikant-Pyarelal for *Bobby* (1973), and also face innuendos of being less talented among the two, when all his movies as solo composer failed. Shanker never admitted it, but with without Jaikishan, Shailendra and Lata, his music too dwindled irrevocably. He faced the humiliation of forty of his films as composer sinking without a trace. When death came in 1987, Shanker was still awaiting his second coming.

SACHIN DEV BURMAN: 'SIMPLY' PEERLESS

Have thirty years gone by without the music of Sachin Dev Burman? I wonder. Such is the youthfulness of his tunes that he seems a live presence even today. Age-wise, he may have belonged to the first-generation composers, but his tunes have a contemporariness that puts him ahead of the fourth generation. SD composed 'Meet na mila re man ka' when he was all of sixty-seven years old!

He remains my favourite composer. I don't quite know why, as I have a penchant for classical compositions, the very kind that SD frowned upon, maintaining that film music is not the place for a composer to demonstrate his classical prowess. It could be because I have often failed to identify a composition as an SD tune. There never was a pattern to his tunes, orchestration or choice of singers. It was always with surprise, often amazement that I discovered that SD had tuned the song that caught my ear. In this ability to spring a surprise on the unsuspecting listener with his sheer variety, he was unparalleled.

This ability to compose what the film needed, and not get identified with one kind of music (such as Naushad's classical image and Madan Mohan's ghazal fascination) was what made SD the only composer in Bollywood who was much sought after right till his death. Had SD lived longer, son RD would have faced the predicament of competing with his father for the top slot. Hadn't SD proved, with his 'Megha chaaye aadhi raat' (Sharmilee, 1971) in the same year that RD tuned 'Raina beeti jaaye' (Amar Prem), that he was not going to retire so that his son could take over? In matters pertaining to music, SD had no favourites, his son included.

I'll attempt to showcase the bewildering range of his music by contrasting the music of two films released in the same year at various points in his long journey as composer. Let's start with Navketan's *Baazi*, the film with which he became a force to reckon with. The jazzy, modern oomph in Geeta's voice in 'Tadbeer se bigdi hui taqdeer bana le' and 'Suno gajar kya gaaye' was totally new, a break with her earlier image of a singer of bhajans and weepy numbers. The score had heavy orchestration, something rare for those years, but you don't feel it is cacophony. SD retained the focus on simplicity even in club songs. Contrast this with the melody-backed score of *Buzdil* (1951) the same year. If *Baazi* was Geeta all the way, *Buzdil* was a Lata show. 'Jhan jhan jhan jhan paayal baaje' was an early Lata classical stunner, carrying the notes of the rare Raag Nat Bihag. 'Rote rote guzar gayi raat re' by Lata again is typically SD, melody and feeling fused together in simple harmony. *Buzdil* remains my all-time favourite Lata–Burman score.

Cut to 1955. In *Munimji*, you have Kishore Kumar in excellent form, singing a robust *'Jeevan ke safar mein raahi'*. It was under SD's baton that Kishore found his mooring as singer, evident in the fact that out of twelve songs in the film, the lone Kishore solo is best remembered. The film also had Hemant Kumar and Geeta Dutt sweetly hum *'Dil ki umangen hain jawaan'*, a tune that represents SD's belief that his tunes should be simple enough to be hummed by his servants. SD gave music in fourteen films for Dev Anand's banner, Navketan, becoming a father figure to the banner itself, conveying so well through his music the spirit of hope that pervaded all their films. Minus SD's music, Navketan would have been unremarkable.

As counterpoint to *Munimji*, 1955 also saw SD compose a completely antithetical score for *Devdas*, where his songs went a long way in creating the atmosphere of doom. Talat Mehmood's *'Mitwa lagi re yeh kaisi'* was a free-flowing song without beats. SD cast it in Raag Hemant, conveying the hero's sense of despondency so well. Lata's *'Jise tu qabool karle'* has an unusual, yet captivating structure in the *antara*. Rafi's *'Manzil ki chaah mein'* is less known, but has a heart-wrenching funereal feel to it, so apt for the mood of the movie.

It must have been the music of *Devdas* that made Guru Dutt pick SD over O.P. Nayyar for his true classic *Pyaasa* (1957). SD used Rafi brilliantly to convey the compassionate but embittered poet in the nazm *'Tang aa chuke hain kashmakash-e-zindagi se hum'* and that dirge to mankind, *'Yeh duniya agar mil bhi jaaye to kya hain'*, but switched to Hemant Kumar's voice for articulating the angst of the failed lover in *'Jaane woh kaise log the'*. But the tour de force in *Pyaasa* is Geeta Dutt's *'Aaj sajan mohe ang laga lo'*, the most authentic adaptation of the Bengali kirtan for Hindi films. SD's use of the flute and Geeta's vocals make the song transcend the eroticism of Sahir's lyrics. With *Pyaasa*, SD made the point that serious music need not be classical in orientation. In the same year, *Paying Guest* saw SD on home ground, composing a delightfully light score. While Kishore was endearing in *'Maana janab ne pukaara nahin'*, Lata enchanted with *'Chaand phir nikla'*. Asha and Kishore came together for the bubbly *'Chod do aanchal zamaana kya kahega'*. The music fitted the breeziness of the story to a T.

It was SD that Bimal Roy wanted to convey the predicament of *Sujata* (1959), the untouchable girl brought up as an outsider in a high-caste family. Roy wanted a message of hope, and SD's score captures the yearnings of the heroine beautifully. The abandonment of Sujata as a child in the lullaby '*Nanhi kali sone chali*'; the yearnings of the young girl who is still an outsider in the family in '*Kaali ghata chaaye mora jiya tarsaaye*'; the hope of love and fulfilment in '*Jalte hain jiske liye*'—*Sujata* was Burman-da's most gentle score of the decade. Not as dark as *Pyaasa*, yet more serious than Navketan scores, SD chartered a third course with this film that would continue into the 1960s. Guru Dutt's *Kaagaz Ke Phool* in the same year saw SD immortalize Geeta Dutt with the wistful '*Waqt ne kiya*'. He turned to Rafi again for conveying the intensity of Kaifi Azmi's lyrics in '*Dekhi zamaane ki yaari*'. With *Kaagaz Ke Phool*, SD bid goodbye to the dark, melancholic part of his music, which he composed superbly, but perhaps did not enjoy.

In 1963, SD decided to end his six-year stand-off with Lata, and invited her for the songs of Bimal Roy's *Bandini*. Lata sang '*Mora gora ang lai lai*' and '*Jogi jab se tu aaya mere dwaare*' with all her allure, firmly ensconcing herself as SD's lead singer for all the years to come. Once he had his 'Lota' back, SD had no qualms about relegating Asha back to her club songs, even after Asha had given '*Ab ke baras bhejo bhaiyya ko babul*' all that she had. SD himself sang the most moving of all numbers in *Bandini*, '*More saajan hain us paar*', which comes at the most defining moment in the film. If *Bandini* banked on his folk expertise, SD composed a predominantly classical score for *Meri Surat Teri Aankhen*, getting Manna Dey to give his lifetime best to the Ahir Bhairav composition '*Poocho na kaise main ne rain bitaaye*'. Rafi came a distant second in the Bhairavi number '*Naache man mora magan tigda dhiggi dhiggi*'. SD earned our awe with the way he got Lata-Rafi to emote '*Tere bin soone nain hamaare*', arguably the best duet of the pair in that decade, set to the notes of an unobtrusive Raag Khamaj. The way he juxtaposes the flute and xylophone in the interlude pieces is truly awesome.

S.D. Burman fell seriously ill while composing for *Guide* (1965), after having completed just one song. Dev Anand steadfastly refused to consider any other composer, including assistant Jaidev who had decisively proved his calibre for Navketan's own *Hum Dono* four years earlier. When SD expressed fears of never recovering enough to compose, Dev Anand replied gallantly that he would then release the film with just the one song that SD had composed. Perhaps this loyalty had something to do with SD's recovery, and the superb score for *Guide* that Dada went on to compose, his best for Navketan ever. With *'Kya se kya ho gaya'*, *'Din dhal jaaye raat na jaaye'* and the outstanding *'Tere mere sapne ab ek rang hain'*, Rafi helped Burman every inch. Lata showed her love for the senior composer with the emotion she put into *'Piya tose naina laage re'*, a gem of a Tilang composition if ever there was one, and *'Mose chal kiye jaaye saiyyan be-imaan'* in Raag Jhinjoti. With the Lata–Kishore duet *'Gaata rahe mera dil'* to boot, SD proved how far ahead he was of the competition. I can't still get over the shock that *Guide* lost to Shanker–Jaikishan's *Suraj* that year for the popular Filmfare awards. There could be no worse proof of the devious methods SJ resorted to, to stay in the limelight.

I would dare to hypothesize that SD was hit hard by lack of recognition for *Guide*. The next few years had nothing memorable from him. His music for *Teen Devian* (1966) and *Jewel Thief* (1967) was lacklustre, the only time he seemed to have lost his grip on melody. R.D. Burman 'assisted' him to create the super-hit songs of *Aradhana*. But the man who came to Bombay in his mid-forties to try his luck in Hindi films was made of much sterner stuff. He found his footing again in small-budget *Jyoti* (1969) with Manna Dey and Lata aiding him in the bewitching duet *'Soch ke yeh gagan jhoome'*.

With *Talaash* (1969), he was getting back in form, mounting a beautiful Raag Baarwa composition in the folk tradition with Lata's *'Khayi hain re humne kasam'*. He was even better in *Gambler* (1971), getting Kishore Kumar to sing a *ghazalish 'Dil aaj shayar hain'* when Rafi played truant about the recording. Rafi ceased to matter to S.D. Burman after this episode. With songs such as *'Megha chaaye aadhi raat'* (*Sharmilee*, 1971) and *'Jaise Radha ne maala japi'* (*Tere Mere Sapne*, 1971) both in Lata's vocals, it looked like the old man was ready for his second innings.

When *Abhimaan* (1973) came his way, SD created the magic of *Guide* yet again, with all seven songs in the film becoming super hits. He could, at sixty-seven and with two heart attacks behind him, melodiously traverse the range between Kishore's trendy *'Meet na mila re man ka'* and Lata's mellow *'Piya bina piya bina'*.

Come to think of it, I believe S.D. Burman is the only composer who managed to compose hit scores for films, as against hit songs that other composers had. Burman-da deservedly won the Filmfare Award for *Abhimaan*, nearly twenty years after his first award for Talat Mehmood's Raag Jaunpuri strains in '*Jayen toh jayen kahaan*' (*Taxi Driver* (1954). *Abhimaan* restored a measure of dignity and faith to the awards that had been so politicized by Shanker–Jaikishan. With renewed confidence, Burman-da created more melodies such as '*Yeh kaisa sur mandir hain*' (*Prem Nagar*, 1974) and '*Sun ri pawan, pawan puruvaiyya*' for *Anuraag* the following year, both sung by Lata.

As late as 1975, a few months before he passed away, SD came up with a youthful score for *Chupke Chupke* ('*Ab ke sajan sawan mein*', Lata). He could do it only because he had learnt early enough to place faith in the opinions of his driver and cook on the tunes he composed, and thus have his ears close to the ground. Thirty years on, he remains the best, simply.

Madan Mohan: Uncrowned King of Melody

Hamaare Baad Ab Mehfil Mein Afsaane Bayaan Honge
Bahaaren Hum Ko Dhoondengi Na Jaane Hum Kahaan Honge

By the time he tuned this song for *Baaghi* (1953) in his third year as composer, Madan Mohan had the foresight to see that while connoisseurs would appreciate his music and he would gain the respect of his peers, he would never have the popular appeal of S.D. Burman, Shanker–Jaikishan or O.P. Nayyar. However, he sustained himself on his faith and belief alone for two decades, producing superb music, before disillusionment caught up with him. It was an embittered man who composed something as evocative as '*Dil dhoondta hain phir wohi fursat ke raat din*' (*Mausam*, 1975) as his swan song.

That he was a composer of class became evident as early as 1951, when you hear Lata's '*Preetam meri duniya mein*' in *Ada*, his second film, where Lata sang for him for the first time. There was a piercing quality to his tunes, something enhanced rather than diluted by their strong classicism. Hadn't he quit the army in pursuit of his first love, music, preferring to hold the baton rather than the gun? It did not take him long to prove to us that his choice was right. His early films had some real stunners in Lata and Talat's vocals. Consider this sample: Talat's *'Meri yaad mein tum na aansoo bahana'* set to Raag Jaunpuri in *Madhosh* (1951), Talat again in *'Main paagal mera manwa paagal'* in Raag Kedar for *Aashiana* (1952), and Lata in *'Badi barbaadiyan lekar meri duniya mein pyar aaya'* (*Dhun*, 1954) and *'Chaand madham hain aasmaan chup hain'* (*Railway Platform*, 1955).

The song that got him public acclaim was ironically not in his favourite Lata's voice, but that of Geeta Dutt's in *Bhai Bhai* (1956), where Geeta infused *'Aye dil mujhe bata de'* with a seductive allure that she had come to perfect in those years. The film was Madan's fifteenth as composer, his first hit. Never mind that his own favourite was the other stunner in the film, Lata's *'Qadar jaane na mora baalam'*, the song that had Begum Akhtar ring up Madan and sing it to her over and over again, long distance! Thus, as early as 1956, it became clear to Madan Mohan that what the public wanted was not what he wanted.

This addiction to sophistication sometimes made him lose track of the appropriateness of his score to the theme of the film. Nowhere is this more evident than in his tunes for *Dekh Kabira Roya* (1957), an out-and-out comedy for which Madan composed a serious classical score. *'Kaun aaya mere man ke dwaare'* (Raag Raageshri, Manna Dey), *'Humse aaya na gaya'* (Raag Bageshri, Talat), *'Meri veena tum bin roye'* (Raag Ahir Bhairav, Lata), *'Tu pyar kare ya thukraaye'* (Raag Bhairavi, Lata) and *'Bairan ho gayee rain'* (Raag Jaijaiwanti, Manna Dey)—each is a gem on its own, each my favourite, but did they belong to the screenplay of *Dekh Kabira Roya*? The film required a breezy score (something like in *Chalti Ka Naam Gaadi*), which Madan was not interested in. Many of his songs stood out for their sheer melody, but they seem out of sync with the respective storyline. *'Preetam daras dikhao'*, the Lata-Manna Dey duet in Raag Lalit that inspired O.P. Nayyar enough to literally recreate it for *Kalpana*, was composed by Madan for *Chacha Zindabad* (1959), another comedy that also had Lata's *'Bairan neend na aaye'*, in Raag Kaafi.

When the theme in the film was sombre, as was much of his music, Madan Mohan outclassed all his peers. Who else could have composed *'Unko yeh shikayat hain'* and *'Yun hasraton ke daagh'* to so effectively convey the predicament of the heroine who finds herself in a *kotha*? With *Adalat* (1958), Madan Mohan found his groove as the architect of the filmi ghazal, earning the sobriquet '*Ghazalon Ka Shehzaada*' from Lata Mangeshkar.

And it was Lata who articulated the spirit of Madan's music best till the very end. The Lata–Madan Mohan partnership bequeathed to music lovers a treasure trove of ghazals and geets through the 1960s. '*Hain isi mein pyaar ki aabroo*' in Raag Charukeshi (*Anpadh*, 1962) had Naushad declaring he would exchange all his songs for just that one composition of Madan. Raj Khosla's suspense thriller *Woh Kaun Thi* (1964) had Madan create the exquisite '*Jo humne daastan apni sunayi aap kyon roye*', besides the atmospheric '*Naina barse rimjhim rimjhim*'. Two years later, he repeated the magic in *Mera Saaya*, with '*Tu jahaan jahaan chalega*' (Raag Nand) and Lata's best Bhimpalasi song, '*Nainon mein badra chaaye*'. In Chetan Anand's *Haqeeqat* (1964), it was in Raag Hamir that Madan cast '*Zara si aahat hoti hain*'. It had to be Madan as composer for the movie *Ghazal* (1964), where he gave us '*Nagma-o-sher ki saugaat*'. So prodigious is the Lata–Madan output that it is difficult to say who nourished whom. It is only clear that without the other, each would have been incomplete.

Starting with a fondness for Talat's voice, Madan had slowly switched to Rafi for putting over his songs for the hero. So Rafi embellished many of Madan's tunes, from '*Tujhe kya sunaoon main dilruba*' (*Aakhri Dao*, 1958), inspired by Sajjad Hussain's earlier composition for Talat '*Yeh hawa yeh raat*' (*Sangdil*, 1953), through '*Tumhaari zulf ke saaye mein shaam kar loonga*' (*Naunihal*, 1967) to '*Tum jo mil gaye ho*' (*Hanste Zakhm*, 1973). Rafi left an impact as late as in *Laila Majnu* (1976), released a year after Madan Mohan's death, with '*Barbaad-e-mohabbat ki duaa saath liye ja*', despite the fact that the composer had for long continued to believe that Talat was a better singer. Madan composed Talat Mehmood's last hit song '*Phir wohi shaam wohi gham*' for *Jahan Ara* (1964), where he unsuccessfully tried to resurrect the singer's fading career by giving him three solos. For all the efforts that he took to lovingly craft every tune, the movie, like so many others before and after, sank without a trace.

For Chetan Anand's *Heer Ranjha* (1970), a movie whose dialogues were entirely in verse, Madan composed a befittingly poignant score. Lata was simply brilliant in '*Milo na tum toh hum ghabraye*,' Madan's subtle Raag Bhairavi. She was as endearing in '*Do dil toote do dil haare*', set to Maand. But it was Rafi who caught the ear with '*Yeh duniya yeh mehfil mere kaam ki nahin*'. Was Madan conveying his own angst in Rafi's vocals? Because by the time *Heer Ranjha* was released, he was a cynical man, increasingly dependent on alchohol for solace. That his one-time guru S.D. Burman felt that only Madan could have scored for the movie so well was of no great comfort. Peer acclaim was no longer sufficient to cope with public rejection.

The only award he won came too late, when his score for *Dastak* (1970)—a movie he had scored without taking any fee, as a mark of his affection for heroine Rehana Sultan—fetched him the National Award. Rehana's regard for him, Majrooh's sensitivity and Lata's support resuscitated Madan enough to produce yet another classy score with '*Mayee ri main kaase kahoon*', '*Hum hain mataa-e-koocha o bazaar ki tarah*' and the outright classical number '*Baiyan na dharo*'. But it couldn't quite reverse his growing alienation from the tinsel world.

Mausam was a film that came his way because of a contract he had with the producer, and not because director Gulzar actually chose him to compose. Madan knew this, and yet put whatever soul was left in him to come up with something as mesmerizing as '*Dil dhoondta hain phir wohi fursat ke raat din*' in two versions, a duet (Lata–Bhupinder) and a solo (Bhupinder). There hasn't been another song in Hindi films that so achingly captures the regret for opportunities lost. He did not live to see the film released, succumbing to the despair that was gnawing at him for years on 14 July 1975. Like Khemchand Prakash before and R.D. Burman after, Madan's last film, released posthumously, was a resounding hit. And his reputation as the emperor of ghazals has only grown in the three decades since.

O.P. Nayyar: The Tunesmith of Hope

There is no greater injustice done to the man than the nickname 'Rhythm King', his ubiquitous 'tonga' beats notwithstanding. For the fifteen years he was at the top, O.P. Nayyar's music epitomized the brighter side of life, the possibility of joy amidst life's vicissitudes. Sure, there was a sameness to his fast-paced catchy tunes, but it seldom diminished their instant appeal. Nayyar put paid to all competition and criticism by the most potent weapon of all: sheer popularity. In an age where good film music had to be classical in orientation, he had the gumption to steer clear of the trend and compose simple, folk-based tunes or go Western in style.

Omkar Prasad Nayyar was recognized early as a genius, having become an AIR artiste in Lahore when he was just eleven. By the time he was fifteen, he was composing songs on AIR. Partition brought Nayyar to Amritsar and onwards to Bombay, where he got his break with D. Pancholi's *Aasmaan* (1952) at a close friend's recommendation. He got Geeta Roy to sing the delightful Behag piece '*Dekho jaadu bhare more nain*' and the stylish '*Dil hain diwana*', furthering Geeta's newfound 'modern' image. *Aasmaan* flopped, and so did his next two films. In Guru Dutt's *Baaz* (1953), Nayyar got Geeta to vocalize '*Aye watan ke naujawan*' and '*Taare chandni afsaane*' brilliantly, but jettisoned her in favour of Asha for all fourteen songs of *Cham Chama Cham*, his next film. When Asha too did not help him click, OP was all set to go back to Amritsar, when Geeta recommended him for Guru Dutt's *Aar Paar* (1954). A grateful OP put his heart and soul into the film, coming up with a super-hit score, albeit largely inspired from Western tunes.

It was in Geeta's vocals that OP soared to stardom, with the breeziness of '*Babuji dheere chalna*' and '*Ye lo main haari piya*' coming as a welcome break to a nation that was recovering from the classical impact of *Baiju Bawra* and *Anarkali*. He proved his calibre by composing the racy duet '*Sun sun sun sun zaalima*' (Rafi–Geeta) even as he got Geeta to render the slower, sad version '*Ja ja ja ja bewafa*' in total contrast. Nayyar consolidated his success with the light scores of Guru Dutt's *Mr. and Mrs. 55*, followed by *CID* (1956). Not just Geeta, Nayyar also helped Rafi find a new facet to his singing by composing eminently hummable duets '*Udhar tum haseen ho*' (*Mr. and Mrs. 55*) and '*Aankhon hi aankhon mein ishaara ho gaya*' (*CID*). By 1956, Nayyar's music had become the new norm in the industry, with producers requesting even senior composers to tune at least one number with the 'OP effect'.

The next big moment in OP's career came when B.R. Chopra gave him *Naya Daur* (1957), a film that had a serious social message. And what lustre OP brought to the score without making it too serious, a feat only he could have managed. If '*Ude jab jab zulfein teri*' was Punjabi gusto at its best, '*Maang ke saath tumhaara*' was lilting in its light-heartedness, a totally fresh image for both Dilip Kumar and Vyjayanthimala after the dark, brooding *Devdas*.

Nayyar did full justice to Sahir's lyrics *'Saathi haath badhaana'*, the Rafi–Asha duet that epitomized the spirit of the 'man versus machine' theme of the film. He also did a Naushad in the complex Rafi bhajan *'Aana hain toh aa'*, making the point subtly that his catchy style was a matter of choice, and not ability. *Naya Daur* fetched him his only Filmfare Award as best music director, and was a professional turning point for Asha Bhonsle who sang for a big heroine for the first time. It wasn't surprising then that they would get emotionally involved, forging a professional relationship that would create magic in the years to come.

In *Tumsa Nahin Dekha* (1957), Nayyar helped Shammi Kapoor craft a new image of the carefree, boisterous young man. *'Chhupnewale saamne aa'* and the title song *'Tumsa nahin dekha'* were typically OP, with an unrestrained Rafi giving expression to the suppressed sexuality of the Hindi film hero, without sounding coarse. Asha added her own oomph in *'Dekho kasam se'*, making *Tumsa Nahin Dekha* the most youthful score of the decade. Shanker–Jaikishan in the 1960s only furthered what Nayyar had achieved for Shammi, and for the Hindi film hero, through this score.

Even as he kept the flag of peppy music flying high, OP startled us with the serious music he composed, and excellently at that, for three films in 1958. In *Sone Ki Chidiya*, he composed the sterling ghazal *'Pyaar par bas toh nahin hain'*, getting Talat Mehmood to give it soul. He banked on Rafi's ability to emote the philosophical *'Raat bhar ka hain mehmaan andhera'*, and tapped the sweetness in Asha's voice in her duet with Talat *'Sach bata tu mujh pe fida'*. All three songs were very un-Nayyar like, surprising in the felicity with which he could take on the melody school of composers. In *Phagun*, he composed all fourteen songs in Raag Pilu, yet making each sound very distinct. The solos *'Piya piya na laage mora jiya'*, *'Sun ja pukar'* and *'Chhun chhun ghungroo bole'* saw Asha Bhonsle shed any diffidence she had as the younger sister of Lata, and emerge confidently as a singer in her own right. The Rafi–Asha duet *'Main soya akhiyan meeche'* is a classic, with the novelty of Asha's humming substituting instruments in the interludes.

OP could pick the hits of *Howrah Bridge* (Asha's *'Aayiye meherbaan'*; Geeta's *'Mera naam Chin Chin Choo'*) out of his bowler hat effortlessly. He only needed effort for something as tuneful as *'Chota sa baalma'*, the Raag Tilang bandish he got Asha to render for *Raagini* (1958), the closest Asha came to matching the Lata impact in that decade. *Raagini* saw OP going classical, with Kishore lip-synching to Rafi's '*Man mora baawra*', Salaamat and Amaanat Ali singing the pure classical '*Ched diye mere dil ke taar kyon*', and none other than Ustaad Aamir Khan rendering '*Jogia mere ghar aaye*'. All this from a man who really did not understand raags! Nayyar's erudition was something he acquired by absorbing the best of other composers. He had no qualms about adapting Madan Mohan's '*Preetam daras dikhao*' and recreating it as '*Tu hain mera prem devta*' (Rafi–Manna Dey) in the same Raag Lalit for *Kalpana* (1960). Or casting S.D. Burman's Kedar nazm '*Tang aa chuke hain kashmakash-e-zindagi se hum*' in *Pyaasa* as '*Humko tumhaare ishq ne kya kya bana diya*' in *Ek Musafir Ek Haseena* (1962).

By the end of the decade, OP was in a serious dilemma. What trade wanted were his lighter tunes (*Aar Paar*, *Naya Daur*, *Tumsa Nahin Dekha*, *Howrah Bridge*) but what he wanted to compose was something more mellow, such as Asha's semi-classical mujra '*Bekasi hadh se jab guzar jaaye*' in Raag Des for *Kalpana*. It took him the best part of three years and many flops, before he could bounce back with a third way. In 1961, he did not score for a single film. But in *Ek Musafir Ek Haseena* the following year, he had found a via media. If '*Aap yun hi agar humse milte rahe*' was a teasing Asha–Rafi duet in Raag Kedar that the market sought, '*Humko tumhaare ishq ne kya kya bana diya*' was something OP wanted to compose. He gained further confidence when the songs of Joy Mukherjee–Asha Parekh starrer *Phir Wohi Dil Laya Hoon* (1963) succeeded. '*Aanchal mein saja lena kaliyan*' (Rafi) and '*Aankhon se jo utari hain dil mein*' (Asha) typify the Nayyar of the 1960s: more serious, yet not too complex, and always accessible to the layperson. Nayyar returned but once to his boisterousness, in *Kashmir Ki Kali* (1964), to hold his own against Shanker–Jaikishan's monopoly over Shammi Kapoor scores. '*Tareef karoon kya uski, jisne tumhe banaya*', sang Rafi, as true for the composer as the heroine! With the super-success of *Kashmir Ki Kali* (which included such epiphanies as Rafi-Asha's '*Diwana hua baadal*'), he was back in reckoning as a top-notch composer. *Mere Sanam* (1965) had an unabashed lift from *Come September* in '*Pukarta chala hoon main*', but Nayyar staved off criticism by getting trusted Asha to sing her best song of the 1960s, '*Jaayiye aap kahaan jaayenge*', a song that set Lata humming!

Which brings us to one of the most amazing facets of Nayyar. He achieved all that glory in an era where every composer worth his salt needed a Lata to vocalize his creations. Nayyar is the only exception, never using Lata's voice for any song as a result of an early misunderstanding, the versions of which vary. Lata has maintained a diplomatic silence over this controversy. Publicly, Nayyar has maintained that his songs needed a more rounded, full-throated voice of the likes of Shamshad or Geeta. That he abandoned Geeta in favour of Asha is another matter, though he admitted honestly later that love knows no reason, only a season!

While that season lasted, he groomed Asha into a complete singer, testing her range in compositions as varied as the wistful '*Poocho na hamein hum unke liye*' (*Mitti Mein Sona*, 1960), the ebullient '*Balma khuli hawa mein*' (*Kashmir Ki Kali*), the brooding '*Woh hanske mile humse*' (*Baharein Phir Bhi Aayengi*, 1966), the sultry '*Woh haseen dard de do*' (*Humsaaya*, 1968) and '*Akeli hoon main piya aa*' (*Sambandh*, 1969). This last happened even as their real-life *sambandh* had run into rough weather, for reasons that are still not clear. Many musical partnerships, not all of them romantic, ended in bitterness in the tinsel world. Perhaps long-term intimacy craved for a change, a newness that could only be found elsewhere.

Nayyar put up a brave front in the face of his fall out with Asha, but the creative part of him was exhausted with her exit from his life. Much like C. Ramchandra without Lata, Nayyar was musically a lesser man without Asha. He sustained himself on his legendary pride for a few years, and then went into hibernation. But not before he gifted Asha with a song that helped her articulate her angst: '*Chain se humko kabhi aapne jeene na diya*' (*Pran Jaaye Par Vachan Na Jaaye*, 1973), a song that won her her fourth Filmfare Award.

His brief re-entry in the 1990s with *Nischay* and *Zid* was forgettable. He decided then to quit music and dedicate his life to healing others through homeopathy. The man who added colour to people's lives through his tunes had become a recluse, until death came on 28 January 2007 to remind people of his genius.

Salil Choudhury: East Meets West

He considered himself the Pele of film music. And not without reason. In his amazing ability to blend the melody of the East with the grandeur of the West, Salil-da was unparalleled. Long before fusion music became fashionable, he integrated Western notes into Indian melodies so seamlessly that it is only with an effort that you tune into the chords, melody and countermelody in his tunes. What hits you straight is their unalloyed sweetness.

There is a restraint to his music, an understatement of emotion that impacts you subtly, yet lastingly. The impact is a combination of the singer, lyrics, tune and, never the least with Salil, the musical arrangement. Take the song from *Chhaya* (1961), '*Aansoo samajh ke kyon mujhe aankh se tumne giraa diya*'. Talat's rendering is superb, Rajinder Krishan's lyrics astounding, but the real heartbreakers are the violins and cello in the background. To comprehend his true genius, one has to pay attention to the way he used background music in all his songs to accentuate the feeling.

Not a tall feat for a man who in his early teens had learnt to play the flute exceedingly well. Growing up amidst the tea gardens of Assam, Salil was immersed in the folk songs of Bengal as well as the records of Western classical music his father would play. Both these influences would permeate his compositions, often seamlessly. He could, for instance, westernize the background music of a totally Indian melody such as '*O sajna barkha bahaar aayee*' in *Parakh* (1960), or, just as easily, give an unusual Bhairavi movement to the Mozart-inspired '*Itna na mujh se tu pyaar badha*' (*Chhaya*). The total effect was typically mind-blowing. He was unapologetic about adapting Western symphonies or Rabindra Sangeet into his film compositions, arguing that even Shakespeare plagiarized!

By the time Salil entered Hindi films as composer with his score for Bimal Roy's *Do Bigha Zameen* (1953), he had spent his youth in composing songs for the freedom movement in Bengal and in writing Bengali poems and lyrics with a strong plea for justice, the result of his involvement with the Indian Peoples' Theatre Association (IPTA), the cultural wing of the communist movement in the 1940s. Salil made peace with the 'love-and-romance preoccupation' in Hindi films by turning a revolutionary in his compositions and musical arrangements. He was the first choice as composer for films with a strong social theme though. '*Dharti kahe pukaar ke*' (Manna Dey–Lata) in *Do Bigha Zameen* reflects the hopes of the peasant poignantly. Raj Kapoor chose

Salil over Shanker-Jaikishan for his powerful *Jaagte Raho* (1956), made when SJ were ruling the industry. Salil got Mukesh to articulate '*Zindagi khwaab hain*', a touchingly cynical view of life so in sync with the movie's theme.

Recognition, however, came to him for the score of *Madhumati* (1958), the film that fetched Salil his first and only Filmfare Award. It remains his most popular score. Possibly because, in *Madhumati*, Salil was composing for a movie that had two superstars: Dilip Kumar and Vyjayanthimala, something rare for the gifted composer. '*Aaja re pardesi*' is an unusual composition—Raageshri in the Indian system of raags, but also the 7th chord as the basic melody, 'the chord of incompletion' in Salil's own words. The effect is so mesmerizing that C. Ramchandra called up Salil to congratulate him on making Lata sound as fresh as a teenager. The most moving song in the score is however the Rafi solo '*Toote huye khwabon ne*,' a typically restrained Darbari Kaanada composition. Lata–Manna Dey's '*Chadh gayo paapi bicchua*' had Salil bring his expertise with folk music into full play, getting Lata to transcend the eroticism of the lyrics with her characteristic poise.

Though Salil used Rafi, Mukesh, Talat, Manna Dey and later Kishore as male playback for his tunes, he was unwilling to look beyond Lata as his lead female playback. Lata was his professional obsession, one he reserved his best tunes for. The regard was mutual, with Lata picking his '*O sajna barkha bahaar aayee*' as one of ten favourites for her silver jubilee selection, and steadfastly maintaining that he was a genius. A genius that found best expression in her voice, in solos such as '*Ja re ja re ud ja re panchi*' (*Maya*, 1961), '*Machalti aarzoo khadi hain baahen pasaar*' (*Usne Kahaa Tha*, 1961), and '*Saathi re tujh bin jiya udaas re*' (*Poonam Ki Raat*, 1965), where the whole orchestration is again Western, heightening the mood of the song beautifully. Salil's work in the 1960s is best remembered for his Lata compositions, and she continued to be vital to him well into the next decade with '*Naa jiya laage naa*' (*Anand*, 1970), '*Raaton ke saaye ghane*' (*Annadaata*, 1972), '*Rajnigandha phool tumhaare*' (*Rajnigandha*, 1974) and '*Na jaane kyon*' (*Chhoti Si Baat*, 1975).

Lata was an obsession, but not a restricting one for him. He was as capable of producing magic in the voices of others too. Talat sang his early songs '*Raat ne kya kya khwaab dikhaaye*' in Ek

Gaon Ki Kahaani (1957) and '*Aankhon mein masti sharab ki*' for *Chhaya*. Mukesh had a longer spell with Salil, immortalizing himself and the composer with '*Kahin door jab din dhal jaaye*' for *Anand* (a song Talat confessed to this author he desperately wanted to sing), and '*Kayi baar yun bhi dekha hain*' (*Rajnigandha*). Rafi featured in almost every Salil film, but only his solo in *Madhumati* is popular. For some reason Salil was not comfortable with him, and didn't have much to say about Rafi as a singer. Salil discovered Kishore's playback talent late, but had the grace to admit he had underrated Kishore when he sang '*Koi hota jisko apna*' soulfully for *Mere Apne* (1971). Manna Dey sang Salil's two best-known songs, '*Aye mere pyaare watan*' (*Kaabuliwaala*, 1961) and '*Zindagi kaisi hain paheli*' (*Anand*).

'I want to create music that transcends all borders', Salil once said. He did that for two decades by blending East and West in Hindi films with a finesse no one could match. He also proved that music is beyond barriers such as language, by composing for over twenty-five Malayalam films. His score for *Chemmeen* (1965) made him as popular in the south as in Hindi films. Perhaps the south gave him more recognition than Bollywood, where the composer, much like peer Madan Mohan, never did get big banners. His songs were loved, but the films were usually forgettable. By the late 1970s, Salil had lost his enthusiasm to compose, because R.D. Burman and Laxmikant–Pyarelal had changed the tone and tenor of film music. Salil decided to retire, moving to Calcutta, and continuing to experiment with composing music and writing scripts for television serials and documentaries. He died in Calcutta in September 1995.

They Kept Melody Alive

The 1950s and 1960s would not be the golden era of music were it also not for the richness and creativity in melody that a host of composers sustained and built upon, if not exactly pioneered. They were the second-line tunesmiths whose contribution was more in terms of keeping the spirit of melody alive, rather than extending the contours of the genre. Perhaps for this reason none of them became an icon like the others we've considered so far, immense as their talent was and prodigious their work.

ROSHAN: Roshan broke through early in his career, with his second film *Bawre Nain* (1950) which had Mukesh and Geeta Roy hum '*Khayalon mein kisi ke*' and Rajkumari match Geeta Bali's on-screen zest in '*Sun bairi balam sach bol re*'. Two years later, he established himself as a composer of class, getting Lata to render '*Aeri aali piya bin*' in Raag Yaman for *Raag Rang*, making Talat give that velvety touch to match the melody of the superb piano notes in '*Main dil hoon ek armaan bhara*' (*Anhonee*) and by composing the Meera bhajan '*Aeri main to prem diwani*' in Raag Bhimpalasi for Lata again in *Naubahaar*. Is it any wonder then that from among all the talent available to her in the 1950s, Lata chose Roshan as composer for her own film *Bhairavi*, a project that never took off? The only other hit Roshan had in the decade was again in Lata's voice, in the little-known film *Aji Bas Shukriya* (1958), where Lata's song '*Saari saari raat teri yaad sataaye*' stood out.

Despite some very classy tunes in the 1950s, Roshan had to wait a full decade before he saw big-time success with the score of *Barsaat Ki Raat* (1960). Rafi's '*Zindagi bhar nahin bhoolegi woh barsaat ki raat*' put him on par with Madan Mohan as far as ghazals were concerned. In composing '*Na toh karwaan ki talaash hain*', Roshan earned the sobriquet of the master of qawwalis, making this genre of songs respectable in films.

Roshan posed a stiff challenge to Madan Mohan in the 1960s with ghazals such as '*Ab kya misaal doon main tumhaare shabab ki*' (Rafi, *Aarti*, 1962), '*Jurm-e-ulfat pe hamen log sazaa dete hain*' (Lata, *Taj Mahal*, 1963), '*Jo baat tujh mein hain*' (Rafi, *Taj Mahal*), '*Man re tu kaahe na dheer dhare*' (Rafi, *Chitralekha*, 1964), '*Dil jo na keh saka*' (Rafi, *Bheegi Raat*, 1965) and '*Rehte the kabhi jinke dil mein*' (Lata, *Mamta*, 1966). Lata and Rafi were the pillars for his ghazals, but he banked on Manna Dey for his classical compositions ('*Laaga chunri mein daag*', *Dil Hi To Hain*, 1963) and Mukesh for his folk-based tunes ('*Oh re taal mile nadi ke jal mein*', *Anokhi Raat*, 1967). The words '*kya hoga kaun se pal mein koi jaane naa*' in the latter song were prophetic, as Roshan succumbed to a heart attack without completing the score of the film.

HEMANT KUMAR: The true measure of Hemant Kumar's musical virtuosity can only be comprehended when you consider him as composer, his awesome reputation as singer notwithstanding. Simplicity and generosity were his hallmark as a man, and his tunes had an innocence and sweetness that only he could have created. Steeped as he was in Rabindra Sangeet and classical music, he could transmute his grasp and knowledge in an uncomplicated way into his film compositions that made them utterly melodious, contributing to their instant appeal.

The simplicity came through in his very first film *Anandmath* (1952), in the shloka '*Jai jagdish hare*' that he sang with Geeta Roy. Two years later, *Nagin* catapulted him to fame, the nation mesmerized by the snake-charmer effect of Lata's '*Man dole mera tan dole*'. The way he used the claviolin to produce the '*been*' effect in the song was astounding. The score was typical of his kind of music—no grandeur, but ample charm. But those were years when the top slot in music was already occupied by Naushad and Shanker-Jaikishan. So Hemant Kumar was left with little choice but to compose for small-budget movies. Like many other talented composers in that era, his songs are well known, but the movies they were featured in obscure. '*Chhup gaya koi re door se pukar ke*', the arresting Lata solo in *Champakali* (1958) is a case in point.

Perhaps it was this neglect that made him turn producer with *Bees Saal Baad* (1962), loosely based on *The Hound of the Baskervilles*. It certainly paid dividends to his music, because in the atmospheric Lata solo '*Kahin deep jale kahin dil*' he had his next big hit after '*Man dole*'. The 1960s brought him more recognition, as he composed a score for Guru Dutt's *Sahib, Bibi aur Ghulam* (1963) that tellingly captured the desolation of the movie. '*Koi door se aawaaz de chale aao*' and '*Na jao saiyan chuda ke baiyan*' had Geeta Dutt achieve her career best under his baton. *Kohraa* (1963) had his own best solo, '*Yeh nayan dare dare*'. In 1966, Hemant composed something as apt as Lata's '*Kuch dil ne kaha, kuch bhi nahin*' and his own '*Ya dil ki suno duniyawalon*' for Hrishikesh Mukherjee's sombre *Anupama*. But his best-ever score came three years later for *Khamoshi*, where listeners had the predicament of choosing their favourite from three heart-tugging melodies. '*Hamne dekhi hain un aankhon ki mehekti khushboo*' is lyricist Gulzar at his best. '*Tum pukar lo*' in Hemant's own voice is arguably the most haunting solo of the decade. And in getting Kishore Kumar to render the sublime '*Woh shaam kuch ajeeb thi*', Hemant Kumar proved Kishore's calibre as a serious singer much before any other composer.

Like many other composers of the golden era, Hemant was too committed to melody to shift gears to the rhythm wave of the 1970s. He continued to do an odd film or two, but couldn't quite recreate the magic of yore. A few years before his death in 1989, Hemant Kumar was in the news when he refused the Padma Shri, saying it came too late.

RAVI: You wonder at the wilful ways of stardom when you reflect on how much composer Ravi's tunes have meant to you, and how unrecognized in the industry his genius was. From a naughty score in *Dilli Ka Thug* ('M-A-D mad, mad maane paagal', Kishore and Asha, 1958) through the classical numbers in *Ghunghat* ('Mori chham chham baaje paayaliya', Lata, 1960) to the all-time great 'Chaudhvin ka chand ho' (*Chaudhvin Ka Chand*, Rafi, 1960), he proved his versatility early in his career. Both the man and his tunes were never flamboyant, and he didn't work with big banners, except with B.R. Films for whom he reserved some of his best work in *Gumraah* ('Chalo ek baar phir se ajnabee ban jaaye hum dono', Mahendra Kapoor, 1963), *Waqt* ('Aage bhi jaane na tu', Asha Bhosle, 1964) and later *Nikaah* ('Dil ki yeh aarzoo thi koi dilruba mile', Mahendra Kapoor–Salma Agha, 1980). Having learnt early as Hemant Kumar's assistant that lyrics and tune are more important than the singer, Ravi could make an impact even with singers he was not too happy about—Mahendra Kapoor and Salma Agha, both the producer's choice. When he had a free hand, he produced masterpieces: 'Sab kuch lutaa ke hosh mein aaye toh kya kiya' (*Ek Saal*, 1957, Talat), 'Aye mere dil-e-nadaan' (*Tower House*, 1962, Lata), 'Tora man darpan kehlaye' (*Kaajal*, 1965, Asha) and 'Raha gardishon mein har dam' (*Do Badan*, 1966, Rafi). He won the Filmfare Award for best composer twice, for *Gharana* (1961) and again for *Khaandan* (1965). As sweet natured as his tunes, Ravi chose to focus on all that he got rather than what he didn't from the industry, managing thus to retain his grip on melody for more than two decades.

JAIDEV: It is difficult to hear Jaidev's music without feeling pained at the raw deal he got from the industry. Surely the man who created 'Allah tero naam ishwar tero naam' (*Hum Dono*) deserved more recognition and success? Unlike peer Madan Mohan, Jaidev did not even have the satisfaction of the industry waking up to his genius posthumously. Till the very end and after, he remained unsung.

This, despite creating some of the most piercing, if complex, melodies over three decades. Lata has gone on record to say how tough it was to sing his compositions, and how sweet the end result was! She should know best, because it is in her voice that he created his best work. From the wistful *'Subah ka intezaar kaun kare'* in *Joru Ka Bhai* (1955) and the sublime *'Allah tero naam'* to the passionate *'Tu chanda main chandni'* (*Reshma Aur Shera*, 1972), Jaidev came alive when she was in his recording room. Rafi sang Jaidev's best-known ghazal *'Kabhi khud pe kabhi haalaat pe rona aaya'* in *Hum Dono*. The film was Jaidev's only big-banner effort, Navketan having opted for him only because he was S.D. Burman's assistant and as a reward for his loyalty to them. What a pity that despite creating the score of a lifetime, Dev Anand had no qualms about jettisoning Jaidev once Dada Burman recovered. *'Abhi na jao chod kar'* (Rafi–Asha), *'Main zindagi ka saath nibhata chala gaya'* (Rafi), *'Prabhu tero naam'* (Lata), *'Jahaan mein aisa kaun hain'* (Asha)—was there ever a more erudite, classier score in a Navketan film?

The same sophitication was evident even in B-grade films that he got to score for, never mind that S.D. Burman reprimanded him for his penchant for intricate compositions. Jaidev was too honest to make anything but gold, musically. *'Dekh li teri khudai'* sang Talat in *Kinare Kinare* (1963). *'Nadi naare na jao shyam'* teased Asha in *Mujhe Jeene Do* (1963). *'Yeh dil aur unki nigahon ke saaye'* warbled Lata in *Prem Parbat* (1973). Much as the public loved these songs, the composer continued to languish. After a while, he could not afford established voices for his songs. His true greatness could be seen in what he got rank newcomers to give. *'Koi gaata main so jaata'* (Yesudas, *Alaap*, 1977), *'Tumhen ho na ho mujhko to itna yakeen hain'* (Runa Laila, *Gharonda*, 1977), *'Seene mein jalan aankhon mein toofan sa kyon hain'* (Suresh Wadkar, *Gaman*, 1979) and *'Zindagi mere ghar aana'* (Bhupinder–Anuradha Paudwal, *Dooriyan*, 1979) are all as exquisite as anything Jaidev composed in Lata, Asha or Rafi's voices.

But it was inevitable that despair would set in. For a while, he drew sustenance from alcohol and the company of friends. But in the end, he died a lonely man, not too long after he won his third National Award, after *Reshma Aur Shera* and *Gaman*, for the score of Amol Palekar's *Ankahee* (1984).

VASANT DESAI: Vasant Desai's musical presence in the golden era of Hindi film music is much larger than the number of films he composed for. Such is the lasting impact of his tunes. So what if he got his most famous film *Jhanak Jhanak Paayal Baaje* (1955) as a gift from Naushad, who turned producer Shantaram away saying that Rajkamal's in-house composer Desai was as good a classical composer? Vasant Desai measured up to Naushad's opinion of him, most notably seen in the way he composed two very different Bhairavi numbers, 'Mere aye dil bata' and the Meera bhajan 'Jo tum todo piya'. One was a cry of anguish, the other an ode of surrender, both piercing in their impact.

The song one associates most with Desai is the other bhajan 'Aye malik tere bande hum' from Shantaram's classic *Do Aankhen Barah Haath* (1957). The Punjab government of the day declared the song as the official prayer in all schools in the state, something rare in an era when film music was still just gaining respectability. The other Lata solo 'Saiyan jhooton ka bada sartaj nikla' and the chorus song 'Umad ghumad kar aayee re ghata' have a delightfully earthy feel, proving that Desai could compose superbly what the theme wanted. His third notable work in the 1950s was the out-and-out classical score for *Goonj Uthi Shehnai* (1959) where he got Ustaad Bismillah Khan to play the shehnai in the songs and background music. With the two Lata solos 'Tere sur aur mere geet' in Raag Behag and 'Dil ka khilona haaye toot gaya' in Raag Bhairavi, and Rafi's monumental 'Kehdo koi na kare yahaan pyaar' in Raag Jogiya, Desai seemed poised for greater things at the turn of the decade.

But as fate would have it, he found the going tough in the 1960s, with his films flopping badly. *Ashirvad* (1968) was the only film that got musical notice, with Lata's Todi refrain in 'Ek tha bachpan' leaving a mark. To Desai goes the credit of composing in this film the first 'rap' number in Hindi films with 'Rail gaadi chuk chuk chuk chuk', sung with aplomb by Ashok Kumar. In his twenty-seventh year as composer, Vasant Desai was still able to create something as youthful. Two years later came his last hit *Guddi*, where he created magic in the voice of debutant Vani Jairam with 'Bole re papihara', the definitive Miyan Ki Malhar composition in films and an iconic rain song. The film also had an authentic Raag Kedar piece in 'Hum ko man ki shakti dena', another favourite school prayer song. A few years and some unremarkable films later, he died a sudden death in an accident in 1976.

THIRD-GENERATION COMPOSERS: THE BRAVEHEARTS

They had the going tough in two ways: one, they inherited the rich legacy of their illustrious forefathers and were taking over the baton knowing very well they would be compared to the best ever. Second, and unfortunately so, they came of age as composers in the 1970s, an era when music had become peripheral to films. The work of Kalyanji–Anandji, R.D. Burman and Laxmikant–Pyarelal, the triumvirate that ruled the 1970s, has to be seen in the light of these contexts. Perhaps one can get a true picture of their immense talent only when one realizes that they gave their share of good music despite such constraints. To live with the realization that the best is over, and yet do what one can to further the cause of music must not have been easy. Khayyam and Ravindra Jain are included here only because they were torchbearers of melody in an era that made it almost impossible to have good music.

KALYANJI–ANANDJI: GENTEEL ART

Having grown up in the years when they were most popular, I thought I knew the music of this composer duo well. However, in going back to Kalyanji–Anandji's work, I had a triple surprise awaiting me. One was the realization that though they are generally recognized as composers of the Bachchan era, their best work happened earlier, between 1960 and 1970. Second, I discovered the true range and depth of Mukesh as a singer in their compositions. Third, the phenomenal poetry lyricist Indeewar wrote for them, which made me wonder how the man could have agreed to write for the Bappi Lahiri films in the 1980s.

Perhaps the true extent of their talent can be gauged from the fact that unlike their role models Shanker–Jaikishan, who fumbled in the face of the challenge posed by others to their suzerainty, Kalyanji–Anandji scaled ever newer peaks musically and commercially even while facing stiff competition from their erstwhile assistants Laxmikant–Pyarelal. And this they achieved without ever resorting to any manipulative tactics, in all their three decades of popularity. Both brothers had a strong spiritual grounding, believing that fate played a role in everything that happened. This helped them keep their heads on their respective shoulders at all times, winning them the respect and, something rare in Bollywood, the affection of people in the industry.

Kalyanji was noticed early for his talent as Hemant Kumar's assistant in *Nagin* (1954), where he played the imported claviolin to produce the *'been'* effect in the chartbuster *'Man dole mera tan dole'*. Four years later, it was with the Hemant Kumar–Lata duet *'O neend na mujhko aaye'* in *Post Box 999* (1958) that Kalyanji had his first hit. Next year, he teamed up with brother Anandji to create another Hemant–Lata melody in *'Tumhen yaad hoga kabhi hum mile the'* for their first film as duo, *Satta Bazaar* (1959). They achieved their first hit score with the Raj Kapoor–Nutan starrer *Chhalia* (1960) where Mukesh sang *'Dum dum diga diga'*, *'Chhalia mera naam'* and *'Mere toote hue dil se'*, all in Shanker–Jaikishan mould. It was in Mukesh's voice that Kalyanji–Anandji would later find their identity; with him they would create their best work.

Their unhooking from the SJ fascination came as early as in *Dulha Dulhan* (1964), where they created the Tilak Kamod gem *'Humne tujhko pyaar kiya hain jitna'*, sung as solos by Lata and Mukesh. Lata brought to the song her classical finesse, and Mukesh his feeling. It is a tough choice, but I'd pick the Mukesh version as the hallmark of this duo's music: tunes steeped in the Indian tradition, but defined most by feeling. The following year saw them enter the big league with *Himalay Ki Godh Mein*, winning the Cine Music Directors' Association award for best score against competition from *Suraj*, *Guide* and *Mere Sanam*, all scored by senior composers. *'Main toh ek khwaab hoon'* and *'Chand si mehbooba ho meri'* are Mukesh classics, but Kalyanji–Anandji's virtuosity was also seen in the way they composed for Lata the happy and sad versions of the same song as *'Ik tu jo mila saari duniya mili'* and *'Ek tu na mila saari duniya milen bhi toh kya hain'* respectively, both to the strains of Raag Charukeshi. In *Upkar* (1967), they created the most popular patriotic song in Hindi films, *'Mere desh ki dharti'*, in Mahendra Kapoor's voice, earning for Manoj Kumar the nickname Mr Bharat. The same film had the Manna Dey hit, the philosophical *'Kasme waade pyar wafa.'* They also depended on Rafi's ability to create hits in *'Pardesion se na akhiyan milana'* (*Jab Jab Phool Khile*, 1965) and in *'Akele hain chale aao'* (*Raaz*, 1967).

But their best was yet to come. With the score of *Saraswatichandra* (1968), they left no one in doubt about their awesome talent. Each song in the film is a musical ocean in itself, each was equally popular at the time. Did Mukesh ever sing anything more mellifluous than '*Chandan sa badan*', set to the muted notes of Raag Yaman? Kalyanji paid tribute to the music of his home town, Kutch, by composing the popular garba number for Lata, '*Main toh bhool chali babul ka des*'. Talking of Indeewar, I wonder whether the lyricist ever wrote anything as sublime as '*Chod de saari duniya kisi ke liye yeh munasib nahin aadmi ke liye*' for Lata to immortalize. Not surprisingly, Kalyanji–Anandji became the first music directors in Hindi cinema to receive the National Award for best music for their score of *Saraswatichandra*.

Not that it made them at all complacent. In 1970, they straddled the two worlds of authentic art and commercial success effortlessly. In the year when their idols Shanker–Jaikishan faced their biggest failure in *Mera Naam Joker*, Kalyanji–Anandji had a huge hit in *Johny Mera Naam*. Kishore Kumar had burst upon the scene, and the duo utilized him aptly for zesty numbers such as '*Nafrat karnewalon ki seene mein pyar bhar doon*' and '*Palbhar ke liye koi hamen pyar karle*'. The Asha–Kishore duet '*O mere raja*' was also hugely popular. If *Johny Mera Naam* was their bow to the market, they also had the classy melody-backed scores of *Safar* and *Purab Aur Paschim* to show. *Safar* brought to the fore the serious singer in Kishore Kumar, with the dark and brooding '*Zindagi ka safar*' and the mellow '*Jeevan se bhari teri aankhen*' representing a facet of him that was underutilized throughout his career. Lata, a strong presence in all their films, had the poignantly beautiful '*Hum the jinke sahaare*'. In *Purab Aur Paschim*, the honesty in Mukesh's voice haunts you long into the night in '*Koi jab tumhaara hriday tod de*', making Indeewar's moving lyrics very real.

The 1970s saw Kalyanji-Anandji at the peak of commercial success, composing popular, if uninspiring music. In an era when music had become incidental to most storylines, they had a string of hits from *Zanjeer* ('*Yaari hain imaan mera*', Manna Dey, 1973) through *Don* ('*Khaike paan Banaraswala*', Kishore, 1978) to *Muqaddar Ka Sikander* ('*O saathi re*', Asha and Kishore solos, 1979), but the scores were musically unremarkable. Like many composers of the era, they found creative satisfaction in composing for small-budget movies that allowed scope for music. It is only in *Kora Kagaz*

('*Mera jeevan kora kagaz*', Kishore, 1974), which fetched them their only Filmfare Award for best composer, or in the songs '*Pal pal dil ke paas*' (*Blackmail*, Kishore, 1973), '*Apne jeevan ke uljhan ko*' (*Uljhan*, Lata and Kishore solos, 1975) and '*Baandhi re kaahe preet*' (*Sankoch*, Sulakshana Pandit, 1976) that you find them musically inspired.

The 1980s began with a bang for the duo, with *Qurbani* (1980) becoming a musical blockbuster, though the most popular Nazia Hassan number '*Aap jaisa koi mere zindagi mein aaye*' was composed by Biddu. They were certainly hurt with Feroz Khan for including the song in the movie, but they chose to take it in their stride by composing the other hit '*Laila o Laila*' (Amit Kumar–Kanchan). Thereafter, they went overboard to remain saleable, even composing something as coarse as '*Saat saheliyan khadi khadi*' (*Vidhaata*, 1982, Kishore, Anuradha Paudwal and Alka Yagnik) and '*Mere angne mein*' (*Laawaris*, 1982 Amitabh and Alka Yagnik solos). In Feroz Khan's *Jaanbaaz* (1986), Kalyanji's son Viju Shah used the synthesiser to make their tunes '*Har kisi ko nahin milta yahaan pyar zindagi mein*' (Manhar–Sadhna Sargam) and '*Pyar do pyar lo*' (Sapna Mukherjee) catchy. They composed for close to a hundred films in that decade, but it is only in something as unsung as '*Haathon ki chand lakeeron ka*' (*Vidhaata*, Suresh Wadkar–Anwar) that you glimpse their magic of yore. By the end of the decade they realized their time was over, and paved the way for Viju Shah to take over with the synthesiser-dominated, youthful score of *Tridev* (1989).

Rahul Dev Burman: Prisoner of His Image

It is thirteen years since he left us, succumbing to a cardiac arrest caused by years of rejection and loneliness. Thirteen years when one facet of his music has only grown in iconic status, thanks to the remix phenomenon. Like in life, Rahul Dev Burman continues to remain prisoner of his image posthumously as the man who most successfully Indianized pop and jazz for Hindi films. For much of the youth today and many of the older generation, '*Piya tu ab toh aaja*' and '*Dum maro dum*' typify RD's music.

I believe RD stumbled upon the jazz route in his quest to find his own moorings in the face of father Sachin Dev Burman's towering presence. *Teesri Manzil* (1966) with '*Aaja aaja main hoon pyar tera*' clicked, and RD got stuck with a brand of music where rhythm and pace were more important than melody. This was further compounded when Dev Anand approached RD to compose for *Hare Rama Hare Krishna* (1971), knowing that only RD could fire the imagination of the youth with something as devil-may-care as '*Dum maro dum*'. The song became a cult, and RD was trapped further in that image. He was too raw to take a firm stand in the first few years, and there never was a right time to relinquish that image publicly in the 1970s. Till the end, he remained a man who couldn't quite succeed with what he truly wanted to compose.

We only have to rewind to 1961 to substantiate my point. The very first song he tuned as independent composer is the Lata melody '*Ghar aaja ghir aayee badra*' set to Raag Maalgunji. Four years later, in *Bhoot Bangla*, for all the jazz of Manna Dey's '*Aao twist karen*', it was again Lata's '*O mere pyar aaja*' that caught our ear for its soothing impact, the saxophone under RD's baton almost matching Lata's sweetness. The bhajan '*O Ganga maiyya*' in *Chandan Ka Palna* (1967) was such an authentic Raag Jogiya composition that RD was one of the nominees that year for the prestigious Sur Singar Samsad Award for best classical song! What came in the way of RD winning it was his newfound pop image, what with '*O mere sona re*' and '*Aaja aaja*' from *Teesri Manzil* still ruling the airwaves then. *Baharon Ke Sapne*, released the year after, had RD compose two outstanding melodies for Lata: '*Aaja piya tohe pyar doon*' with its soft strumming electric guitar replacing the tabla for rhythm, and '*O more sajna o more balma*', an early RD stunner in Raag Nand.

If any more proof of what RD really wanted to compose is needed, one only has to turn to the two mellow numbers in the riotous comedy *Padosan* (1968). '*Kehna hain kehna hain*' gave a glimpse of the special rapport that would develop between RD and Kishore Kumar over the years. There was an undercurrent of melancholy in the song that made it really exquisite, putting it way ahead of all other numbers in the movie. RD saw the need for the rollicking '*Ek chatura naar*' (Manna Dey–Kishore) and the comic '*O meri pyari Bindu*' (Kishore), but could find creative satisfaction only with something as subtle as '*Kehna hain*'. Also noteworthy in the film is the rarely heard Lata solo '*Sharm aati hain magar aaj yeh kehna hoga*' in RD's favourite Raag Khamaj.

'*Piya tu ab toh aaja*' (*Caravan*, 1971) and '*Dum maro dum*'

(*Hare Rama Hare Krishna*) certainly gave RD much-needed confidence that he could make it on his own. But it was with the melody-backed score of *Amar Prem* the same year that RD proved he had come of age as a composer of class. '*Raina beeti jaaye*', with an unusual combination of Raags Todi and Khamaj, stands out as Lata's best classical solo in that decade. Moreover, RD converted an entire generation Rafi fans into Kishore fanatics with the score of *Amar Prem*. Kishore truly arrived as a playback singer with '*Chingari koi bhadke*' set to Raag Bhairavi, '*Kuch toh log kahenge*' with its base in Khamaj and '*Yeh kya hua*' with shades of Raag Kalavati. *Amar Prem*, while showcasing Kishore's virtuosity, was more importantly a tribute to RD's composing skill and faith in Kishore as singer.

RD, much like his father, had the knack of drawing out the essence of a raag in a song without making it complex. *Buddha Mil Gaya* (1971) sank as a film, but '*Aayo kahan se Ghanshyam*' (Manna Dey) and '*Jiya na laage mora*' (Lata) both attest to this ability, as does his classical composition '*Beeti na bitayee raina*' in *Parichay*, which fetched Lata and Bhupinder the National Award. RD himself was passed over for the best composer award. Had he got it, he may have found the courage to give free rein to the serious composer in him.

As it turned out, 1972 was the year that slotted RD as the composer of youth, with '*Duniya mein logon ko*' (RD-Asha, *Apna Desh*), '*Dekha na haaye re socha na*' (Kishore, *Bombay To Goa*), '*Jaan-e-jaan dhoondta phir raha*' (Kishore-Asha, *Jawani Diwani*), '*O mere dil ke chain*' (Kishore, *Mere Jeevan Saathi*) and '*Hawa ke saath saath*' (Kishore-Asha, *Seeta Aur Geeta*) all becoming chartbusters. He, however, came closest to composing what he wanted to in little-known *Lakhon Mein Ek* with the Kishore-Lata duet '*Chanda o chanda*' and in *Rampur Ka Laxman* with the arresting '*Gum hain kisi ke pyar mein*' (Kishore-Lata again). In what was an incredibly successful year, RD very likely came to grief, realizing that success needed only a part of him, a part at odds with his core desire.

From then on, RD played it safe. His big-banner movies had only one kind of music. Thus it was that *Yaadon Ki Baraat* was his biggest hit in 1973, revolutionizing what popular film music would be all about. Thrilling as '*Chura liya hain tumne jo dilko*' and '*Lekar hum deewana dil*' were, it is elsewhere that one finds his best even in that year. '*Wada karo nahin chodoge tum mera saath*' (Kishore-

Lata, *Aa Gale Lag Jaa*), '*Diye jalte hain*' (Kishore, *Namak Haram*), '*Kiska rasta dekhein*' (Kishore, *Joshila*) and '*Panna ki tamanna hain*' (Lata–Kishore, *Heera Panna*) were all infinitely superior compositions.

It was only in Gulzar's films that RD managed to bridge the dichotomy between class appeal and mass adulation. With *Parichay* began a long association between the writer–director and the composer that was to last right till RD's demise. Such was the tuning between the two that they often instinctively understood what the other wanted. Hence, RD could soar high without any constraints in '*Is mod se jaate hain*' (Lata–Kishore, *Aandhi*, 1975), '*Naam gum jaayega*' (Lata–Bhupinder, *Kinara*, 1977) or '*Aaj kal paon zameen par nahin padte mere*' (Lata, *Ghar*, 1978). In '*Mera kuch saaman*' a decade later (*Ijaazat*), RD ensured a National Award for best playback singer to wife Asha Bhonsle. While Gulzar walked away with the award for best lyricist for the same song, RD had to remain content in their glory.

Which brings us to the special bond that existed between Asha and RD. After O.P. Nayyar's exit from Asha's life, it was RD who helped Asha find her vocal identity through his youthful numbers. Right from '*O mere sona re*' (*Teesri Manzil*) to '*Katra katra milti hain*' (*Ijaazat*), Asha remained crucial to the experimental side of his music. She sang the sexy, tuneless '*Mera naam hain shabnam*' (*Kati Patang*), the evocative '*Sapna mera toot gaya*' (*Khel Khel Mein*, 1975) and all the jazzy numbers in *Yaadon Ki Baraat* and *Hum Kisi Se Kam Nahin* (1977). However, RD continued to be reluctant to look beyond Lata for his melodious numbers. It was only in the 1980s that Asha got something musically weighty as the Behag-based '*Piya baawri piya baawri*' (*Khubsoorat*, 1980), the delightfully classical '*Roz roz daali daali*' in Kalyan (*Angoor*, 1981) or the ghazal '*Aur kya ahd-e-wafa hote hain*' (*Sunny*, 1984). It was an aggrieved Asha who went on record to say that even RD reserved his best tunes for Lata, a grievance not without some justification, given that even in *Sunny*, RD had reserved the better number '*Jaane kya baat hain*' for Lata. By the time RD turned towards the serious singer in Asha, his best was already over.

Despite the youthful, hit scores of *Love Story* (1981) and *Betaab* (1983), I believe that by the 1980s, RD was in the throes of a serious identity crisis. He had exhausted his capacity to create westernized jazzy scores, and he had had too many instances of his more melodious scores being rejected, mostly because the films were badly made, or did not have the right star cast. *Kudrat* (1981) is a case in point. '*Hamen tumse pyar kitna*' is a beautiful thumri in Bhairavi by Begum Parveen Sultana that fetched her the Filmfare Award for best singer, but the film itself bombed despite good music. *Masoom* (1982) had some good melodies that fetched RD a Filmfare Award, but it earned him only critical acclaim. *Sanam Teri Kasam* (1983) bombed as a movie, so RD couldn't draw comfort from his more hip score in it either. Meanwhile, Bappi Lahiri had taken on the mantle of the disco king, leaving RD very unsure of which kind of music he should focus on. In *Saagar* (1985) he tried a via media between the two styles of his music, with 'O Maria' as the typical RD number and '*Saagar kinare*' being the more musical, mellow kind. When *Saagar* failed at the box office, RD found himself being written off. Kishore Kumar's death in 1987 was a blow that shattered him further. When Subhash Ghai replaced RD with Laxmikant–Pyarelal in *Ram Lakhan* (1989), RD suffered his first heart attack. He recovered enough to compose for *Ijaazat* with friend Gulzar and wife Asha as the two pillars of his strength, but for all the waves it made, *Ijaazat* could not resuscitate his career.

Diminished in body and mind, RD plodded on with whatever assignments came his way for the next few years. He had always been shy of crowds; in the last few years only more so. Vidhu Vinod Chopra's *1942–A Love Story* was a good opportunity for him to come back with a bang composing his kind of music. A valiant RD did give it his best in songs such as '*Ek ladki ko dekha to aisa laga*' (Kumar Sanu), '*Kuch naa kaho*' (both Kumar Sanu and Lata solos) and '*Pyar hua chupke se*' (the song that fetched Kavita Krishnamurthy a Filmfare Award for best singer) but it came too late for him to revive his spirit. He succumbed to a heart attack on 4 January 1994, even as the soundtrack of the movie was making waves.

LAXMIKANT–PYARELAL: THE LONG-PLAYING DUO

With 488 films over a period of thirty-five years no wonder Laxmikant–Pyarelal earned the nickname Long-Playing. Their record as the most successful composer duo is unparalleled. LP reached the top in the 1960s when old-timers Naushad and

Shanker–Jaikishan were very much around. Over the next twenty years, they kept close competitors Kalyanji–Anandji and R.D. Burman at bay. And they were composing hits along with fourth-generation composers Nadeem–Shravan and Anand–Milind in the 1990s. As late as 1993, just four years before death snatched Laxmikant away and ended the partnership, LP remained a force to reckon with in Bollywood.

It is inevitable that such quantity demanded a price in terms of quality. Despite some really good music in the first two decades of their career, LP are not accorded the status of legends in Bollywood. They also have the dubious distinction of having scored the maximum number of movies where music was just cacophony. But even if one focuses only on the work they did between 1963 and 1983, one is surprised at how often they produced remarkable music, even if intermittently. That they had top banners—Raj Kapoor, Manmohan Desai, Manoj Kumar and Subhash Ghai—vying for their music and no less a person than Lata Mangeshkar endorsing them throughout their career speaks for their glittering talent.

The special musical vibes that existed between Lata and LP for a good part of the duo's career is legendary. While they were playing instruments as part of an orchestra when barely into their teens, Lata recommended them for Naushad and C. Ramchandra's troupe of musicians. While LP paid Lata out of their own pocket for the songs of their early film *Sati Savitri* (1964), Lata boosted their confidence no end by naming its song '*Jeevan dor tumhi sang baandhi*' as one of her ten favourites in the special silver jubilee record she released in 1967. It is for LP that Lata sang her first cabaret number '*Aa Jaan-e-jaan*' in *Inteqam*. They also played a crucial role in bringing Lata back to the RK banner for the songs of *Bobby*, ending a rift that was created years ago. They have publicly acknowledged their gratitude to her, saying that *Didi* (Lata) converted their four-anna compositions into sixteen-anna bounties. Lata has sung the maximum solos for this composer duo, running to over 600. Indeed, take away Lata's songs from their repertoire, and you take away LP's best.

The best that came through as melodiously as '*Jyot se jyot jagaate chalo*' (*Sant Gyaneshwar*, 1964), '*Suno sajna papihe ne*' (*Aaye Din Bahaar Ke*, 1966), '*Kareeb aayi nazar*' (*Anita*, 1967), '*Bindiya chamkegi*' (*Do Raaste*, 1969), '*O ghata saanwari*' (*Abhinetri*, 1970),

'O mitwaa' (Jal Bin Machli Nritya Bin Bijli, 1971), 'Bandhan toote na sanwariya' (Mome Ki Gudiya, 1972), 'Akhiyon ko rahne de' (Bobby, 1973), 'Haay haay yeh majboori' (Roti Kapda Aur Makaan, 1974), 'Main Tulsi tere aangan ki' (Main Tulsi Tere Aangan Ki, 1978), 'Bhor bhaye panghat pe' (Satyam Shivam Sundaram, 1978), 'Parbat ke us paar' (Sargam, 1979), 'Sheesha ho ya dil ho' (Aasha, 1980), 'Solah baras ki baali umar ko salaam' (Ek Duje Ke Liye, 1981) and 'Ho Ramji bada dukh deena' (Ram Lakhan, 1989). The film music buff can see the contours of the LP era spanning twenty-five years in these songs alone.

Not that LP's creativity was limited to Lata. After all, it was in Rafi's voice that they created history with the music of *Dosti* (1964), the film that straightaway put them in the top bracket. *Dosti* was a film that many composers had turned down, not wanting to risk their name for a story of friendship between two young men, one crippled, the other blind, both unknown names. Rafi, always known to support new composers, gamely sang 'Chahoonga main tujhe sanjh savere', 'Meri dosti mera pyar' and the most arresting 'Jaanewalon zara', fetching LP their first Filmfare Award for best composer in the process. LP had many hits with Rafi in the years to come, be it the frothy 'Mast baharon ka main aashiq' (Farz, 1967), the brooding ghazal 'Huyi shaam unka khayal aa gaya' (Mere Humdum Mere Dost, 1968), the lamenting 'Khilona jaan kar tum toh' (Khilona, 1970), the incredibly romantic 'Aaj mausam bada beimaan hain' (Loafer, 1973), the teasing 'Pardah hain pardah' (Amar Akbar Anthony, 1977) and his last hit, 'Dard-e-Dil' (Karz, 1980). The last, one of their most inspired compositions for him in an otherwise Kishore-dominated score, was LP's way of acknowledging Rafi's contribution to their success.

Kishore Kumar gave an early hit to LP with 'Mere mehboob qayamat hogi' (Mr. X in Bombay, 1964), but had to wait a full five years for his next LP hit 'Mere naseeb mein aye dost' in the Rajesh Khanna starrer *Do Raaste* (1969). In the 1970s, LP, like every other composer, switched to Kishore as lead male playback. They utilized Kishore's ability to give a light, romantic feel to his renditions to the fullest in songs like 'Yeh jeevan hain' (Piya Ka Ghar, 1972), 'Mere dil mein aaj kya hain' (Daag, 1973), 'Dekh sakta hoon main kuch bhi hote huye' (Majboor, 1974), 'Aap ke anurodh pe' (Anurodh, 1976), 'My name is Anthony Gonsalvez' (Amar Akbar Anthony) and their tour de force for Subhash Ghai, 'Om shanti om'

(*Karz*), the harbinger of the disco era. Kishore sang a plethora of songs for them over this period, but LP could not produce the RD magic in his voice, and therefore the number of his hits for them is relatively low.

LP's contribution to encouraging new singers is phenomenal. Some of their most popular songs were sung by newcomers who were either introduced by the duo, or who came into prominence singing songs composed by them. Shailendra Singh ('*Main shaayar toh nahin*', *Bobby*), Suresh Wadkar ('*Mere kismat mein tu nahin shaayad*', *Prem Rog*, 1982), Anuradha Paudwal ('*Tu mera jaanu hain*', *Hero*, 1983), Kavita Krishnamurthy ('*Tumse milkar na jaane kyon*', *Pyar Jhukta Nahin*, 1983) all benefited by singing LP's songs when many composers preferred more established singers. Ghazal singer Pankaj Udhas reached a new high when he sang '*Chitthi aayi hain*' for LP in *Naam* (1986). That LP could create big hits with new voices was another feather in their cap.

Some of their most tuneful numbers are duets, and it will be a grave injustice to them if we don't revisit some of these. '*Woh jab yaad aaye*' (Rafi–Lata, *Parasmani*, 1963), '*Khoobsoorat haseena*' (Kishore–Lata, *Mr X in Bombay*), '*Tum gagan ke chandrama*' (Manna Dey–Lata, *Sati Savitri*), '*Ek ritu aaye ek ritu jaaye*' (Manna Dey–Lata, *Sau Saal Baad*, 1966), '*Sawan ka mahina pawan kare sor*' (Mukesh–Lata, *Milan*, 1967), '*Yeh dil tum bin kahin lagta nahin*' (Lata–Rafi, *Izzat*, 1969), '*Accha toh hum chalte hain*' (Kishore–Lata, *Aan Milo Sajna*, 1970), '*Ik pyaar ka naghma hain*' (Lata–Mukesh, *Shor*, 1972), '*Hum tum ik kamre mein bandh ho*' (Shailendra Singh–Lata, *Bobby*), '*Main na bhooloonga*' (Mukesh–Lata, *Roti Kapda Aur Makaan*), '*Aaja teri yaad aayi*' (Lata–Rafi, *Charas*, 1976), '*Dafliwaale dafli baja*' (Lata–Rafi, *Sargam*), '*Zindagi ki na toote ladi*' (Lata–Nitin Mukesh, *Kranti*, 1981), '*Hum bane tum bane ek duje ke liye*' (Lata–S.P. Balasubramaniam, *Ek Duje Ke Liye*), '*Mohabbat hain kya cheez*' (Lata–Suresh Wadkar, *Prem Rog*) and '*Man kyon behka*' (Lata–Asha, *Utsav*, 1984) are just some examples.

To avoid the clash of egos that was the undoing of Shanker-Jaikishan, LP worked out a neat division of work. Laxmikant was in charge of tune, Pyarelal responsible for orchestration. The former would tune something catchy or melodious as the situation demanded, and the latter would take care of the musical arrangement for the song. It is impossible to separate the tune from the music in their songs, so well did the two blend their talents. Can you decide easily what held you spellbound in '*Ik pyaar ka naghma hain*': Laxmi's tune or Pyare's violin? The same is the case with '*Dard-e-Dil*' from *Karz*. It was a ghazal in tune, but a pop song in orchestration, which is what made it irresistible.

Bewildering as the range and number of songs mentioned above may seem, it is a fact that melody was largely absent from LP's recording room after Reshma's poignant folk number '*Lambi judaai*' in *Hero*. In composing for 250 films in twenty years, they had exhausted themselves. The mid-1980s saw them churn out insipid music in film after film, taking on more and more assignments to beat the Bappi Lahiri onslaught. The only break from cacophony came with *Utsav*, where they abandoned their loud and flashy orchestra in favour of the flute to accompany Suresh Wadkar's melodious voice in '*Saanjh dhale gagan tale*'. The Hindi remake of K. Viswanath's *Shankarabharanam* as *Sur Sangam* (1985) was an opportunity to compose some soothing classical numbers, but LP couldn't give the time that such effort required. Their score for the film was utterly lacking in melody, despite the presence of Pandit Rajan and Sajan Misra and Lata.

With *Tezaab* (1988) started the most inferior phase in LP's career musically as the duo went overboard in catering to the lowest common denominator in their attempt to remain at the top. '*Ek do teen*' (Alka Yagnik, *Tezaab*), '*One two ka four*' (Mohammed Aziz, *Ram Lakhan*), '*Jumma chumma de de*' (Sudesh Bhonsle, *Hum*, 1991) and that super hit of the era, '*Choli ke peeche kya hain*' (Ila Arun–Alka Yagnik, *Khalnayak*, 1993) saw them playing more and more to the gallery. The duo left no stone unturned in beating back the challenge posed by the next-generation composers Nadeem–Shravan and Anand–Milind, but they cheapened their music beyond redemption in the process. Their attempt to resurrect their faltering image with the semi-classical score of *Bhairavi* (1995) was a non-starter, as the film and its music went unnoticed. The next three years saw more listless music from them, until Laxmikant succumbed to a persistent kidney problem in 1998. There was some talk that Pyarelal would compose solo, but it was not to be, as he was rudderless without Laxmikant, and himself kept indifferent health. There never could be a Pyarelal without a Laxmikant.

Khayyam: The Pole Star of Melody

Why feature Khayyam as a composer of the 1970s and 1980s? After all, he started off way back in 1953. Reason: his music stood out in the 1970s, his films were commercially more successful, and it is only in a decade where melodiousness was fading fast that you recognize Khayyam's genius, and his hallmark—integrity to melody. The 1950s and 1960s were years where everyone made good music. The times forced them to. It required a Khayyam to keep melody in film music alive in the 1970s, and more so in the following decade. And he paid a price for it by not getting the recognition his talent deserved.

His tryst with melody began with his very first film *Footpath* (1953) where Talat sang the ghazal '*Sham-e-gham ki kasam*', a song that defines the music of that decade no less than many others. But the presence of Dilip Kumar and Meena Kumari could not prevent the film from failing, and Khayyam's music went unrecognized. Five years later, Raj Kapoor was delighted with his compositions for the left-leaning *Phir Subah Hogi*, but despite Sahir's evocative lyrics in '*Woh subah kabhi toh aayegi*' (Mukesh–Asha), the film sank, yet again depriving Khayyam stardom. *Shola Aur Shabnam* (1961) had Khayyam give sheen to Kaifi Azmi's lyrics in '*Jeet hi lenge baazi hum*' (Rafi–Lata, both sounding utterly melodious) and the famous Rafi solo '*Jaane kya dhoondti rehti hain yeh aankhen mujh mein*'. What distinguished Khayyam's music was the superior quality of poetry in all his songs. For him, the purpose of music was to make the lyrics come alive. He had the sagacity to keep his tunes simple, instruments minimal. As we shall see, some of the best poetry in Hindi films was set to music by Khayyam.

Shagun (1964) was the same story all over again—superb songs in a box office misfire: if '*Tum apna ranjh-o-gham*' (Jagjit Kaur, who later became his wife) was a Pahadi set to the ghazal format, '*Parbaton ke pedon par*' (Rafi–Suman Kalyanpur) was a Pahadi literally making you feel elevated. Suman Kalyanpur sang '*Bujha diye hain khud apne haathon*', Khayyam's restrained Bhairavi ghazal, and Talat Mehmood teamed up with Mubarak Begum for the teasing duet '*Itne kareeb aake bhi*' in Raag Kedar. Undeterred by the film's commercial failure, Khayyam went on to compose yet another dulcet Pahadi in Lata's voice for Chetan Anand's *Aakhri*

Khat (1966): '*Baharon mera jeevan bhi sawaaron*'. There was nothing remarkable from him for the next eight years (he did not compose for movies between 1967 and 1973), but when he came back, it was with something as soothing as the Ahir Bhairav bhajan '*Tu hi saagar tu hain kinara*' for *Sankalp* (1974), the song with which Sulakshana Pandit dared to dream of becoming a singing star. For Khayyam, good tidings were just round the corner.

Kabhi Kabhie (1975) was his much-delayed vehicle to stardom. Yash Chopra wanted a composer who could do justice to the angst of the failed lover–poet hero, and he risked Khayyam. '*Main pal do pal ka shaayar hoon*' (Mukesh) and '*Kabhi kabhie mere dil mein*' (Mukesh and Lata solos) made for yet another Sahir–Khayyam coup. The two numbers lifted an otherwise unremarkable score to a new plane. The music and the film succeeded, and Khayyam became sought-after. If *Kabhi Kabhie* was a compromise to commercialism, Khayyam returned to pure melody in little-known *Shankar Hussain* (1977), reclaiming his identity with two Lata gems: '*Aap yun faaslon se*' and the ethereal '*Apne aap raaton mein*'. Even in an insipid melodrama like *Khandan* (1979), Khayyam gave something as memorable as '*Yeh mulaaqat ik bahaana hain*' (Lata), while small-budget *Noorie* (1979) had Lata singing the delectable '*Chori chori koi aye*'.

Ironically, Khayyam's best efforts were reserved for the 1980s, a decade that saw music plumb new depths. In *Umrao Jaan* (1981), he brought to the fore the mature singer in Asha, getting her to sing four beautiful ghazals in a scale below her normal pitch, making Asha sound all the more alluring. '*Dil cheez kya hain*' was the biggest hit, but '*Justju jiski thi*' and '*Yeh kya jageh hain doston*' were weightier. Asha was superb, and so was Talat Aziz in the lone male ghazal '*Zindagi jab bhi teri bazm mein*'. Khayyam deservedly won the National Award for best composer that year. *Umrao Jaan* remains the movie he is most remembered for. *Bazaar* (1982), where Talat Aziz and Lata sang the most lyrically beautiful duet of the decade, '*Phir chidi raat baat phoolon ki*', was even better. Lata's '*Dikhayee diye yun*' and Jagjit Kaur's '*Dekh lo aaj humko jee bhar ke*' are equally haunting.

He continued to compose till the early 1990s, but the soul went missing in the last decade. Kamaal Amrohi's *Razia Sultan* (1983) bombed, but Khayyam succeeded in giving us another atmospheric Lata beauty in '*Aye dil-e-nadaan*'. It could well have been his swan song.

Ravindra Jain: Genius Underutilized

He has made music for over a hundred films in three decades. Half a dozen of them have been remarkable. Yet, Ravindra Jain figures prominently in the nostalgia for melody, as his music made a difference to the general ambience of decline in the 1970s and the 1980s. As the favoured composer of the Rajshri banner, he dared to bring classical music back to films in *Chitchor* (1976), in the voices of Yesudas and Hemlata, both unknown to Bollywood then. '*Jab dweep jale aana*' and '*Tu jo mere sur mein*' are an oasis of melody in the otherwise barren desert that music had become. Even in a totally obscure film such as *Kotwaal Sahab* (1977), Jain could compose a complex, chord-based melody such as '*Saathi re bhool na jaana mera pyaar*' (Asha Bhonsle). *Akhiyon Ke Jharokhon Se* (1978) ran only because of Jain's tuneful and breezy score, with the title song by Hemlata becoming very popular.

Similarly, his score for Raj Kapoor's *Ram Teri Ganga Maili* was a whiff of freshness and originality in an era of coarseness spearheaded by Bappi Lahiri. Lata did the composer a grave injustice when she publicly declared at the HMV function of *Ram Teri Ganga Maili* that the music of Raj Kapoor's films was determined by RK alone, irrespective of the composer. RK may well have had a say in the tunes, but in composition and orchestration, the Lata solos '*Ek dukhiyaari kahe*' and the classic '*Ek Radha ek Meera*' could have only come from a man who had composed '*Shyam teri bansi pukare Radha naam*' (Jaspal Singh–Aarti Mukherjee) a full decade earlier in *Geet Gaata Chal*. The film also had the last authentic Pahadi tune in Hindi films—'*Husn pahadon ka*' (Suresh Wadkar–Lata). Ravindra Jain deservedly won the Filmfare Award that year for best composer. It was his moment, as he had achieved one big yardstick of success—being chosen as composer for the RK banner. However, his best was over with the film, as he couldn't repeat the magic for RK's *Henna* (1991), where an ageing Lata sounded laboured. The film and its music failed.

FOURTH-GENERATION COMPOSERS: THE FOLLOWERS

Of the composers of the 1980s and 1990s featured here, most are essentially followers. Both Bappi Lahiri and Rajesh Roshan gave the music that the times needed, lacking perhaps the conviction, if not the talent, to set a new trend in that bleak decade, the 1980s. Roshan Junior tried to keep his music decent; Bappi gave up even that struggle. In the process, it was film music, and the music lover, that lost, almost irrevocably. The next-generation composers such as Anand–Milind, Nadeem–Shravan and Jatin–Lalit all began well, but were quick to play the game by the rules of success.

That A.R. Rahman from the south could zoom past everyone else with his ingenious blend of melody and technology speaks for the talent and conviction of that man certainly, but far more importantly, it also puts paid to the argument that music in the 1980s became what it did because people loved it. Rahman is, for all practical purposes, the last Titan in Hindi film music because he proved again what Naushad always believed: that a composer had the power and the responsibility to mould people's tastes.

BAPPI LAHIRI: SUCCESS AT ANY COST

The much-maligned composer of the 1980s has the unenviable reputation of plunging music to an all-time low in that decade. Producing assembly-line music for an average of twenty-five films a year, beating competition from RD through a price war, blatantly plagiarizing tunes, composing for the most banal lyrics conceivable, it is no wonder that he remains everyone's favourite whipping boy when it comes to music of the era. But perhaps it is unfair to blame the tragedy of film music in the 1980s on him alone. The all-round decline was a phenomenon much larger than what one man wrought.

It was never a question of ability with Bappi. After all, someone who could accompany his illustrious parents on the tabla at the age of four must have been a prodigy. It was just that he wanted to succeed at any cost in a decade where melody was scarcely needed. The first few films of Bappi had some noteworthy numbers, even if they sounded too close to RD's style. '*Abhi abhi thi dushmani*' (Lata, *Zakhmee*, 1975), the favourite 'college farewell' song '*Chalte chalte mere yeh geet*' by Kishore in *Chalte Chalte* (1976), the Kishore–Lata title song in *Phir Janam Lenge Hum* (1977), Yesudas's '*Maana ho tum behad haseen*' (*Toote Khilone*, 1978), the Lata–Bhupinder duet '*Saiyan bina ghar soona*' (*Aangan Ki Kali*, 1979) and the classical Yesudas–Lata tandem song '*Zid na karo*' (*Lahu Ke Do Rang*, 1979) all showcase a different Bappi. Sadly for him, he got nowhere composing these songs.

Breakthrough came unexpectedly with '*Hari om Hari*' (Usha Uthup, *Pyaara Dushman*, 1980) that made Bappi stumble upon the disco route to stardom. The fallout: '*Ramba ho*' (Usha Uthup–Bappi, *Armaan*, 1981), '*I am a disco dancer*' (Vijay Benedict, *Disco Dancer*, 1982), '*Jawaan-e-jaaneman*' (Asha, *Namak Halaal*, 1982), '*Disco station disco*' (Asha, *Hathkadi*, 1982). So far, it wasn't too bad.

The worst phase of the Bappi era came with the Chennai-based Padmalaya Films' first venture with Jeetendra and Sridevi, *Himmatwala* (1981). With ample support from Anjaan and Indeewar, Bappi inflicted songs like '*Nainon mein sapna*' (Kishore–Lata), '*Taaki, taaki o taaki*' (Kishore–Asha) and '*Wah wah wah khel shuroo ho gaya*' (Kishore–Asha). When Sridevi's gyrations made the movie a hit, Bappi's music got legitimized. What followed were a slew of such scores in *Justice Choudhury* ('*Mama mia, pom pom*', Kishore–Asha, 1983), *Mawaali* ('*Jhopdi mein charpaayee*', Kishore–Asha) and *Tohfa* ('*Pyar ka tohfa tera*', Asha–Kishore, 1984). Even by the generally sad standards of the era this was lamentable stuff. That Bappi composed the romantic '*Inteha ho gayi*' (Kishore–Asha, *Sharaabi*, 1984), the lingering classical number '*Dard ki raagini muskura ke ched di*' in Raag Abhogi Kaanada for Lata in *Pyaas* (1984) or the soft lorie '*Aaja nindiyaa aaja*' (Lata, *Bhavna*, 1984) was of no consequence. Trade wanted only a certain kind of music from Bappi, and he was only too happy to oblige. As late as 1993, Bappi composed the double entendre '*Angnaa mein baba*' (Kumar Sanu–Alka Yagnik) for *Aankhen*. Mercifully, the massive success of the teenage love story *Maine Pyar Kiya* (1989) had turned the tide against the Bappi kind of music, and the composer faded out in the early 1990s.

Rajesh Roshan: Trendy Tunes

'*Pyaar ki kashti mein*' (*Kaho Naa Pyaar Hain*, 1999) may have set the nation swinging to his music and revived his fortunes in Bollywood, but the best of Rajesh Roshan happened more than two decades earlier as a youngster stepping into the formidable shoes of father Roshan. Roshan Junior got noticed for his very second film *Julie* (1975) where he composed a modern score to pose a challenge to the LP-RD-Kalyanji-Anandji triumvirate that ruled Hindi film music then. The songs of *Julie* became hits, Kishore's sultry '*Dil kya kare jab kisiko*', Preeti Sagar's '*My heart is beating*,' Kishore-Lata's '*Bhool gaya sab kuch*' all finding favour with the youth of the era. Rajesh Roshan won the Filmfare Award for *Julie* as a rank newcomer, something rare in Bollywood.

Having the wisdom to not get bogged down by his father's reputation for ghazals and qawwalis, Rajesh Roshan composed music that was trendy, without becoming unmusical. '*Kya mausam hain*' (Lata-Kishore-Rafi, *Doosra Aadmi*, 1977), '*Thoda hain thode ki zaroorat hain*' (Kishore-Lata, *Khatta Meetha*, 1977), '*Tu pee aur jee*' (Kishore, *Des Pardes*, 1978) and '*Uthe sabke kadam, dekho rum pum pum*' (Lata-Amit Kumar, *Baaton Baaton Mein*, 1979) are all examples of his style in the 1970s. The one notable exception was his sober score for *Swami* (1977), where he surprised listeners by adapting Bade Ghulam Ali Khan's thumri '*Kaa karoon sajni*' for Yesudas to vocalize. Purists frown upon this adaptation, but *Swami* is remembered most for this song.

Rajesh Roshan could infuse melody even in Amitabh Bachchan films that had little scope for music. In *Mr. Natwarlal* (1979), he got Amitabh to sing the endearing children's song '*Mere paas aao mere doston*' which is the closest the Big B ever came to sounding musical. *Kaala Paththar* (1979) had the hummable '*Ek raasta hain zindagi*' (Kishore-Lata). Even in that box-office turkey *Yaraana* (1981), Kishore, under Rajesh's baton, gave us what was arguably his best solo in that decade, the mellow '*Chhookar mere man ko*'. *Khuddar* (1982) too succeeded because of the songs, with the Kishore-Lata duet '*Angrezi mein kehte hain ke I love you*' catching the fancy of the public.

Since the early 1980s, a majority of Rajesh Roshan's compositions have been for films produced by his brother Rakesh Roshan. Starting with the youthful score of *Aap Ke Deewane*

(1980), he went on to compose some good melodies such as *'Tujh sang preet lagaayi sajna'* in *Kaamchor* (1982). After Rakesh Roshan turned director in the late 1980s, Rajesh Roshan saw big-time success with his brother's films such as *Karan Arjun* (1995), *Kaho Naa Pyaar Hain* (1999) and *Koi Mil Gaya* (2003). In the history of Bollywood, he's the only composer to have won his second Filmfare Award (*Kaho Naa Pyaar Hain*) twenty-five years after the first.

Musically, the films of the 1990s may not be his best, but they finally got him superstar status. For melody, however, one has to turn to his songs in small-budget movies directed by Mahesh Bhatt like *Daddy* (1990) where Talat Aziz poignantly sang *'Aaina mujh se meri pehli si soorat maange'* or *Papa Kehte Hain* (1996) where *'Ghar se nikalte hi'* had an innocence that reminds us of dad Roshan.

A.R. RAHMAN:
THE LAST TITAN OF THE TWENTIETH CENTURY

Rahman was to film music of the 1990s what RD was two decades earlier. Amidst a flurry of new talent all around, A.R. Rahman stands tall as the man who caught the imagination of music lovers, his grand mix of melody and technology creating a sensation.

Mani Ratnam's Tamil movie *Roja* (1992) was dubbed in Hindi a year later, and a new kind of music came to Bollywood. It didn't matter that the tunes had a south Indian feel. It was enough that they were trendy, melodious and remarkably original. *'Dil hain chhota sa'* gave Rahman a grand presence in Bollywood much before he scored his first Hindi film *Rangeela* (1995). Then followed a dubbing wave beginning with *Kaadhalan* (1993) being dubbed as *Hum Se Hain Muqabla* (*'Urvasi, Urvasi'*). *Gentleman* (1993) in Hindi was credited to Annu Malik, who used Rahman's tunes without compunction. *'Roop suhana lagta hain'* was a note-for-note translation of Rahman's *'Ottagathai kattikko'*. Never before had a composer from the south, who did not know Hindi, created such an impact in Bollywood.

With *Rangeela*, a musical blockbuster, Rahman gave a fresh lease of life to the ever-youthful Asha in *'Yaayi re yaayi re'* and *'Tanha tanha'*. Rahman's amazing hold on rhythm, his command over electronic instruments and his ability to blend superbly Indian classical and Western music (as in the song *'Haaye rama* yeh kya ho gaya') were beyond compare in Bollywood, and he became the most sought-after composer. The movies he composed were few, but his influence was felt more in what other composers crafted, as producers wanted a 'Rahman effect' to the tunes, irrespective of who the actual composer was.

Three years and a few hits later, Rahman stormed Bollywood yet again with his sufiana score of *Dil Se*, Mani Ratnam's first Hindi venture. Rahman knew very little Hindi, but it did not stop him from converting Gulzar's lyrics into shimmering musical notes in the songs '*Chhaiyya chhaiyya*' (Sukhwinder Singh and Sapna Awasthi) and Lata's '*Jiya jale*'. With *Dil Se*, Rahman's music took on a truly pan-Indian character, and he became the only Indian composer whose name became more important to the film than the producer's and director's. Subhash Ghai acknowledged this when he confessed he named his *Taal* (1999) only after the music of Rahman. *Taal*, with its trendier and flashy dance-floor score ('*Ishq bina*' and '*Taal se taal mila*'), stayed at the top of the charts for a full year.

Lagaan (2001) had a score that was earthier, but no less catchy for that. Concentrating more on the spirit of the movie, Rahman composed '*Ghanan ghanan*', '*Mitwa tujhko kya dar hain re*', the garba-influenced '*Radha kaise na jaale*' and the rousing patriotic number, '*Chale chalo*', this time to Javed Akhtar's lyrics. *Lagaan* was Rahman's diplomatic answer to those accusing him of being a better craftsman than an artiste.

Hailed as the biggest phenomenon of the 1990s in not just Bollywood but in Indian films, Rahman's music, however well put together, at times seems to lack soul. Rahman himself probably realizes this keenly, looking for opportunities to make more meaningful music such as in Deepa Mehta's *1947: Earth* ('*Bheeni bheeni*', Hariharan, 2001), Ashutosh Gowarikar's *Swades* (A.R. Rahman, '*Yeh des hain tera*', 2004) in the new millennium. But all criticisms notwithstanding, even his worst detractors acknowledge him as a phenomenon.

THE 1990s: A DECADE OF NEW TALENT

ANAND–MILIND: Sons of composer Chitragupt who gave many melodies in the 1960s, this duo showed promise in *Qayamat Se Qayamat Tak* (1988), with some fresh and tuneful music for the

Aamir Khan–Juhi Chawla debut. '*Papa kehte hain bada naam karega*' (Udit Narayan's debut) became a sort of anthem for the youth of the time, while '*Ghazab ka hain din*' (Alka Yagnik–Udit) and '*Aye mere humsafar*' (Alka–Udit) too created waves. The tunes were simple; the orchestration minimal, a relief unavailable to the listener for long. There was an innocence about the score that could only be attributed to the all-round newness. However, Anand–Milind failed to retain their grip on melody for too long, impatient as they were for commercial success. Their second film *Dil* (1990) had some melodious tracks such as '*Mujhe neend na aaye*' (Anuradha Paudwal–Udit) and '*O Priya Priya*' (Anuradha–Suresh Wadkar), but in '*Khambe jaisi khadi hain*' they gave an early warning of the course their music would take. '*Dhak dhak karne laga*' (Anuradha–Udit, *Beta*, 1991) and '*Tu tu tu tu tu taara*' (Kumar Sanu–Sushma Shreshta, *Bol Radha Bol*, 1992) marked them as composers of crass music. Getting associated with the David Dhawan banner didn't help either. Despite the large number of films they composed for, they were out of the reckoning by the late 1990s.

NADEEM–SHRAVAN: The only composer duo without a past connection in Bollywood, Nadeem–Shravan created history of sorts when all six songs in their debut *Aashiqui* (1990) became popular—a feat achieved only by S.D. Burman for *Guide* and *Abhimaan*. '*Saason ki zaroorat hain jaise*' and '*Ab tere bin jee lenge hum*' put newcomer Kumar Sanu in the limelight as the new Kishore Kumar. Nadeem–Shravan went from strength to strength with other hit scores such as *Dil Hain Ki Maanta Nahin* (title song, Kumar Sanu–Anuradha, 1991), *Saajan* ('*Mera dil bhi kitna paagal hain*', Kumar Sanu–Alka, 1991) and *Deewana* ('*Sochenge tumhe pyar karen ke nahin*', Kumar Sanu, 1992) in the early 1990s, and established a reputation for bright, melodious music. Following differences with godfather Gulshan Kumar of T-Series, they walked out of the banner and continued conjuring hits with *Raja Hindustani* ('*Aaye ho mere zindagi mein tum bahaar banke*', Udit Narayan and Alka Yagnik solos, 1996) and *Pardes* ('*Yeh dil deewana*', Sonu Nigam, 1997). Their music had a sophistication that was unique, and they were the most promising duo of the decade till the time Nadeem was charged with Gulshan Kumar's murder, and he scooted to London. They came together to create the hit score of

Dhadkan ('*Tum dil ki dhadkan mein*', Abhijeet and Kumar Sanu, 2001), but haven't been able to sustain the partnership long-distance.

ANNU MALIK: Son of composer Sardar Malik of *Saranga* fame, Annu Malik is the other major composer of the decade. Though *Sohni Mahiwal* (1984) was noticed for its music, it took Annu ten years to arrive with the lilting score of Mahesh Bhatt's *Phir Teri Kahani Yaad Aayi* (1993). '*Baadalon mein chup raha hain chand kyon*' (Kumar Sanu–Alka) and '*Shayarana si hain*' (Alka) were notable for their melody. Then followed the hugely successful *Baazigar* where he came up with super-hit songs like '*Yeh kaali kaali ankhen*' and '*Baazigar o baazigar*'. He also gave ample indication of his plagiarizing instincts as he moulded the old LP tune '*Khoobsoorat haseena*' (*Mr. X in Bombay*) as '*Aye Mere Humsafar*' (Vinod Rathod–Alka). Known as much for shooting his mouth off in the media as for his music, Annu Malik found the plagiarism route to success easier, retaining his name for the songs of *Gentleman* (1993) even as all tunes were A.R. Rehman's in the Tamil original, and lifting Nusrat Fateh Ali Khan's '*Mera piya ghar aaya*' for *Yaarana* (1996). Talented but inconsistent, he surprised his critics with '*Sandesen aate hain*' (*Border*, 1997) and with the surprisingly melodious music of *Refugee*. Despite hit scores for over a decade now, if there's one thing that eludes Annu Malik it is respectability.

JATIN–LALIT: This duo made an impact even in their small-budget debut *Yaara Dildara* way back in 1990, with the song '*Bin tere sanam*' (Udit Narayan–Kavita Krishnamurthy). Erstwhile arrangers for R.D. Burman, their tunes have a likeness to his—*Pehla nasha, pehla khumaar*' (Udit–Sadhana Sargam, *Jo Jeeta Wohi Sikandar*, 1992) and '*Waada raha sanam*' (Abhijeet–Alka Yagnik, *Khiladi*, 1994) are both in the RD mould—but still manage to sound fresh. They zoomed to the top with *Dilwale Dulhaniya Le Jaayenge* (1995), '*Tujhe dekha to yeh jaana sanam*' (Kumar Sanu–Lata) becoming the anthem for new-age lovers. With *Sarfarosh* ('*Zindagi maut na ban jaaye*', Roopkumar Rathod–Sonu Nigam and '*Hoshwalon ko khabar kya*', Jagjit Singh, 1999), they emerged as composers who could shine in their own light. Their run of musical hits continued into the new century (*Kabhi Khushi Kabhi Gham*, 2002), but the partnership came apart in 2005. Whether they'll beat the jinx of duos failing when they go solo is yet to be seen.

Twenty-First-Century Composers

The new millennium has brought to the fore more new talent. Shankar–Ehsaan–Loy, the first composer trio in Bollywood, broke through with their peppy score for *Dil Chahta Hai* (2001) but finally came out of their 'jingles' groove to compose what is arguably the most melodic score in the new millennium, *Kal Ho Na Ho* (2003). *Bunty Aur Babli* (2005) had the yuppie generation gyrating to their modern qawwali '*Kajra re*' (Shankar Mahadevan–Alisha Chinai–Javed Ali), and they seem to have cornered some big banners. Ismail Darbar has a reputation out of proportion with the volume of his work. Despite the hit songs of *Devdas* (2002), he is yet to recreate the magic of the songs in *Hum Dil De Chuke Sanam* (1999). M.M. Kreem who impressed us with his unusual '*Tu mile dil khile*' (Kumar Sanu–Alka Yagnik, *Criminal*, 1995) shows promise in the new millennium, if his songs '*Jadoo hain nasha hain*' (Shreya Ghoshal, *Jism*, 2003) and '*Dheere jalna*' (Sonu Nigam–Shreya Ghoshal, *Paheli*, 2005) are anything to go by. Himesh Reshammiya's '*Just chill*' (*Maine Pyar Kyon Kiya*, 2005) and other chartbusters may have set the discotheques afire, but his songs have already begun to sound repetitive. Whether he will break away from the Rahman groove and compose anything original is anyone's guess. Newcomer Shantanu Moitra, who composed the critically appreciated score of *Hazaaron Khwaishein Aisi* (2003) and the melodious '*Piyu bole*' (Shreya Ghoshal–Sonu Nigam, *Parineeta*, 2005), is a ray of hope, but his conviction for melody is yet to be tested.

DEV ANAND REMEMBERS S.D. BURMAN

His sprawling office in Anand Studios has books and files everywhere. He is seated in a corner, dressed impeccably in formals, with the famous scarf round his neck. Nothing about him suggests he is touching eighty-four. Like his favourite composer and mentor Sachin Dev Burman, Dev Anand is a man who moves with the times. He tells me he is working on a new script for his next film. He is excited when I tell him about my book, and wishes me good luck. For the next forty minutes, I have a tough time keeping pace with the speed of his thought and articulation. In his presence, I can comprehend why he is called evergreen. Dev Anand reflects on the music of Navketan and his association with Sachin Dev Burman. After all, the two are so closely intertwined.

How did Dada Burman come to be associated so closely with Navketan?

I was responsible for that. When I saw the film *Shikari* for which he had scored music, I was completely bowled over. After he composed music for *Vidya* where I starred with Suraiya, I was very clear I wanted him for Navketan. I met Dada at his residence, and he graciously agreed to my request that he compose for Navketan's first film *Afsar*. Thus was born a great partnership, one that lasted till his death.

What about his music attracted you?

I was always attracted to the melody of Bengal. In Dada Burman's music, I found an innovative mix of the melody of Rabindra

Sangeet and very modern rhythms. Also, his music was full of hope; it had an optimism that suited my themes very well. The music of *Afsar* did not click, but I wanted only him to compose for *Baazi*. Look at what an amazingly trendy score he composed for the film! I remember, '*Tadbeer se bigdi huyi taqdeer bana le*' was such a hit that in Jodhpur, air force personnel would go to the theatre every night and ask the manager to play only that song repeatedly. In Bombay, people used to throw money at the screen every time Geeta Bali appeared for that song. After *Baazi*, there was no question of us looking at anyone else to compose music for Navketan.

But others composed for Navketan too. *Aandhiyan* had sarod maestro Ali Akbar Khan as music director.

That was my brother Chetan Anand's decision. He preferred someone with a strong classical base, as his themes were more serious—which is why he parted company with Navketan after the first few years. Left to my choice, I wouldn't have asked anyone but Dada to compose music. What amazing effects he got from Kishore for me in *Funtoosh* and many other films for other banners! He had the courage to be different from all the others, who would not want Kishore to sing their songs.

He also made Rafi sing so many beautiful songs for you.

Yes, Rafi sang all the songs in *Kaala Paani*, *Kaala Bazaar*, *Tere Ghar Ke Saamne* and also *Guide*. Only the duet '*Gaata rahen mera dil*' in *Guide* had Kishore, but the song was partially composed by R.D. Burman. Dada would always try something new; he never wanted to be predictable. So after he successfully made Kishore my voice in the early 1950s, he switched to a more serious kind of music from *Kaala Paani*, which needed Rafi. But if you ask me, I'll say Kishore's voice suited me best. He understood the spirit of Navketan's music totally, like Dada Burman did. I maintain that Kishore, at his best, was better than every other singer, including Rafi.

If S.D. Burman had become so critical to Navketan, how come Jaidev came to compose the music of *Hum Dono*?

Well, it was Navketan's way of acknowledging Jaidev's loyalty to them. He had started in Navketan as assistant to Ali Akbar Khan in *Aandhiyan*, and when Khan saab decided to become a full-fledged sarod player, Jaidev stayed back in Navketan to assist Dada Burman. He was extremely talented, and would add to Dada's tunes and orchestra very significantly. Jaidev would keep asking me for an independent break, and when *Hum Dono* was being planned, I conceded his request, after speaking to Dada. Dada was only too happy that his assistant was getting a big break with Navketan. Jaidev made brilliant music in *Hum Dono*. '*Main zindagi ka saath nibhata chala gaya*' is my motif in life. That's the way I have lived life.

And yet you went back to Burman-da for *Tere Ghar Ke Samne* and other films?

Yes. Because you see, Burman-da was not just a composer for me. He was a father figure to Navketan. I depended on him for all aspects of the film, not just music. I would consult him on the script and ask him whether it is okay to make a film on a particular theme. I cannot forget what his music did for Navketan in the first few years. And even later, right till *Prem Pujari*, didn't he make brilliant music? '*Rangeela re*' by Lata is my all-time favourite among all the Navketan songs. It has melody, and yet a trendy feel. I had no need to look beyond him for my films. For *Hare Rama Hare Krishna*, it was Dada who proposed that I use Pancham, because he was not comfortable composing for the theme of the film. As long as Dada was alive, I used other composers only for very strong reasons, and always with his consent.

After his death, I used Pancham initially. He gave superb music in *Heera Panna*, but I moved on to Rajesh Roshan and many other composers in later years because I strictly believe one must move with the times. But there hasn't been another composer who has meant so much to me since Dada Burman. I still miss him.

DOWN MEMORY LANE WITH PYARELAL

The first thing that strikes you when you meet Pyarelal is that he seems remarkably fit and raring to go. It comes as quite a surprise, considering all the reports in the industry about his failing health. When asked, he says mischievously that his 'well-wishers' in the industry had blown his health problems out of proportion. He is bursting with excitement at the prospect of composing for the Royal Philharmonic Orchestra in London, and shows me the notations he is making for the 100-piece orchestra proudly. Fresh from a recording with Sonu Nigam and Shreya Ghoshal for a forthcoming film, he raves about both singers. Pyarelal seems very much a man of the present, and it is with an effort that he rewinds to the past, to reminisce about late partner Laxmikant and other composers in Hindi films.

Let's start with your association with Laxmikant-ji...

I was fortunate that a person of his calibre and nature became my partner in music, and we did so much work together. It is God's grace that we lasted together for more than forty years, and only his death separated us. I don't want to say much about him because I feel words cannot do justice to who he really was. And I don't want to be dramatic and say 'he was my right hand' or anything of the kind. He was a full-fledged musician by himself, and so was I. We were two independent, complete musicians who came together, and stayed together to create some truly wonderful music in films. We began composing in 1963, but had started playing in the orchestra for other composers in 1953. I was twelve then, Laxmi-ji was four years older.

Laxmi-ji was an excellent mandolin player, and I was good at the violin. He was passionate about Indian classical music; I was drawn towards Western music from an early age. Our complementary strengths brought us together and gave our music a lot of variety. When '*laxmi*' and '*pyar*' come together, who can stop them or harm them? By nature, he was an extremely sweet person who just did not say 'no' ever. Any request, any demand would have Laxmi-ji say '*ho jaayega*' or '*dekh lenge*'; never '*nahin hoga*'. This characteristic of him was an important reason for our success, as we earned the goodwill of so many people in the industry. A great musician, a kind human being.

Along with Laxmi-ji, I had another L in my life that helped me (and Laxmi-ji) succeed very early. Lata Mangeshkar. Didi was the pillar on which we achieved name and fame at a very early stage. She sang our best compositions. I used to literally live in her house in the early 1950s, picking up music from her genius brother Hridaynath Mangeshkar and from Didi herself. Her blessings have seen us through tough times.

Of course, I wouldn't have come into music in the first place, were it not for my father Pandit Ramprasad Sharma. He taught me to play the violin from the age of five, and instilled a deep respect for Indian and Western classical music in all his children. I would say there hasn't been another instrumentalist or arranger as great as him in the industry. He was superb in playing the trumpet ('*Suhaani raat dhal chuki*' has his trumpet in the background), the violin and many other instruments. He taught people what he knew without any reservations, often without charging a fee. He had a passion for imparting knowledge. Do you know he taught so many slum children to play the violin and trumpet? Today, many of them are big arrangers in films, and have made a lot of money and name. The whole film industry is full of people who learnt some instrument or the other from him, and there are many composers—from Naushad, C. Ramchandra and Hridaynath Mangeshkar to Annu Malik and Uttam Singh—who learnt the art of making notations from him. My father cared only for music, so he did not get the recognition or name due to him. But with God's grace, I have fulfilled his dream of a successful career in music.

In your early years, you and Laxmikant-ji assisted many composers. What was that experience like?

(*Even before I finish the question, he interjects agitatedly*): I want to make one thing clear. I don't like the word 'assist'. An assistant composer in this industry is no less than the main composer. It's just that he works under another composer, helping that composer with the tune, the orchestra, the words, everything. Ghulam Mohammed assisted Naushad. But when he got a chance to compose for a top film like *Pakeezah*, didn't he prove his mettle forcefully? We ourselves assisted Kalyanji–Anandji for many years. We helped them make their music better, but it is not that we learnt music from them. An assistant composer is not an apprentice. It's just that he's taking his time before launching on his own. Jaidev-ji assisted S.D. Burman for so many years. Didn't he make great music as composer in *Hum Dono*? What about Madan Mohan who assisted C. Ramchandra? Was he any less as composer? I'd say Madan Mohan was among the top four composers in the industry. I was fortunate to have played for him for so many years, and also 'assisted' him! I have even assisted Naushad saab, and played the violin for so many of his songs.

As a composer, how do you view Naushad saab's contribution to film music?

He chose his films carefully, and made music in a manner that ensured that each one was a landmark film. *Rattan* brought folk music to films, *Baiju Bawra* initiated the classical music era and *Mughal-e-Azam* was Urdu poetry and music at their best. Naushad saab gave a big stature to music in films. Everything about his music was grand, which helped establish the importance of music and musicians in the industry. But I'll say this. In music, there's no composer who is better or worse than any other. Some are successful, some aren't. The reasons are many. Naushad saab was lucky that he had the best names in the industry backing his films. A.R. Kardar, Mehboob Khan, Vijay Bhatt, Dilip Kumar, Shakeel Badayuni and 'assistant' Ghulam Mohammed all played a role in making his music popular. Sajjad Hussain was as talented as Naushad, but he did not get the kind of backing that Naushad did. '*Phir tumhari yaad aayi aye sanam*' in *Rustom Sohrab* is the best qawwali in Hindi films for all times, but Sajjad remained unsung despite all his talent.

I love Naushad saab's music, though I don't agree with his point that one need not look beyond Indian classical music for good music. He too gave Western music in *Dastaan* and again in *Jadoo*. A composer has to give what the story or the situation demands. You cannot impose your preferences on the story.

Which composer would you rate as the best in the 1950s and 1960s?

Look, I don't believe in comparisons. Like I said before, each composer brings to music all that he has, and it is not his fault if sometimes the films don't do well, or the composer doesn't get his due. Having said that, I'd say that Laxmi-ji and I liked Shanker–Jaikishan the most. They are the only composers whom we never assisted or played for. Isn't it strange that both Laxmi-ji and I liked the same composer duo best? Just shows how much we were in sync when it came to matters musical. So fond of them we were that both of us used to copy all their mannerisms.

What was it that Shanker–Jaikishan had which other composers didn't?

You tell me what they didn't have. Is there a single flaw you can see in them as composers? Is there any other composer who consistently gave good music in so many films? Is there a single kind of music they've not made? If Naushad saab composed *Baiju Bawra*, Shanker–Jaikishan followed with *Basant Bahar*. What superb music they gave for Raj Kapoor films! In fact, I'll be honest and say that while we won the best composer award for *Dosti* in 1964, I liked Shanker–Jaikishan's score for *Sangam* better!

They never copied anyone else. If fifty songs in the 5000 they made sound similar to other composers' songs, I'd not call it copying. Working in the same industry, it happens sometimes that without your consciously knowing it, you've picked up someone else's tune.

Why did their partnership not last, the way yours with Laxmi-ji did?

Shanker and Jaikishan came together because Raj Kapoor had seen their work as assistants to Ram Ganguly during the making of *Aag*. They did not grow up together the way Laxmi-ji and I did. Insiders know that very early in their career, they had started composing separately. Shanker would create some songs in a film and Jaikishan would create some others. Except for RK Films, where they were salaried employees on the payroll, they rarely worked together on the music of any film. Only their name appeared as Shanker–Jaikishan. In contrast, there is not a single song in our entire career where Laxmi-ji and I have not worked together. Maybe that's why we stayed together also. But in spite of their composing separately, they were able to give their music a distinct identity, a brand. That was their greatness.

What about Sachin Dev Burman, who was also very popular?

S.D. Burman belonged to the R.C. Boral–Pankaj Mullick tradition of music, a school that borrowed heavily from Rabindra Sangeet and the folk music of Bengal and Assam. Hemant Kumar too came from this school. Most of S.D. Burman's hits are Rabindra Sangeet adaptations or folk variations. So I wouldn't call him very original. Hemant Kumar was an excellent composer and a great singer, but unfortunately he did not get his due in the industry. C. Ramchandra, who 'assisted' S.D. Burman, was a very creative, original composer. He brought the Western influence to films with '*Aana meri jaan Sunday ke Sunday*' in *Shehnai*, but also composed what I consider the best *lorie* in Hindi films till date, '*Dheere se aaja ri akhiyan mein*' in *Albela*. He composed the beautiful ghazals of *Anarkali*, but was also the man who made a 'tuneless' and 'wordless' song such as '*Eena meena deeka*' into a super-duper hit. I have played the violin in this song. I feel sad that Anna Saheb, like Hemant Kumar, did not get his due.

Would you say Roshan and Madan Mohan constituted the 'ghazal school' of music?

I'd say Sajjad Hussain, Roshan, and Khayyam belonged to the same line of music, the one that emphasised melody and poetry. Roshan was extremely melodious, a true genius in ghazals, yet fame eluded him. He died early too. I'll not include Madan Mohan in this line. Madan saab was very versatile, composing every kind of music, though he is considered to be the *shehzada* of ghazals. He too did not get the fame and success due to him, but at least today people are aware of Madan Mohan's greatness. Roshan and Khayyam saab continue to languish in the by-lanes of film music. Perhaps because they came to be too closely identified with a particular kind of music. It is not enough for a composer to create good music. It is equally important that they don't become predictable.

What about the next generation of composers, people who came into prominence in the 1960s, such as Kalyanji–Anandji?

They were great. I should know, because Laxmi-ji and I assisted them for many years, even after we started composing on our own. Kalyanji–Anandji created very simple tunes that appealed to everyone. They did not want complex melodies or rhythms for their songs. They gave a lot of importance to words in a song, and made music that was appropriate to the situation in the film. For all these reasons, their songs became very popular. They would always give a lot of freedom to Laxmi-ji and myself to improvise on their tunes, and were very generous with their praise. When we (Laxmi and I) became popular, they were very happy for us, and blessed us. I wouldn't call them trendsetters in music, but they made good, hummable tunes.

And R.D. Burman?

What can I say about R.D. Burman that can do justice to the sheer genius of the man? He was simply superb. I believe he is the only composer who gave three totally different kinds of music in three different films. It is amazing that the same man composed for *Padosan*, *Kati Patang* and *Mehbooba*. The Pancham–Kishore–Rajesh Khanna combination was truly divine. So many songs by him in the 1970s were such hits. He was extremely knowledgeable about the use of instruments, recording techniques etc. He gave music that was very futuristic. What he composed thirty years ago in *Hum Kisi Se Kam Nahin* is being remixed today.

But there was a time when RD seemed to have lost his grip on music. He just couldn't compose anything that was successful. People felt you had overtaken him in popularity.

Well, it can happen to anybody. After all, making music is a creative process, and there may come a time when any composer, no matter how great, can feel stuck. But I'd say this about Pancham: he never slipped from the twenty-fifth floor to the fifth. If he wasn't at his best, he slipped to the twentieth floor only. Never below that. The same goes for Laxmikant–Pyarelal. We too had our share of flops, our mistakes, but we never fell too low.

A few months before he died suddenly, Pancham rang me up excitedly to tell me that he had composed some really good tunes for *1942–A Love Story*. 'Pyare, tu sun na, tujhe pasand aayenge'— these words kept echoing in my ears when I saw the film. I can't tell you how terrible I felt that he was no more.

But commercially you have succeeded more than others?

There are many reasons for this. First, we did not have too many ego issues between us. Second, Lata Mangeshkar sang maximum number of hit songs for us. Third, Kishore Kumar too sang a huge number of good songs for us. While his songs with S.D. Burman and R.D. Burman are legendary, what he sang for us is in no way less. From *'Mere mehboob qayamat hogi'* in *Mr. X in Bombay* to *'Zindagi ki yahi reet hain'* in *Mr. India*, Kishore's songs for us have always been hits. If LP have succeeded, it is on the strength of teamwork between singer and composer. Remember the hits Rafi saab sang for us in our first hit film *Dosti*?

It is believed that many composers of the 1990s—Nadeem–Shravan, Anand–Milind or Annu Malik have followed the LP school of music. What do you think?

I don't want to cast aspersions on any new-generation composer. If their music sounds similar to ours, it could be because in the 1970s and 1980s, we composed music for all the banners that continue to make films today. Be it Yash Chopra, Subhash Ghai, Dev Anand, Manoj Kumar or Raj Kapoor, we've done music for them all. So it is possible that others who came after us to compose for the same banners were influenced by our style.

What do you feel about the current generation of composers, the ones who began in the 1990s?

A lot of new talent came to the fore in the 1990s. Anand–Milind, Nadeem–Shravan, Jatin–Lalit and, of course, A.R. Rahman. Annu Malik finally succeeded in the 1990s. But somehow, I feel that there is still a void. Every genre of music—classical, ghazal or film music—is defined by a few legendary names in each generation. I don't think such legends have happened in the last twenty years in Hindi films.

Is there any composer today who you feel is particularly good?

A.R. Rahman showed tremendous originality in the first five years of his career. I loved the songs of *Roja*. What innovative use of instruments, what freshness in the tunes! *Bombay* and *Thiruda Thiruda* (Tamil) were also very good. The latter film, in my opinion, is Rahman's best till date. It is my personal opinion that Rahman has not been subsequently able to build on that freshness. Shankar–Ehsaan–Loy are good too. Their music has a bubbly, youthful appeal.

I don't want to pass a judgement on the music of any of the present-day composers, because I don't think they are solely responsible for the kind of music that's made today. I'd blame the lack of good stories for the absence of freshness and originality in film music. Aren't all stories similar these days? Earlier, filmmakers such as Raj Kapoor, Manoj Kumar or Subhash Ghai all made films that had very different storylines. So our music for each of them had to sound different. Thus we were always searching, always creating. From the mid-1980s, good stories have become scarce in films. So how can there be great music? If film music has to have a complete resurgence, films with diverse themes must be made.

PART II
The Songwriters

Lyricists: The Spirit of a Song

Perhaps the least acknowledged of the composer–singer–lyricist triumvirate in the music industry, lyricists have often had to be content with life in the shadow of the composer and the singer. They haven't usually generated that degree of awe and adulation from film music lovers. Possibly because we are a country with a much stronger oral tradition than a written one, compounded by our high levels of illiteracy.

I myself was guilty of ignoring the lyricists, until the time I started writing this part of the book. Usually, I liked a song or didn't like one depending on the tune and the way it was sung. Only if I liked the song did I pay attention to the lyric. It is only when I began writing about the lyricists featured here that I learnt to focus on the words of the song primarily, and realized the significance of the lyrics in making the song what it was. Moreover, in the course of my research for this section, I painfully discovered the extent to which lyricists—even stalwarts such as Majrooh Sultanpuri, Shailendra and Sahir Ludhianvi—are marginalized in Hindi films. Getting any reference material about them was truly a Herculean task. While composers merit at least a tribute in the print media on their birth and death anniversaries, lyricists remain unsung even on those occasions. For writing about the work of many lyricists, I have had to depend on my own internal resources, my thoughts and feelings about their work, more than was the case with regard to composers. In the process, I have had the joy of knowing the genius in each of the eleven lyricists featured here.

Starting with Kidar Sharma who wrote the immortal songs of Saigal's *Devdas*, this section takes you through the voluminous, and very often brilliant, work of some of the best lyricists in Hindi cinema, right through to Javed Akhtar. It concludes with an interview with eminent lyricist Gulzar, who candidly shares his thoughts on the work of his lyricist colleagues. There have been many more lyricists in Hindi cinema who have written great, and extremely popular, songs. It is just that their contribution to enlarging the boundaries of the film song lyric hasn't been as significant as the eleven lyricists featured here. And that, like much else in this book, is a purely subjective point of view.

FIRST-GENERATION LYRICISTS

Kidar Sharma and Dina Nath Madhok were the first to make the film song sound different from traditional poetry associated with theatre. In their hands, the film song became friendlier, written in a language that the layperson could relate to, and thus achieved mass appeal. They were the first 'lyricists' of Hindi cinema, in the true sense of the term. Both Sharma and Madhok were all-round cinematic personalities, which probably made them better lyricists. Kavi Pradeep brought to his film songs a strong social orientation, something different in a medium preoccupied with romantic love even in its early years. All three made vital, but very distinct contribution to film lyrics in the 1930s and 1940s, the first years of the film song.

KIDAR SHARMA: ARTICULATOR OF MISERY

He was the man who wrote the searing lyrics for Saigal to immortalize in *Devdas* (1935). Need anything more be said for him as a lyricist? Yet, Kidar Sharma, the poet–lyricist is subsumed by his other identities as producer, director, and dialogue and screenplay writer. Love, longing and despair were the motifs in almost all his films, and it is in penning songs of unrequited love that he shone best.

'*Na main kisi ka na koi mera/Chaaya chaaron ore andhera/Ab kachu soojhath nahin/More ab din beetat nahin/Dukh ke ab din beetat naahin,*' he wrote at Saigal's behest. R.C. Boral was a pioneer composer, Saigal a maestro, but Kidar's poetry had as much a role in bringing the angst of Devdas alive. As screenplay and dialogue writer for the film, he also replaced the theatrical manner of speaking dialogues with a natural conversational style.

In his own way, Sharma was a revolutionary. Gaining a formidable reputation with the songs of *Devdas* and *Vidyapati*, Sharma left New Theatres over differences with Debaki Bose and shifted to Bombay, writing for Ranjit Movietone. He was always keen on film-making and made his first film *Chitralekha* in 1941, where he had composer Jhande Khan set his iconoclastic lyrics '*Tum jaao jaao bhagwan bane/Insaan bane to jaane/Tum unke jo tumko dhyaye/Jo naam rathe moti paaye/Hum paap kare aur door rahe/*

Tum paar karo to maane' to Raag Bhairavi to be rendered by Ram Dulari. Perhaps Sahir was inspired to recreate the same sentiment in the later version of *Chitralekha* (1964) where Lata sang *'Sansaar se bhaage phirte ho/Bhagwan ko tum kya paaoge'*.

Kidar Sharma's contribution to film music was bigger than the songs he wrote. He gave the struggling Roshan a much-needed break in *Baawre Nain* (1950). Sharma's lyrics stand out particularly in two duets in the film. One of these—*'Jinhe mitna ho woh mitne se dar jaaya nahin karte/Mohabbat karnewaale gham se ghabraaya nahin karte/Khayalon mein kisi ke is tarah aaya nahin karte'*—was sung by Geeta Roy and Mukesh. The other duet by Mukesh and Rajkumari, who also had her biggest hit in this film with the folksy *'Sun bairi balam sach bol re'*, introduced the conversational style of singing in Hindi films:

Mujhe sach sach bata do
Kya?
Ke kab dil mein samaaye the
...
Tumhe kisne kaha hai mere sapnon mein aane ko?
Tere sapnon mein aate hain teri kismat jagaane ko

If *Baawre Nain* was Roshan's launch pad, the other composer who got a break with Kidar Sharma's films is Snehal Bhatkar. This talented composer is best remembered for the songs of Sharma's *Hamari Yaad Aayegi* (1961). The title song in the film became a legend in the voice of Mubarak Begum who stepped in because Lata was too busy. Never was Sharma's pen as piercing as in *'Yeh bijli raakh kar jaayegi tere pyar ki duniya/Na phir tu jee sakega aur na tujhko maut aayegi/Kabhi tanhaiyon mein yun hamari yaad aayegi...'*

Kidar Sharma was a man who found his calling in nurturing new talent. Raj Kapoor, Geeta Bali, Madhubala and Mala Sinha were his discoveries. Roshan and Snehal Bhatkar owed their success to him. Rajkumari and Mubarak Begum had their most popular songs in his films. As late as 1964, Suman Kalyanpur delivered a big hit in the ghazal Sharma penned for his film *Fariyad*: *'Haal-e-dil unko sunana tha/Sunaya na gaya'*.

Sharma retired from active film-making after *Fariyad*, though he continued to write lyrics for documentaries on Doordarshan and a few stray movies. The popular song *'Hum honge kaamyaab ek din'* was written by him and composed by Bhatkar for Doordarshan. Towards the end, he was an embittered man who felt letdown by the fact that he had been denied the recognition that many of his protégés were getting from the government. He wrote his autobiography, *The One and Lonely Kidar Sharma*, in his last years, but did not live to see it published, passing away in 1999.

D.N. MADHOK: HARBINGER OF JOY

Much like Kidar Sharma, Dina Nath Madhok was a multifaceted artiste. He directed no less than eighteen films between 1932 and 1954. He too was instrumental in bringing many composers into the limelight, Naushad being the foremost. He wrote dialogues and screenplay for many movies, but it is as lyricist that D.N. Madhok attained stardom. If Kidar Sharma was the voice of pain, Madhok was the harbinger of hope. His lyrics always had a spirit of optimism pervading them, even when he wrote about despair. His poetry was ultimately about the joy of living.

He was without peer in conveying the effervescence of romantic love. Not surprisingly, the 1940s belonged to him and he earned the sobriquet *Mahakavi* Madhok. He wrote songs that were simple in style but universal in appeal such as '*Panchi jaa/Peeche raha hain bachpan mera/Usko jaake laa*'. Suraiya's childlike innocence had inspired Madhok's lyrics in this song for Naushad in *Sharda* (1942). Earlier, it was Madhok who spotted the talent of Naushad and got him a break as composer in *Prem Nagar* (1940). It was with Madhok's lyrics that Naushad soared to stardom with the path-breaking songs of *Rattan*. Recall Zohrabai singing with sweetness and gusto Madhok's words '*Jaaoge jaane na doongi main rasta rok loongi/Haan saiyan ke paiyan pad jaaoongi roke kahoongi/Akhiyan milake jiya bharmaake chale nahin jaana...*' Or Ameerbai bringing her charm to '*Mushkil se hamne bhulaye the woh din/Phir aake cheda balam ne/Phir se dhadak gayi chhatiyan haay rama/Mil ke bichad gayee akhiyan...*' in the same film.

Madhok's brilliance was by no means confined to Naushad. He was already a popular lyricist by the early 1940s, with hits such as *Pardesi* (1941), *Bhakt Surdas* (1942), and *Tansen* (1943). The first singing diva of Bollywood, Khursheed, sang Madhok's ghazal in *Pardesi* for composer Khemchand Prakash: '*Pehle jo mohabbat se inkaar kiya hota/Yun humko na duniya se bezaar kiya hota/Maloom agar hota anjaam mohabbat ka/Na dil hi diya hota na pyar kiya hota...'* Bhakt Surdas had Khursheed and Saigal in healthy competition, with the former singing the classical song *'Panchi baawra'*, and Saigal, the popular bhajan *'Madhukar Shyam hamare chor'*.

Madhok understood the music of his home state Punjab only too well, and penned something as lustrous as *'Tu kaun si badli mein mere chand hain aaja/Taare hain mere zakhm-e-jigar in mein samaa ja'* for Master Ghulam Haider to tune and Noorjehan to sing in *Khandan* (1942).

While his detractors say Madhok was a wheeler-dealer, peddling one composer's cancelled tunes to another, he also had a reputation for helping many a composer with tunes for his own lyrics, as the tune would often occur to him along with the words. He would tap the rhythm on his cigarette tin and hum the tune, which many a grateful composer would improvise. In his last directorial venture *Bilwamangal* (1954), he got composer Bulo C. Rani to tune his ghazal *'Hum ishq ke maron ko/Do dil jo diye hote/Hum ne na kabhi unke/Ehsaan liye hote'* into something extra-sweet for Suraiya.

By the early 1950s though, Madhok's time was over, caused in part by his increasing waywardness (he was reportedly too fond of alcohol). The second-generation lyricists such as Majrooh Sultanpuri, Shakeel Badayuni and Sahir had also come into prominence by then. He wrote his last popular songs for the Dilip Kumar–Madhubala starrer *Tarana* (1951), in which Anil Biswas soulfully composed Madhok's prescient words *'Aankhon mein neend thi magar/Soye nahin the raat bhar/Dilko laga hua tha dar/Haay savera ho gaya/Woh din kahaan gaye bataa'* for Lata to render.

Pradeep: Poetry for a Cause

To dub him the poet of patriotism is being unfair to Kavi Pradeep, the popularity of his nationalistic *'Aye mere watan ke logon'* notwithstanding. A closer look at Pradeep's work in Hindi films reveals that his true concerns went beyond patriotism. Most of his songs reflect his anguish over the plight of the poor, rising sectarian violence in society and the vanishing spirit of universal brotherhood. He, much before Sahir, used his pen with a sense of responsibility towards larger causes in society, within the constraints of commercial Hindi cinema. It is a measure of his acumen, and the tragedy of this country, that his words written half a century ago remain very contemporaneous.

Pradeep was no doubt a consummate poet, writing for all occasions of life with equal felicity, but what set him apart was the way he articulated the vision of a free, secular and just India even before independence. You are awestruck at his perspicacity as you hear Ashok Kumar and Renuka Devi give feeling to his song '*Ek naya sansar basaa lein/Ek naya sansar.../Aisa ek sansar ke jisme dharti ho azaad/Ke jisme jeevan ho azaad/Ke jisme bharat ho azaad*' in the film *Ek Naya Sansar* way back in 1941.

Two years later, Pradeep penned the even more daring '*Door hato aye duniyawalon Hindustan hamara hain*' for *Kismet* (1943) while the Quit India movement was in full swing, cleverly disguising his call for direct action to throw the British out by substituting the words '*German ho ya Japani*' at the critical stage of the song. He, however, knew even then that, much as freedom was important, the real enemy lay within. For him, freedom was only the first step in the struggle for a more equitable, just and dignified life for the poor. It is in the other song in *Kismet*, '*Ghar ghar mein Diwali hain mere ghar mein andhera*', that one feels the intensity of the man's angst with the ills of Indian society:

Charon taraf laga hua meena bazaar hain
Dhan ki jahan pe jeet garibon ki haar hain
Insaniyat ki bhes mein phirta hain lutera
Ji chahta hain sansar mein main aag laga doon
Soye huye insaan ki qismat ko jaga doon
Thokar se udaa doon main daya-o-dharm ka deraa

Never has a woman in Hindi cinema so boldly called for an overhaul of the existing social order. Ameerbai Karnataki's feisty rendition of Anil Biswas's tune highlights the power of Pradeep's words tellingly. Pradeep's uniqueness also lay in the fact that his social concerns came through in the lyrics he penned for purely commercial Hindi films.

The revolutionary in him was going strong even after independence, and he used his pen with remarkable foresight in the film *Jaagriti* (1954) to caution the younger generation against slipping into complacency, now that freedom was here. The words, set to music by Hemant Kumar and sung by Rafi, hit you with their relevance to twenty-first-century India:

Hum laaye hain toofan se kishti nikaal ke
Is desh ko rakhna mere bachcho sambhaal ke
...
Aaram ki tum bhool bhulaiya mein na bhoolo
Sapnon ki hindolon pe magan hoke na jhoolo
Ab waqt aa gaya mere hanste huye phoolon
Utho chalaang maar ke aakaash ko choo lo

He normally confined himself to writing in Hindi, except when he wrote about the scourge of communalism, an issue he felt deeply about. For such songs, Pradeep would delve into his knowledge of Urdu and create a potent combination of Hindi and Urdu, symbolizing the commonness between the two languages. Pradeep himself sang many of these poignant lyrics, using the raw honesty of his voice to give them more weight as in the ballad from the film *Amar Rahe Yeh Pyar* (1961):

Aaj ke insaan ko yeh kya ho gaya
Iska purana pyar kahaan par kho gaya
Kaisi yeh manhoos ghadi hain
Bhaaiyon mein jang chidi hain
Kahin pe khoon kahin par jwaala
Jaane kya hain hone waala

In later years, a mellower Pradeep turned his attention away from political causes to more personal ones. His lyrics now were about exhorting the beaten individual to face the trials and tribulations of life with fortitude, as in the popular Mukesh number from *Sambandh* (1969), 'Chal akela': *Hazaaron meel lambe raaste tujhko bulaate/Yahaan dukhde sehne ke waaste tujhko bulaate/Hain kaun sa woh insaan yahaan par jisne dukh na jhela*'.

Recognition from the government came in the form of many awards, the Dadasaheb Phalke Award being the last, just before his death in 1998. For all the glory, Pradeep maintained a low profile, always concerned more over the loss of idealism in India than his personal achievements.

SECOND-GENERATION LYRICISTS

Each of the five lyricists featured here are legends in their own right, their role in giving form and substance to the film song no less than that of the stalwart composers of the golden era. Majrooh Sultanpuri, Shakeel Badayuni, Sahir Ludhianvi, Shailendra and Kaifi Azmi were no mere lyricists. They were men who fundamentally cared for their fellow human beings, using their experiences, feelings, intelligence and their convictions to articulate the human condition, reflect the hopes, aspirations and frustrations of a generation coming of age during and after independence. It is this tuning in with the people that, more than anything else, accounts for the contemporary relevance of their lyrics, two generations later. It is what gives each of them a stature far beyond the films they wrote for.

MAJROOH SULTANPURI: THE BRIGHTER SIDE OF LIFE

Easily the most versatile lyricist in Hindi cinema, Majrooh Sultanpuri was also the most prolific without ever being profane. In a career spanning half a century, he is the only lyricist who wrote songs for heroes ranging from Saigal to Shah Rukh Khan and leading ladies from Nargis to Madhuri Dixit with aplomb, relinquishing, somewhere along the way, his initial qualms about film music being too flippant. Majrooh wrote about love and romance for 350 films and 2000 songs without sounding jaded, coming up with something as innocent as *'Pehla nasha, pehla khumaar'* (*Jo Jeeta Wohi Sikandar*, 1992), or as effervescent as *'Aaj main upar aasmaan neeche'* (*Khamoshi*, 1996) when he was well into his seventies. He breathed his last in 2000 even as *Jaanam Samjha Karo*, the Asha Bhonsle–Leslie Lewis indipop album he penned lyrics for, had youngsters the age of his grandchildren swinging.

Not many lyricists have made such a glorious debut. When A.R. Kardar gave him a break in *Shahjehan* after hearing him in a mushaira, Majrooh wrote the last Saigal classic *'Jab dil hi toot gaya'*. Saigal loved the song so much he wanted it played in his final journey, which happened soon after the film's release. Much of Majrooh's early work had a melancholic tenor, justifying his name *'majrooh'*, meaning the wounded. Sample the words from

'*Jab dil hi toot gaya*', '*Maloom na tha hum ko/Mushkil hain meri raahein/Armaan ke bahe aansoo/Hasrat ne bhari aahein/Har saathi choot gaya/Hum jeeke kya karenge*' or from the song '*Uthaye jaa unke sitam*' in *Andaaz*, which came three years later, and where Majrooh wrote: '*Yehi hain mohaabat ka dastoor aye dil/Woh gham de tujhe aur tu duaayen diye jaa/Uthaye jaa unke sitam.*' Talat Mehmood debuted in Hindi films singing Majrooh's words '*Aye dil mujhe aisi jagah le chal jahan koi na ho*' for Anil Biswas in *Aarzoo*.

Influenced by left-wing ideology, Majrooh took an anti-establishment stand against Nehruvian politics just after independence in a couplet he recited, and paid the price for it by spending a year in jail, put behind bars by the Bombay government of Morarji Desai in 1950, just when he was getting to be in demand as a lyricist. When he came out, he was a chastened man who had decided on a career as songwriter to make both ends meet. From then on, Majrooh kept his activism strictly out of his film lyrics. In sharp contrast to his early work, Majrooh's lyrics from the mid-1950s reflect a buoyancy and light-heartedness that established him as a lyricist of romance. He worked consistently with O.P. Nayyar and S.D. Burman, penning hits like '*Babuji dheere chalna*' (Geeta Dutt, *Aar Paar*, 1954), '*Aye dil hain mushkil jeena yahaan*' (Rafi–Geeta, *CID*, 1956), '*Hum hain raahi pyaar ke*' (Kishore, *Nau Do Gyarah*, 1957) and '*Chod do aanchal zamana kya kahega*' (Kishore–Asha, *Paying Guest*, 1957). From frowning upon film music as flippant, Majrooh had made peace with the dictates of success, penning the frivolous '*C-A-T cat, cat maane billi*' for *Dilli Ka Thug* (1958). His lyrics went a long way in giving Shammi Kapoor the boisterous hero image, in songs such as '*Chhupnewale saamne aa*' (Rafi, *Tumsa Nahin Dekha*, 1957) and the title song in *Dil Deke Dekho* (Rafi, 1959).

Popular as they were, many songs of Majrooh in the 1950s did not make a special impact lyrically. It was only in serious themes such as *Sujata* (1959) that he brought to bear his erudition with the glorious lines of '*Jalte hain jiske liye*' (Talat for S.D. Burman). Majrooh was established enough by the turn of the decade to not confine himself to any particular kind of music. Thus the 1960s found him at his versatile best, writing different kinds of songs for varied composers. In *Aarti* (1962), Majrooh betrayed his early communist leanings with something as sublime, yet powerful as '*Bane ho ek khaak se/Ke door kya kareeb kya/Lahoo ka rang ek hain/*

Ameer kya gareeb kya/Gareeb hain woh isliye/Ke tum ameer ho gaye/ Ke ek badshah huaa/To sau fakir ho gaye/Khata yeh hain samaaj ki/ Bhala bura naseeb kya'. His lyrics for Mamta (1966) also stand out. Could Roshan have achieved his career best without Majrooh's words, you wonder as you hear the Lata scorcher 'Rehte the kabhi jinke dil mein/Hum jaan se bhi pyaaron ki tarah/Baithe hain unhi ke koochen mein/Hum aaj gunahgaaron ki tarah'.

After Roshan, Majrooh brought out the buried poet in him for Madan Mohan, to come up with something as exquisite as 'Teri aankhon ke siva duniya mein rakha kya hain' (Rafi and Lata solos, Chirag, 1969). Much like Madan Mohan, Dastak (1970) was a labour of love for Majrooh, where he penned his most authentic Urdu ghazal in 'Hum hain mataa-e-koocha o baazaar ki tarah'. The poignant last verse in the song goes 'Majrooh likh rahe hain woh ahl-e-wafa ka naam/Hum bhi khade huye hain gunahgaar ki tarah'. It may well have been the last time Majrooh wrote something from the heart.

Majrooh adroitly managed to stay ahead of all competition in the 1960s by writing for blockbusters such as Teesri Manzil and Jewel Thief. His sexually charged 'Aaja aaja main hoon pyaar tera' and 'O haseena zulfon waali' for R.D. Burman helped the latter arrive. Starting with Dosti, he also helped newcomers Laxmikant–Pyarelal in their initial phase with other hits like the title song in Paththar Ke Sanam (Rafi, 1967) and 'Chalkaaye jaam' (Mere Humdam Mere Dost, Rafi, 1968). It is a mystery why LP later switched to Anand Bakshi as their lead lyricist.

As R.D. Burman zoomed to the top in the 1970s, Majrooh remained in the limelight as his preferred lyricist. With 150 films behind him, Majrooh could still write something as youthful as 'Raat kali ik khwab mein aayi' (Kishore, Buddha Mil Gaya), 'Lekar hum deewana dil' (Kishore–Asha, Yaadon Ki Baraat) and 'Yeh ladka haaye allah kaisa hain deewana' (Asha–Rafi, Hum Kisi Se Kum Nahin). For Burman Senior, Majrooh wrote the more mature songs of Abhimaan, 'Piya bina piya bina' and 'Ab toh hain tumse' signifying the crowning glory of a partnership between the lyricist and composer that lasted eighteen years.

The 1980s were unremarkable for Majrooh, despite work in over forty films between 1980 and 1988—perhaps because RD's fortunes slipped rapidly in that decade. 'Poocho na yaar kya huaa' (Asha and Rafi, Zamane Ko Dikhana Hain, 1981), 'Hamen tumse *pyar kitna*' (Parveen Sultana and Kishore solos, *Kudrat*, 1981) and '*Jeevan ke din chote sahi*' (Kishore, *Bade Dilwala*, 1983) all proved Majrooh was in good form, but he needed a successful RD to bring out his best in those years. It was the decade when the lyricist seemed at a loss for the first time.

Only till Nasir Hussain's son Mansoor Khan's *Qayamat Se Qayamat Tak* (1988). In '*Papa kehte hain bada naam karega*' Majrooh bounced back with startling freshness, without RD, with newcomers Anand–Milind. At sixty-nine, he could capture the innocence and headiness of teenage love in all its splendour with '*Akele hain toh kya gham hain*'. Followed a slew of love songs. '*Kya karte the sajna tum humse door rehke*' (Anuradha–Anwar, *Lal Dupatta Malmal Ka*, 1989), '*Saathiya, tune kya kiya*' (Chitra and SP Balasubramaniam, *Love*, 1991), '*Bin tere sanam mar mitenge hum*' (Udit–Kavita, *Yaara Dildara*, 1991) and '*Pehla nasha, pehla khumaar*' (Udit–Sadhna Sargam, *Jo Jeeta Wohi Sikandar*, 1992) all proved Majrooh was ready to tune in with the taste of the 1990s, for RD's assistants Jatin–Lalit and other fourth-generation composers. When the opportunity presented itself, Majrooh could still coin something as beautiful as '*Woh toh hain albela*' in the small-budget *Kabhi Haan Kabhi Naa* (1992).

But it was a decade when newcomers ruled the roost in the music industry and an embittered Majrooh had to see Javed Akhtar and Sameer steal a march over him, winning one Filmfare Award after another for their songs. He drew solace from being awarded the Dadasaheb Phalke Award in 1993 for his contribution to Hindi cinema. As the first lyricist to get it, it was a moment of triumph for the veteran. He could have chosen to call it a day then, but like most artistes, lingered on, writing popular, if trite lyrics right until his death in 2000.

SHAKEEL BADAYUNI: GENIUS IN THE SHADOWS

When you think of Naushad with due reverence, spare a thought for Shakeel Badayuni. For what would Naushad have brought his musical weight to bear on, were it not for Shakeel's poetry? To acknowledge Naushad's greatness as composer is to also pay tribute to the genius of Shakeel.

As you traverse the songs he penned for Naushad from *Dard* (1947) till *Sanghursh* (1968), you are so amazed at the consistency of Shakeel's brilliance that you wonder who inspired whom to scale ever-newer peaks in music. No other composer–lyricist partnership was as committed to each other, lasted as long, or produced as many outstanding songs. Shakeel was Naushad's discovery; it was the composer who got the struggling poet a break in Kardar's *Dard*, ending days of poverty for young Shakeel's large family. Shakeel never forgot that, and always underplayed his contribution to Naushad's glory in the 1950s. Unlike Sahir who was wont to shoot his mouth off, Shakeel was content to write good, and often great, poetry for the composer to tune.

Shakeel used his experiences of deprivation with painful intensity in his early lyrics. His poetry stood out most for the quality of despair, giving vent to feelings of dejection, frustration and often a muted anger with the almighty for the plight of his protagonists. This last lent his poetry a blazing intensity, as in the song '*Beech bhanwar mein*' in his very first film *Dard*: '*Bekas ke ghamkhaar tumhi ho/Jo kuch ho sarkaar tumhi ho/Dil ka sukoon jeene ka sahara/Duniya ne sab chheena shah-e-madeena.*' Naushad used the same Raag Darbari to highlight Shakeel's angry articulation of his grievance in *Baiju Bawra* where '*O duniya ke rakhwaale*' bristles with the poet's intensity. Shakeel's words contribute as much to the potency of the song as Rafi's pathos-drenched vocals. *Baiju Bawra* was a film that required Shakeel to use pure Hindi, and the man came up with trumps, penning a bhajan as authentic as '*Man tarpat Hari darshan ko aaj*'. It was for Naushad again that Shakeel wrote the ghazal '*Na milta gham toh barbaadi ke afsaane kahaan jaate*' in *Amar* (1954, Lata). Was it any wonder that contemporary Sahir considered Shakeel the best ghazal writer in Hindi cinema?

Shakeel confined all his creativity to love, romance and dejection, resisting all temptation to write about social causes. Among the quartet of Majrooh, Shailendra, Sahir and Shakeel that ruled Hindi film lyrics in the 1950s and 1960s, Shakeel was the only one to steer clear of political leanings. Sahir may have not liked Shakeel's preoccupation with matters of the heart alone, but he had the grace to admit that Shakeel was truly brilliant in that genre. Nowhere is that brilliance more sparkling than in all the songs of K. Asif's *Mughal-e-Azam*, where Shakeel had to help Naushad surmount the popularity of *Anarkali*, the same theme that was a musical hit seven years earlier. Shakeel reached his zenith as lyricist in the film, with each song a lyrical cosmos in itself, the line '*pyar kiya toh darna kya*' easily the most popular. Anarkali challenging Emperor Akbar in his court with her public declaration of love for prince Salim hasn't lost any of its spirited defiance fifty years on, thanks in no small measure to Shakeel's words: '*Aaj kahenge dil ka fasana/Jaan bhi lele chaahe zamana/Maut wohi jo duniya dekhe/Ghut ghut kar yun Marna kya*'.

If it was defiance in this song, it was Shakeel's trademark dialogue with the Lord in '*Bekas pe karam kijiye sarkaar-e-madeena*', Naushad's Kedar tune that found a place among Lata's first list of personal favourites in 1967. While each song leaves you impressed, it is in the other Lata solo at the end of the film, *Khuda nigehbaan ho tumhaara/Dhadakte dil ka payaam lelo*, that Shakeel's words, topped by Ram Lal's Shehnai and Naushad's Yaman notes, move you to tears.

After *Mughal-e-Azam*, everything Shakeel wrote seemed less. Of course, there were many flashes of brilliance in later years, the title song of *Chaudhvin Ka Chand* being a case in point. Shakeel also wrote '*Mere mehboob tujhe meri mohabbat ki kasam*' (*Mere Mehboob*), '*Ek shahenshah ne banwa ke haseen Taj Mahal*' (*Leader*), '*Guzren hain aaj ishq mein hum us makaam se*' (*Dil Diya Dard Liya*) and '*Dil ki kashti bhanwar mein aayi hain*' (*Palki*), all for Naushad, but with the slide in the fortunes of the composer, Shakeel's poetry went unnoticed. With *Mughal-e-Azam*, the best of Naushad was over, and all of Shakeel's verve couldn't reverse the fortunes of either. His hits for Hemant Kumar in *Sahib, Bibi Aur Ghulam* and *Bees Saal Baad* and for Ravi in *Do Badan* kept him going, but lyrically, what he wrote for others came nowhere close to the magic he created for Naushad.

Luckily for him, death came early, in 1970, and he was spared the redundancy that many stalwarts of music of the previous two decades, including Naushad, had to face. Perhaps he was bidding adieu to the world in his last hit song '*Aaj puraani raahon se*' in *Aadmi*, where he wrote with uncanny prescience: *Jeevan badla duniya badli, mann ko anokha gyaan mila/Aaj mujhe apne hi dil mein ek naya insaan mila/Pahuncha hoon wahaan nahin door jahaan/Bhagwaan bhi meri nigaahon se*'.

SAHIR LUDHIANVI: THE VOICE OF THE OPPRESSED

His name evokes awe and respect on par with Lata Mangeshkar or Naushad, something no other lyricist has quite managed. Sahir did not write lyrics for songs; he wrote intense poems that composers gladly accepted for their tunes. Lyricist–director Gulzar put it very well: Sahir was the one lyricist who never conformed to the norms of the film industry, yet found acceptance in Hindi cinema. In almost everything he wrote for 115 films over three decades, you'll sense why.

Tadbeer se bigdi huyi taqdeer banaa le/Apne pe bharosa hain toh yeh daaon lagaa le—fledgling Sahir was aghast when S.D. Burman turned his ghazal into a club song in *Baazi* for Geeta Dutt to waft through. His protests went unheeded by Burman who never brooked any interference, and it was Sahir who repented when the song became a rage. The Burman–Sahir partnership went from strength to strength for the next six years, years when Sahir would explore the various hues of love, longing and life in his poetry with the confidence that Burman's genius would turn them into hits. If *'Thandi hawaayen'* (*Naujawan*, 1951, Lata) and *'Yeh raat yeh chandni phir kahaan'* (*Jaal*, 1952, Hemant Kumar) represented the thrill of first love, *'Jaayen toh jaayen kahaan'* (*Taxi Driver*, 1954, Talat and Lata as solos) and *'Teri duniya mein jeene se toh behter hain ke mar jaayen'* (*House No. 44*, 1955, Hemant Kumar) were about despair and anguish, something Sahir understood only too well, having witnessed the break-up of his parents' marriage as a child. The custody battle that his mother fought and won for him against all odds made Sahir extremely close to her. Scarred by these events, he found solace through poetry even as a teenager in Lahore.

Sahir's lyrics shone whenever he wrote of dejection. Often, Burman's tunes would give them a brighter feel than what the lyricist intended, as in the Kishore Kumar solo *'Jeevan ke safar mein rahi'* (*Munimji*, 1955). Sadly, Sahir's partnership with Burman ended with Guru Dutt's *Pyaasa* (1957). Sahir's claim that his lyrics contributed more to the success of the film than Burman's music angered Burman into banishing him from his team. *Pyaasa* was the movie where Sahir brought out the leftist in him strongly, articulating the disillusionment of India's poor with Nehruvian socialism in *'Jinhe naaz hain Hind par woh kahaan hain'*, besides castigating the crass materialism prevalent in society with *'Yeh duniya agar mil bhi jaayen to kya hain'*.

Even more scathing was his *'Chin-o-Arab hamara'* in *Phir Subah Hogi* (1958) that talked about the end of hope for the poor in independent India. Sahir's poetry was unvarnished, hitting you straight with its cynicism. He never believed in sublimating his emotions or in pleasing the powers that be. Hadn't he come to Bombay in 1949 from Pakistan only to evade the arrest warrant of the then Pakistani regime for his critical poems, seeking an environment where he could speak his mind?

He may have been cynical of politics, but Sahir never lost faith in the collective power of people, a faith that came through optimistically in *'Saathi haath badhaana'* (*Naya Daur*, 1957) with its uplifting lines *'Ek se ek mile to katra ban jaata hain dariya/Ek se ek mile to zarra ban jaata hain sehra/Ek se ek mile to rai ban sakti hain parbat/Ek se ek mile to insaan bas mein karle kismat...'* In a similar vein, he wrote in *Dhool Ka Phool* (1959): *'Tu Hindu banegaa na Mussalman banegaa/Insaan ki aulaad hain insaan banegaa.'*

His leftist views gradually disappeared from his lyrics by the end of the 1950s. The next decade saw Sahir switch to writing more about love and longing, and excellently at that. But not before he had had his say about the preoccupation with romantic love in films with his usual candour in the Sudha Malhotra–Mukesh duet *'Tum mujhe bhool bhi jaao'* for the film *Didi* (1959): *'Zindagi sirf mohabbat nahin kuch aur bhi hain/Zulf-o-rukhsaar ki jannat nahin kuch aur bhi hain/Bhook aur pyaas ki maari hui is duniya mein/Ishq hi ek haqeeqat nahin kuch aur bhi hain.'*

Having said that, Sahir rested his case for larger social causes. By and large, he confined himself to writing ghazals, nazms and romantic geets for the next two decades. There was the typical Sahir edge to whatever he wrote though. The fire he felt towards social causes earlier was now trained towards many existential dilemmas of the individual, including love. Witness his lyrics, sung by Lata and composed by Roshan, exhorting lovers to face up to the demands of love in *Taj Mahal* (1963): *'Taqt kya cheez hain lal-o-jawaahar kya hain/Ishq waale to khudaai bhi luta dete hain/Jurm-e-ulfat pe hamen log sazaa dete hain/Kaise nadaan hain sholon ko hawaa dete hain.'*

If it was S.D. Burman in the 1950s that Sahir wrote his best for, he teamed up with Roshan in the 1960s to give vent to his creativity. From *'Zindagi bhar nahin bhoolegi woh barsaat ki raat'* (Lata and Rafi solos, *Barsaat Ki Raat*) and *'Mann re tu kaahe na dheer dhare'* (Rafi, *Chitralekha*) to *'Duniya karen sawaal to hum kya jawaab de'* (Lata, *Bahu Begum*, 1967), Sahir found in Roshan a composer who could embellish his words with some outstanding tunes. Sahir also wrote memorable lyrics for composer Ravi, creating many hits for the B.R. Chopra banner in *Gumraah* ('*Chalo ek baar phir se ajnabee ban jaayen hum dono*'), *Waqt* ('*Aage bhi jaane na tu*') and *Humraaz* ('*Na munh chhupa ke jiyo*'). Somewhere in between, he also managed to sneak in some outstanding lyrics for Navketan's *Hum Dono*, the only time when Jaidev stepped in as composer for them. Thus was born the most moving bhajan in Hindi cinema, '*Allah tero naam*', immortalized by Sahir, Jaidev and Lata.

Compared to his work in the 1960s, the next decade was unremarkable. Rhythm had replaced lyrics as the determinant of success, and Sahir's punch was not required any more. Though he wrote for over thirty films in the decade, it is only under a lyrically sensitive composer like Khayyam that Sahir roused himself to pen the introspective, if cynical '*Main pal do pal ka shayar hoon*' in Yash Chopra's *Kabhi Kabhie*, with its acute understanding of the ephemeral nature of fame: '*Kal koi mujhko yaad karen/Kyon koi mujhko yaad karen/Masroof zamaana mere liye/Kyon waqt apna barbaad karen.*'

The first lyricist to demand royalties for his songs and get them, Sahir remained a bachelor till the end. His closeness to his mother prevented his many love affairs from fructifying, and he lost a sense of purpose in living after her death in 1976. Four years later, he followed her to the grave, leaving listeners with the words of the qawwali he wrote for B.R. Chopra's *The Burning Train*: *Pal do pal ka saath hamaara/Pal do pal ke yaarane hain...*'

SHAILENDRA: SIMPLE IS BEAUTIFUL

It is perhaps his untimely death at the age of forty-three that has etched him in the memory of many music lovers as the greatest lyricist in Hindi cinema. Shailendra had but sixteen years in which he wrote sparkling lyrics for around 1000 songs before death stalled him in 1966. In retrospect, it seems he was fortunate, as he wrote during an era when the best in film music happened, and exited before the decline began. All his work, therefore, is of sterling quality, an honour that eluded almost every other lyricist.

The Grade B engineer in Indian Railways was discovered by Raj Kapoor in 1948 when he was reciting a poem on partition,

'*Jalta hain Punjab*', at a mushaira. RK approached Shailendra to write for his films, but the leftist Shailendra frowned upon the frivolity of films and declined. A year later, domestic responsibilities forced him to approach RK and thus was born his first song, '*Barsaat mein humse mile tum sajan*', in *Barsaat*. Shailendra went on to become one of the pillars of the RK banner, writing, along with Hasrat Jaipuri, simple but evocative lyrics for all of RK's films right till his death.

It was Shailendra, more than Hasrat, who helped RK's persona of the simple, innocent man in all his films of the 1950s. '*Awara hoon*' (*Awara*), '*Mera joota hain Japani*' (*Shri 420*), and the title song of *Jis Desh Mein Ganga Behti Hain* (1961) were all penned by him. Shailendra, Shanker-Jaikishan, Hasrat Jaipuri and Mukesh all worked in tandem to give the RK banner a distinct musical identity: simple but heartfelt lyrics, catchy tunes and a voice that resonated innocence like no other could. So familiar was Shailendra with the RK school of music by the end of the decade that even in non-RK films that had Kapoor as the hero, Shailendra embellished the characteristic naivety of the hero with his words, as, for example, with '*Sab kuch seekha humne na seekhi hoshiyaari/ Sach hain duniya waalon ke hum hain anari*' (*Anari*). The song fetched him the Filmfare best lyricist award that year.

By then, Shailendra had carved his own niche amongst other weighty names such as Majrooh, Sahir and Shakeel Badayuni. Unlike Sahir and Shakeel, Shailendra never aspired for literary erudition in his lyrics. He wanted to convey the feelings of the common man—joy, hope, love, devotion and dejection—in a manner that enhanced the tune of the composer, but never outshone it. When he wrote about pain, it was with a simple directness as in *Hain sab se madhur woh geet jinhe/Hum dard ke sur mein gaate hain.../Kaanton mein khile hain phool hamaare, rang bhare armaanon ke/Naadaan hain jo in kaanton se daaman ko bachaaye jaate hain*' (sung by Talat for SJ in *Patita*).

In an echo of the Shakeel–Naushad partnership, Shailendra teamed up best with Shanker–Jaikishan. Like SJ, Shailendra's versatility is seen more in the movies outside the RK banner. Talat's '*Aye mere dil kahin aur chal*' (*Daag*), Lata's '*Kisi ne apna banake mujhko muskurana sikha diya*' (*Patita*), Manna Dey's '*Tu pyar ka saagar hain*' (*Seema*) and Rafi's '*Duniya na bhaaye mohe*' (*Basant Bahar*) are some of the best work of Shailendra, all for SJ.

Besides Shanker–Jaikishan he worked regularly with Salil Choudhury and S.D. Burman to produce charming ditties. When Salil composed for Bimal Roy's *Do Bigha Zameen*, it was Shailendra he approached for giving an earthy feel to the songs reflecting the hopes and aspirations of the small peasant. The result was the immortal '*Mausam beeta jaaye*'. Shailendra also wrote all the songs of Bimal Roy's *Madhumati*, covering a range of feelings—the sheer joy of living in '*Suhaana safar aur yeh mausam haseen*', the eroticism of love in '*Chadh gayo paapi bichchuaa*', the sense of unfulfilled longing in '*Aaja re pardesi*', and the despair and finality of death as a separator in '*Toote huye khwaabon ne*'. If Salil got his only Filmfare Award as composer for *Madhumati*, Shailendra surely deserved the best lyricist award?

Shailendra was a melancholic personality, having lost his mother very early in life in an accident. He was only too aware of the transience of life, and his songs of separation and loneliness had a piercing edge. Which is why S.D. Burman sought him out to provide the words for his melancholic scores in *Bandini* ('*O jaane waale ho sake toh laut ke aana*') and *Meri Soorat Teri Aankhen* (*Poocho na kaise maine rain bitaayi*).

No wonder SD wanted Shailendra for all the mellow ghazals of *Guide*, where Shailendra wrote '*Din dhal jaaye raat na jaaye*', echoing the sentiment of *Poocho na kaise*. With '*Tere mere sapne ab ek rang hain*', '*Kya se kya ho gayaa*', '*Aaj phir jeene ki tamanna hain*' and '*Piya tose naina laage re*' to boot, *Guide* stood tall among all musicals of the 1960s, a decade which saw Shailendra's work gain greater depth, more maturity. It was almost as though he knew time was running out. Even as he adroitly managed to remain trendy with '*Yahoo, chahe koi mujhe junglee kahe*', he wrote with feeling for Shanker–Jaikishan's more serious films. '*Yaad na jaaye beete dinon ki*' (*Dil Ek Mandir*), '*Aaj kal mein dhal gayaa*' (*Beti Bete*), '*Humne jafaa na seekhi*' (*Zindagi*) and '*Dost dost na raha*' (*Sangam*) are only some examples of his serious work. For Anil Biswas's swan song *Chhoti Chhoti Baatein*, Shailendra, unusually for him, wrote some very authentic ghazals, like, for example, '*Kuch aur zamaana kehta hain/Kuch aur hain zid mere dil ki/Main baat zamaane ki maanoon/Ya baat sunoon apne dil ki*' rendered by Meena Kapoor.

Shailendra's own swan song came soon after in *Teesri Kasam*, the movie he also produced. Alas! Despite Basu Bhattacharya's restrained direction, Raj Kapoor and Waheeda Rehman's sensitive performances and Shailendra's eloquent lyrics, the movie was a box-office disaster, though it won the President's Gold Medal for best film. The failure snuffed the life out of producer–lyricist Shailendra, who passed away within a few days of its release, unable to cope with the long delay in the making of the film and the lukewarm response it met with.

KAIFI AZMI: A RELUCTANT LYRICIST

Kaifi Azmi the lyricist was always overshadowed by the poet who stood for a humanistic India. A pity that, because a closer look at his work in Hindi films reveals brilliance, an empathy that put him on par with Sahir. There was one difference though. Sahir's lyrics reflected all his passion and social conscience, his film songs often being political statements. They were hard-hitting, and often bitter, a reflection perhaps of his personal angst. Kaifi wrote with equal intensity, but confined his politics to poetry he wrote outside films. As lyricist, Kaifi stood out for his compassionate view of human foibles, his ability to articulate the inner world of people without ever judging them. He was fundamentally an optimist.

The communist party member who had shocked others with his ability to write a ghazal at the age of eleven frowned upon film lyrics, as had other lyricists of the era with a strong social conscience. Like Shailendra, Kaifi accepted work in films only as a means of survival. Unhappy he may have been writing for films, but his integrity as an artiste and his felicity with poetry were reflected amply in most of his lyrics.

Sachin Dev Burman knew that only Kaifi could take over from Sahir for Guru Dutt's dark and semi-autobiographical *Kagaz Ke Phool*. Kaifi wrote what he later confessed to be the one song he is truly proud of: *Waqt ne kiya kya haseen sitam/Tum rahen na tum hum rahen na hum*. Perhaps it's futile to ponder over what gave the song its iconic status: Kaifi's lyrics, SD's tune or Geeta Dutt's singing. It was the first time Kaifi wrote for Guru Dutt, and he packed in his best. Rafi's '*Dekhi zamane ki yaari*' rivalled '*Waqt ne kiya*' in intensity.

It must have been this intensity that made Khayyam, the composer who saw music as something that only adorns and embellishes good poetry, switch from favourite Sahir to Kaifi for *Shola Aur Shabnam*, where Kaifi came up with another scorcher for Rafi: *Jaane kya dhoondthi rehti hain yeh aankhen mujh mein/Raakh ki dher mein shola hain na chingaari hain*. With *Shola Aur Shabnam*, Kaifi acquired a reputation for going beyond literary erudition and stoking powerful emotions in you, emotions you were often surprised at. It is difficult enough to comprehend, let alone articulate the feelings evoked when you hear this stanza from the song '*Kar chale hum fidaa jaan-o-tan saathiyon*', another Rafi gem, in Chetan Anand's war movie *Haqeeqat*:

Raah qurbaaniyon ki na veeraan ho
Tum sajaate hi rehna naye kaafile
Fateh ka jashn is jashn ke baad hain
Zindagi maut se mil rahi hain gale
Baandh lo apne sar se kafan saathiyon
Ab tumhaare hawaale watan saathiyon

Not that Kaifi's intensity was reserved for causes only political. When Hemant Kumar sought him out for the songs of *Anupama* (1966), a sensitive portrayal of the yearnings of a girl unloved by her father, Kaifi's words in '*Kuch dil ne kaha kuch bhi nahin*'—*Dil ki tassalli ke liye jhooti chamak jhoota nikhaar/Jeevan to soona hi raha sab samjhe aayi hain bahaar/Kaliyon se koyi poochta woh hansti hain yaa roti hain/ Aisi bhi baatein hoti hain*—went a long way in conveying the brooding melancholy of the protagonist.

With *Haqeeqat* began a partnership between Chetan Anand, Madan Mohan and Kaifi Azmi, encompassing some of Kaifi's best work in the 1960s and 1970s. *Heer Ranjha* was a landmark in Hindi cinema, as Kaifi wrote the entire script in verse. Rafi came through despondently in Madan Mohan's custody only with the aid of Kaifi's lyrics in '*Yeh duniya yeh mehfil/mere kaam ki nahin*'.

Leftist that he was, words of pain came to Kaifi effortlessly. He was at his creative peak when writing about the predicament of the dispossessed. His underlying optimism about human nature kept his empathy intact, and thus he could pen a ghazal that captured the angst of the prostitute heroine in Chetan Anand's *Hanste Zakhm*, a ghazal Madan Mohan turned into a classic in Lata's voice: *Aaj socha toh aansoo bhar aaye/Muddate ho gayee muskuraaye*.

Kaifi wrote with acute compassion about the need for relationships to sustain and nurture people through the vicissitudes of life. Nowhere is this compassion more in evidence than in the songs of *Arth* (1982), a movie that sought to bridge the divide between commercial and art cinema. Made with integrity by Mahesh Bhatt, it made commercial cinema aware of the sensitive artiste in Kaifi's daughter Shabana Azmi. Less acknowledged is Kaifi's contribution to the movie, with songs like '*Jhuki jhuki si nazar*', '*Koi yeh kaise bataye*' and '*Tum itna jo muskuraa rahe ho*', tuned and sung by Jagjit Singh. There never has been another ode to the redemptive power of relationships as poignant as the last-mentioned song.

Kaifi's last years were not his happiest. He was troubled over the rising sectarian violence in the country, a theme he had so eloquently explored through the National Award–winning script of *Garam Hawa* in 1973. The destruction of Babri Masjid in 1992 stirred him to write the poem 'Ram Ka Doosra Banwaas', pleading for sanity in times when passions were running high. When Mumbai burned in the riots following the demolition, he resolutely refused to move out of his residence in Janki Kutir in Juhu, ignoring even daughter Shabana's pleas that he does so in the interest of safety. For him, it would have been abandoning all that he stood for. A decade later, a frail and ill Kaifi wouldn't let even hospitalization deter him from responding to the Gujarat carnage with his poem 'Meri Awaaz Suno' that he had first used in the film *Naunihal* (1967). It was his last clarion call, literally from deathbed. He breathed his last on 10 May 2002, still holding on to the dream of a better India.

THIRD-GENERATION LYRICISTS

Their work has to be seen in the context of the milieu in which they wrote. Gulzar, Anand Bakshi and Javed Akhtar blossomed into full-fledged lyricists in the 1970s and 1980s, musically uninspiring years. Unlike the lyricists of the golden era who were inspired to write great poetry because of great music, these three wrote good, at times great poetry despite bad films and indifferent music. Gulzar, more than others, played a leading role in keeping poetry going in this era through the films he produced and directed. Anand Bakshi was the most prolific and sought-after lyricist of the 1970s, who, despite brilliance, conformed to trends rather than create them. By sheer volume, Bakshi ousted every other lyricist from the scene. Javed Akhtar bravely jettisoned his career as scriptwriter in that dim decade of the 1980s, choosing poetry in an era that had no need for it. Together, they constitute the last generation of legendary lyricists.

GULZAR:
ILLUMINATOR OF THE INTERPERSONAL TERRAIN

Here is a lyricist who believes that the personal is political. For Gulzar, the interpersonal world has been as significant, as potent a determinant of the human condition as larger social and political causes. For over four decades now, Gulzar has brought his gentle wit, compassion and optimism to take us a wee bit further into the mysterious world of love and longing. His songs that amplify and explore the nuances and tangles of relationships do not provide us easy answers, but do take us a little closer towards understanding, acceptance and hope.

And to think that we could have almost been denied him, were it not for the tiff that S.D. Burman had with Shailendra while scoring *Bandini*, which led to the young assistant director of Bimal Roy stepping in to pen his first song '*Mora gora ang lai lai*', a song with which Burman ended his six-year stand-off with Lata. There couldn't have been a more auspicious beginning for Gulzar's career as lyricist. That he was a poet in the making is amply clear in the way he articulated the dilemma of the heroine caught between tradition and new-found love: *Ek laaj roke paiyyan/Ek moh kheeche baiyyan/Jaaoon kidhar na jaaoon/Humka koi batai de.*

It took him the best part of six years to find his bearings as a songwriter. It was with *Khamoshi* that Gulzar took off as lyricist, writing about what fascinated him most: relationships, and doing it in a manner that was daringly defiant. '*Humne dekhi hain un aankhon ki mehekti khushboo*' raised many literary eyebrows for the alleged faux paus of 'dekhi hain khushboo', but Gulzar was unfazed. When the song clicked, he found his identity as lyricist. The song remains his finest, at once a plea for love to exist, and an assertion: '*Sirf ehsaas hain yeh rooh se mehsoos karo/Pyaar ko pyaar hi rehne do koi naam na do.*'

Gulzar struck an early rapport with Salil Choudhury when he wrote '*Ganga aaye kahaan se*' (*Kabuliwala*), something that found fruition in his lyrics for *Anand*, scored by Salil. It's a tough task to choose between Mukesh's '*Maine tere liye hi saat rang ke*' and Lata's '*Na jiya laage na*', but the former, with its wider canvas of love in its entirety, better represents the bold strides the lyricist was taking.

Salil Choudhury it was who composed Gulzar's lyrics for the latter's first film as director, *Mere Apne*. The film, a sensitive exploration of an old woman's life, loneliness and death against the backdrop of gang wars among unemployed youth, was also a deeply moving statement about the futility of violence as a weapon for justice. Gulzar's lyrics in the memorable '*Koi hota jisko apna*' made you feel the desolation of the gang-leader hero, who introspects on the connections between violence and the absence of love in his life.

The 1970s witnessed Gulzar at his peak as director and lyricist. His lyrics contributed in no small measure to the impact of his two most powerful films, both with Sanjeev Kumar in the lead. In *Mausam*, the only film where Gulzar worked with Madan Mohan, the Bhupinder solo '*Dil dhoondta hain phir wohi fursat ke raat*' stands out for the grace with which it paints the vulnerability of an old and repentant Sanjeev who comes back to a hill station after years, only to be assailed by memories of youth, romance and guilt over his jettisoning his beloved.

In the other film, *Aandhi*, Gulzar deftly wove a story of estrangement between a couple against the backdrop of politics. The most moving moment in the film is when the couple meet after years, and wonder whether they could have made different choices, choices that may have given them less fulfilment individually, but more happiness together. Arguably Gulzar's most poignant lyric, '*Tere bina zindagi se*' stands tall among the ones created by the RD–Gulzar partnership. Kishore Kumar and Lata are at their sublime best with words that reflect the agony and regret of choices made: '*Kaash aisa ho, tere kadmon se, chunke manzil chalen/Aur kahin door kahin/Tum gar saath ho manzilon ki kami toh nahin.*'

Not that Gulzar did not write great poetry for films he did not direct. When he worked with Basu Bhattacharya, who had a keen eye for the shades of man–woman relationships within the institution of marriage, Gulzar brought his own insights about relationships to the songs. '*Mujhe ja na kaho meri jaan*' (Geeta Dutt, *Anubhav*, 1971), '*Hasne ki chaah ne intna mujhe rulaaya hain*' (Manna Dey, *Aavishkar*, 1974) and '*Pehchaan toh thi pehchana nahin*' (Chandrani Mukherjee, *Grihapravesh*, 1979) represent a body of work that is unusually intense for Gulzar, though less popular. His words in '*Pehchaan toh thi*'—*Main jaag rahi thi sapnon mein/Aur jaagi huyi bhi soyi rahi/Jaane kin bhool-bhulaiyyon mein/ Kuch bhatki rahin kuch khoyi rahin/Jeene ke liye main marti rahin/Jeene ka ishaara samjha nahin*—is a sensitive statement about the oppression a woman feels inside the institution of marriage.

Gulzar won his first Filmfare Award for best lyricist for *Gharonda*, where he wrote for composer Jaidev the breezy '*Do deewane shehar mein*' (Bhupinder–Runa Laila) and the starkly beautiful '*Ek akela is shaher mein*' about the ruthlessness of Mumbai, its relentless pace, something only truer three decades later: '*In umr se lambi sadkon ko/Manzil pe pahunchte dekha nahin/Bas daudti phirti rehti hain/Hamne toh theherrte dekha nahin.*'

Of course, Gulzar's most memorable partnership was with his favourite composer Pancham. Theirs was a friendship born out of similar struggles in the initial days and a deep professional regard for each other. It is only with something as mood lifting as '*Aaj kal paaon zameen par nahin padte mere*' (Lata, *Ghar*, 1978) that RD could fly with his notes. In working with Gulzar as lyricist and director, RD gave expression to the serious composer in him with songs like '*Naam gum jaayega*' (Lata–Bhupinder, *Kinara*, 1977).

Beginning with *Parichay* ('*Beete na bitaaye raina*, Lata–Bupinder), the Gulzar–Pancham team gave us unforgettable numbers through *Aandhi* ('*Is mod se jaate hain*', Kishore–Lata), *Ghar* ('*Aap ki aankhon mein kuch*', Kishore–Lata), *Kinara* ('*Meethe bole boley*', Bhupinder–

Lata), *Golmaal* ('*Aanewaala pal jaanewaala hain*', Kishore), *Angoor* ('*Roz roz daali daali kya likh jaaye*', Asha), *Masoom* ('*Do naina aur ek kahaani*', Aarti Mukherjee) and *Ijaazat* ('*Mera Kuch Saamaan*', Asha). The last fetched Gulzar a National Award for best lyricist, and also the Filmfare Award. Written in free-flowing verse without meter, the song was a challenge for RD to compose and Asha to sing. '*Katra katra milti hain*', also from *Ijaazat*, has Gulzar exhort us to cherish moments of longing for love as yet another form of happiness: '*Paake bhi tumhaari aarzoo ho/Shaayad aisi zindagi haseen hain/Aarzoo mein behne do/Pyaasi hoon main pyaasi rehne do.*' At a time when film lyrics and music had coarsened to a point of no return, Gulzar retained his integrity as lyricist and wrote '*Yaara seeli seeli*' and other haunting songs for *Lekin* (1990), winning both the Filmfare Award and the National Award for best lyricist that year.

His second innings as film-maker in the 1990s had him move to more political themes, such as terrorism in *Maachis* (1996) and political corruption in *Hu Tu Tu* (1999). Though made with integrity, something was missing in both films, perhaps the ease and comfort with which he told a story of relationships. Even in *Maachis*, it is only in '*Chod aaye hum woh galiyaan*' that you feel the pain on behalf of the young terrorists-in-the making, for the lost innocence of the world they have left behind.

After *Maachis*, Gulzar's lyrics took a turn for the worse. The imagery that was so effortless earlier seemed forced and jaded; the writing laboured. For all the waves '*Chhaiyya chhaiyya*' (*Dil Se*) made, despite the man's ability to remain relevant and popular in the age of techno-music with something as trendy as '*Kajra re*' (*Bunty Aur Bubli*), there is a hollowness to his lyrics that is saddening at the very least. He himself seems aware of this, as lately he has declared that films don't excite him any more. Perhaps the poet was ruing his own lost innocence in *Chod aaye hum woh galiyaan*?

ANAND BAKSHI: HIGH-VOLUME POETRY

The most prolific lyricist in Bollywood, Anand Bakshi wrote nearly 4500 songs over four decades, an unbeatable record for any other songwriter anywhere in the world. Much like his favourite composer duo Laxmikant–Pyarelal for whom he wrote in approximately 250 films, Bakshi's prodigious output was not always consistent in quality. But there's no denying that the 1970s belonged to him as lyricist, and that he remained a force to reckon with well into the twenty-first century, until a few months before his death in 2002.

Ex-army man Bakshi wanted to be a playback singer, and settled for writing lyrics only because he made no headway as singer. Not that the going was easy as lyricist, in an age when stalwarts Majrooh, Sahir, Shakeel and Shailendra were at their peak. It was also a time when Shanker–Jaikishan worked only with Hasrat and Shailendra; Naushad did not look beyond Shakeel. A determined Bakshi persevered, and got noticed first for his song 'Mere mehboob qayamat hogi' in Mr. X in Bombay (1964) with newcomers LP. The following year, he had a big hit in 'Pardesiyon se na akhiyan milana' in Jab Jab Phool Khile. But it was with the songs of Milan (1967) that Bakshi came into his own as lyricist, 'Ram kare aisa ho jaaye' (Mukesh) and 'Saawan ka mahina pawan kare sor' (Mukesh–Lata) marking his own style. Bakshi steered clear of the Shakeel–Sahir fascination for Urdu, or even Shailendra's penchant for literary Hindustani. Keen that his songs appeal to the layperson, Bakshi kept his lyrics simple and colloquial.

The song 'Achcha toh hum chalte hain' (Kishore–Lata, Aan Milo Sajna, 1970) is a case in point. In a music sitting for the film with the composers LP, Bakshi got stuck and decided to call it a day, getting up uttering the words 'achcha toh hum chalte hain'. 'Phir kab miloge?' queried LP, and Bakshi saw light, converting the casual conversation into a cute duet. Then there is the anecdote of how Raj Khosla wanted Laxmikant–Pyarelal to tune the title song of Main Tulsi Tere Aangan Ki without the lyrics being ready, and how Bakshi, with his famed flash of inspiration, said the next line should be 'koi nahin main tere saajan ki', to the immense relief of the composers. It was this spontaneity that LP so valued, never looking beyond him for their songs in the following decades, but for an odd exception here and there. And what a treasure-trove of songs the trio created during the decade.

Some of Bakshi's most popular work happened for LP in the 1970s. 'Yeh jeevan hain' (Kishore, Piya Ka Ghar, 1973), 'Hum tum ek kamre mein bandh ho' (Lata–Shailendra Singh, Bobby, 1973), 'Gaadi bulaa rahi hain' (Kishore, Dost, 1974), 'Dekh sakta hoon main kuch bhi hote huye' (Kishore, Majboor, 1974), 'Ke aaja teri yaad aayi' (Rafi–Lata, Charas, 1976), 'Humko tumse ho gayaa hain pyaar kya kare' (Rafi, Kishore, Mukesh and Lata, *Amar Akbar Anthony*, 1977), 'Dafli waale dafli bajaa' (Lata–Rafi, *Sargam*, 1979) and 'Darde-dil, dard-e-jigar' (Rafi, *Karz*, 1980) were all the outcome of this partnership. In between all these hits, Bakshi managed to pen the philosophical 'Aadmi musafir hain' for *Apnapan* (1978), the song that fetched him his first Filmfare Award for best lyricist, in an era when songs with depth were the exception. When you look at all the work that Bakshi did for LP in the 1970s, you wonder whether there was anything else that was musically significant.

There certainly was, and it was Bakshi's work for the other star composer of that decade, R.D. Burman. Beginning with *Kati Patang* (1970), the composer and lyricist struck an equation that was to result in many hits in the coming years. Bakshi's work with RD was more varied, as he wrote all kinds of songs for RD to tune: philosophical, sad, peppy and modern. Bakshi's lyrics helped RD craft for himself the image of composer for the swinging youth of the era, with songs such as the sexy 'Mera naam hain Shabnam' (Asha Bhosle, *Kati Patang*, 1970), the rebellious 'Dum maaro dum' (Asha, *Hare Rama Hare Krishna*, 1971) and the raunchy 'Mehbooba mehbooba' (R.D. Burman, *Sholay*, 1975). What is less known is that within the ambit of strictly commercial cinema, Bakshi wrote some of his most intense lyrics for the same RD. 'Jis gali mein tera ghar na ho baalma' (Mukesh, *Kati Patang*, 1970), 'Chingaari koi bhadke' (Kishore, *Amar Prem*, 1971), 'Zindagi ke safar mein guzar jaate hain jo makaam' (Kishore, *Aap Ki Kasam*, 1974) and 'Saawan ke jhoole pade' (Lata, *Jurmana*, 1979) are cases in point. The closest Bakshi came to true poetry was again in a film which had music by RD, *Namak Haram* (1973), where Kishore excelled himself in that paean to friendship 'Diye jalte hain' and in vocalizing the poet's longing in 'Main shayar badnam'.

His ability to move with the times made Bakshi the sought after lyricist for all the teenage love stories of the early 1980s. Working with RD and LP, Bakshi made us feel the exhilaration, the tentativeness and the innocent longing of first love in songs such as 'Solah baras ki baali umar ko salaam' (Lata, *Ek Duje Ke Liye*, 1981), 'Yaad aa rahi hain' (Amit Kumar–Lata, *Love Story*, 1981), 'Kya yahi pyaar hain' (Kishore–Lata, *Rocky*, 1981), 'Tu mera jaanu hain' (Anuradha Paudwal–Manhar, *Hero*, 1983) and 'Jab hum jawaan honge' (Shabbir Kumar–Lata, *Betaab*, 1983). His lyrics were nondescript in scores of movies in that decade, but he could occasionally muster enough energy to write something out of the ordinary, even in a vendetta movie such as *Meri Jung* (1985)—*Zindagi har kadam ek nayee jung hain*.

By the end of the 1980s, Bakshi had given up the *jung* for respectability as lyricist. The next decade saw him hit an all-time low in terms of quality, stooping to write songs as coarse as '*Jumma chumma de de*' (*Hum*), '*Choli ke peeche kya hain*' (*Khalnaayak*), '*One two ka four*' (*Ram Lakhan*) and '*Tu cheez badi hain mast mast*' (*Mohra*). Bakshi was unabashed about this part of his work, blaming it on the times. The latter half of the decade saw him revert to his pet theme—romantic songs in the Yash Chopra and Subhash Ghai blockbusters, effortlessly tuning with the fourth-generation composers Jatin–Lalit, Nadeem–Shravan and A.R. Rahman. '*Tujhe dekha to yeh jaana sanam*' (*Dilwaale Dulhaniya Le Jaayenge*), '*Dil toh paagal hain*' (same film), '*Yeh Dil, Deewaana*' (*Pardes*), '*Ishq bina kya jeena yaaron*' (*Taal*) and '*Humko hamin se churaa lo*' (*Mohabbatein*) were some of Bakshi's most popular songs in the last phase of his career.

In one of his last interviews, he rued the fact that there was no scope for serious lyrics any more in films. He couldn't recall when he last wrote a sad song. Perhaps he was right about the times being unfavourable to serious poetry, because when he tried to do just that in *Yaadein* (2001), the film bombed. The title song, '*Baatein bhool jaati hain/Yaadein yaad aati hain*', sung with feeling by Hariharan, was Bakshi's last flicker.

JAVED AKHTAR: IN PURSUIT OF FIRST LOVE

It was *1942—A Love Story* in the early 1990s that put the erstwhile scriptwriter, who assiduously built Amitabh's persona as the 'angry young man' in the 1970s through his screenplays in partnership with Salim, in the reckoning as a top lyricist of Bollywood. You wonder why Javed Akhtar's work as lyricist in the preceding decade is almost invisible, though he wrote quite a few memorable songs, beginning with '*Yeh kahan aa gaye hum*' and '*Neela asmaan so gaya*' in *Silsila* (1981). Perhaps it had to do with the overall decline in music in the 1980s. Javed started out his career as lyricist in a decade when even established lyricists such as Indeewar had succumbed to writing '*Jhopdi mein charpayee*' (*Mawaali*, 1982).

If *Silsila* gave you a taste of the man's flair for poetry, small-budget *Saath Saath* the following year confirmed that the man who wrote feisty screenplays could also turn a sublime poet. After all, the son of Jan Nisar Akhtar, who wrote simple but potent lyrics for O.P. Nayyar in the 1950s and 1960s, knew he'd be measured against his father's output. If '*Kyon zindagi ki raah mein majboor ho gaye*' (Chitra Singh) was a pain-lashed lament over the loss of ideals and the consequent estrangement in a relationship, '*Tumko dekha to yeh khayal aaya*' (Jagjit Singh) was about all the longing, all the uncertainties of first love. Barring *Arth*, Jagjit rarely came close to sounding so effective in films, and young Javed's words—*Aaj phir dil ne ek tamanna ki/Aaj phir dil ko humne samjhaaya/Zindagi dhoop tum ghanaa saaya*—had much to do with it.

Javed captured the idealism of youth, their spirit of 'raring to go' brilliantly in the song '*Zindagi aa raha hoon main*' in *Mashaal* (scored by Hridaynath Mangeshkar, sung by Kishore, 1984), with the telling words 'Mere haathon ki garmi se/Pighal jaayengi zanjeerein/ Mere qadmon ki aahat se/Badal jayengi taqdeerein/Umeedon ke diye lekar/Ye sab tere liye lekar/Zindagi aa raha hoon main'. A pity the film bombed, despite convincing performances by Dilip Kumar and Anil Kapoor, and the best solo of Kishore Kumar in his last years.

With *Saagar* (1985) began Javed's tryst with commercial cinema, and the fledgling lyricist showed an ability to manage the tightrope between artistic integrity and commercial success, penning '*Jaane do na*' as his bow to trade, even while writing the more polished '*Sagar kinaare dil yeh pukaare*'. This was followed by more tepid songs in *Arjun* (1985), *Mr. India* (1987) and *Tezaab* (1988), all three taking the lyricist on a spiral of popularity, even as he was steadily rubbishing poetry with lyrics as trite as '*Mammaiyya kero kero kero mamma*' (*Arjun*), '*Hawaa hawaai*' (*Mr. India*) and '*Ek do teen*' (*Tezaab*). Mercifully, Javed seems to have realized this himself, and took a long break of five years before he came up with genuine poetry in *1942—A Love Story*. In '*Kuch na kaho*' and '*Pyaar hua chupke se*' you find again the promise he displayed in *Saath Saath* a decade earlier.

With this film, Javed emerged as a full-fledged lyricist, marching ahead of all competition (particularly from lyricist Sameer of *Aashqui, Saajan, Dil* and *Deewana* fame) and acquired an awesome reputation, only cemented with the hauntingly moving '*Sandese aate hain*' for *Border* (1997). In its evocative quality, the song comes close to Kaifi Azmi's '*Hoke majboor usne mujhe bhulaaya hoga*' for *Haqeeqat* three decades earlier. With the song that fetched him his second National Award as lyricist, Javed put paid all criticism that his lyrics sound like improvised scripts. But his best was yet to come, and he got there with '*Panchi nadiyaan pawan ke jhoke*' for *Refugee* in 2000. One hadn't heard such a tender plea for universal brotherhood in a long time. Deservedly, Javed Akhtar won his fourth National Award as lyricist for this song, giving lyrics a new relevance and respectability into the twenty-first century. In an age of techno-music, Javed could blend philosophy and youthfulness seamlessly as in *Har ghadi badal rahi hain roop zindagi/Chaon hain kabhi kabhi hain dhoop zindagi/Har pal yahaan jee bhar jiyo/Jo hain sama kal ho na ho*, the title song of *Kal Ho Na Ho*. Thus, at sixty-two, the most successful scriptwriter of the 1970s is into his third innings in Bollywood as the most sought-after lyricist of the new millennium.

GULZAR ON THE POETS OF HINDI FILM MUSIC

There is warmth in his eyes, a compassionate look so reminiscent of his lyrics of yore. He surprises me by beginning the meeting with an apology for his manager's act of asking me to send proof that I really am who I say I am. Then he proceeds to inquire unobtrusively about how I came to write the book. When I ask him if I can tape our conversation, he replies with a twinkle in his eyes that he'll speak the truth and nothing but the truth. He goes on to say he is relieved I want him to speak about other lyricists, and not about himself. Warm, approachable and self-effacing, writer, poet, producer, director and lyricist Gulzar speaks on lyricists of Hindi cinema down the ages.

What would you say about the contribution of first-generation lyricists Kidar Sharma and D.N. Madhok?

I am glad you're asking me to talk about these pioneers. Somehow their work as lyricists has been forgotten by the film industry, which seems to believe that lyrics started with Shailendra, Majrooh and Sahir. The fact is that there were many creative songwriters before the 1950s, Kidar Sharma and Dina Nath Madhok being the two most popular.

To appreciate the true contribution of Kidar Sharma, you have to understand the context in which songs emerged in films. Music came to films from the Indian tradition of songs being part of any narrative in theatre. The first-generation lyricists came from a strong theatre background. The people who wrote and sang kathas and nazms became the ones who wrote geets and ghazals.

Early twentieth century was a time when Urdu had gained prominence; so many songwriters were Urdu poets.

From the same Urdu tradition came Kidar Sharma, who pioneered the use of imagery in film songs. He created many beautiful and popular songs using the imagery of *'chaand'* and *'panchchi'* such as K.L. Saigal's *'Panchchi kaahe hoth udaas'* or *'Mere roothe huye chanda'* (*Bawre Nain*). Conveying feelings in songs through the use of imagery was Kidar Sharma's original contribution. However, he still confined himself largely to the classical Urdu style in the beginning.

D.N. Madhok was responsible for bringing our folk tradition, the music of the common man, into films in a big way. The songs that were sung by the farmer to welcome spring; the mother to her child while feeding or putting it to sleep; songs of the different festivals...all these were incorporated into film lyrics by Madhok saab. While classical music was there in films even in the silent era through the live orchestra that performed in the pit, folk entered films only after Madhok incorporated it. He made film music the music of everyday culture. That's why I consider him a true genius. Also, he had amazing variety: he wrote ghazals and geets; brought the dialects of Purabi, Bhojpuri and Avadhi into films. Film lyrics as a distinct art form began with Madhok. He was a singer and composer too. He also tuned many songs he wrote, though the composer took the credit.

Kidar Sharma achieved fame also as a director of films. He brought his creative imagery even into making films. Madhok too made films, but he was a far better lyricist than film-maker. In the 1940s, Madhok was the most sought-after lyricist. Another man who was the voice of the masses in the first generation of lyricists is Kavi Pradeep, who used the film medium so effectively to articulate urgent concerns of the common man. *'Door hato aye duniyawalon Hindustan hamara hain'*—who can deny the power of these lyrics, even if the standard of poetry was not great? Pradeep was a man of the masses. He wrote in folk style, sang folk tunes and talked about social concerns in a language that stirred the common man.

From the next generation of lyricists, who would you say was the best?

The Indian People's Theatre Association (IPTA), which began as a protest movement and played a crucial role in the freedom struggle, threw up a lot of poets. Sahir Ludhianvi, Majrooh Sultanpuri and Shailendra all came from IPTA into films. Shakeel Badayuni, though not from IPTA, started writing for films at the same time. All four played an important role in the evolution of lyrics.

Shailendra was the best among them all. In my view, he was the lyricist who understood films as a medium distinct from poetry and theatre perfectly, and adapted to it beautifully. For his ability to know the medium, understand the situation, get into the shoes of his characters, and writing in a language suiting the character, he was without peer. Shailendra, like D.N. Madhok, could write in a variety of dialects.

Shakeel Badayuni was extremely popular and wrote beautiful ghazals, but his language remained the same in all his films. So with Majrooh, who wrote 'C-A-T- *cat, cat maane billi*' to suit the situation of the song, but used the same language, the same vocabulary with a heavy Urdu base most often. Shailendra would give a regional flavour to his lyrics depending on where the story is situated. His songs for stories from the south would have a feel of the south; if the film was set in Uttar Pradesh, he'd write in Bhojpuri or Avadhi. For a story set in the north, he could write pure Hindustani or Urdu as the situation demanded.

Also, Shailendra was the only lyricist who found an effective way of merging his personal beliefs with his lyrics, without in any way sermonizing or propagating an ideology. The only other poet who succeeded in doing this was Sahir, but Shailendra did so without rejecting the film medium. Let me give you an example. He was a leftist and a trade unionist. He actually refused to write for films initially because he thought the medium was elitist. But under Raj Kapoor, who made films reflecting the struggles and hopes of the common man, Shailendra found a way of being true to his personal beliefs and to the film medium simultaneously. '*Dil ka haal sune dilwaala*' is a great example of this ability. So is '*Mera joota hain Japaani*'. Notice that the latter song was never a slogan. Only a simple man articulating a simple truth. That was Shailendra's greatness. I'd go as far as to say that among all the lyricists of Hindi cinema, only Shailendra became a part of the film medium, expertly and successfully. All others remained poets who wrote for films.

Sahir Ludhianvi merged his poetry and social conscience in all his songs, but he totally refused to learn the film medium, and wrote only what he wanted. He is the only poet whom the industry accepted as he is, with his language, his vocabulary and his imagery. Sahir is also the only poet whose songs became successful because of his lyrics, and not because of the tune or singer, as was usually the case. In the history of Hindi cinema, this phenomenon of a lyricist succeeding entirely on his own terms happened only with Sahir.

I believe that in any song that becomes a hit, the primary factors are the rhythm and the tune. The words follow. In fact, the quality of the words depends on how much it matches the melody and the beat. That is why I consider the role of the lyricist as secondary to that of the composer. With Sahir, however, the songs succeeded on the merit of his words alone. The tune and the beat came only next. His words had a persona of their own. For instance, *'Pedon ki shaakhon pe soyi soyi chaandni aur thodi der mein thhak ke laut jaayegi'* in the film *Jaal*. This language, this kind of expression did not exist in films till Sahir saab came. He gave a new meaning to romanticism in films.

It was Sahir saab again who fought for visibility to lyricists on All India Radio, in those days when radio was the means of entertainment for people, and programmes based on film songs were extremely popular. He raised the issue of the lyricist being ignored while credits for the song were being announced. If the singer and composer could be mentioned, why not the lyricist, argued Sahir, and finally AIR conceded the point. For that the lyricist community will always be grateful to him.

Your views on Kaifi Azmi as lyricist?

Kaifi saab wrote for very few films. He was not a full-time lyricist, you see. He had a much bigger responsibility of keeping IPTA and the Progressive Writers' Association (PWA) alive, keeping the values of the communist movement alive. He was a crusader for the underprivileged, and spoke his mind on many issues affecting the nation. As lyricist, I liked his songs in Guru Dutt's *Kaagaz Ke Phool*.

And Anand Bakshi, the lyricist who wrote the maximum number of songs in Hindi films?

There is one thing that came through in all of Bakshi saab's voluminous work: his honesty, sincerity and gusto as an ex-serviceman. Like a true soldier, Bakshi was totally committed to the task of writing lyrics. He also had the overwhelming energy of a Punjabi, which kept him going for years. Bakshi was rather like a man sitting on the edge of a well that is full to the brim. A man who has the rope and bucket in his hand, and who keeps pouring water into the hands of anyone in need of water. Let me tell you it's not at all easy to keep churning out songs, and Bakshi saab's ability to write so consistently for so many years is truly amazing. The only drawback was that he did not seem to have a choice about what he wrote. But then, he was like a soldier. He delivered what was asked of him, with a cheerful smile. His lyrics reflect his nature. There's no snobbery, no bitterness, no judgement about others. And he wrote all kinds of songs, for so many composers. I remember, in the late 1970s, about 70 per cent of all songs played on Vividh Bharati were written by Bakshi. Such was his mega presence in the industry.

What about the lyricists of the 1980s and 1990s?

I like the work of some lyricists who did not get too much name in the industry. Nida Fazli, Shahryar, Naqsh Lyallpuri and Neeraj did some good work in the 1970s and early 1980s. Neeraj wrote very well for S.D. Burman, but was a man with a burning desire to contribute something concrete to the people of his village, which is why he joined politics. I respect his convictions and admire his decision.

Javed Akhtar and Nida Fazli are people with grounding in poetry, who came from a tradition of literature into films. That is the reason why they wrote well in the 1980s and 1990s. Javed Akhtar started late as lyricist, but managed to make the transition from scriptwriter to lyricist smoothly.

Looking back at your own career as lyricist, what would you say in retrospect?

When I started writing lyrics, I had the advantage of so many masters to learn from. I have tried to imbibe a little of what I like about their style in my lyrics, but still create an identity for myself. I have written a lot about relationships, not with any finality or from the point of view of an expert, but from the outlook of one who is engaged in the search for answers.

One thing I learned from Shailendra is to write about deeper issues in a light-hearted fashion. I believe you can sing with a sense of humour about serious social problems; you need not convert it into a lament. '*Goli maar bheje mein*' (*Satya*) is an example. The lyrics are frivolous, but it is a song of many layers. So it is with many of my other songs. '*Ghapla hain*' (*Hu Tu Tu*) is funny, but it is actually about the menace of booth capturing.

I am also happy with the songs I have written for children. I think my style has been to write songs that children can play with; songs that are really a game. Earlier, children's songs used to be full of serious social messages. My song in *Masoom*, '*Lakdi ki kaathi*', is pure fun. So is my theme song for the television character Mowglee, '*Jungal jungal pataa chala hain chaddi pehenke phool khila hain*'. I'll confess humbly that I've learnt this art of writing for children from Sukumar Ray, whom I consider the greatest poet for children.

I am really glad that today I am working for youngsters, the directors and composers of today. I am still learning. To write as per today's norms and the new values is a challenge. There definitely is a change of vocabulary; a change of expression. The nature of stories in films too has changed; concepts of what is good music have changed. So how can you expect the words to be similar to what was written two or three decades ago? I don't want to keep going back to the 1960s and 1970s, because too much nostalgia for the past can make you miss what is good about the present. I admire the music made in those years, I love hearing those songs, but I also think the music of *Bunty Aur Babli* is energetic and youthful, something that reflects the pace of life today. Sure, we don't have the melody of *Baiju Bawra* today, but neither was the energy of '*Kajra re*' there in the 1950s! I think I've been able to see what is good about each age. It is one reason why I continue to be relevant to films, at my age.

PART III

The Playback Singers

Singers: The Voice of a Song

The playback singer is possibly closest to the hearts of music lovers, as it is the singer's voice that lends fruition to the composer's tune and the lyricist's words; it is the voice that makes the song come alive for the listener; it is in the same voice that the song is etched in the listener's memory. Thus, it is not without reason that playback singers are the 'stars' of the music industry, much more in the limelight than either composers or lyricists. Barring Naushad in the earlier era and Rahman today, no composer has mattered so much to the listener as Saigal, Lata, Asha, Mukesh, Rafi and Kishore have.

I myself woke up to Hindi film music way back in the early 1980s as Geeta Dutt's *'Thandi hawa kaali ghata'* (Mr. & Mrs. 55) hit me like a thunderbolt one evening, simultaneously ending my fascination for Western pop music and beginning my enduring romance with Hindi film music. For that reason, she remains my eternal favourite. Subsequently, I discovered the magic of all other singers, then composers, and finally lyricists. I know cognitively that without the composer's tune filled in by the lyricist's words, there would be no song for the singer to sing. Knowing that doesn't, however, make the slightest difference to the fact that I like Geeta Dutt more than S.D. Burman, Mohammed Rafi more than Madan Mohan, or Sonu Nigam more than Shankar–Ehsaan–Loy.

In the male-dominated music industry in Bollywood, women find a place only with their voices. Saraswati Devi and Usha Khanna notwithstanding, the world of composers and lyricists has been overwhelmingly male, and continues to be so in the twenty-first century. Perhaps women wanted to make the point that given an entry, they could prove themselves equal, if not superior. After all, except Saigal, all other superstars of the 1930s and 1940s—Noorjehan, Shamshad Begum, Suraiya—were women. And among the singers of the next generation, Lata and Asha have sung more than, and outlasted all other male playback singers.

Between themselves, the singers featured in this section, spanning three generations, have not only given expression to the Hindi film song, but have also made it something larger, something greater than what the composers and lyricists intended. They, more than composers or lyricists, have kept the nation's love affair with Hindi film music going for over seventy-five years. Aptly, the book concludes with a trip down memory lane in the words of the nightingale of India, Lata Mangeshkar, no doubt the last word in film songs.

FIRST-GENERATION SINGERS

They were explorers, pioneers in the truest sense of the word. They had their heyday in the 1930s and 1940s, before recording techniques became refined and convenient. Even as Saigal sang in 1933, the first institution in playback singing was born. Given that Saigal, Noorjehan and Suraiya were also actors, who probably could not devote themselves fully to singing, you are simply amazed that their voices come across so beautifully. Shamsad Begum, with her spontaneity before the mike, proved early that playback singers would be the real superstars in the years to come. Taken together, these four first-generation singers shaped the identity of the film song in the early years, before the golden era of Hindi film music.

K.L. Saigal: The First Institution in Playback

The most revealing moment for me in the course of writing this book, also the most joyous, has been my discovery of Kundan Lal Saigal. In a span of just two weeks, Saigal, with his awesome voice and astounding range, replaced Lata Mangeshkar in my mind and heart as the best playback singer ever in India, a belief, a conviction rather, which I had held on to for two decades. As Saigal's bass, slightly nasal but utterly melodious voice comes through in the strains of *'Dukh ke ab din beetat naahin'* and *'Babul mora naihar chootho hi jaaye'*, I wonder why it took me so long to appreciate his genius.

Perhaps Saigal appeals to you only when you are into your late thirties, when you are not looking for mere dazzle, but a mellower, lasting impact. I remember as a teenager I used to be amused at my neighbour getting ecstatic with Saigal's *'Ek bangla bane nyaara'*. Too slow and too morbid, I thought. Today I find the same song mesmerizing. Many of Saigal's songs evoke in me an intensity of feeling that's hard to describe, one that is almost fearsome in its grip. Saigal, I now believe, is the only playback singer who simultaneously speaks to your head and heart. His technical finesse is superb. Combined with his feeling-laden voice, he is truly without peer.

Without peer he was in the 1930s. It was a decade when

sound had just come to films in India, when recording techniques were still rudimentary. To Saigal goes the credit of defining, and excellently at that, the possibilities of playback singing. In blazing a trail, he set impossibly high standards for others to match, let alone exceed. His contemporaries (Surendra, G.M. Durrani and C.H. Atma) tried, but they could only be followers. The next generation of playback singers—Mukesh, Talat, Kishore and Rafi—were content to model themselves after him. By the mid-1940s, Saigal was not just a superstar. He was the first institution in playback singing.

That here was history in the making was amply clear when his first non-film record containing the *bandish 'Jhulana jhulaao ri'* set to Raag Jaunpuri reportedly sold no less than five lakh pieces in 1932, in an era when record players were owned by very few. As you listen to Saigal navigate the complex *taans* with astonishing ease, you understand why classical musician Ustaad Faiyyaaz Khan conceded that here was a magic even classical artistes feared. This despite the fact that Saigal had only the sketchiest training in music! B.N. Sircar of New Theatres gladly accepted Saigal as part of his company, and thus began Saigal's tryst with stardom as actor and singer.

A year later, in *Yahudi Ki Ladki,* Saigal sang the most definitive Ghalib ghazal *'Nukta cheen hain gham-e-dil'*. Many others have sung it in films later, but Saigal's Bhimpalasi shades to this ghazal make it tower over all other versions. With little training in classical music, Saigal created the first classical ghazal in Hindi films with this song. Yet, he uses his voice only to enhance the beauty of Ghalib's verse; never to overpower it. With the sensitivity of a true artiste, Saigal knew where to draw the line.

With *Devdas* (1935), Saigal became a national icon. He succeeded as an actor too in the film, but all his acting talent paled before the impact of his singing voice. Through two songs, *'Baalam aaye baso more man mein'* and *'Dukh ke ab din beetat naahin'*, Saigal brought alive the doom and despair of Devdas compellingly. The latter song in Raag Des is a study in understatement. A lesser singer could have become maudlin in the interlude, where Devdas laughs at himself over the wreck he has become, but Saigal conveys despair artfully, deftly stopping short of self-pity. As his biographer Raghava Menon puts it in the book *Pilgrim of the Swara,* Saigal was too sensitive an artiste to define all your feelings for you. He took you into the world of feelings sure, but left you to navigate your course there.

Saigal's supreme effort at singing was, of course, R.C. Boral's Bhairavi Thumri *'Babul mora naihar chooto hi jaaye'* in *Street Singer* (1938). In terms of authenticity and feeling, no other Bhairavi, not even Naushad's own composition for Saigal, *'Jab dil hi toot gaya'*, comes close to matching this Boral–Saigal masterpiece. Saigal, playing the protagonist, insisted that this song be recorded live as he is walking the streets, though playback was well in vogue by then. Saigal knew that it was through his voice that he conveyed the truths of his characters, and the truth of the street singer needed a live recording. The director complied, and the song was recorded live with Saigal walking the streets, singing and playing the harmonium, while a mike followed him in a truck just behind! No other singer would have dared a live recording. No other singer, therefore, has sung as intense a Bhairavi.

By the late 1930s, New Theatres was in shambles, and Saigal, like many others, moved from Calcutta to Bombay and joined Ranjit Movietone. But not before he gave us yet another unforgettable song—the effervescent *'Main kya janoo kya jadoo hain'* set to the notes of Yaman Kalyan by Pankaj Mullick. You only have to attempt the second *'kya'* in the above line to realize how effortless Saigal made really tough taans seem. In Bombay, Saigal smoothly adjusted to new composers Khemchand Prakash (*Tansen*), Gyan Dutt (*Bhakt Surdas*), and Naushad (*Shahjehan*). The hits he sang for each of these composers were proof that the Saigal magic was largely his own, and not confined to the compositions of Boral or Mullick. When Saigal left New Theatres, it was the latter that dwindled irretrievably. The singer went on to achieve newer peaks in Bombay, embellishing many a composer's tunes with his characteristic intensity, and giving a fillip to their careers in the process. *'Diya jalao'* in Raag Deepak, *'Baagh lagaa doon sajani'* in Megh Malhar and *'Kaahe gumaan karen'* in Pilu were his gifts to composer Khemchand Prakash in *Tansen* (1943). *'Madhukar Shyam hamaare chor'* (*Bhakt Surdas*, 1942) is Gyan Dutt's most renowned song. For Naushad, composing for Saigal in *Shahjehan* (1946) meant a break with his folk-oriented tunes, as he got the emperor of melody to put over something as weighty as *'Jab dil hi toot gaya'* or *'Aye dil-e-bekaraar jhoom.'*

My own personal favourite of the Saigal of the 1940s is,

ironically, in a film for which he returned to Calcutta just that once—*My Sister* (1944). In '*Aye kaatib-e-taqdeer mujhe itna bataa de*', scored by Pankaj Mullick, Saigal comes closest to the magic he created in '*Dukh ke ab din*' and '*Babul mora*'. The way he articulates the lament '*Kya maine kiya hain*' in the song leaves you spellbound. If Bhairavi it has to be in the 1940s, I'd pick '*Aye kaatib-e-taqdeer*' over '*Jab dil hi toot gaya*' as the better one, exemplifying all that Saigal's music stood for. It is possible that in the two years between *My Sister* and *Shahjehan*, Saigal's health had deteriorated sharply. He was always too fond of alcohol, and in the later years used to insist that only after consuming what he mockingly called 'Kaali Paanch' could he sing at all. Naushad pleaded with Saigal to record when sober, and the singer agreed, saying he'd compare the versions he rendered with and without alcohol, and decide which one was better. When Naushad played the two versions of '*Jab dil hi toot gaya*', Saigal picked the sober one as better, and was amazed to be told that. '*Kaash tum pehle aate mere zindagi mein*' was his response to Naushad. He succumbed to cirrhosis of the liver soon after.

In a career spanning sixteen years, Saigal recorded 110 Hindi film songs. Yet, he has the stature of a legend; he is considered the father of playback singing. He was lucky to have lived and died in an era when all that mattered was how, never how much.

NOORJEHAN: THE ORIGINAL SINGING DIVA

She was part of Hindi cinema as singing star for just five years, 1942 to 1947, achieving in that brief period a glory that came close to Saigal's. Partition took her away to Pakistan, paving the way for Lata Mangeshkar to rise as the new phenomenon. Six decades later, it seems irrelevant to go back to that oft-repeated poser: would Lata have become the voice of the century had Noorjehan stayed back in India? But only till you hear what Naushad called 'the brighter voice' warble '*Jawan hain mohabbat*' in *Anmol Ghadi* (1946). As the honey-sweet, yet strong voice of Noorjehan compels your attention, the question comes back to haunt you: what if she had not migrated to Pakistan?

Barely thirteen when Ghulam Haider made her sing for his Punjabi film *Gul-e-Bakawali* in 1939, Noorjehan tellingly proved her musical prowess in the film. Three years later came *Khandaan*

(1942), her Hindi debut as heroine. Glowing looks combined with a radiant voice got her instant notice, particularly the song '*Tu kaunsi badli mein mere chand hain aaja*' composed again by Ghulam Haider. Sweeter than any other female voice at the time, it was also extremely flexible, the result of early classical training from the reputed singer Kajjan Bai that made Noorjehan seem effortless even in the complex tune '*Ud jaa panchi ud jaa*' in the same film. Most importantly, with a confidence unusual for her age, she was able to infuse each song with a sparkle, a spirit of optimism that was so typical of her home state Punjab. Like Saigal, her voice was her route to stardom. It mattered little if she acted well or not.

Sajjad Hussain groomed her further with the songs in *Dost* (1944). As you hear her articulate '*Badnaam mohabbat kaun kare*', you are struck with the awareness of how much Lata moulded her singing after Noorjehan. The same ease, the same melody, the same control. But there was also something extra in Noorjehan. The sadness and despair she conveyed were very real, but finally transitory. In her singing, there was always a quality of defiance, a will to fight back, something that even as pathos-soaked a melody as '*Bulbulon mat ro yahaan*' in *Zeenat* (1945), composed by Hafiz Khan in that raag of despair, Darbari, could not restrain. The song is a tribute to Noorjehan's classical virtuosity, an example of why she won the acclaim of many classical musicians of the era.

This spirit of indomitable optimism found its fullest expression in what is certainly her most popular score, *Anmol Ghadi*. Naushad tapped the gold in her throat like no other composer could, showcasing all her strengths within the ambit of songs in the same film. If '*Jawan hain mohabbat*' needed impishness and abandon, '*Awaaz de kahaan hain*' is a study in restraint, where the singer had to turn to her classical training to use her strength and melody in the upper octave, in the process outclassing co-singing star Surendra's mellow rendition. If the song became the best duet of the decade, it is only because of Noorjehan. Less popular, but making a quiet impact was '*Aaja mere barbaad mohabbat ke sahare*', where you again realize how much Lata borrowed Noorjehan's 'throw of words' to create a lingering effect, at least initially.

Anmol Ghadi turned out to be Noorjehan's brightest moment in Hindi cinema. A year later, she was packing her bags along with director-husband Shaukat Hussain Rizvi to move to Pakistan, even as both sides of the newly created border were reeling under the spell she cast in the songs of *Jugnu* (1947), where she starred with Dilip Kumar. Many composers and singers in India hold that it is Noorjehan who lost by the move, cramping her style into a largely Punjabi–Urdu school of music once in Pakistan, though she had a long career as Prima Donna of the Pakistani film industry. But what this side of the border lost hits you powerfully each time you hear her Bhairavi ghazal '*Hamein toh sham-e-gham mein kaatni hain zindagi apni*' in *Jugnu*. With that one song, she achieved everything any other singer in Hindi cinema subsequently has.

SURAIYA: FAME, GLORY AND LONELINESS

The last singing star of Hindi cinema, Suraiya's voice and looks conveyed the innocence of a bygone era. In her heyday (1947–50) she became a rage, people queuing outside her Marine Drive residence and causing traffic jams just to get a glimpse of her. She was also the highest paid female star of her time. Through all that fame, all the adulation, Suraiya retained her ability to be what she essentially was: humble and self-effacing. Almost as though she herself was bemused at what made her so popular, so sought after. Her singing had a quality of tentativeness to it, always a trifle uncertain, much like her real life persona. Perhaps it is that uncertainty that contributed to her allure.

A child of eleven when Naushad made her sing for heroine Mehtab in *Sharda* (1942), Suraiya had to stand on a stool to reach the mike! The song was, aptly as it turned out, '*Panchi jaa peeche raha hain bachpan mera*'. After that, there really was no time for looking back, as the following year she made her debut as heroine. She acted and sang in a handful of films in the next two years, but it was as second lead to Noorjehan in *Anmol Ghadi* (1946) that she hit big time. Suraiya, for all her tentativeness, was able to leave a mark in the film in the face of some awesome singing by Noorjehan. In '*Socha tha kya kya ho gaya*' people glimpsed an artiste who was a contrast to the confident and brilliant Noorjehan, but as appealing for the very innocence and diffidence she conveyed. Naushad tapped this diffidence artfully again in *Dard* (1947), where Suraiya was again playing second lead, this time to Munawar Sultana. Only she could have conveyed that state of supplication in Naushad's early Darbari Naat *'Beech bhanwar mein aan fasaa hain'*.

While Saigal wanted to act with her and she did three films with him, Suraiya flatly refused to record any duet with him, believing she was no match for him as singer. So, for their last film together, *Parwana* (1947), composer Khurshid Anwar had to be content with recording only solos for each of them. Similarly, Suraiya went public saying Noorjehan was born to sing, while she herself only had singing greatness thrust upon her! Not that it made a difference to her snowballing popularity. After Noorjehan's exit in 1947, Suraiya zoomed past all heroines of the era (Nargis, Kamini Kaushal, Madhubala et al) only on the basis of her singing star status. She had three whopping hits—*Pyar Ki Jeet* (1948), *Badi Behen* (1949), and the film that had young Dharmendra returning to watch her dozens of times, *Dillagi* (1949). Her most popular songs are from these films. *'Tere nainon ne chori kiya'* and *'O door jaane waale'* (*Pyar Ki Jeet*) and that beauty *'Woh paas rahen ya door rahen'* (*Badi Behen*) were courtesy Husnlal–Bhagatram, while Naushad with his famed ability to catch the pulse of the masses, composed her biggest hit, *'Tu mera chaand main teri chaandni'* (*Dillagi*). The last was a duet with Shyam, but only Suraiya remains in public memory. By the time *Dastaan* (1950) was released, Suraiya had matured as a singer, taking in her stride the Western orchestration Naushad created for the film, rendering with assurance the delightful waltz duet with Rafi *'Tara ri yara ri'*.

It was here that fate took a turn. Her love affair with Dev Anand that lasted through the seven films they acted in had reached a critical point, and Suraiya, unable to stand up to her grandmother's opposition to the match, called off the engagement. Something died in her, maybe the desire to belong to the world of stardom. She continued acting and singing, but the films did badly and the songs failed to impact. It was only in something as close to life as the doomed love story in *Mirza Ghalib* (1954) that she revived herself to put her heart and soul into. Musically, *Mirza Ghalib* saw her peak, her renditions of Ghalib etching them in the public mind in a manner that no other singer since could surpass. Prime Minister Jawaharlal Nehru publicly complimented Suraiya, saying, *'Ladki, tumne Ghalib ki rooh ko zinda kar diya.'* Composer Ghulam Mohammed trusted Suraiya to do justice to the Yaman-based *'Nukta cheen hain gham-e-dil'*, *'Yeh na thi hamari kismet'* in a faster tempo than usual, and of course, the immortal *'Dil-e-nadaan tujhe hua kya hain'* in Raag Des. The last is a duet where Talat too is brilliant, but Suraiya reached her pinnacle as singer in the lines *'Humko unse wafa ki hain ummeed, jo nahin jaante wafa kya hain'*.

Lata's rise as the premier playback singer too had its fallout on Suraiya's singing. With Lata around, there strictly was no need for a singing heroine. It is ironical that Suraiya sang better and better in the 1950s, but her songs did not get any acclaim, because the films flopped. *'Mera dildaar na milaaya'* in *Shama Parwana* (1954) was eloquent in feeling, perhaps because Suraiya was articulating a personal angst with the Lord. Ghulam Mohammed again gave her the lilting and complex *'Dhadakte dil ki tamanna'* in *Shama* (1961), but the film sank without a trace. Sajjad Hussain, who never believed in any other singer except Noorjehan and Lata, gave Suraiya *'Yeh kaisi ajab daastan ho gayi hain'* in *Rustom Shorab* (1963). After breathing life into the song with her voice that was still in top form, Suraiya stunned everyone by calling it a day, retreating to her private world of memories and reminisces with a few close friends. As years went by, she faded from public memory, until her death in 2004 when the world paused to recall the voice that reminded one of tinkling bells.

SHAMSHAD BEGUM: FIRST SUPERSTAR OF PLAYBACK

For a generation whose idea of the perfect voice is Lata Mangeshkar, Shamshad Begum is but a name, perhaps familiar because of the remixed versions of many of her racy numbers. Yet, Shamshad was the first superstar female playback singer, who, much before Lata had entered the fray, had producers and composers vying for her dates, willing to pay her an astronomical 1000 rupees per song in the late 1940s! Between 1944 and 1949, Shamshad, with her full-throated and spirited, if nasal, voice had zoomed past phenomenally talented peers such as Zohrabai and Ameerbai to reach the peak.

That hunter of fresh talent, composer Ghulam Haider had spotted her early, when she was singing devotional songs on AIR Lahore in 1937. He gave her a break in a few of his Punjabi films, and then came the Hindi film *Khazanchi* (1941), where Shamshad's free-flowing voice helped him create a sprightly, vibrant kind of music. Not confined by the rigour of classical training, Shamshad used the power and throw of her voice to delightful effect in the songs '*Ek kali naazon se pali*' and '*Saawan ke nazaaren hain*'. In the next four years, Shamshad slowly but surely inched past contemporaries Ameerbai and Zohrabai, who had sweeter, more rounded voices and were classically trained, but couldn't match Shamshad's spirit of abandon before the mike. Composers Khemchand Prakash and Shyam Sunder followed Ghulam Haider in giving her many breaks.

But to really make it big, Shamshad had to wait till her foray into the Naushad camp with '*Udan khatole pe ud jaaoon*' (*Anmol Ghadi*, 1946), her duet with Zohra, where she made her presence felt, in spite of singing stars Noorjehan and Suraiya dominating the score. In the following three years, it was in Naushad's custody that she sang hit after hit, gaining superstardom in the process. Bewitched by what he called the 'transparency' in Shamshad's voice, Naushad dumped Zohra, who had given him his career-making hit '*Akhiyaan milaake*', without a qualm, and made Shamshad his lead singer. And what an array of songs Shamshad sang for him until Lata intervened! From '*Badal aaya jhoom ke*' (*Shahjehan*, 1946) through '*Hum dard ka afsana*' (*Dard*, 1947) and '*Dharti ko aakaash pukare*' (*Mela*, 1948), till '*Chandni aayi banke pyar*' (*Dulaari*, 1949) there was no stopping the Shamshad juggernaut, and she went from strength to strength.

Of all her songs for Naushad in the 1940s, I'd pick her *Mela* solo '*Taqdeer bani bankar bigdi*' as representative of how much she had evolved as a serious singer. In this song, Naushad moderates the sharp edge to her voice beautifully, and makes Shamshad sound sweet and tragic. Little did she know that the words were prophetic, as Naushad was already besotted with Lata's voice, even as he was drawing the best out of Shamshad. The very next year, Lata would replace Shamshad as his lead female playback in *Andaaz*. In 1948, Shamshad also sang brilliantly for Raj Kapoor's first film *Aag*. If one were to look beyond Naushad, it was for Ram Ganguly, the newcomer composer of *Aag*, that she sang her best solo, '*Kaahe koyal shor machaaye re*'. But alas! Raj Kapoor had a row with Ganguly and dropped him for his next venture *Barsaat*, and Shanker–Jaikishan brought in Lata. Thus, Shamshad's end began in the same year that she achieved her best.

'*Duniya badal gayee, meri duniya badal gayee*' she mourned in the duet with Talat in *Babul* (1950), her last film for Naushad as lead playback. By then, Lata's '*Uthaaye jaa unke sitam*' (*Andaaz*) and '*Barsaat mein humse mile tum sajan*' (*Barsaat*) had proclaimed the arrival of a new revolution in film music. Shamshad was around throughout the 1950s, seeing all the composers whom she had helped kick-start their careers (C. Ramchandra and Madan Mohan to name two) sideline her and go for Lata. She tried valiantly to ward off the Lata onslaught, even going to the extent of learning classical singing at that late stage, but had to be content with the stray songs that came her way, from O.P. Nayyar and Naushad. Lata's meteoric rise shook Shamshad's poise, and her voice had an even sharper edge to it in the songs she rendered in the 1950s. From '*Bachpan ke din bhula na dena*' (*Deedar*, 1951) to '*Teri mehfil mein qismat aazmakar hum bhi dekhenge*' (*Mughal-e-Azam*, 1960), Naushad paired Shamshad and Lata a dozen times, each to Shamshad's disadvantage. The latter song was Shamshad's last straw, as she had no clue that her voice would go on Nigar Sultana in the film. She gave up the fight thereafter.

Nayyar used Shamshad's famed abandon to good effect in many songs such as '*Kabhi aar kabhi paar*' in *Aar Paar* (1954), '*Boojh mera kya naam re*' (*CID*, 1956) and '*Leke pehla pehla pyar*' (*CID*, with Rafi and Asha). Shamshad was able to be her unrestrained self while singing for Nayyar, as she knew he would not use Lata. Even then, Shamshad knew only too well that Nayyar preferred Geeta and Asha for the sultry–sexy effect they could bring to his creations. By the early 1960s, Shamshad, like many others before her, had just faded away. She came back just once more with a flash of spirit to render the tangy '*Kajra mohabbatwaala*' with Asha for Nayyar in *Kismet* (1968). For all practical purposes, it became her swan song.

SECOND-GENERATION SINGERS

Hindi film music would never have become the art form that it did, were it not for each of the legends featured in this part. They represent the best of this genre; their voices are the stuff that all nostalgia is made of. They shaped the golden era—the 1950s and 1960s—as much as the legendary composers and lyricists of that era did. If there is one difference, it is that many of these singers outlasted the composers and lyricists, going on to define the best even in the following decades.

LATA MANGESHKAR: THE VOICE OF MELODY

Much as I have looked forward to writing about Lata Mangeshkar, now that the moment is here, I find myself riddled with doubts and anxieties. What can I say that hasn't been said before? Will I be able to write about the longest career in film music in one section of one chapter of a book and do justice to her? Most importantly, how do I even begin to articulate all that her music has meant to me for two decades?

Perhaps in going back to her music, I'll find a way to move beyond this sense of being paralysed? As I randomly started playing Lata's early hits, it occurred to me that one way to address the odds is to write about particular songs of Lata at different stages of her sixty-year career, songs that were, for some reason or the other, defining moments in her music and also the history of playback. For, in tracing Lata's career, you are in effect charting the course of film music in Hindi cinema.

Some caveats are called for at the outset. I place no claim to objectivity in the selection of songs. It is, like much of this book, totally personal, more a result of what comes to my mind about Lata's music at this time than any carefully balanced account of Lata's contribution to the emergence of playback as an art form. The latter would merit a full-length book, the third after Raju Bharatan's incisive, if finally unflattering biography of the crooner and Harish Bhimani's sanitized version of her life and times. Secondly, I am writing only about the part of her work that I know, which I guess is probably 60 per cent of her output. Having said that, here I venture.

I'd start with Khemchand Prakash's Chaya Nat composition for *Ziddi* (1948), '*Chanda re ja re ja re*', a song Lata conceded was a feat to compose, given the long mukhda. If it has to be Khemchand Prakash, why not the historic '*Aayega aanewala*' from *Mahal* (1950), you might well ask. The reason is that the *Ziddi* number came at a time when Lata didn't know whether she'd make it at all in Hindi films. '*Chanda re ja re ja re*' was the first major test for Lata's technique and range, complex melody that it was. Knowing that it was still make-or-break for her, Lata came through with flying colours, rendering it with poise, melody and feeling. The song made Anil Biswas and Naushad shed their tentativeness about Lata.

For 1949, the year Lata ousted Shamshad Begum from the Naushad camp with '*Uthaaye ja unke sitam*' rendered patently in the Noorjehan idiom, I'd pick Anil Biswas's *Laadli* number '*Tumhaare bulaane ko jee chahtaa hain*' as the tougher challenge that only Lata could have managed. She artfully subordinates the classical orientation of the song to an overlay of innocence that the words merit. It is a pity that so many of the songs Lata sang for Anil Biswas were in films that sank without a trace, thereby rendering the songs themselves obscure.

Even as '*Aayega aanewala*' was ruling the airwaves, proclaiming the new voice of the century, Lata was striving to put her Noorjehan origins behind her. It is with something as mellifluous as '*Baharein phir bhi aayengi*' in *Lahore* (1950) for composer Shyam Sunder that she made you lose your sleep, leaving no one in doubt that though she may have started as someone stepping into Noorjehan's shoes, she had no intention of staying there. Lata's rendition and Shyam Sunder's composing skills produced something so melodious that the fiercely original Madan Mohan was inspired to tune something very similar as '*Baharein humko dhoondengi na jaane hum kahaan honge*' three years later in *Baaghi*. '*Baharein phir bhi aayengi*' highlights the inherent sadness in Lata's voice that lent itself best to songs conveying feelings of pain and dejection.

Cut to 1952 and *Baiju Bawra*. Lata had just one classical solo against Rafi's overwhelming presence in the film. Was she intimidated? Never! Putting all that she had into '*Mohe bhool gaye saanwariyaa*', she ensured that she got her share of the public adulation for the music. So immersed was she in the pathos of Naushad's Bhairav that she was overcome with emotion while recording the number. No wonder the song put her at the top of the classical wave the film spawned. For, by the time of *Baiju Bawra*, Lata had perfected the art of using her classical training in an unobtrusive, but highly effective manner to heighten the feelings of the song.

Like she did in C. Ramchandra's classy ghazal for *Anarkali* the following year. Of all the Lata ditties in the film, I'd pick '*Mujh se mat pooch mere ishq mein rakha kya hain*' as the song that enlarged Lata's already vast range in singing. Here was an authentic ghazal, and a difficult one at that. Note the way Lata articulates the word '*daagh-e-dil*' in the first stanza of the song and you know she hadn't forgotten Dilip Kumar's prickly remark that Maharashtrians give Urdu a flavour of *daal-chawal*. She had proceeded to master Urdu, and how! Her diction is flawless in all the songs of *Anarkali*. I also wonder whether her tenderness towards C. Ramchandra accounted for her extra-sweet rendition.

Have you ever wondered why not many women classical singers sang in films even at the height of the classical era in Hindi cinema? In the Shanker–Jaikishan tuned '*Man mohana bade jhoote*' (*Seema*, 1955), you have the answer. Lata handles the intricate taans in Jaijaiwanti with aplomb, always in tune, always melodious. What Bhimsen Joshi or Ustad Amir Khan were called upon to do was possible in the voice of Lata for the women. '*Kambhakt kabhi besuri nahin hoti*,' said no less a maestro than Ustad Bade Ghulam Ali Khan, lovingly of Lata, and what better example of her quest for perfection than '*Man mohana*'? Sadly, composer Shanker and Lata grew steadily apart in the coming years.

I may not subscribe to the popular view that Lata has sung the best Meera bhajans in films, but I don't have an answer to why I am moved to tears each time I hear '*Jo tum todo piya*' from *Jhanak Jhanak Paayal Baaje* (1955). Vasant Desai's Bhairavi tune has something to do with it, but so does the anguish in Lata's voice, the dignity she lends to Meera's act of total surrender to Krishna. Of all the Meera bhajans she's sung, I'd rate this one as the truest in feeling.

'*Aaja re pardesi*' merits mention in this list for reasons other than just how convincingly Lata articulates the feeling of 'incompletion' as composer Salil Choudhury put it. The song marks a victory for Lata in the battle she fought with *Filmfare* for creating a separate category of awards for singers. She had boycotted all Filmfare Award functions as part of the battle, and 1958 was the year when *Filmfare* conceded her point and gave the first award for Best Playback Singer, deservedly, to her for '*Aaja re pardesi*'. The next year, Lata used her pull to institute a separate award for male playback singers.

It is no secret that Lata thought very highly of Madan Mohan as composer. And Madan Mohan lived for Lata's voice, one that could convey just the right shade of inhibition, which was the hallmark of all Madan Mohan compositions for Lata. She called him *Ghazalon Ka Shehzaada*, and you agree with her each time you hear '*Unko yeh shikayat hain*' from *Adalat* (1958). What grace, what dignity Lata brought to the act of silent suffering through the song, probably voicing the predicament of a large majority of Indian women!

Not that she stood for silent suffering alone. In the stances she took on various issues in life and in her songs, you find enough evidence that the charge against Lata, that she succeeded because through her voice she stymied the desires of women, is unfounded. In *Mughal-e-Azam*, her voice resonates with defiance in the song '*Pyar kiya toh darna kya*'. Other tunes in the film are more melodious, more musical, but I'll choose this song for putting paid to an image of Lata.

When sitar maestro Pandit Ravi Shankar tried his hand at composing for films with the award-winning *Anuradha* (1960), it was but natural that he'd bank on Lata's vocals. She sang four solos for him in the film, each a beauty, each a reflection of the composer's and the singer's finesse in matters classical. I'd pick '*Kaise din beete*' as the best, for the complex metre it has, and the tune set to the rare Raag Manjh Khamaj. Lata captures the vulnerability and the loneliness of the protagonist brilliantly. No wonder Pandit Ravi Shankar was left with a sense of loss while composing Gulzar's *Meera* (1979), though Vani Jairam gave the songs everything she had. Having sung two non-film records of Meera bhajans for brother Hridaynath, Lata had declared in the 1970s that she would sing Meera only if composed by him.

The year was 1961. The industry was abuzz with the word that Jaidev, who had got the opportunity of a lifetime to compose Navketan's *Hum Dono*, was all set to invite classical musician M.S. Subbulakshmi to sing the bhajan he'd tuned for the film.

Lata had parted ways with Dada Burman and assistant Jaidev a few years earlier, but when she heard about this bhajan, she sent a discreet word to Jaidev that she'd be happy to record it for him. And '*Allah tero naam*' happened. In her voice, it sounds transcendental, making you believe no one, not even MS, could have brought you as close to the sublime in yourself. But the episode also proves that Lata was only human, not beyond feeling a sense of threat and acting on it, despite her twelve years at the top.

Madan Mohan's ghazal fascination was in full flow in the 1960s, aided staunchly by Lata. Together, they created the really atmospheric gems in *Woh Kaun Thi* (1964). Has there ever been another ghost story that used ghazals to enhance the mood of suspense? Lata is scintillating in all the songs, particularly '*Lag jaa gale*'. Her voice captures that moment in eternity when you simultaneously feel the joy of being together and the pain of impending separation. '*Lag jaa gale*', I'd say, is the peak of the Lata–Madan jugalbandi in filmi ghazal.

Paradoxically, it was around this time that Lata's singing began to sound a little detached from feelings. The technique was still superb, the perfection intact. But something was missing, perhaps a genuine engagement with the theme of the song, the emotion of the lyric. Could it be that the early 1960s were years when she realized that her music was all she would have? Did her bitter break with C. Ramchandra leave her with a sense of aloneness; a gnawing realization that shores unvisited thus far will only recede further in the horizon? We can only surmise. What is clear is that '*Aaj phir jeene ki tamanna hain*' (*Guide*), '*Tu jahaan jahaan chalega*' (*Mera Saaya*) and '*Rehte the kabhi jinke dil mein*' (*Mamta*) all have something missing. That they all are considered classics only tells us that Lata, even at less than 100 per cent, was better than all others.

She was probably ready for something different, something that would be a fresh challenge to her abilities as singer. I was intrigued to see Lata choosing R.D. Burman's *Padosan* song '*Bhai battoor*' as one of her favourites. A careful listening made me realize that in the half-notes he gets her to sing in the beginning, Lata did something new, something unusual. Also, with its fast tempo and boisterous feel, the song was a curtain raiser for the era of Westernized songs, a revolution RD would spearhead in the

1970s. She may have had qualms about something as blatantly sexy as '*Aaja aaja main hoon pyar tera*' in *Teesri Manzil*, conceding that it required Asha's dazzling and uninhibited singing, but there was no way Lata was going to allow herself to be sidelined in the new-wave music of the 1970s.

So when Laxmikant–Pyarelal, who'd managed to earn her approval early in their career, composed the cabaret number '*Aa jaane jaa*' picturised on Helen in *Inteqam*, Lata gamely agreed to sing it, stepping for the first time into the territory that had been conquered by younger sister Asha Bhonsle, now that Geeta Dutt was out of the reckoning. The song is a study on how one can sound seductive without ever seeming coarse, or even boisterous. Cabaret it definitely is, but one that is uniquely Lata's. Her instincts told her that trends were changing, and she couldn't hold on to her dos and don'ts as fixedly as she had in the 1950s. *Padosan* and *Inteqam* were two films that told the world that Lata would adapt, and remain on top.

Which wasn't difficult for her, given that the 1970s demanded much less out of every musician. Lata sang for all the heroines of the decade—Hema Malini, Rekha, Zeenat Aman and even the thirteen-year-old Dimple Kapadia in *Bobby* (1972). But her singing was unremarkable, a pale shadow of what she achieved in the previous decades. It wasn't that she didn't give her best to the songs. It was only that the best was no big deal in the 1970s. With rhythm replacing melody as the mainstay of music, Lata's technique and grip on music were underutilized. It was a decade when Asha Bhonsle emerged out of the shadow of elder sister, lending the swing and zing to R.D. Burman's youthful tunes. It was also the decade when there was a craving for newer voices in playback. Vani Jairam, Preeti Sagar and Runa Laila all had their brief tryst with fame. Musically diminished she might have been, but Lata was still number one at the end of the decade.

So, which songs would one pick from the 1970s for Lata? I'll limit myself to just two. The first is the *Amar Prem* beauty '*Bada natkhat hain re*'. Lata herself has said she prefers this song to '*Raina beeti jaaye*'. The reasons are not hard to guess. S.D. Burman had taken over from RD to compose this song, believing RD was too young to comprehend that the situation needed a tune that would do justice to the heroine's suppressed feelings of maternal love, which she knows will not fructify. And he composed a Khamaj tune that does just that. It is one of those songs where Lata subordinates technique to feelings, and is all the more effective for it. Perhaps the heroine's predicament came close to Lata's own?

The second Lata song I'd choose for the decade is from the Rajesh Roshan-composed *Swami* (1977). *'Pal bhar mein yeh kya ho gaya'* is an example of what Lata alone could bring to even the music of the 1970s. Modern, yet melodious, joyful, yet tentative, Lata is outstanding in the song. Given that Roshan Junior was still a fledgling composer, the credit for making the song extraordinary rests more with Lata.

What passed for music in mainstream Bollywood of the 1980s was but a travesty. Lata would have done better to retire before the Bappi era in film music. But sing she did, and a lot for Bappi Lahiri himself. Finally, time had begun to tell on her voice, which had acquired a shrill tone, something that only as seasoned a composer as Khayyam could moderate with *'Dikhayee diye yun'* in *Bazaar*. The song is among the handful in that decade that still deserved Lata. But more than *'Dikhayee diye'*, it was in Raj Kapoor's *Ram Teri Ganga Maili* that Lata regained her poise as singer. Among the four solos she sang, I'd vote for the least popular Bhairavi bhajan *'Ek Radha ek Meera'* as something that needed Lata and only Lata. It brought back a little of the Lata of yore, with its classical rigour and devotional feel. Lata's voice in *Ram Teri Ganga Maili* lent heroine Mandakini a dignity that Raj Kapoor wouldn't let her have, in the way he filmed her body. The song in question was also the one that got composer Ravindra Jain into the RK banner, as Raj Kapoor offered him the assignment after hearing Jain sing it at a private function. Lata was, however, unforgiving of Ravindra Jain for having promoted Hemlata as singer, and was always ill at ease with him. But there is no denying that *Ram Teri Ganga Maili* was Lata's best effort in the 1980s.

The last time, in my opinion, that Lata shone musically in Bollywood was in the film she herself produced, *Lekin* (1990). With music from Hridaynath Mangeshkar, Lata, now sixty-one years old, worked harder to give the songs whatever she could. I'd select the slow version of *'Kesariya balma'* as a befitting tribute to a singer who rose to become an institution in her lifetime. Notwithstanding the fact that it is a straight lift from a folk tune of Rajasthan, Hridaynath embellishes the song with Lata's famed ability to bring alive pathos. *Lekin* could have become Lata's dignified swan song. She would then have retired when her phenomenal talent was a live presence, not a distant memory. But Lata, like superstars in all arenas in India, could not bring herself to quit in time. She set herself up in competition with Anuradha Paudwal in the early 1990s, who left no stone unturned in fighting the Mangeshkar monopoly with the help of T-Series baron Gulshan Kumar. Lata outlasted that phase sure, but was anything she sang worth the price of staying on? A.R. Rahman, on the strength of his vastly superior recording technique, may have made Lata sound hummable as late as in 1998 with *'Jiya jale'* (*Dil Se*), but wouldn't even her most ardent fan admit that she no longer sounded like a nightingale?

GEETA DUTT: STRAIGHT FROM THE HEART

Was there ever a playback singer who conveyed feelings better? Geeta (Roy) Dutt may have had the sketchiest of training, but she succeeded as a singer because she knew that playback singing is not so much about technique as it is about taking the listener along into the world of feelings. In her ability to be true to the mood of the song, her capacity to evoke the same mood in the listener, Geeta was supreme. It was on the strength of this ability that she was able to hold her own against so phenomenal a talent like Lata Mangeshkar between 1947 and 1957, the first decade in Hindi cinema for both. Lata seemed perfect; Geeta rang true.

Composer Hanuman Prasad chanced upon her voice and gave her a couple of lines to sing for the film *Bhakt Prahlad*. Sachin Dev Burman was so impressed that he insisted on giving Geeta a break in the film *Do Bhai* (1947). The reluctant producer Chandulal Shah agreed for a recording, telling Burman he'd retain the song only if he was happy with the results. Fifteen-year old Geeta was unfazed, and proceeded to render '*Mera sunder sapna beet gaya*' with faith in herself and a pronounced Bengali lilt in her voice. As she began singing, Chandulal couldn't believe his ears; he hadn't heard a singer who could thus bring alive the pathos in the words. A star was born and Geeta surged ahead of all others, even Lata, in the next two years. Only Shamshad Begum retained her premier position with the help of Naushad.

Unfortunately, Geeta's early work, between 1948 and 1950, is lost to the world, at least to the generation born in the late 1960s.

After *Do Bhai*, only the songs she sang in the Dilip Kumar–Nargis starrer *Jogan* (1950) for composer Bulo C. Rani are available as records. What a depth of feeling Geeta brought to the Meera bhajans in the film! She ranks '*Mat jaa jogi*' as her best solo, and you can't but agree as the raw pain of *Jogan* pierces through you in Geeta's most evocative Bhairavi. '*Pyaare darshan deejo aaj*', '*Main toh giridhar ke ghar jaaoon*' and '*Aeri main to prem diwaani*' are all sung with an authenticity that makes you wonder how someone in just her late teens could sing with such grasp of the sublime. But then, Geeta was gifted. Every other Meera rendition in Hindi films, even Lata's, comes only a close second in emotional appeal. When you hear the songs of *Jogan*, you also realize how unfair to Geeta any comparison with Asha Bhonsle is. For all her virtuosity, Asha would just not have rung true in *Jogan*.

But 1950 also saw Lata's '*Aayega aanewala*' in *Mahal*, after which no other female singer mattered. S.D. Burman came to Geeta's rescue, giving her an image makeover with the fast, jazzy numbers of *Baazi* (1951). It is a mark of Geeta's versatility that she went Western in style, sounding utterly vivacious in '*Tadbeer se bigdi huyi taqdeer bana le*'. The song became a rage, Geeta Roy's vivacity matched every inch by Geeta Bali on-screen. *Baazi* proved a hit on the strength of that song alone, and Geeta found a new facet to her singing that would help her ward off the mighty Mangeshkar. The song was also personally special for Geeta, as director Guru Dutt saw her at the recording and fell head over heels in love with her. They were married in 1953.

With S.D. Burman's club song '*Soch samajh kar dil ko lagaana*' in *Jaal* (1952), Geeta carved a slot for herself that was impregnable. The same year, newcomer O.P. Nayyar made Geeta sing the melodious '*Dekho jaadu bhare more nain*' and the stylish '*Dil hain deewana*' in his debut *Aasmaan*. The film bombed but Geeta had noticed Nayyar's potential, and recommended him for Guru Dutt's *Baaz* (1953), where she sang the seductive '*Taare chaandni afsaane*', the patriotic '*Aye watan ke naujawan*' and the introspective '*Aye dil aye deewaane*' with equal felicity. In terms of versatility and class, *Baaz* ranks as the best Nayyar–Geeta collaboration. However, the film was a box-office disaster, and Geeta's brilliant effort went unnoticed.

It was with Guru Dutt's *Aar Paar* that Nayyar succeeded as composer, with the full backing of Geeta in the four solos and three duets she sang for him. '*Ae lo main haari piya*' and '*Babuji dheere chalna*' may be the two most popular songs to which Geeta brought her by-now-famous sexy–sultry effect, but the Nayyar–Geeta combination peaks in the rarely heard solo '*Jaa jaa jaa jaa bewafa*', Nayyar's only original composition in the film, where the bigger hits were all borrowed from Western tunes. With amazing dexterity and restraint, Geeta manages to convey just the right shade of dejection, in what could have turned morbid in the vocals of a lesser singer. The only other Nayyar composition that came anywhere close to tapping the serious singer in Geeta is '*Preetam aan milo*' (*Mr & Mrs 55*), where Geeta had to contend with the impact C.H. Atma had earlier created in the non-film version of the song. But never one to get caught in the proving game, Geeta could infuse the song with an originality that left even Nayyar amazed. What a pity that the song remains buried under the other catchy Geeta solos '*Thandi hawa kaali ghata*' and '*Neele Aasmaani*' in the film. In a way the same fate befell the composer and the crooner. Both reserved their best for serious songs; both found that what trade wanted from them was something frivolous and easier.

With S.D. Burman, Geeta found more opportunities to emerge as a complete singer. When Burman wanted the folk effect of Bengal, he turned to Geeta, as in the duet '*Aan milo shyam saanware*' with Manna Dey in *Devdas*. In Guru Dutt's *Pyaasa*, Burman exploited Geeta's potential, within the scope of a single film, like no other composer did. '*Jaane kya tuney kahi*' needed just the right amount of oomph, whereas '*Aaj sajan mohe ang lagaa lo*' required Geeta to transcend the patent eroticism of the lyrics and convey a love that was ultimately spiritual. Till date, there hasn't been another singer who sounded so convincing in two totally antithetical renditions. One needn't look beyond *Pyaasa* for proof of Geeta's versatility. Yet, for all the stunning effects she gave him in *Pyaasa*, Burman relegated Geeta to an odd song here and there, jumping on to the Lata bandwagon. But when he fell out with Lata, he needed Geeta for the lorie '*Nanhi kali sone chali*' in *Sujata*. Though Asha Bhonsle had replaced Lata as his lead playback singer in *Sujata*, Burman knew that only Geeta's vocals could envelop you in the warmth of maternal love. The same year, he also composed for Geeta her most poignant solo in Guru Dutt's *Kaagaz Ke Phool*. Kaifi Azmi's lyrics '*Waqt ne kiya*' needed the singer to convey restlessness and wistfulness simultaneously, a feat Geeta managed deftly. The song is about longing and a quest; equally, it is also about compassion, something that Geeta's generous spirit had in abundance. 'Waqt ne kiya' merits a place among the ten best solos of that decade.

Phenomenal as Geeta's work for Nayyar and Burman is, her range and versatility are exemplified by her solos for many other composers, some relatively unknown. Dhani Ram–Sudarsanam surprised us by revealing Geeta's ability to sing classical music with 'Baat chalat nayi chunari rang daari' in Bhairavi for *Ladki* (1953). Aroon Kumar gave Geeta 'Chand hain wohi', a soft melody in *Parineeta* (1953). Fully aware that Sajjad Hussain had ears for no one but Lata, Geeta sang his bhajan 'Darshan pyaasi aayi daasi' in *Sangdil* (1953) with a longing that even Lata would yearn for. In *Anarkali* (1953), the only Geeta solo 'Aa jaane wafa aa', composed by Basant Prakash, has you riveted, even in the face of all those Lata beauties scored by C. Ramchandra. Hemant Kumar's own version of the tandem number 'Na yeh chaand hoga' pales in comparison to Geeta's in *Shart* (1954). Anil Biswas, normally sold on Lata, had Geeta render his 'Bulbul mere chaman ke' in *Heer* (1956). Little-known Sailesh Mukherjee could extract from Geeta a complex melody such as 'Tehero zarasi der toh' in *Savera* (1958), a film that surprisingly had Lata sing the faster numbers. And these songs comprise only a fraction of the beauties Geeta sang through the decade.

Would she have sung more, lasted more, had she not been constrained by an insecure husband who needed his wife to hide her talent under a bushel only so that his could shine brighter? Guru Dutt not only prevented her from singing for other banners, but tormented Geeta also by his involvement with Waheeda Rehman. Left with a ruined career and a teetering marriage, Geeta found solace in alcohol, her natural ability to feel intensely now requiring blunting. Composers who may have preferred her mature vocals to Asha's had no choice but to groom Asha to take over, as Geeta was just not available for rehearsals or recordings. By the early 1960s, the music industry had reconciled itself to her exit. Geeta had refused to playback for Waheeda, consenting to sing only for Meena Kumari in the home production *Sahib, Bibi aur Ghulam*. As late as 1962, composer Hemant Kumar could get Geeta to portray the doom and desperation of *chhoti bahu* hauntingly in the solos '*Na jao saiyan chuda ke baiyaan*' and '*Koi door se aawaaz de chale aao*' in the film. Geeta had merged her personal pain into her singing with searing results.

Guru Dutt's suicide in 1964 shattered Geeta, and she suffered a nervous breakdown. As she recovered, she had to support their three children by performing live shows, as Guru Dutt had accumulated huge debts. Geeta's drinking continued unabated, and she was in and out of hospitals. It was not long before liver cirrhosis and a lack of desire to live sapped her life. She died in 1972, at the age of forty-one. But not before she bequeathed to us three songs in *Anubhav* (1971), which continue to haunt the listener even today. Time and circumstances had taken their toll, but Geeta's ability to emote was still intact. '*Meri jaan mujhe jaan na kaho*', '*Koi chupke se aake*' and '*Mera dil jo mera hota*' convey an optimism that is uplifting, yet all the more heart-rending for that. It was her last bow.

Asha Bhonsle: Redefining Musical Boundaries

To call her the most 'versatile' singer is to do her a grave injustice. For Asha Bhonsle's music has, over the six decades she's been performing, symbolized something much larger and deeper. In her music as in life, Asha stands for questioning imposed identities, for challenging and redefining boundaries. Personally and professionally, she made choices that went against the grain time and again. In facing up to all odds, persevering despite disapproval, and finally achieving success and glory on her own terms, Asha is inspirational, and not just for women.

Her music is an expression of all that she is. Backed by amazing training and technique for sure, but bound by neither. There has always been something more, something which is intrinsic to her personality: a zest for living, desire to *live* life instead of glossing over it, which gives her singing a joie de vivre that lasts till date, when she's in her mid-seventies. Asha's music has also gained from her ability to be non-judgemental about changing trends, her readiness to move with the times. She's worked with four generations of composers, singers and lyricists, yet carries her experience lightly, using it to adapt to the contemporary, never to judge.

She was only fourteen when she eloped and married, little

aware she'd have to use her voice to earn a living. Forced to seek work by an errant husband at a time when Lata Mangeshkar was getting to be a sensation, Asha had to sing whatever came her way, coping with the knowledge that what she got was not even second best, as Geeta Dutt was still going strong. She did the only thing she could: give the songs she got her best. Only, her best was up for comparison at all times with Lata, and all of Asha's talent and grit could not help the fact that her songs *were* less than those of Lata's, who had composers vying with each other to give her their best creations.

How Asha survived the first eight years of her career (1948–56) is anybody's guess. Perhaps, as breadwinner to her family, she had no choice. Her luck turned in 1957 for two reasons. O.P. Nayyar, the only composer to have made it in Hindi films without Lata's vocal aid, decided to make her his lead singer in *Naya Daur*, giving Asha the first chance to playback for a big star like Vyjayanthimala. When her duets with Rafi in the film clicked, Nayyar decided on Asha as his only female playback from then on. Second, Sachin Dev Burman had a tiff with Lata after *Paying Guest* and decided to banish her from his recording room. Burman would have preferred Geeta to replace Lata as his lead singer, but Geeta was too preoccupied with her marriage to give the taskmaster what he wanted. So he settled for Asha.

It was in the custody of Nayyar and Burman that Asha began the slow and daunting process of emerging out of Lata's shadow. The results were visible instantly. Asha proved that given half a chance, she could do wonders. In *Nau Do Gyarah*, S.D. Burman had composed '*Dhalki jaaye chundariyaa*' with Lata in mind, but Asha took over and sang it in style, giving it an identity all her own. Nayyar's Tilang composition in *Raagini* (1958), '*Chota sa baalma*', tested her classical prowess, even as she had the formidable task of matching the Talat magic in her version of the ghazal '*Pyar par bas to nahin hain*' that Nayyar composed for *Sone Ki Chidiya* (1958). Asha triumphed in both, impressing the sceptics with her ability to emote serious songs.

It is no surprise that Asha's best songs in the years 1958 to 1963 were either for Nayyar or for Burman. She did sing '*Ashqon se teri humne*' in *Dekh Kabira Roya* (1957) for Madan Mohan and '*Dil shaam se dooba jaata hain*' in *Sanskar* (1958) for Anil Biswas, but to overcome her diffidence in that phase, she needed to know that she was the preferred singer for the composer. An assurance she had only with O.P. Nayyar. So it was Nayyar who tapped the gold in Asha's throat best in these years, never having divided loyalties like even Burman did. Any understanding of how much Asha evolved as singer in the 1960s is best evidenced from the songs she sang for Nayyar.

Exuding a raw sensuousness in '*Aayiye meherbaan*' (*Howrah Bridge*) and '*Piya piya na laage mora jiya*' (*Phagun*), Asha began the process of getting the Hindi film heroine own her sexual identity on screen. '*Bekasi had se jab guzar jaaye*', Nayyar's Des ghazal, required a very different classical grip and restraint that Asha adroitly managed. '*Poocho na hamein hum unke liye*' (*Mitti Mein Sona*, 1960) and '*Aankhon se utari hain dil mein*' (*Phir Wohi Dil Laaya Hoon*, 1963) are the best examples of the strides Asha had taken in Nayyar's custody as a serious singer. Perhaps it was inevitable that they would get emotionally involved with each other. Asha had walked out on her husband, and was in need of an emotional anchor that Nayyar willingly provided. As their love blossomed, so did their music. '*Jaayiye aap kahaan jaayenge*' (*Mere Sanam*, 1964), '*Yehi woh jagah hain*' (*Yeh Raat Phir Na Aayegi*, 1965), '*Woh hanske mile humse*' (*Baharein Phir Bhi Aayengi*, 1966), '*Zara haule haule chalo more saajna*' (*Saawan Ki Ghata*, 1966) and '*Woh haseen dard dedo*' (*Humsaaya*, 1968) were all the outcome of the Nayyar–Asha emotional and musical tuning. But by the turn of the decade, Nayyar's reign at the top had come to an end, and the relationship had turned sour. The exact reasons are not known, but Nayyar did not let Asha part without giving her a song that would sum up where their relationship had reached: '*Chain se humko kabhi aapne jeene na diya*' (*Pran Jaaye Par Vachan Na Jaaye*, 1973), for which Asha won a Filmfare award that she refused to collect.

Secure as Nayyar's leading voice, Asha could cope with S.D. Burman's volte-face in favour of Lata in *Bandini* (1963), after Asha had put her heart and soul into his songs for all of six years. '*Nazar laagi raaja tore bangle par*' (*Kaala Paani*, 1958) '*Kaali ghata chaaye mora jiya tarsaaye*' (*Sujata*, 1959), '*Gaa mere man gaa*' (*Lajwanti*, 1959) and '*Ab ke baras bhejo*' (*Bandini*, 1963) are representative of her best for SD as his leading voice. Though he publicly praised Asha's quick grasp and control, what Burman missed in Asha's voice that made him broker peace with Lata is a mystery.

However, by the mid-1960s, Asha was no longer as vulnerable as she was in 1957. Besides Nayyar, she also had composer Ravi who preferred her voice to Lata's, and gave her some real gems. The title song in *Yeh Raaste Hain Pyaar Ke* (1963), '*Tora mann darpan kehlaye*' (*Kaajal* 1965), '*Aage bhi jaane na tu*' (*Waqt*, 1965) and '*Jab chali thandi hawa*' (*Do Badan*, 1966) all indicate that rich as the Asha–Ravi collaboration was, it remained unacknowledged in the industry, perhaps because Ravi, despite his talent, did not rise to dizzying heights of fame like Nayyar and Burman did.

When she sang for R.D. Burman in *Teesri Manzil* (1966), Asha was already seeking an identity beyond Nayyar. Paradoxically, the film was originally to be scored by O.P. Nayyar. What freshness RD brought to Asha's voice in the duets with Rafi '*O mere sona re*' and '*O haseena zulfon waali jaan-e-jahan*'! Of course, the real sizzler was '*Aaja aaja main hoon pyar tera*' where Asha Bhonsle gave Asha Parekh an image makeover with her uninhibited singing. The song was a trendsetter, the first with an overtly sexual feel that was sung by the heroine, and not the vamp. RD realized that with Asha's support he could move out of S.D. Burman's shadow and chart an independent path for himself as the composer of youth. He, however, waited a full four years before he experimented again with Asha's vocals for the cabaret number '*Mera naam hain Shabnam*' in *Kati Patang*. The song had no tune, but used the oomph in Asha's voice to full effect. The following year, RD got the chance he wanted when Dev Anand offered him *Hare Rama Hare Krishna*, where he got Asha to articulate the hedonistic world-view of the hippie culture in '*Dum maro dum*'. Would any other singer have dared to sing something so iconoclastic with such aplomb? But then, Asha had decided early that she was not going to live life fearing social disapproval.

Was Nayyar's split with Asha in the early 1970s an outcome of his growing insecurity in the face of the magic Asha helped RD create? It is possible. For when she walked out on Nayyar, Asha sought succour in RD, and married him soon after. Nayyar was a man diminished after Asha's exit from his life, and could just not create good music. But with her characteristic resilience, Asha moved on, professionally and personally. If the 1960s belonged to Nayyar, the 1970s were ruled by RD, resting on his two pillars: Asha and Kishore.

Asha's voice by now had acquired a roundedness that made

her sound sweeter. Under RD's baton, she sounded luscious, without being overly boisterous in songs such as '*Aao naa gale lagao naa*' (*Mere Jeevan Saathi*, 1972), '*Chura liya hain*' (with Rafi, *Yaadon Ki Baaraat*, 1973), '*Jaan-e-jaan dhoondta phir raha*' (with Kishore, *Jawani Diwani*, 1973), '*Neend churaake raaton mein*' (with Kishore, *Shareef Badmaash*, 1973), '*Chori chori sola singaar karoongi*' (*Manoranjan*, 1974) and '*Sapna mera toot gaya*' (with RD, *Khel Khel Mein*, 1975). The pop–jazz revolution RD unleashed with the help of Asha and Kishore reached its pinnacle in *Hum Kisise Kum Nahin* (1977) where Asha straddled with equal ease the westernized ABBA-inspired disco '*Mil gaya humko saathi mil gaya*' (with Kishore) and the desi qawwali '*Hain agar dushman*' with Rafi. Talk about versatility!

RD may have composed Asha's most popular tunes in the 1970s, but her best was by no means restricted to him. If you're still harbouring the 'good-for-cabaret' prejudice, just pause to hear Shanker's (of Shanker–Jaikishan fame) classical Yaman duet '*Re mann sur mein gaa*' in *Lal Paththar* (1971) where Asha confidently takes on Manna Dey's erudition, and emerges the winner. This even as she sang '*Dum maro dum*' for RD the same year! Or listen to '*Ambar ki ek paak suraahi*' that Asha emoted for Ustad Vilayat Khan in *Kadambari* (1974). Asha is superbly mellow here, doing full justice to the philosophical mood of the song. If you're still not convinced, get hold of Jaidev's Bhairavi melody '*Zehar detaa hain mujhe koi*' in the little-known *Wohi Baat* (1977). Jaidev was a staunch Asha votary, having proved her mettle as serious singer as early as 1961 with '*Jahaan mein aisa kaun hain*', the slow version of '*Abhi na jao chod kar*' that Asha rendered with such empathy in *Hum Dono*. If Asha, even in the 1970s, remained stuck in the groove of the fast, sexy numbers, it was certainly not because of dearth of talent. It was mainstream cinema that slotted her, unable as it was to look beyond Lata for melody.

Perhaps there was a reason, even if minor. All the years of singing Nayyar's boisterous music and RD's pop tunes had made Asha sound a trifle salacious even when not quite required. If at all there was a flaw in her singing, it was this need to overdo her oomph bit. What was it that made Lata's voice a shade superior for you, even when you realized that Asha was far more varied in her repertoire? Composer Anil Biswas put it unflatteringly, saying Asha's voice has body, Lata's, soul.

Unfair? So thought hubby R.D. Burman who set out to prove in the late 1970s that Asha was a complete singer in her own right. In sharp contrast to his numbers for her in the first part of the decade, RD tuned wistful melodies for Asha in a slew of films at the turn of the decade. When you listen with an open mind, you realize that this is the time when Asha edged past Lata, her voice sounding better than ever before in these RD numbers: '*Aisa ho toh kaisa hoga*' (Ratnadeep, 1979), '*Yeh saayen hain yeh duniya hain*' (Sitara, 1980), '*Piya baawri piya baawri*' (Khubsoorat, 1980), '*Sajti hain yun hi mehfil*' (Kudrat, 1981), '*Roz roz daali daali kya likh jaaye*' (Angoor, 1982), '*Hamen raaston ki zaroorat nahin hain*' (RD's original version of the Lata–Kishore duet '*Saagar kinare*', Naram Garam, 1982) and '*Aur kya ahd-e-wafa hote hain*' (Sunny, 1984). The films were obscure, but wasn't Asha delectable in each of these numbers? Pity that despite all these stunners that RD created, the credit for giving Asha 'respectability' is ascribed to Khayyam for his ghazals in *Umrao Jaan*.

Khayyam did create history of sorts by bringing to the fore the ghazal singer in Asha. Lowering her pitch by half a note, he gave Asha's voice a resonance not heard before or after. Asha grabbed the opportunity to sing for superstar Rekha in the lead role, and gave her lifetime best to all songs of *Umrao Jaan*. '*Dil cheez kya hain*' may have been in the traditional mujra mould, but even her worst critic cannot deny the authenticity of poetry and feeling she brought to the two slower ghazals, '*Yeh kya jageh hain doston*' and '*Justuju jiski thi*'. After *Umrao Jaan*, there was no substance left in any unfavourable comparison with Lata. It took long, the journey was arduous, but Asha had finally established herself as an equal. Acceptance of this reality came in the form of the National Award for best singer to her that year.

But the award came at a time when Asha's relationship with RD was strained, a result of RD's unhappiness with Asha singing for Bappi Lahiri, who had successfully mounted a challenge to RD. RD was sore that Bappi was making it to the top copying his style. However, Asha, always flowing with the trends, was too much of a professional to stop singing for Bappi. Though hurt, RD realized the unfairness of his expectation from Asha after a while, and composed a totally fresh-sounding score for her in *Ijaazat*, with the support of trusted friend and colleague Gulzar's lyrics. With songs as arresting as '*Katra katra milti hain*' and '*Mera kuch saamaan*', RD proved he was only down, certainly not out. '*Mera kuch saamaan*' may have been only an improvisation over the earlier RD–Gulzar–Asha effort '*Hothon pe beeti baat aayi hain*' in *Angoor*, but so welcome was Asha's singing in the melody-less Bollywood of the 1980s that she won her second National Award as singer for the song. That RD was passed over for the best composer award for the same film is but one of those ironies.

Strangely, *Ijaazat* saw the beginning of an enforced sabbatical for Asha. The late 1980s were years when the next generation of singers had appeared on the horizon, and composers preferred the newer voices of Kavita Krishnamurthy, Alka Yagnik or Anuradha Paudwal. Asha, still in peak form, found this banishment tough to cope with. She sang an odd number for RD now and then, but he had ceased to matter in Bollywood by the early 1990s. His last bow, *1942–A Love Story* was a hit, but had no song from Asha.

Though hit hard by RD's sudden demise, Asha bounced back soon enough with the new sensation A.R. Rahman, who offered her the songs in *Rangeela*, going on the young, sexy Urmila Matondkar. Rahman could have settled for a younger voice, but something told him that Asha, then sixty-two, was still superior to all of them. And did Asha take us back to the era of RD's '*Ek main aur ek tu*' in '*Tanha tanha*' under Rahman's baton! She also had the yuppie generation of the era swinging to '*Ho jaa rangeela re*'. *Rangeela* did for Asha what *Maine Pyar Kiya* had done for Lata six years earlier. Asha was suddenly in demand, now that the top composer of the time had cast his vote for her. With her usual savvy, Asha adapted to fourth-generation composers Jatin–Lalit, Nadeem–Shravan and of course, A.R. Rahman. But like in the case of Lata, the revival of her career did not demand anything new or different from her musically. After all, what could the music of the 1990s need that Asha didn't have, having worked with the trendsetters in the decades gone by? She is still youthful, still sexy at the turn of the century in '*Mujhe rang de rang de*' (*Thakshak*, 1999) or the title song of *Jaanam Samjha Karo* (1999). But it is very likely that only through remixing RD's early hits does she feel a connection to her glorious past, her true music.

MUKESH: ARTICULATOR OF MELANCHOLY

There hasn't been, at least after Saigal, another voice in Hindi cinema that could articulate melancholy better. Mukesh left us over thirty years ago, but each time you hear his sonorous, masculine, yet vulnerable voice express the anguish of the failed lover, the despondency of a purposeless life, the ache of his loss assails you afresh. It can't be just a coincidence that the emotions he articulated best—gloom, sorrow and despair—went out of fashion in Bollywood after his death. Perhaps there was a realization that in no other voice would these feelings ring as true. For hadn't Saigal himself, upon hearing Mukesh in 1945, proclaimed him the emperor of pain?

The song was *'Dil jalta hain toh jalne de'* tuned by melody maestro Anil Biswas for the film *Pehli Nazar*. Biswas had worked on Mukesh for a long time to get the Saigal effect that the singer wanted, having idolized Saigal from his early teens. For all the authenticity of expression that Mukesh brought to the song, producer Mazhar Khan was not happy with the result, believing Mukesh's voice did not fit the hero Motilal. Mukesh pleaded with him to retain the song only for the first show of the film. If the audience didn't like it, Mazhar Khan could scrap the song. The audience loved the song, and Mukesh emerged winner after four years of struggle.

He was not trained in music, and had a tendency to sing slightly off-key. But Anil Biswas knew that Mukesh's very rawness gave his voice a moving honesty, and set out to groom him in all seriousness as an original singer, not just a clone of Saigal. Starting with *'Jeevan sapna toot gaya'* (*Anokha Pyar*, 1948), Biswas was instrumental in making Mukesh find his own identity. Be it the duet *'Zamaane ka dastoor hain yeh purana'* (with Lata, *Laajawab*, 1950) or *'Aye jaan-e-jigar'* (*Araam*, 1951) Mukesh sounded superbly melodious while singing for Biswas, something no other composer, not even Naushad, was able to extract from him. Sadly, the films Biswas scored for in the 1950s sank without a trace and the best of Mukesh's singing remained buried.

Naushad, like Biswas, was mesmerized by the simplicity and directness in Mukesh's voice. In *Anokhi Ada* (1948), Mukesh had an opportunity to pit his talent against singing star Surendra, who was still basking in the glory of his songs in *Anmol Ghadi*. However, the moment you hear the resonant voice of Mukesh begin the ghazal *'Kabhi dil dil se takrata toh hoga'*, you are clear he was in a different league altogether. There was an innocence to Mukesh's articulation that brought alive the hurt. It did not matter that he sang for the second hero Prem Adib. Mukesh's impact was beyond the actor he sang for. Was he any less alluring in 'Bhoolne waale yaad na aa' in Anokhi Ada than in 'Mera dil todnewaale' in Mela (1948), where he sang for Dilip Kumar? In fact, Dilip Kumar was reluctant to act in Mela, till he heard Mukesh's opening lines in 'Mera dil todnewaale'. So bowled over was Dilip that he signed the film on the spot! Dilip's restraint as actor was only helped further by Mukesh's compelling honesty, as evidenced in the first hit, 'Gaaye ja geet milan ke', that Mukesh sang for Dilip in Mela.

Andaaz (1949) was the high point of the Naushad–Mukesh–Dilip association. Modern in approach, Naushad's four solos for Mukesh, all going on Dilip Kumar, were instrumental in the roaring success the film achieved. Mukesh had to work extra-hard, rehearsing 'Toote na dil toote na' no less than twenty-three times before Naushad felt satisfied. Dilip was originally unhappy with what he considered 'simple' tunes, wanting something comparable to Lata's 'Uthaaye jaa unke sitam', but Naushad was convinced the songs would click. How right he was! Nearly fifty years later, the most vivid memory of Andaaz is of Dilip singing 'Jhoom jhoom ke naacho aaj' on the piano, never sounding as natural as in Mukesh's voice.

A full year prior to Andaaz, Mukesh had already tuned in as Raj Kapoor's voice in Aag (1948), RK's first film as director. 'Zinda hoon is tarah ke gham-e-zindagi nahin' was Mukesh's first hit for Kapoor. Even as Andaaz was being made, RK was already mounting Barsaat, where newcomers Shanker–Jaikishan were getting Mukesh to put over the only duet in the film, 'Chod gaye baalam', with newly discovered Lata. The song cemented the bond between RK and Mukesh further, something that was in full evidence in Awara (1950). Too much has been said about the music of RK films, so we shall not dwell on it here. The true greatness of Mukesh as singer can only be comprehended when we focus on all that he achieved over and above the RK banner. RK films gave him popularity no doubt, the simple tunes 'Awara hoon' (Awara) and 'Mera joota hain Japani' (Shri 420) catching the imagination of the audience, national and international. But Mukesh did not grow as singer through RK films. That happened elsewhere.

In childhood friend turned composer Roshan's breakthrough film Bawre Nain (1950), for instance. 'Teri duniya mein dil lagta *nahin'* was a heart-stopper, showcasing Roshan's grip on melody as much as Mukesh's. Roshan, who knew Mukesh since their days together at school, composed for Mukesh what sounded best in his voice, not just what would appeal to the public. '*Taara toote duniya dekhe*' (*Malhaar*, 1951), '*Dil ki pareshaniyan*' (*Humlog*, 1951) and the vintage '*Ek jhooti si tasalli woh mujhe deke*' (*Shisham*, 1952) are pointers to the early Roshan–Mukesh magic. As fate would have it, Mukesh's most melodious songs of the 1950s, sung for Anil Biswas and Roshan, are all but forgotten in the blaze of the RK songs.

Mukesh himself caused his straitjacketing as the man of simple tunes. Just as his playback career was taking off, the acting bug bit him, and he announced to the public that they would hear his voice only for himself as singing star. His launch pad was to be opposite Suraiya in *Mashooqa* (1953), which got him nowhere. The film took two years in the making, and Mukesh agreed to the producer's demand that he'd not do playback until the film was released. Talat and Rafi had, in the meanwhile, surged ahead, composers using their voice even for songs they would have preferred Mukesh to sing, had he been available. The years 1954–56 were his lowest, with no composer except Roshan and Anil Biswas giving him songs, but in films that went unnoticed. Mukesh tried to turn producer in a desperate bid to salvage his career, but the film, *Anurag*, was never released, though the solo '*Kise yaad rakhoon kise bhool jaaoon*' tuned by Mukesh himself became popular. Piercing in impact, the song probably articulated Mukesh's real dilemma of having to choose between acting and playback.

Raj Kapoor came to his rescue, giving Mukesh a breather with '*Mera joota hain Japani*'. But even as the song made waves in India and Russia, Mukesh found no other composer approaching him with work. Financially in ruins, he had to see his children being turned away from school because he couldn't pay their fees. Until Salil Choudhury started Mukesh on the road to recovery with the hedonistic '*Zindagi khwab hain*' in RK's *Jaagte Raho* (1956), the only film Salil scored for RK. Mukesh grabbed the lifeline with all his might, and proved he could sound fabulous in an RK film even if the song was not on picturized on Raj Kapoor. It was Salil again who created a sensational impact with Mukesh as Dilip's voice in *Madhumati* (1958), when Talat had long replaced Mukesh as

Dilip's own favourite. '*Suhana safar aur yeh mausam haseen*' heralded a second spring for Mukesh, once more as the voice of Dilip Kumar. The same year, Shanker insisted on Mukesh as Dilip's playback in *Yahudi* for '*Yeh mera deewanapan hain*', proving in the bargain that Mukesh was perfectly capable of giving hits, if only the producer and the hero would let him. Khayyam brought back Mukesh poignantly as the voice of Raj Kapoor in the sensitive socialist film *Phir Subah Hogi* with '*Woh subah kabhi toh aayegi*' in the company of Asha Bhonsle. Topped by composer Dattaram's *Parvarish* solo '*Aansoo bhari hain*' in mellow Yaman that Mukesh emoted for Raj Kapoor, 1958 was truly a comeback year for Mukesh.

'*Sab kuch seekha humne na seekhi hoshiyaari*' in *Anari* (1959) fetched him the Filmfare award, thus becoming a watershed in Mukesh's career. Still recovering from the mess that he had created in his life, Mukesh sang it with scorching intensity. The song heralded a long second innings that lasted right till his untimely death. Mukesh took his playback career very seriously from then on, determined to ensure that his family never faced a financial crisis again. The 1960s were busy years for him, and he emerged as a playback singer in his own right. His voice, always resonant with feeling, now also had depth, probably the result of having faced life's vicissitudes.

This richness of expression is what made '*Saranga teri yaad mein*' (*Saranga*, 1960), composer Sardar Malik's only claim to fame, so sonorous. It just did not matter that the hero in the film was little-known Suresh Kumar. Mukesh had reached a point where who he sang for was of little consequence. The song became a hit because it was in Mukesh's voice. When S.D. Burman summoned him reluctantly for the *Bambai Ka Babu* (1960) backgrounder '*Chal ri sajni ab kya soche*', little did he know that Mukesh would outclass something as intense as Rafi's '*Saathi na koyi manzil*'. '*Chal ri sajni*' was originally conceived by Burman for Kishore, but the latter turned it down, fearing it would be inconsequential in the face of all the weighty Rafi numbers! Three years later, in *Bandini*, Burman pit Mukesh's background solo '*O jaane waale ho sake toh laut ke aana*' against his own atmospheric '*More saajan hain us paar*', totally unprepared for Mukesh stealing a march over him in the charts. The fact was that, by the early 1960s, Mukesh did not need any famous face to make his songs click. Even in *Jis Desh*

Mein Ganga Behti Hain, it is RK who needed Mukesh to convey the image of the simple, innocent man through '*Hoton pe sachchayee rehti hain*'.

After *Anari* (1959), Mukesh had disengaged his vocal persona from the screen image of RK. He succeeded in creating hits on the strength of his voice alone. '*Mujhko is raat ki tanhayi mein awaaz na do*', the solo that newcomers Kalyanji–Anandji had tuned for debutant Dharmendra in *Dil Bhi Tera Hum Bhi Tere* (1960), and '*Bhooli huyi yaadon*', tuned by Madan Mohan and picturized on old-timer Pradeep Kumar in *Sanjog* (1961), are but two examples. Like S.D. Burman, Madan Mohan too had underrated Mukesh.

Shanker–Jaikishan emulators Kalyanji–Anandji gladly took to Mukesh's voice. The songs Mukesh sang for this duo rank among their best compositions, and Kalyanji, gentleman that he was, conceded in an interview that Mukesh was their ladder to success and recognition in the 1960s. His '*Chandan sa badan*' fetched them their only National Award for *Saraswatichandra* (1968), at a time when it made all the difference to their career. Yet, '*Chandan sa badan*' is only the first among equals Mukesh sang for them over the decade. '*Mere toote huye dil se*' (*Chhalia*, 1960), '*Humne tujhko pyar kiya hain jitna*' (*Dulha Dulhan*, 1964), '*Main toh ek khwab hoon*' (*Himalay Ki Godh Mein*, 1965), '*Jis dil mein basaa tha pyar tera*' (*Saheli*, 1965), '*Waqt karta jo wafa*' (*Dil Ne Pukara*, 1967) and, never the least, '*Koi jab tumhara hriday tod de*' (*Purab Aur Paschim*, 1970) should tell us how much this duo counted on Mukesh to hold their own against competition from idols Shanker–Jaikishan on the one hand, and erstwhile assistants Laxmikant–Pyarelal on the other.

Shanker–Jaikishan, enchanted as they were with Rafi, used Mukesh only sparingly in the 1960s. But Mukesh never gave them anything less than his best, whether it was '*Teri yaad dil se bhula ne chala hoon*' (*Hariyali Aur Raasta*), '*Dost dost na raha*' (*Sangam*), or '*Duniya bananewaale*' (*Teesri Kasam*). Even when they hit their all-time low with RK's *Mera Naam Joker*, Mukesh revived their insipid score with '*Jaane kahaan gaye woh din*'. He displayed the same seriousness for Laxmikant–Pyarelal when they turned to him for '*Jyot se jyot jagaate chalo*' (*Sant Gyaneshwar*, 1964), the song with which Mukesh himself found his devotional voice, or even '*Tum bin jeevan kaise beeta*' in *Anita* (1967), so typically Mukesh in execution. All this even while delivering much-needed hits to second-line composers such as S.N. Tripathi ('*Jhoomti chali hawa*', *Sangeet Samraat Tansen*, 1962) or Usha Khanna ('*Chand ko kya maaloom*', *Lal Bangla*, 1966).

No account of Mukesh's work in the 1960s can overlook what he gave his two oldest well-wishers, Anil Biswas and Roshan. In Biswas's last film *Chhoti Chhoti Baatein*, Mukesh brought back the distinct melody of yore in '*Zindagi ka ajab fasana hain*', the duet with Lata. For Roshan, Mukesh sang the chorus-backed background solo '*Oh re taal mile nadi ke jal mein*' in *Anokhi Raat* (1967), relegating Rafi's '*Mile na phool toh kaanton se dosti karli*' to second place. The song was Mukesh's tribute to the composer–friend who had never lost faith in his vocals. Roshan died during the making of the film.

Mukesh survived the melody-devoid world of the 1970s with the help of long-time admirer Salil Choudhury, who came up with a song that would easily rank as Mukesh's best in that decade: '*Kahin door jab din dhal jaaye*' for the young Rajesh Khanna in *Anand*. Only Salil would have dared to use Mukesh on Khanna, when Kishore was already a rage as Khanna's playback after *Aradhana* and *Kati Patang*. Mukesh captured the introspective mood and the subtle sadness of the song so well that after *Anand*, everything he sang in that decade seemed less, even Salil's own compositions '*Kai baar yun bhi dekha hain*' in *Rajnigandha* (1974), which fetched him the National Award for best singer, and '*Yeh din kya aaye*' (*Chhoti Si Baat*, 1975).

Mainstream Hindi film had swung to the new rhythm of R.D. Burman who had never believed in Mukesh. The only time Mukesh succeeded as a mainstream hero's voice was in *Kabhi Kabhie* (1976). As the jilted poet–lover Amitabh's voice, Mukesh sensitively conveyed his cynicism and despair over a flippant world in the song '*Main pal do pal ka shaayar hoon*', proving yet again that within this genre of music, he was invincible. All of Kishore's zest, all his freshness in the other songs couldn't dim the Mukesh lustre in *Kabhi Kabhie*.

Death came suddenly in 1976, in the form of a heart attack while on a concert tour in Detroit, USA. It was almost as though he sought it out, steadfastly ignoring pleas by family and warnings by doctors to not overexert himself. In hindsight, he couldn't have asked for a better time to die. Having succeeded as top hero Amitabh's voice with a National Award for the title song of *Kabhi*

Kabhie to boot, his family financially secure and son Nitin Mukesh ready to take over, Mukesh didn't fight death, preferring to not outlive the era of melody. His last recorded song was, appropriately enough, for alma mater RK films, the Laxmikant-Pyarelal tuned '*Chanchal sheetal nirmal komal*' in *Satyam Shivam Sundaram* (1978).

TALAT MEHMOOD: CUSTODIAN OF THE FILMI GHAZAL

His voice belongs to another era, when gentleness was a virtue in music. Talat Mehmood's music falls on your ear rather like soft petals on wet earth. Quietly, and with a melody that is *felt* more than heard. In his short spell at the top, Talat Mehmood, more than any other male singer, gave a vocal identity to the filmi ghazal. If Madan Mohan was the emperor of ghazals in Hindi films, Talat was undoubtedly the crown prince. Talat's true contribution lay in not just what he sang for films; it was as much in institutionalizing a particular kind of music in the subcontinent: quiet, polished and utterly melodious. An industry intoxicated with rhythm in the 1970s may have shunted him out, but the crooner lived on in the voices of a whole generation of ghazal singers ranging from Mehdi Hassan to Jagjit Singh, who considered him their inspiration.

Not surprising, considering the fact that he had cut his first disc at sixteen, and was already a rage in the ghazal format before he came to films. His HMV release '*Tasveer teri dil mera behlaa na sakegi*' in 1946 had New Theatres beseeching him to join them, and Talat started his career in films with them. But his stint as singer with New Theatres did not quite click and he moved to Bombay in 1949 in search of greener pastures. The time was just right. The film industry had recovered from the aftermath of partition; Hindi cinema was in search of a voice that could replace Saigal's, particularly in articulating the ghazal. Talat, who had idolized Saigal from his childhood, seemed the apt choice. Anil Biswas, having given Mukesh a start with '*Dil jalta hain*' now turned to Talat for '*Aye dil mujhe aisi jagah le chal*' in *Arzoo* (1950). Talat could not have asked for a better break. Biswas, enamoured with the quiver in Talat's voice, insisted that it lent his voice a distinct allure. The song became hugely popular and other composers, Naushad included, queued up for the 'velvety' effect.

Talat's career got off to a flying start as the voice of the gentle lover Dilip Kumar in songs such as 'Mera jeevan saathi bichad gaya' for Naushad in *Babul* (1950), 'Seene mein sulagte hain armaan' for Anil Biswas in *Tarana* (1951), 'Yeh hawa yeh raat yeh chandni' for Sajjad Hussain in *Sangdil* (1952), 'Aye mere dil kahin aur chal' for Shanker–Jaikishan in *Daag* (1952) and 'Sham-e-gham ki kasam' for Khayyam in *Footpath* (1953). What set Talat apart from every other singer was also his flawless diction in Urdu, and the way he enhanced the poetry in the song with his articulation. By 1953, Dilip Kumar was so besotted with Talat's voice that he would plead with producers to have Talat as his playback. An early misunderstanding with Naushad saw the senior composer banish Talat from his recording room, and so Dilip reluctantly settled for Rafi's voice in *Deedar* and subsequent films scored by Naushad. But whenever he had a choice, he would vote for Talat. Thus followed other gems such as 'Sapnon ki suhaani duniya ko' for Shanker–Jaikishan in *Shikast* (1953) and 'Mitwaa laagi re' for S.D. Burman in *Devdas* (1955). In the first half of the decade, Dilip's image as the gentle, tragic lover was helped in no small measure by Talat's vocals.

Talat succeeded initially as Dev Anand's voice too with hits such as 'Hain sab se madhur woh geet' in *Patita* (1953) and the S.D. Burman classic 'Jaayen toh jaayen kahan' in *Taxi Driver* (1954), before Dev, in a bid to create for himself a distinct identity from Dilip Kumar, settled on Kishore Kumar as his playback. Madan Mohan created the Kedar classic 'Main paagal mera manwaa paagal' for Talat to go on Raj Kapoor in *Aashiana* (1952), but the film bombed. Despite Roshan's exquisite 'Main dil hoon ik armaan bhara' in *Anhonee* (1952), Talat did not click as the voice of Raj Kapoor, whose persona had come to be enmeshed with the simplistic style of Mukesh after *Awara*. But such was the Talat magic in those years that it did not matter whether the films did well or not. His songs stood out on the basis of the lustre he brought to them alone. Even on a tepid Bharat Bhushan, Talat could create a mesmerizing impact in *Mirza Ghalib* (1954) with the ghazal 'Phir mujhe deedar-e-tar yaad aaya'. By this time, Talat had emerged as a formidable rival to Rafi.

But the acting bug had bit Talat badly, and he naively believed he could succeed as actor too because of his dashing looks. He acted in a dozen films, but the only ones that got any notice are *Dil-e-Naadaan* (1953), scored by Ghulam Mohammed, and *Sone Ki Chidiya* (1958), which had music by O.P. Nayyar. This foray into acting made producers and heroes wary of him, and much like Mukesh, Talat found he neither had films nor songs after a while. 'Zindagi denewaale sun' in *Dil-e-Naadaan* and 'Pyar par bas to nahin hain' (*Sone Ki Chidiya*) are both Talat classics that were also picturized on him, but the audience rejected Talat on-screen even as they adored him behind the mike. Shammi Kapoor, for whom Talat had sung the early stunners 'Chal diyaa kaarwaan' in *Laila Majnu* (1953) and 'Aye gham-e-dil kya karoon' in *Thokar* (1954), advised Talat to quit acting and focus on singing, and a chastened Talat finally took that advice. He had realized he was no match for Dilip Kumar's talent, Dev Anand's charm or Raj Kapoor's innocence.

But Rafi had established himself very firmly in the meanwhile, and Talat could not quite regain his earlier position as playback singer. He had to be content with an odd song here and there. This was the time when his sublime rendition of a Madan Mohan beauty, 'Humse aaya na gaya', in *Dekh Kabira Roya* was picturized on comedian Anoop Kumar! Even S.D. Burman, for whom Talat had immortalized 'Jaayen toh jaayen kahan', now wanted Rafi for the *Sujata* number 'Jalte hain jiske liye', and it was only on the insistence of Bimal Roy that Talat got to sing it. Dilip Kumar wanted Talat for the *Yahudi* solo 'Yeh mera deewaanapan hain' but composer Shanker prevailed upon him to let Mukesh sing it. Dilip was again keen that Talat sing 'Suhana safar aur yeh mausam haseen' in *Madhumati*, but this time Talat himself declined, saying Mukesh needed that break much more than him, given that Mukesh's career was in the doldrums and that he was hard up for money. The famed gentleness of Talat was not confined to his voice alone.

He was a compassionate man, and it is this generosity of spirit that could so move you to tears in the ghazal 'Aansoo samajh ke kyon mujhe' in *Chhaya* (1961). Composer Salil Choudhury was always more fond of Talat than Rafi, and got Talat to explore his range in *Chhaya* with songs as varied as the delightful solo 'Aankhon mein masti sharaab ki' and the charming duet with Lata, 'Itna na mujh se tu pyaar badha'. But even the popularity of the songs of *Chhaya* could not place Talat firmly back in the saddle. Madan Mohan valiantly tried to revive Talat's career by getting the crooner to sing all major songs in *Jahan Ara* (1964), much against the producer's desire to have Rafi as lead singer. Madan Mohan even paid Talat out of his own pocket for the songs! '*Phir wohi shaam wohi gham*' saw Talat in top form, gracing the tune with a wistfulness that was inimitable. '*Teri aankh ke aansoo pee jaaoon*' was Talat's own lament at the slide in his fortunes. But all his grace could not help the film suceed. *Jahan Ara* sank without a trace, and both Madan Mohan and Talat Mehmood never quite recovered. The last straw was Manoj Kumar dubbing Talat's portion of the duet '*Kaisi haseen raat*' with Mahendra Kapoor's voice in *Aadmi* (1968). The soundtrack had the song in Rafi and Talat's voice, the film in Rafi and Mahendra Kapoor's! Talat decided to call it a day, choosing to retreat to the world of memories than stay and fight back.

He continued to perform live shows and record non-film ghazals well into the 1980s until failing health made him retire completely. When asked by this author, in what turned out to be his last interview for *The Metropolis* in 1993, about why he quit so early, Talat replied that he could not perform in an era where music had become just noise. He categorically stated that he was happy with whatever he achieved, and was secure in the knowledge that he will be remembered as long as there is nostalgia for melody in film music. At seventy, Talat seemed to see little point in regrets, and chose to derive joy by recalling the brighter moments of his career in Hindi films. Five years later, on 9 May 1998, Talat, with the same quiet dignity that marked his music, breathed his last, leaving his fans with the strains of '*Meri yaad mein tum na aansoo bahana*' to console themselves.

MOHAMMED RAFI: SINGER FOR THE SOUL

No other male playback singer attained such glory in Hindi films. For twenty years (1949–69) Mohammed Rafi's voice defined melody and success in film music in a manner akin to Saigal in the 1930s. After all, wasn't it with Saigal's blessings that Rafi started his bid for a career in music at the tender age of fourteen, having performed live as stopgap in a show while Saigal waited for power supply to be restored? Yet, for all his admiration of Saigal, even as a struggler in Bombay in 1944, Rafi's singing was remarkably original. It was on the strength of this originality and the richness of his tone that Rafi ruled Hindi film music like a colossus for twenty years. The generation of today, distanced in time, may swear by Kishore Kumar as the best, but they would be surprised to be told that Kishore himself venerated Rafi as singer. It is no coincidence that the end of the Rafi era in 1969 saw the end of melody in music for good measure.

Honed by Naushad

He may have been discovered by Shyam Sunder for the Punjabi film *Gul Baloch* and the Hindi *Gaon Ki Gori* in the early 1940s, but to Naushad goes the credit of polishing the uncut diamond that Rafi intrinsically was. As early as 1948, Naushad had demonstrated Rafi's grip on music and the gold in his voice with '*Yeh zindagi ke mele*' in *Mela*. The next year, he showcased Rafi's as the ultimate voice of romantic yearning with '*Suhani raat dhal chuki*', the stylish Pahadi he composed for *Dulaari*. That Rafi could make such an impact on a nonentity hero like Shyam should have told us that here was a phenomenon in the making. *Dastaan* (1950) saw a delightful and bubbly facet of Rafi in the duet '*Tara ri yara ri*' with Suraiya, this time as Raj Kapoor's voice. But Naushad had to wait till *Deedar* (1951) to switch wholesale to Rafi, jettisoning trusted Mukesh in favour of the more rounded, richer voice. It was with *Deedar*, a full year before *Baiju Bawra*, that Rafi arrived as playback singer, helped immensely by the fact that he was the voice of top star Dilip Kumar. '*Huye hum jinke liye barbaad*' plumbed new depths of despair with finesse, feeling and utter melody. Naushad exploited the richness of Rafi as singer further in '*Meri kahani bhoolnewale*' and the duet with Lata, '*Dekh liya maine*'. After *Deedar*, even Talat, who had an edge over Rafi till then, had to be content with second place.

Baiju Bawra was but the crowning glory in the Naushad–Rafi takeover of filmdom. Banking on his early classical training under Ustads Abdul Wahid Khan and Ghulam Ali Khan, Rafi proceeded to give the classical compositions of Naushad an authenticity that even the far better trained Manna Dey feared. What came through so tellingly in '*Man tarpat hari darshan ko*' and '*O duniya ke rakhwaale*' was not just Rafi's brilliance as singer, but equally important, his deep faith in religion, and his humility and compassion as a person, qualities everyone who knew him attest to. Perhaps these qualities are what gave his singing a heart-warming quality ever so often. *'Insaan bano, karlo bhalayee ka kaam'* created such an impact only because the person singing it epitomized the very same qualities. With *Baiju Bawra*, not only did Rafi become a superstar, but he also began the trend of creating superstar actors on the merit of his voice alone. Bharat Bhushan was only the first.

Every composer's singer

Even as he became Naushad's lone male voice, the two sustaining and building on the classical wave that *Baiju Bawra* spawned, Rafi was already exploring another facet to his singing, this time under the baton of newcomer O.P. Nayyar, whose compositions, in sharp contrast to Naushad's serious music, spoke of the joys and triumphs of life. Rafi's skyrocketing fame in the mid-1950s is due in no small measure to Nayyar's breezy and extremely catchy songs for him. '*Sun sun sun sun zaalima*' (with Geeta in *Aar Paar*), '*Dil par hua aisa jaadoo*' (*Mr & Mrs 55*), '*Aankhon hi aankhon mein ishaara ho gaya*' (with Geeta in *CID*) and '*Maang ke saath tumhaara*' (with Asha in *Naya Daur*) brought to the fore the lighter, lilting, yet melodious side of Rafi's voice. Rafi's solos for Nayyar in the 1960s are far better, but it is with these early Nayyar compositions that Rafi emerged as a more versatile singer, a facet that many other composers, Shanker–Jaikishan and Sachin Dev Burman included, capitalized on.

S.D. Burman woke up to Rafi reluctantly, barely giving him a handful of songs till 1956. However, for Guru Dutt's *Pyaasa*, Burman had to turn to Rafi, as Nayyar had already positioned Rafi as Guru Dutt's voice in earlier films. Moreover, *Pyaasa* required a singer with range and feeling, something only Rafi had. '*Yeh duniya agar mil bhi jaaye toh kya hain*' and '*Jinhe naaz hain Hind par woh kahan hain*' demanded from Rafi a moderation of his classicism and an accent on feeling, which Rafi managed adroitly, coming through with just the right touch of pathos for articulating the cynicism of a failed poet and lover. More than the songs, it is in singing the various nazms of Sahir that Rafi shines in the film, '*Tang aa chuke hain kashmakash-e-zindagi se hum*' being the best. In sharp contrast to the dark, brooding feel he gave to these numbers, Rafi was delightfully impressive in the lighter songs '*Hum aapki aankhon mein*' (with Geeta) and '*Sar jo tera chakraaye,*' a song after the Nayyar style of using Rafi's voice for comedy. After *Pyaasa*, SD became a staunch Rafi votary, relegating favourites Hemant Kumar and Kishore Kumar to the second slot.

What followed was a veritable feast of Rafi gems under SD's baton. As Dev Anand's voice, Rafi sang some of his most memorable solos for SD in the 1950s and 1960s. '*Hum bekhudi mein*' (*Kaala Pani*, 1958) deserves special mention as the first full-fledged ghazal that Rafi sang, much before he became the ghazal samraat. '*Apni toh har aah ek toofan hain*' (*Kaala Bazaar*, 1960) and '*Saathi na koi manzil*' (*Bambai Ka Babu*, 1960) were some of Rafi's best solos for SD who masterfully restrained Rafi from becoming overly emotional, as he was often wont to while singing sad songs. Rafi continued to sing hits for Burman well into the 1970s, but for some inexplicable reason, SD never acknowledged Rafi's contribution to his music. How indispensable Rafi had become for Burman by the late 1950s can be gauged from the fact that though he had made Kishore Dev Anand's playback in all the early Navketan films, after *Kaala Paani*, Rafi ruled Navketan for a full eight years, right till *Guide* (1965), where, with the solos '*Din dhal jaaye*', '*Kya se kya ho gaya*' and the surpassingly beautiful '*Tere mere sapne ab ek rang hain*', Rafi made the point tellingly that he was as critical to SD's music as to Naushad's.

Shanker–Jaikishan ignored Rafi in the early 1950s, preoccupied as they were with Mukesh in Raj Kapoor films, and with their preference for Talat as the voice of Dilip Kumar (*Daag*) and Dev Anand (*Patita*). This was despite Rafi having given them a hit in their very first film *Barsaat* with '*Main zindagi mein hardam rota hi raha hoon*'. Even in the latter half of that decade, they used Rafi only sparingly, perhaps in an effort to be different from top rival Naushad. *Basant Bahar* had more songs from Manna Dey than from Rafi but Rafi put his heart and soul into '*Duniya na bhaaye mohe*' for them in the film. Asked to choose between Manna's '*Sur na saje*' and Rafi's '*Duniya na bhaaye*', one is in no doubt that the latter is more arresting, though '*Sur na saje*' is the better composition. '*Sur na saje*' is a testimony to Shanker the composer, '*Duniya na bhaaye*' a tribute to the singing prowess of Rafi. The same year, Rafi gave another hit to Shanker–Jaikishan with '*Aaye bahaar banke lubhaa kar chale gaye*' in *Raj Hath*.

By the end of the 1950s, every other male singer had to

reconcile to the fact that producers and composers wanted Rafi first. Instances of songs originally recorded in other's voices being re-recorded at the last minute in Rafi's voice were many, 'Chal ud jaa re panchi' in Bhabhi (1957) being a case in point. The song was recorded first by Talat. Manna Dey was to originally sing the duet with Lata 'Tere bin soone' in S.D. Burman's Meri Soorat Teri Aankhen (1963), but Rafi took over at the last minute at the producer's instance. By the early 1960s, there was only one male playback singer who mattered. Talented composer Roshan saw commercial success only with Rafi's ghazal 'Zindagi bhar nahin bhoolegi' in Barsaat Ki Raat (1960), a full decade after he started composing. Madan Mohan, for whom Rafi had sung superbly the ghazal 'Humsafar saath apna chod chale' (with Asha) in Aakhri Dao (1958) tried to bring back Talat Mehmood as the ghazal king with the songs of Jahan Ara, but failed miserably, despite great compositions and great singing. A chastened Madan plumped for Rafi, achieving name and fame with the songs Rafi sang for him throughout the decade.

Ghazal samraat

Rafi's contribution to shaping the filmi ghazal in the early 1960s in the custody of Roshan and Madan Mohan is colossal. 'Ab kya misaal dooni' (Aarti, 1962), 'Jo baat tujh mein hain' (Taj Mahal, 1963), 'Dil jo na keh sakaa' (Bheegi Raat, 1965), 'Caravan guzar gaya' (Nayi Umar Ki Nayi Fasal, 1965), 'Hum intezar karenge' (Bahu Begum, 1967) and 'Mile na phool toh' (Anokhi Raat, 1968) all represent Roshan's best work, all in Rafi's voice. Enamoured with Mukesh and Talat, Roshan too had previously ignored Rafi.

It is a revelation that Rafi sang the maximum number of solos (82) for Madan Mohan. An overwhelming number of these happened in the 1960s, after Madan reckoned with Rafi's popularity and switched from Talat and Manna Dey. It was just as well, because only Rafi could have roused the dormant patriotism in each of us with the clarion call 'Ab tumhare hawale watan saathiyon' in Haqeeqat (1964). After that, there was no other male singer for Madan right till the end. Here's a sampling of the hits Rafi gave this luckless composer: 'Rang aur noor ki baaraat' (Ghazal, 1964), 'Kabhi na kabhi' (Sharabi, 1964), 'Tu mere saamne hain' (Suhagan, 1964), 'Aapko pyar chhupane ki' (with Asha, Neela

Akaash, 1965), '*Ek haseen sham ko*' (*Dulhan Ek Raat Ki*, 1966), '*Aapke pehloon mein aakar ro diye*' (*Mera Saaya*, 1966), '*Tumhari zulf ke saaye mein*' (*Naunihal*, 1967, the ghazal that Rafi named his best for Madan Mohan), '*Teri aankhon ke siva*' (*Chirag*, 1969), '*Yeh duniya yeh mehfil*' (*Heer Ranjha*, 1970) and '*Tum jo mil gaye ho*' (*Hanste Zakhm*, 1973).

He made superstars

Rafi created superstars out of ordinary actors with his vocal virtuosity. In those musically rich decades, no hero could do without Rafi hits. Rajendra Kumar, who had moulded himself after Dilip Kumar, piggybacked to stardom on the vocals of Rafi. From the popular Rafi–Lata duet '*Jeevan mein piya tera saath rahen*' in Kumar's first hit *Goonj Uthi Shehnai* (1959) began a slew of chartbusters that Rafi sang for him. '*Teri pyari pyari soorat ko*' (*Sasural*, 1961, Shanker–Jaikishan), '*Mere mehboob tujhe*' (*Mere Mehboob*, 1963, Naushad), '*Yaad na jaaye*' (*Dil Ek Mandir*, 1963, Shanker–Jaikishan), '*Yeh mera prem patra padhkar*' (*Sangam*, 1964, Shanker–Jaikishan), '*Tum kamsin ho nadaan ho*' (*Ayee Milan Ki Bela*, 1964, Shanker–Jaikishan), '*Aye phoolon ki rani*' (*Aarzoo*, 1965, Shanker–Jaikishan) and '*Baharon phool barsaao*' (*Suraj*, 1966, Shanker–Jaikishan) were all songs that contributed to making Rajendra Kumar 'Jubilee' Kumar. Old-timers insist that Rafi used to sing differently for every actor, and just by hearing his song, they could say whether the actor was Dev Anand, Rajendra Kumar or Dilip Kumar.

Shammi Kapoor owed his boisterous, youthful image totally to Rafi's voice. O.P. Nayyar created that image with the peppy '*Chhupnewale saamne aa*' and other songs of *Tumsa Nahin Dekha*. Usha Khanna, moulding herself in the Nayyar idiom, created the hit songs of *Dil Dekhe Dekho*. Composer Ravi furthered this image with '*Baar baar dekho*' in *China Town* (1962). All, of course, in the voice of Rafi. The biggest Shammi Kapoor hit was, however, yet to come. '*Yaahooo, chahe koi mujhe junglee kahe*' in *Junglee* (1963) was the start of a new trend, where Shanker–Jaikishan, in a bid to outdo O.P. Nayyar's popularity, got Rafi to sing extra-loud. Nayyar's '*Tareef karoon kya uski*' (*Kashmir Ki Kali*, 1963) in Rafi's vocals had just made waves. *Junglee* proved a smash hit, starting a trend of popular but loud music, with Rafi still at the top but no longer as musical. Other Shammi Kapoor songs such as 'Lal chadi maidan khadi' (Jaanwar, 1965), 'Kisko pyar karoon' (Tumse Achcha Kaun Hain, 1967), 'Aji aisa mauka phir kahaan milega' (An Evening In Paris, 1967), 'Badan pe sitaare lapete hue' (Prince, 1969) and 'Chakke pe chakka' (Brahmachari, 1969) had Rafi in demand more than ever before, but all lowered the quality of music and took away something of his magic. That he sang something as soothing as 'Ehsaan tera hoga mujh par' for the same Shammi Kapoor was no consolation.

Naushad, unmindful of changing trends, kept composing melodies for Rafi to go on Dilip Kumar well into the 1960s. From 'Zindagi aaj mere naam se' in Son of India (1962) to 'Koi saagar dil ko' in Dil Diya Dard Liya (1966), Naushad had Rafi in top form as the voice of Dilip Kumar, but the movies failed and the long run at the top for the thespian and the composer came to an end by the end of the decade. Nayyar made more serious, yet hummable music throughout the decade in Rafi's voice for actors Joy Mukherjee and Biswajeet. It is on the strength of solos such as 'Humko tumhaare ishq ne' (Ek Musafir Ek Haseena, 1962), 'Banda parwar thaamlo jigar' (Phir Wohi Dil Laaya Hoon, 1963), 'Pukarta chala hoon main' (Mere Sanam, 1965) and 'Dil ki awaaz bhi sun' (Humsaaya, 1968) that Biswajeet and Joy Mukherjee had their brief tryst with fame in the 1960s. Young Dharmendra's career got a boost with something as achingly sweet as 'Aap ki haseen rukh pe aaj naya noor hain' in Baharein Phir Bhi Aayengi (1966), arguably Nayyar's best solo for Rafi in the decade.

Launching new composers

Rafi helped launch the careers of two of the most creative and successful third-generation composers. Laxmikant–Pyarelal zoomed to the top very early in their career because Rafi generously agreed to sing for their film *Dosti*. His atmospheric solos 'Chahoonga main tujhe' and 'Jaanewaalon zara' fetched the singer and the composer duo Filmfare awards that year. Laxmikant–Pyarelal always remained grateful to Rafi, banking on him for hits even in the Kishore era.

R.D. Burman broke through on the strength of Rafi's vocals with the jazzy score of *Teesri Manzil*. Rafi played a bigger role than Asha in the success of the film, singing not only 'Aaja aaja main hoon pyaar tera' and other duets with Asha with aplomb, but also the lingering solo *'Tumne mujhe dekha hokar meherbaan'* that lent RD's score respectability. Despite this, RD never believed much in Rafi, and brought the singer's long spell at the top to an end by getting Kishore Kumar to render the hit songs of *Aradhana*.

End of suzerainty

Rafi was hit hard by the sudden ascent of Kishore Kumar after *Aradhana*, more so as he had, in the same film, given his best in the two duets *'Gunguna rahen hain bhawre'* with Asha and *'Baaghon mein bahaar hain'* with Lata, as the voice of the same Rajesh Khanna. But R.D. Burman had, without the knowledge of SD, got Kishore Kumar to sing the faster *'Mere sapnon ki rani'* and *'Roop tera mastana'*. It was Kishore Kumar's moment after twenty years of waiting in the wings as playback singer, and all of Rafi's awesome talent couldn't reverse the relentless march of time. With the Kishore hits of *Kati Patang* and *Amar Prem*, R.D. Burman almost single-handedly ended the Rafi era in Hindi films. Dada Burman was undecided even in *Gambler* (1971), giving Rafi the evocative *'Mera man tera pyaasa'* even as he tested Kishore with *'Dil aaj shaayar hain'*, but bowed to the new sensation in *Sharmilee* (1971) and *Abhimaan* (1972). In much the same way that composers jettisoned Mukesh and Talat in 1952 in favour of Rafi, every Rafi loyalist switched over to Kishore in the early 1970s.

Even a cursory look at his output during the decade is enough to dispel any myth that Rafi was past his prime. *'Door rehkar na karo baat'* (*Amaanat*, 1970, Ravi), *'Unke khayal aaye toh'* (*Lal Paththar*, 1971, Shanker–Jaikishan), *'Na tu zameen ke liye'* (*Dastaan*, 1972, Laxmikant–Pyarelal), *'Nazar aati nahin manzil'* (*Kaanch Aur Heera*, 1972, Ravindra Jain) and *'Teri galiyon mein na rakhenge kadam'* (*Hawas*, 1974, Usha Khanna) are some of his best solos, all sung in the Kishore era. Ironically, much of his work in the early 1970s was more melodious than the loud shrieking that he was asked to indulge in during the 1960s. An embittered Rafi confessed to Naushad that he felt like calling it a day in the face of all composers going for Kishore wholesale. Naushad advised him to quit when he was riding high. Fortunately, Rafi took that advice.

A comeback too late

The first step in staging a comeback was a gift from ardent Rafi supporter Madan Mohan, who insisted that Rafi be the voice of young Rishi Kapoor in *Laila Majnu* (1976), a year after Kishore had phenomenally succeeded as the voice of college-going Rishi in *Khel Khel Mein*. Madan was convinced that *Laila Majnu*, with its tragic theme, needed Rafi alone. '*Barbaad mohabbat ki duaan*' was Rafi's comeback vehicle, and Rafi put his heart and soul to give Sahir's words and Madan's tune a life of its own. As it turned out, it was Madan's parting gift to Rafi, as the composer died during the making of the film. When the movie clicked, Rafi emerged as Rishi Kapoor's voice, and went on to sing a string of hits for the star. '*Pardah hain pardah*' (*Amar Akbar Anthony*) and '*Dafliwaale*' (*Sargam*) were the precursors to his true comeback song, '*Dard-e-dil*' (*Karz*), where Rafi sounded bewitchingly youthful, trendy and melodious. Rafi loyalists Laxmikant–Pyarelal had not forgotten that he had literally 'made' them with the songs of *Dosti* when the two were still raw. They even mounted Rafi as Amitabh's voice in *Dostana* (1979) with '*Mere dost kissa yeh kya ho gaya*' and gave him the chartbusting '*John Jani Janardan*' for Amitabh in *Naseeb* (1981).

Even R.D. Burman, who never had much to say about Rafi, brought him back for the qawwali '*Hain agar dushman*' and '*Kya hua tera waada*' (*Hum Kisi Se Kum Nahin*). The latter fetched Rafi his sixth (and last) Filmfare Award. '*Maine poochha chand se*' in *Abdullah* (1980) was RD recasting an earlier Rafi song, but this time it went on to become a hit.

When death came unexpectedly on 31 July 1980, Rafi was well on his way for what seemed a long second innings. He may have been lucky to die when he was again on the rise, but the world lost melody irrevocably that rainy day. With Rafi went a whole gharana of music, as senior colleague and admirer Manna Dey put it. It is any wonder that the 1980s turned out to be the worst decade in Hindi film music? It was almost as though the music industry lost the desire to create melody after Rafi. Again much like Saigal, his death too spawned a whole bunch of Rafi clones, his influence lasting almost three decades after his death in the voice of Sonu Nigam, the latest sensation in playback.

Kishore Kumar: The Man Who Enacted Music

The last legend of playback in Hindi cinema was never just a singer. Kishore Kumar is a live presence twenty years after his death precisely because he was always a performer, an enactor of music. It took him all of twenty-one years in the industry to achieve fame and glory as singer; years spent more in front of the camera than behind the mike. Thus he had what no other singer in Hindi films, barring Saigal, had: a knack for making the song literally come alive. This ability to 'perform' music, rather than just sing it, accounted for his mystique; it is what enabled him to oust as monumental a talent as Rafi in 1969 and stay at the top for the next eighteen years, till death stilled his energy. For Kishore, singing was not training, never technique. It was always total involvement.

A reluctant hero

To Khemchand Prakash goes the credit of discovering his voice with the song 'Marne ki duaaen kyon mangoon' for Dev Anand in *Ziddi* (1948). Kishore, always a fan of Saigal, sang this number after the Saigal fashion. Not that it launched him as singer, as those were years when Mukesh was at the top, soon to be followed by Talat. The music of the late 1940s and early 1950s was serious in nature, classical in orientation and Kishore, with his 'plain', untrained voice, and only his spontaneity to aid him in front of the mike, found no takers. Acting offers came his way because he was presentable and had a youthful innocence about him, and Kishore was too raw to decide what he wanted. Always a prankster, he found that his penchant for playing the fool came in handy to carve for himself a light-hearted, comic image as actor. This proved to be a double-edged sword, as he found his acting career going great guns, but at the cost of his singing. He was typecast as actor and singer for the breezy, comic numbers, and no song that marked him as a singer of potential came his way in the first seven years of his career. Such was the aversion to his voice in the early 1950s that Kishore had to beg and plead with Salil Choudhury to let him sing the duet 'Chota sa ghar hoga' for the film *Naukri* (1954), a film which had Kishore himself as the hero!

Sachin Dev Burman as mentor

Only Sachin Dev Burman dared to cast Kishore Kumar as playback for Dev Anand, having heard him hum in the bathroom once while visiting his brother Ashok Kumar. Burman was impressed with the open-throated voice and decided to test Kishore on Dev Anand, beginning with '*Mere labon mein chhipe*' in *Baazi* (1951). It is with Burman's solo '*Jeevan ke safar mein raahi*' for Dev Anand in *Munimji* (1955) that Kishore proved he was a singer first, an actor only next. The joie de vivre that one came to associate with his music began with this song. Out of twelve songs in the film, many of them intricate classical compositions, only Kishore's lone solo had the public humming. The very next year, Burman took the risk of giving Kishore a sentimental song '*Dukhi man mere*' in *Funtoosh*, again for Dev Anand. Kishore sang the song in his own style, having emerged out of the Saigal shadow by then. The song clicked, but Kishore didn't. He had signed a slew of comedy films as hero, and had no time to focus on singing. He settled for singing his own songs and the odd number that Burman would invite him to sing for Dev Anand.

Navketan's *Nau Do Gyarah* the following year saw Kishore in top form, conveying the spirit of the song '*Hum hain raahi pyar ke*' with innocence and melody. Dev Anand was very convincing in the voice of Kishore, crafting his image of the carefree, yet essentially kind-hearted hero with the help of Kishore's vocals in *Paying Guest* (1957). The teaser '*Maana janaab ne pukaara nahin*' was a rage among the youth, and Kishore brought his bubbly spontaneity to the duet '*Chod do aanchal*' with Asha. It looked like Kishore would find acceptance as playback singer at least as the voice of Dev Anand. But alas! S.D. Burman switched to Rafi wholesale from Dev Anand's next film *Kaala Paani*. He made excellent music with Rafi over the next eight years for Navketan, but Kishore was sidelined. Burman came up trumps for the comic score of Kishore's own film *Chalti Ka Naam Gaadi* (1958). '*Ek ladki bheegi bhaagi si*' was the first explicitly sexual song the hero would sing to the heroine, ten years before *Aradhana*'s '*Roop tera mastana*'. The songs of *Chalti Ka Naam Gaadi* were all cute, all hits, yet Kishore as singer stagnated.

Comic hero turns composer

It must have been the desire to sing the kind of songs he truly wanted to that made Kishore turn composer for the film *Jhumroo* (1961). '*Thandi hawa yeh chandni suhaani*' was a facet of him that was well known by then but the real surprise was his rendition of the '*Koi humdum na raha*'. Melodiously walking the thin line between sounding sensitive and becoming sentimental, Kishore gave this song a feeling of lingering regret than deep sadness. He was all the more effective for that. The song was an early pointer to the sensitive artiste in the man, one who dared to make the offbeat *Door Gagan Ki Chaon Mein* three years later.

The theme of bonding between a widower father and his handicapped son provided Kishore the opportunity to bring the serious composer and singer in him out of the closet. '*Koi lauta de mere*' and '*Aa chal ke tujhe*' represent Kishore at his sensitive best, but the rarely heard '*Jin raaton ki bhor nahin*' stuns you with the levels of sadness Kishore's voice could plumb, without ever going maudlin. The film was a commercial success, yet Kishore remained unsung as singer.

Not even Burman's return to Kishore with the duet '*Gaata rahen mera dil*' in *Guide* made a difference. '*Yeh dil na hota bechara*' in *Jewel Thief* (1967) was popular, but again in the familiar Kishore–Dev Anand mould. Burman was aware that Kishore was underutilized, but he was never known to fight industry norms too strongly. Rafi was the last word in music as late as 1969, and Burman was content to have him as lead playback even in *Talash* (1969). The late 1960s saw Kishore caught between the devil and the deep sea. As singer he seemed to be getting nowhere. As actor, his career had run aground, age catching up with him and the public ready for something else. His acting in the riotous comedy *Padosan* (1968) was brilliant, his singing for R.D. Burman even better. '*Kehna hain kehna hain*' must rank as the best solo of Kishore for another composer in the era, *Aradhana* included. But Kishore was tired of acting (he had done seventy-odd films by then) and he was beginning to lose hope of succeeding as a playback singer. He contemplated giving it all up and returning to his native village Khandwa, but elder brother Ashok Kumar advised him to quit acting and concentrate on playback as a career. Fortunately, Kishore stayed back.

Stardom as the voice of Rajesh Khanna

The year 1969 is a sort of watershed in the history of Hindi film music. It was the year Kishore took over from Rafi as lead male playback with the songs of *Aradhana*, but before we get there let's spare a thought to the other composer who dared to use Kishore's voice as playback to the still-new Rajesh Khanna. We're talking of Hemant Kumar and '*Woh shaam kuch ajeeb thi*' (*Khamoshi*), evocatively sung by Kishore, the melody as quiet as the river Hooghly on which the song was shot. Like it often happened with him, Hemant Kumar's classic remains buried under all the acclaim the more flamboyant songs of *Aradhana* won, with the same Kishore on the very same Rajesh Khanna. Perhaps it was a harbinger of the times ahead.

Coming to *Aradhana*, it is now widely acknowledged that Pancham, and not S.D. Burman, was the man who recorded '*Mere sapnon ki rani*' and '*Roop tera mastana*' in Kishore's voice. Dada Burman was too ill during the making of the film to protest, and allowed RD to do what he wanted. Hadn't RD proved Kishore's versatility in *Padosan*, and pitted Kishore and Rafi in a tandem number much to Kishore's advantage in '*Tum bin jaoon kahan*' (*Pyar Ka Mausam*, 1969)? Thus the man who believed only in Kishore quietly staged the biggest revolution in Hindi film music, hoodwinking all, including his own father. That Kishore infused both the songs with vitality and freshness that matched Khanna's screen presence to the T is undeniable. However, musically, *Aradhana* is a milestone in Kishore's career only for what it gave him from then on, and not for the songs of the film per se.

In his twenty-first year in the industry, Kishore finally got what he wanted. Every composer wanted his voice; every composer who previously swore by Rafi was willing to discover Kishore's 'merits' as singer. In the face of the storm unleashed by RD with *Aradhana* and cemented further with the raging hits of *Kati Patang*, even as monumental a talent as Rafi couldn't fight back. '*Pyar deewaana hota hain*', '*Yeh jo mohabbat hain*' and that evergreen picnic song, '*Yeh shaam mastaani*' left no one in doubt that Kishore was the new phenomenon in music. If Rajesh Khanna ended the reign of all the heroes who had ruled for two decades, Kishore Kumar, as his voice, ended the reign of Rafi as the voice of all of them. Laxmikant–Pyarelal switched to Kishore with '*Mere naseeb* mein aye dost' in *Do Raaste* (1969) and Kalyanji–Anandji sculpted the erudite '*Zindagi ka safar*' for the Kishore–Khanna team in *Safar* (1970).

In custody of the Burmans

When R.D. Burman's sentimental score for *Amar Prem* was released in 1971, Kishore, with his pain-lashed renditions, made the world aware of what they had overlooked in him a decade ago when he sang '*Koi humdum na raha*'. '*Chingaari Koi Bhadke*' grips you as much for Bakshi's poetry as Kishore's voice, but '*Kuch toh log kahenge*' is Kishore's triumph alone. There hasn't been a better expression of compassion from a male playback singer in Hindi films since.

In Kishore's rise to stardom as playback singer, Sachin Dev Burman's role is next only to that of son Pancham. As Burman Junior was exploring the serious facet of Kishore, Dada Burman was getting him to do what he was always good at, singing youthful, romantic numbers. '*O mere sharmilee*' (*Sharmilee*, 1971) was but an extension of the earlier '*O nigahen mastana*' in *Paying Guest*, but '*Khilte hain gul yahaan*' would have needed a Rafi just two years earlier. Burman extracted gold from Kishore in this song, much as he had done with Asha in the years when he had banished Lata. The final test for Kishore in Dada Burman's custody was in *Gambler* (1971), where he effortlessly took on the Rafiesque '*Dil aaj shaayar hain*' and cast it in a mould all his own. After that, Dada Burman didn't look beyond Kishore, installing him as Amitabh's voice in *Abhimaan* with '*Meet na mila re man ka*' and the pivotal duet '*Tere mere milan ki yeh raina*' with Lata. From the soothing '*Jeevan ki bagiyan mehkegi*' (*Tere Mere Sapne*, 1971) through the naughty '*Pyar ke is khel mein*' (*Jugnu*, 1973) to the anguished '*Badi sooni sooni hain*' in *Mili* (1975), Burman left no part of Kishore's vocal persona unexplored in his last years. He died a happy man in 1975, knowing that his protégé had finally made it.

A complete playback singer at last

Meanwhile, son Pancham was riding an all-time high as the composer of youth, now that the most youthful voice was no longer taboo. Banking on Kishore and Asha, Pancham unleashed a pop–jazz revolution in Hindi film music. *'Dekha na haaye re socha na'* (*Bombay To Goa*, 1972), *'Yeh jawaani hain diwaani'* (*Jawani Diwani*, 1972), *'Lekar hum deewana dil'* (with Asha, *Yaadon Ki Baraat*, 1973) and *'Ek main aur ek tu'* (*Khel Khel Main*, 1975) saw Pancham and Kishore create a new kind of music, one that held sway not only with the youth of that generation, but ever since. The trend culminated with *Hum Kisi Se Kum Nahin* (1977) where *'Bachna aye haseeno'* and *'Mil gaya humko saathi'* saw the composer–singer partnership peak commercially.

Along the way, Kishore helped RD in his quest for respectability by articulating Pancham's mellow tunes such as *'Musafir hoon yaaron'* (*Parichay*, 1972), *'Main shaayar badnaam'* (*Namak Haraam*, 1973), *'Zindagi ke safar mein'* (*Aap Ki Kasam*, 1974) and the classically oriented *'Is mod se jaate hain'* (with Lata, *Aandhi*, 1975). On the strength of RD's conviction that Kishore could render even classical compositions better than anyone else, Kishore gamely took on the challenge of the Shivranjani strains of *'Mere naina saawan bhadon'* in *Mehbooba* (1976). *'Phir wohi raat hain'* (*Ghar*, 1978) required superb control to negotiate the chords-based melody, and Kishore didn't disappoint. *'Aanewaala pal jaanewaala hain'* (*Golmaal*, 1979) needed muted shades of sadness, and Kishore was perfect. Only RD would have dared to use Kishore for *'Aye khuda har faisla'* in *Abdullah* (1980), when he had the option of using Rafi for something right up Rafi's street. Kishore lent the song a rare dignity, even while conveying the feeling of surrender.

Death comes as the end

Kishore's songs for all composers in the 1970s ranging from Kalyanji–Anandji (*Don*, *Muqaddar Ka Sikander*) to Rajesh Roshan (*Julie*, *Doosra Aadmi*) and even Bappi Lahiri (*Sharabi*) were big hits, but came nowhere close to the magic he created under RD's baton. Take way the RD songs from Kishore's repertoire and you take away his best. Laxmikant–Pyarelal used Kishore extensively in the 1970s, but except for rare melodies like *'Yeh jeevan hain'* (*Piya Ka Ghar*, 1972), *'Mere dil mein aaj kya hain'* (*Daag*, 1973) or *'Aapke anurodh pe'* (*Anurodh*, 1977), their creations for Kishore were unremarkable, not defining the crooner the way RD's songs for him did. Even in the unmusical 1980s, RD's compositions for

Kishore had something which no other composer had. '*Hamen tumse pyar kitna*' (*Kudrat*, 1981), '*Humen aur jeene ki*' (*Agar Tum Na Hote*, 1984) and '*Chehra hain ya chaand khila hain*' (*Saagar*, 1985) were among the handful of memorable songs that Kishore sang in the decade, all three composed by Pancham. The RD-Kishore collaboration must rank in the same league as the legendary Madan Mohan–Lata and O.P. Nayyar–Asha partnerships earlier. Like Madan and Nayyar, Pancham too needed his favourite singer for giving his best. He never got over the shock of Kishore's sudden demise in 1987. The only time he composed something akin to the magic of yore was in his swan song *1942–A Love Story*, where Kumar Sanu almost did a Kishore.

The last few years of Kishore were professionally unfulfilling, as the Bappi era left little scope for genuine music. Kishore was unfortunate in that he had barely a decade to establish himself in the annals of fame. By 1979, music had all but disappeared from films. He continued to sing round the clock till his last day, but knew that his best was long over. The last time you heard that familiar spark, that zest for living in his voice was in the song '*Liye sapne nigahon mein*' in *Mashaal* (1984), a song written by Javed Akhtar and tuned by Hridaynath Mangeshkar.

Towards the end he had become the eccentric he was always thought to be, preferring the company of birds and trees to people. There was a part of him that had retreated into some private, unknowable world. The lines of his Pancham-composed solo for *Bemisaal* (1982) seemed to reflect his state of being just before his death: '*Kisi baat par main kisi se khafaa hoon/Main zinda hoon par zindagi se khafa hoon.*'

THIRD-GENERATION SINGERS

They are the reigning voices today, having come into prominence when music returned to Hindi films in the 1990s. Among them, Alka Yagnik, Udit Narayan and Sonu Nigam seem invincible in the first decade of the twenty-first century, in terms of the number of songs they sing and the percentage of hits they deliver. Talented without doubt, they are luckless in the sense of being at the top when nothing great is happening musically. In an age where music is only yet another tool of instant gratification, these singers are constrained to live with the knowledge that for all their success, they are unlikely to leave any legacy for posterity. But then, isn't the whole of Bollywood caught in enacting the theme *kal ho na ho?*

UDIT NARAYAN:
THE VOICE OF THE CHOCOLATE HERO

Isn't it intriguing that the first of the next generation male playback singers appeared on the scene just after Kishore Kumar's death? Nepal-born Udit Narayan made his halting bid for stardom way back in 1978, but had to wait for Mansoor Khan's *Qayamat Se Qayamat Tak* to arrive. That he did so in his own original style is what marks him out, and is perhaps the reason why he has outlasted other, sometimes more talented, singers who came after him. Almost two decades after he created a sensation as the voice of Aamir Khan with his characteristic innocence in '*Papa kehte hain*', Udit remains at the top, secure in the knowledge that he is the preferred voice of the heroes who matter most in Bollywood: the three Khans.

There is a quality of optimism to his voice; a buoyancy that is not in any way restrained by his classical training. The zest and youthfulness in his voice have in no small measure sustained the 'lover-boy' image of the not-so-young Khans for more than a decade now. From '*Aaye ho mere zindagi mein*' (*Raja Hindustani*, 1996) through '*Chand chhupa baadal mein*' (*Hum Dil De Chuke Sanam*, 1999) to '*Yeh taara woh taara*' (*Swades*, 2004), Udit has kept the box office brimming, with a voice that articulates the joy of first love best. This trait made him win admirers down south too, and Udit is the only singer in Bollywood now who is much sought-after in Telugu, Tamil and Kannada films, despite his not knowing any of the languages.

Admittedly, there isn't much variety in his songs, his five Filmfare awards notwithstanding. It is anybody's guess how Udit will sound in a sad song or a ghazal. But then, we're probably talking of something that is passé today. If there is a sameness to many of his songs, perhaps the times are as much to blame. For all his limitations, however, Udit has proved time and again his capacity to deliver hits, and is hence likely to be in the reckoning for years to come.

KUMAR SANU: IN MEMORY OF KISHORE

He was lucky to have emerged at a time when the nation was still grieving the loss of Kishore Kumar, zooming to the top with the Kishore-sounding songs of *Aashiqui* (1990). As the voice that evoked memories of Kishore best, Kumar Sanu had his tryst with superstardom for the best part of the 1990s, at one time entering the Guinness Book of Records for recording an unbelievable twenty-eight songs in a single day! Sanu also holds the record of winning the Filmfare best singer award five times in a row, after which he declined to be nominated, much like Lata Mangeshkar a quarter century ago.

Exposed to classical music from an early age, Sanu's voice had both melody and malleability. Years of singing Kishore Kumar's songs in live orchestras made him sound very similar, and Sanu was wise enough to capitalize on that, never disclaiming his idol's influence. Growing from strength to strength with the songs of *Saajan* ('Mera dil bhi kitna paagal hain', with Alka Yagnik, 1990), *Dil Hain Ki Maanta Nahin* (title song, 1991) and *Deewana* ('Sochenge tumhe pyar karen ke nahin', 1992) under the baton of mentors Nadeem–Shravan, Sanu had his most sublime moment in singing for R.D. Burman's swan song, *1942–A Love Story* (1994). 'Ek ladki ko dekha' represented his peak as singer, something he couldn't surpass in the latter half of the decade, despite hummable songs in scores of films. Sanu himself seemed to be aware of this, and cut down assignments drastically in the new millennium, preferring live shows of his own songs to the beats-based music of Bollywood films. Appropriately enough, his last hit was for Nadeem–Shravan's

Dhadkan (2001). '*Tum dil ki dhadkan mein*' may have well been his swan song for all practical purposes.

ANURADHA PAUDWAL:
A TAKEOVER THAT NEVER WAS

She was probably meant to make a career out of devotional music, given that the first time she sang, it was a Shiv stuti in *Abhimaan*. Hubby Arun Paudwal, assistant to S.D. Burman, had recorded her voice as a dummy, only to be re-recorded by Lata Mangeshkar later. However, Burman-da liked her voice enough to retain it in the film. For someone who had such an auspicious beginning, it is a pity Anuradha's career languished for want of good breaks, and that though she finally did achieve fame, she will be remembered more for her battles to oust the Mangeshkar hold on Bollywood than for the songs she sang.

Not that she didn't have formidable talent. After all, she was initially groomed by no less a composer than Jaidev, who saw her potential and decided to make her sing for *Dooriyan* (1979). Her duets with Bhupinder, '*Zindagi mere ghar aana*' and '*Zindagi mein jab tumhaare gham nahin the*', showed great promise. Here was a voice moulded after Lata, but yet distinct. But like many a singer before her, Anuradha suffered because her vocals did not get worked upon by a host of composers. She remained a bud forever awaiting its moment. She sang through the 1980s, but barring Laxmikant–Pyarelal (*Hero, Ram Lakhan*), other composers wouldn't look beyond Lata or Asha. Anyway, music had ceased to matter in films of the era. Anuradha had to see juniors Kavita Krishnamurthy and Alka Yagnik surge ahead of her with bigger hits.

Until *Aashiqui* and T-Series happened in 1990. Backed by T-Series founder Gulshan Kumar and aided by the talent of Nadeem–Shravan, Anuradha saw glory with the runaway success of all the songs of the film. '*Tu meri zindagi hain*' and '*Nazar ke saamne*' saw her in sparkling form, shedding years of diffidence overnight. Like Sanu, Anuradha went from strength to strength in the early 1990s in films such as *Dil* ('*O Priya Priya*'), *Dil Hain Ki Maanta Nahin* (title song), *Beta* ('*Dhak dhak karne lagaa*') and *Sadak* ('*Tumhe apna banane ki kasam*'). In 1993, it looked like the Paudwal era in Bollywood was well and truly here.

It was at this critical juncture that Anuradha lost her poise, recording too many devotional albums for T-Series and wasting her energy in rivalling Lata's *Shraddhanjali* by re-recording the songs Lata had immortalized for every composer, as against honing her skills as playback singer. As a mark of loyalty to Gulshan Kumar, she declared that she would only sing for T-Series films. For a brief while, she even entertained ideas of turning composer herself, floating rumours that songs credited to Nadeem–Shravan were actually composed by her. Naturally, the composers turned bitter and walked out of T-Series. It was Anuradha who lost in every way. Her mentor Gulshan Kumar was murdered and she found herself without offers, composers having become wary of her. Her attempt at staging a comeback at the turn of the century after a five-year hiatus with songs in *Deewane* and *Pukar* didn't quite take off. She continues to sing an odd number here and there, but stoically maintains that she is happy singing bhajans.

KAVITA KRISHNAMURTHY: HITS ALL THE WAY

Hers is a story of perseverance ultimately paying dividends. Kavita Krishnamurthy may not have been blessed with as good a voice as Anuradha Paudwal, but on the strength of her patience and determination alone, she succeeded in carving a niche for herself in the Bollywood of the 1990s, before marriage shifted priorities. Detractors may find her voice shrill, her songs unremarkable, but Kavita's capacity to churn out hits is phenomenal, and in the final analysis, that has always counted more than anything else in Bollywood.

Laxmikant–Pyarelal brought her into the limelight with the saucy '*Hawa Hawaii*' in *Mr. India* (1987), and Kavita was able to put years of obscurity behind her. What her voice lacked she made up with focussing on expression, with often surprising results. If the '*Hawa Hawaii*' exuberance was one facet of her singing, accentuated further by chartbuster songs such as '*Tu cheez badi hain mast mast*' (*Mohra*, 1994), '*Mera piya ghar aaya*' (*Yaaraana*, 1996), '*Nimbuda*' (*Hum Dil De Chuke Sanam*, 1999) or even '*Dola re dola*' (*Devdas*, 2002), Kavita simultaneously proved her versatility with serious songs such as '*Tu hi re*' (*Bombay*, 1993) and '*Pyaar hua chupke se*' (*1942–A Love Story*, 1994) or the title song of *Hum Dil De Chuke Sanam*. If her classical songs in *Bhairavi* (1995) went unnoticed, she got more than her share of acclaim for the songs of *Khamoshi* ('*Aaj main upar*', 1996) and *Pukar* ('*Kay sera sera*', 2001). Her marriage to violin virtuoso L. Subramaniam and her subsequent move to Bangalore may have made home a bigger priority, but Kavita Subramaniam is uncomplaining, having seen it all in Bollywood between 1987 and 1997.

Sonu Nigam: Hope in the Twenty-first Century

The latest sensation in Bollywood is also, unusually, the most talented. Moulding his voice after that of Rafi initially and topping it with the Kumar Sanu effect, Sonu rules Bollywood in the new millennium as the most versatile and melodious male playback. While Udit and Sanu could rarely rise beyond the composers' tune, Sonu manages to invest even the mundane song with something extra, helped by his unerring grip on melody and feeling. In his voice, there's hope for true music in Bollywood.

For proof, you only need to recall his duets with singer Roopkumar Rathod '*Sandese aate hain*' (*Border*, 1997) and '*Zindagi maut na ban jaayen*' (*Sarfarosh*, 1999). Sonu matches the strong classical grip of Rathod note by note. Unlike Sanu and Udit who are good primarily with romantic ballads, Sonu could take Rajesh's Roshan's adaptation of Madan Mohan's original ghazal '*Baad muddat ke yeh ghadi aayi*' (*Jahan Ara*) and invest it with originality as '*Mujhse naraaz ho toh ho jaao*' (*Papa Kehte Hain*, 1996). Or take the song of *Refugee* (2000), '*Panchchi nadiyan pawan ke jhonken*', where Sonu finally resolves his Rafi–Sanu dilemma and evolves his own third way. The title song of *Kal Ho Na Ho* (2003) is arguably the best male solo of the new millennium as yet. Even in a theme with little scope for music such as *Main Hoon Na* (2004), Sonu makes you sit up and take notice of his qawwali '*Tumse milke hain jo dilka haal kya karen*'. If only he manages to reign in his need to be everywhere (Indipop, classical etc) as if there's no tomorrow, Sonu Nigam is likely to outlast all his contemporaries.

Alka Yagnik: Songstress for all Seasons

With Alka, success was as much a result of tact as talent. Her reign at the top began in the late 1980s, and Alka Yagnik has not let anything spoil it for her. No controversy, no tiffs with composers or producers and of course a voice that's cast in the Lata Mangeshkar mould. For almost two decades now, the *'Mere angne mein'* girl has retained her hold at the top. There isn't a major film today that doesn't have her voice in at least one song.

The 1980s saw her succeed with 'item' numbers such as *'Mere angne mein'* (*Lawaaris*) and *'Ek do teen'* (*Tezaab*), but respectability came with the songs of *Qayamat Se Qayamat Tak*. The duets with Udit Narayan were of course popular, but it is in the verse *'Kaahe sataaye'* that you get a glimpse of a new Alka, one who could emerge as the heroine's voice of the 1990s. Songs in *Saajan* (*'Dekha hain pehli baar'*), *Phir Teri Kahani Yaad Aayi* (*'Shayarana si hain'*) and *Baazigar* (*'Aye mere humsafar'*) took the thin, reedy edge off her voice. Till Anuradha Paudwal was going strong, Alka was content to be second, gamely singing the raunchy *'Choli ke peeche kya hain'* with Ila Arun in her quest for popularity. In 1996, with the songs of *Raja Hindustani*, Alka emerged as the top singer, now that Anuradha's career was beset with problems.

A.R. Rahman took time to switch to her, but with the songs in *Taal* (1999), she became his favourite for Hindi films. *Lagaan* saw her in great form, matching, and at times surpassing co-singer Udit Narayan's skilfulness in her duets *'Mitwaa'* and *'O re chhori'*. Rahman brought the best out from her, be it the forgotten solo *'Mehendi hain rachne waali'* in *Zubeida* (2000) or the hauntingly beautiful *'Sanwariya'* (*Swades*, 2004).

Having lived through years of struggle, Alka wisely accepts that playback music today has to have more zest than melody. *'Pyaar ki kashti mein'* (*Kaho Naa Pyaar Hain*, 1999) and *'Jaane kyon log pyar karte hain'* (*Dil Chahta Hain*, 2001) may not demand much from a singer who has been around for two decades, but Alka seeks solace in the odd skilful composition such as *'Kuch toh hua hain'* (*Kal Ho Na Ho*, 2003) that tests her virtuosity. Like other singers of the present era, Alka has to contend with the knowledge that prodigious her output may well be, but she is only likely to merit a footnote in the history of Bollywood.

MANNA DEY: AN ECHO FROM THE GOLDEN ERA OF HINDI FILM MUSIC

At eighty-six, he is the most senior link with the golden era of music in Hindi films. It occurs to me that rather than me writing about him, it may be a good idea to get him to speak about his own music and the music of that era. An idea all the more tempting given that he lives just two streets away from where I live. All enthusiasm I feel dwindles when I hear his forbidding response to my first call. 'I am too busy, call me later,' he says tersely, before ringing off. It takes me a whole month and a lot of perseverance before he consents to meet me.

There is an air of serenity to his house, rather like much of his music. He greets me warmly in English, all his earlier reserve now gone. Relaxed and alert, he seems much younger than his age. As he reminisces on the years gone by, you are amazed at his clarity of thought, his compassionate wit, and his humility. Over the next two hours, it strikes you that it isn't just his music that belongs to another era. The man himself does. Excerpts from the conversation:

On his early years with music

I came from a joint family, thirty-two people living under one roof. My second uncle was an engineer, and his voice carried a lot of weight. He decided that I should be a lawyer. But then I had already made up my mind that I'd pursue music. I lived in an atmosphere drenched in music, you see. All the stalwarts of classical music in that era would visit my house often. My uncle

K.C. Dey was an extremely popular film musician then. He made music for films and sang in them, but his true contribution was far greater than the films he composed for. He was trained in all forms of classical music—dhrupad, dhamar, thumri, bhajan—everything. He made it a point to present all the richness of classical music in a form that was accessible and enjoyable to the common man. I was very impressed with my uncle, and I learnt the rudiments of music from him. I also underwent classical training from others, but pure classical music never caught my fancy. I was drawn towards my uncle's ability to modify classical music to make it appealing to the layperson. I appreciated the rigour of classical music, but I always knew I didn't want to sing a raag for two hours. I would listen to many classical performances of ustads who visited my house, and also the students who came to learn from my uncle. I was fortunate that I grew up amidst so much good music, and thus was able to tell good music from bad at a very early age.

On finding his own voice

One of my uncle's students was Sachin Dev Burman. Sachin-da had a fantastic voice, powerful and somewhat nasal, which would fascinate me a lot. I knew he had quit the royal family in Tripura to pursue music, and I became a big admirer of him and his style of singing. For a while I would copy all aspects of his singing, including the nasal tone. My uncle was furious, and reprimanded me, saying it's okay to sing Sachin's songs, but you don't need to imitate him. Make any song your own; that's the way you'll grow.

My uncle also prepared me for facing the harshness of the film world—the competition, rivalry, fame and rejection. So when I came to films, I was ready to take successes and failures equally. I came to Bombay in 1942 to be an assistant to my uncle in music direction. But I realized that composing was too difficult a job. I was keen on singing as a career. My break in playback happened by sheer chance, as producer Vijay Bhatt and composer Shankar Rao Vyas came to meet my uncle with a request that he give playback for the film *Ram Rajya* (1943). My uncle refused, saying he would not lend his voice to anyone else. They saw me sitting in a corner, and asked my uncle who I was. When he told them, they wanted me to sing the songs instead. Shankar Rao Vyas himself taught me the songs, and I sang them in the K.C. Dey style. Vijay Bhatt came running to me saying, 'You've got a marvellous voice.' '*Gayi tu gayi Seeta sati*' was my first song as a playback singer.

Though I sang quite a few songs after that in films, it was an era when playback singers were not given any credit, and my songs went unnoticed. So I continued to be an assistant music director to my uncle, and after him to Anil Biswas, Khemchand Prakash and finally Sachin Dev Burman. It was while assisting the latter that I got to sing Kavi Pradeep's '*Oopar gagan vishal*' for the film *Mashal* (1950), my first hit song. It was Burman-da who suggested that I sing it like Ustad-ji, meaning my uncle K.C. Dey. I was noticed by the industry for my full-throated rendition of that song. Incidentally, the tune was not S.D. Burman's, but lyricist Pradeep's, who usually set to tune his own lyrics.

It was not long before I shook off all influences of others from my voice. By the time Anil Biswas's '*Ritu aaye ritu jaaye sakhi*' that I sang with Lata in *Humdard* (1953) happened, my voice was my own. This song is one of my best. There hasn't, in my opinion, been a better classical song ever in Hindi films. Not even Roshan's '*Laaga chunri mein daagh*' (*Dil Hi To Hain*), one of my other favourites, was as good. Anil Biswas, in my opinion, was a composer who mattered most to people who knew music. Sadly, he never saw the dizzying heights of fame like many who were inferior to him did. But his era was the 1940s, when he ruled music in Hindi cinema.

On the road to fame

My next big moment as singer came when I got the songs of *Basant Bahar*. It was composer Shanker (of Shanker–Jaikishan) who insisted that I sing '*Sur naa saje*' while everyone else associated with the film wanted Rafi to sing the song. Shanker remained adamant, and thus I got to sing the song, a great classical number. Jaikishan tuned '*Bhay banjana*' in the same film. But I will now confess that what I got from Shanker and Jaikishan is the bare outline of the tunes. All improvisations, all the intricacies in both songs were my own. Shanker knew I was the only singer capable of making those improvisations at that time. Every other singer—Talat, Mukesh, Kishore—could sing what was given to them. Rafi tried to improvise, but not very successfully. Improvisation required a command over classical music that only I had.

For all that, I was petrified of singing '*Ketaki gulaab juhi champak ban phoole*' with Bhimsen Joshi. I protested to Shanker, saying it is ridiculous that I beat Bhimsen Joshi in that song, as he was a great classical singer in his prime then. But the director and Shanker insisted, and the song was recorded. I couldn't believe it when Joshi saab came and told me after the recording that I sang very well. He, in fact, advised me to become a full-time classical singer!

It is to Shanker that I owe all my really big breaks, as in the Raj Kapoor films *Shri 420* and *Chori Chori*. Shanker overruled RK's preference for Mukesh, knowing Mukesh could not do justice to the dexterity required for '*Dil ka haal sune dilwaala*' or even the duet '*Pyaar hua ikraar hua*' in *Shri 420*. But RK had a thick friendship with Mukesh, and had become too closely identified with Mukesh's voice for me to make a real difference to their pairing. Even '*Aye bhai zara dekh ke chalo*' for *Mera Naam Joker*, for which I won an award, was tuned by Shanker, who again convinced Raj saab that I should sing the song instead of Mukesh. Even at a late stage in his career, when Shanker and Jaikishan had split, Shanker gave me great songs such as '*Re man sur mein gaa*' (*Lal Paththar*, 1971) or the beautiful '*Chham chham baaje re paayaliya*' (*Jaane Anjaane*, 1971). Truly a great composer, one who was always experimenting.

On his favourite songs

I still don't know why Madan Mohan wanted me to sing '*Kaun aaya mere mann ke dwaare*' in *Dekh Kabira Roya*. He had worked more with Rafi, and I was surprised that he wanted me to sing this song. Perhaps because the character in the film, Anoop Kumar, was a classical singer, and Madan felt I would ring true as his voice. For me, the real challenge in the film was the other classical composition in Raag Jaijaiwanti, '*Bairan ho gayi rain*' where I had to prove my vocal virtuosity with all the intricate taans. Madan Mohan also gave me other classical compositions such as the duet with Lata, '*Preetam daras dikhao*' in Raag Lalit for *Chacha Zindabad* (1959). When I asked him once why he wanted me for the song '*Har taraf ab yahin afsaane hain*' in *Hindustan Ki Kasam*, he told me he wanted a cultured and sophisticated voice for the character of an army officer. I was happy. But more than my songs, I love what he composed for Rafi and Lata. Madan Mohan is immortalized in their voices alone. I believe that he did not get his due. He deserved more fame and recognition.

'*Poocho na kaise maine rain bitaayi*' (*Meri Soorat Teri Aankhen*) was a straight lift from a Bengali Nazrul Geet. Burman-da didn't have much of a role in composing it. In fact, I don't consider Sachin Dev Burman to be a great composer of serious songs. Even his '*Jalte hain jiske liye*' in *Sujata* was a Tagore song originally. He was best at light-hearted numbers, the ones he got Kishore or Asha to sing. He had the uncanny ability to look for the extraordinary twist in the ordinary tune. Remember the way he composed '*Jaane kya toone kahi*' in *Pyaasa*? The way the tune moves is delightful. It is one of my all-time favourites in Hindi cinema.

Sachin-da's son R.D. Burman was a more versatile and original composer. Do you know that many songs credited to S.D. Burman were actually composed by RD? My song '*Tere naina talash karen*' (*Talash*, 1969) is a case in point. RD's contribution to that was much more than Sachin-da's. I also love the song '*Aao twist karen*' that RD gave me in *Bhoot Bangla* (1964). It proved that I could as easily sing a Western tune as classical. I believe Pancham is the last genius in Hindi cinema. That is why every composer today composes music like he did a full twenty years ago.

Coming to the lighter songs I've sung, I'd also mention the qawwali from *Waqt* as my favourite. '*Aye meri zohra jabeen*' was based on an Afghan song, and composer Ravi masterfully adapted it to a qawwali. It required restraint and sweetness more than power, as a middle-aged man sang it in the film to his middle-aged wife. Maybe that's why I was chosen over Rafi for this song. I think Balraj Sahani wanted me to sing the song, because I had sung for him the bhajan '*Tu pyaar ka saagar hain*' in *Seema*.

Among my later songs, I'd also mention '*Kasme waade pyaar wafa*' (*Upkar*) as a particularly memorable song, as much for Indeewar's lyrics as for the tune. The day after I sang the song, I got a call from Lata Mangeshkar who told me that she was moved to tears when she heard the song while at a recording. I sang quite a few popular numbers for composers Kalyanji–Anandji, but this is my favourite. Musically, I like Laxmikant–Pyarelal better. One of my best duets with Lata, '*Tum gagan ki chandrama ho*' (*Sati Savitri*, 1964), was composed by Laxmikant–Pyarelal.

On other playback singers

The playback singer I truly feared was Mohammed Rafi. He was an instinctive singer, and I required all my training, all my grounding in classical music to match his impact. While singing duets, I used to be extra-careful, knowing that I have to be on my guard, as the person singing with me is the one and only Mohammed Rafi! I used to tell myself, Manna, your lines have to stand on their own, no matter that the co-singer is Rafi. Among the songs Rafi and I sang, I'd mention O.P. Nayyar's classical duet *'Tu hain mera prem devta'* in *Kalpana* (1960) as my favourite.

I like Rafi best as a playback singer, but I'd say Kishore Kumar had the best voice. When you listen to Kishore's spirited singing, you are often left with a sense of wonder at how the man could make singing sound so effortless. Just Listen to *'Yeh dosti, hum nahin todenge'* in *Sholay* (1975). I have always felt that when my voice comes after Kishore's, it has something lacking. With what confidence Kishore has sung the difficult notes in the song! This without any classical training! He was a genius.

The last word

I do feel I have not got my share of recognition. *'Sur naa saje'*, *'Poocho na kaise maine'* and *'Laaga chunri mein daagh'* were all passed over for best playback singer award. Even the extremely popular *'Aye meri zohra jabeen'* didn't fetch me one. But I choose not to nurse these regrets. Why focus on what you didn't get when what you've got is so much? My music is remembered till date, and remembered with respect. Is there anything else one can wish for? In the end, I consider myself lucky to have been part of an era when some really creative and outstanding music happened. For that I thank God.

LATA MANGESHKAR ON OTHER PLAYBACK SINGERS

The first time I hear her voice on the phone, I am speechless. Could it really be that I am talking to the one and only Lata Mangeshkar? I gather my wits and ask her very tentatively whether she would meet me to speak about her singer colleagues for this book. There's a pause during which I die a hundred deaths. She asks me to call her back the next day, and gives me a specific time to call. The next twenty-four hours are excruciating, and I vacillate between hope and the fear of hearing a no. Next day she is as polite, but asks me to call a couple of days later, telling me she is unwell. I ring off after rambling about how fortunate it will be for my book and me if only she could give me time. She listens with patience, but is noncommittal. And so it goes on for the next four calls, until I, in sheer desperation, tell her (the truth) that I am classically trained in music and that I consider her classical songs in films to be truly extraordinary. This proves to be the clincher, and after the famous pause, she asks me to call her back in ten minutes. When I do so with a thudding heart, she gives me an appointment for that weekend. I am again speechless, and mumble something about being grateful before ringing off. For the next two days, I am on cloud nine. My wife remarks good-naturedly that she's not seen me this happy since the time she met me.

  I ring the doorbell of her unpretentious flat in Prabhu Kunj bang on time. The door is opened by her secretary, who tells me, 'Didi aap hi ka intezaar kar rahi hain.' As I walk into the hall, I find Lata Mangeshkar standing up to greet me with a warm namaste. I instinctively touch her feet, and sit down on the sofa beside her, searching for words to convey all that's happening to me at the moment. She seems to understand, and invites me to talk about the book. I do so, getting over my diffidence by the minute, and soon we are conversing easily. I am keen to start the interview, but she would want to speak only after we've finished tea and snacks. Over the next hour and half, she speaks thoughtfully, sometimes spontaneously, about her colleagues in playback. The nightingale in her own words:

Saigal as inspiration

As a child, I heard Saigal's music before I heard anyone else, barring my father, who was himself a reputed musician. I used to learn classical music from my father at home, and he'd have the final say in what music we kids got to listen. Film music was banned at home, but fortunately for me, my father approved of Saigal and I could listen to his music without censure. I liked Saigal particularly for his diction. Coming from Punjab, he sang Hindi and Urdu without a trace of accent, unlike other singers from Bengal at that time, who sang well, but with a Bengali intonation.

I used to sing Saigal songs all the time those days, whenever I was not practising classical music. I learnt the rudiments of light music solely from listening to Saigal. It wasn't too difficult, as I grew up in an atmosphere of classical music all around me. I believe once you learn classical, you can master every other kind of music. I came to know later that Saigal too had learnt classical music before he came to films. Only then could he have sung something as complex as '*Jhulana jhulao ri*', the non-film record with which he became so popular. Among his film songs, I like '*So ja rajkumari*' best. '*Main kya jaanu kya jaadoo hain*' and '*Baalam aaye baso more man mein*' are my other favourites, which is why I recorded them in my tribute *Shraddhanjali*. I think Saigal's best songs happened in the 1930s under the New Theatres banner. The songs he got in Bombay in the 1940s in films such as *Tansen* and *Shahjehan* weren't too good.

I think he became so popular because he had all the four qualities that any playback singer ought to have. First, he had a god-given voice: powerful, resonant and melodious. His range was phenomenal; he could negotiate all three octaves with ease. Second, he understood music; he knew what good music is all about. Third, he had the ability to sing as the situation in the film demanded. His expression varied according to the need of the song. Fourth, he had good, clear diction, better than all others then. Every other singer of that era had one or the other of these qualities. Only Saigal possessed them all. Finally, I'd say he had the Almighty's blessings with him. It was ordained that he should become a superstar.

One of my regrets in life is that I couldn't meet him in person. He died very soon after I came to Bombay in 1947. I think he was unhappy in his personal life, despite all the success he achieved as a singing star. Among playback singers, Mukesh, Kishore and I were particularly influenced by his style of singing.

The Noorjehan influence

Noorjehan is my favourite among the female singing stars. She was truly a great singer, with a style of singing that was original, and a beautiful voice. She used her voice very well, having been trained in classical music. Also, she was without peer in getting the expression right, something crucial for film music. I fell in love with her voice right from her first songs in the film *Khandaan* (1942). I had the opportunity to meet her first when she came to Kolhapur for the shooting of Master Vinayak's film *Badi Maa* in 1944. I was completely in awe of her, and I used to visit her every day. She knew I could sing, and would often ask me to sing something for her. I was only fourteen then, and she would always bless me after hearing me sing.

Initially, I used to sing like her, because she was my idol. She was better than everyone else at that time. Listening to Noorjehan's songs also helped me get my Urdu diction right. The way you articulate words in a song in very critical to the overall effect of the song. Saigal and Noorjehan were two singers who realized this, and I too learnt it by listening to their songs.

(*In response to my question*) I don't agree with the view that I succeeded because Noorjehan left for Pakistan in 1947. It was God's will that I should achieve name and fame in 1948-49. I really believe that. I was gifted with a good voice, I worked hard with learning and practising music, but ultimately it was not so much what I did as much as what I was meant to do in this lifetime. For some reason, success in music was ordained for me. It had nothing to do with who came or who left the scene.

Other singing stars

Kanan Devi's voice impressed me a lot. It had sweetness and melody, and she sang with feeling. Khursheed also sang well; she had a good grasp of classical music, but sounded a little flat at times. She was not able to give adequate expression to her songs. I liked Anil Biswas's sister Parul Ghosh, too, but despite having a good voice, she did not get enough opportunities.

Suraiya had a sweet voice, and for someone who did not train in music, she sang really well. I believe she had the potential to become a far better singer, but she was content with using only what she intrinsically had. She did not strive to become a complete singer. Singing stars had a more difficult time than us playback singers, because they had to concentrate on both acting and singing. It was not physically possible to concentrate on singing after a hard day of shooting. Suraiya was first an actress, only then a singer. People loved her screen presence more than her songs.

Female playback singers

When I came into the Hindi film industry, Ameerbai Karnataki and Zohrabai Ambalewali were extremely popular. I liked Zohrabai's voice very much. It was a heavy voice, but it had more melody in it than the other voices of the 1940s. Her song '*Akhiyaan milaake*' that I sang for *Shraddhanjali* is my favourite.

Shamshad Begum was the most popular singer in 1947. I feel Shamshad's voice had more sharpness than melody to it. Under Ghulam Haider, she sang the popular songs of *Khazanchi* in the open-throated, Punjabi style in 1941. Later she used the same style of singing in Bombay, and was popular with composers of the Punjabi style of music. She succeeded so enormously because her voice was thinner than others of that era, though she sang only some songs very well, those that required spirit more than melody.

Geeta Dutt and I came at the same time, though she became popular with the songs of *Do Bhai* before I did. Geeta's voice was very charming, with a distinctive Bengali lilt to it. She had good enunciation and diction too. She relied more on instinct than practice, so her songs had a lot of spontaneity. But since she was not trained, I feel the range of songs she could sing was somewhat limited. Also, after I became popular in 1950, most composers gave their better songs to me. So Geeta did not have the advantage of getting the kind of compositions I did. But whatever she got, she sang really well. Not just as a singer, Geeta was a very sweet person too. I had a good personal equation with her.

Asha Bhonsle, I have always maintained, is the singer with the maximum versatility in Hindi films. She could sing (and still can) every kind of song: classical, romantic, sad, bhajan, ghazal, cabaret, everything. I don't think even I can sing as wide a range of songs as she can. I haven't tried either. Asha, like me, had the advantage of a solid grounding in music from our father. She's worked very hard at her music subsequently, which is why she's succeeded so much, and is popular even today.

In response to my comment that Asha may be more versatile, but Lata's voice has a spiritual quality that transcends the lyric of the song often

If I do have that spiritual quality to my singing, it is because I am a god-fearing person, and I have never forgotten that it is His blessings that have given me so much. I have never tried to 'create' a spiritual effect. It can't be done as a technique. It has to come from within, naturally. In the earlier days, often while recording a song, I'd feel a benign presence beside me.

When asked about the impressions of rivalry between her and Asha

It is sheer nonsense. What rivalry can I have with Asha? She's my sister, a part of my household. This talk of competition and enmity between us is a myth, generated by those who are envious of my success and hers. If there were really any truth to it, would we have lived on the same floor all these years? My flat is connected to hers through a passage inside. She visits me often and I visit her as often. If I have achieved much name and fame for my style of singing, she too has achieved as much for her own style. Most importantly, I don't believe anyone else can spoil your chances, or take away what is due to you. It is a ridiculous thought that I could spoil anyone's career or he or she, mine.

Male playback singers

I have always respected Mukesh bhaiyya as a singer and person. He had a beautiful bass voice that was very rich, what I'd call *paak awaaz*, without any blemish whatsoever. He used to work hard with each song until he got the notes and expression perfect. Once he was ready to record, you would be amazed at his control. He used to learn classical music, and I've seen him do *riyaaz* with great devotion. Mukesh did not sing too many songs, but he was lucky that the ones he got were good songs, and they became very popular.

He gave something extra to every song he sang, because of what I'd call the purity of his voice. When I would sing with him or listen to him, I would always be moved by the *sachchai* in his singing. Rather like a Hindu *sant*, if you know what I mean. What I liked most about him was that he was a very kind-hearted, warm and generous person. It was because of his nature that all his songs have a ring of innocence, of truth.

Rafi saab had the best voice among all my contemporaries, the voice with maximum melody. His range too was awesome. I don't know if he had learnt classical, but he sang classical songs so well. 'Madhuban mein Radhika naache re' is one of my favourites. I don't think any other singer in our industry could have sung that song the way Rafi saab did. Though he sang every kind of song, I would often feel that he was best in articulating sadness and pain. I love most of his sad songs and ghazals. I also respected the sheer commitment to work that he had. My God, he used to sing round the clock. He'd leave home early in the morning one day and return home only the next morning! He was far busier than I was.

Manna Dey was of course very good in classical songs. But I sometimes feel he was typecast as the singer of weighty classical numbers, while the fact is that he sang light-hearted numbers also very well. So many comedy songs for Mehmood are in Manna-da's voice, sung brilliantly. I can tell you that giving expression to funny songs is more difficult than singing sad songs. However, I feel Manna-da's voice tended to sound a little aged, and he was preferred for songs picturized on senior actors. For some reason, his voice did not have the youthful energy that Rafi or Kishore's voice did. Therefore, Manna-da did not get too many songs to sing.

Talat Mehmood had a soft, gentle voice that was also extraordinarily sweet. I loved the way he used that sweetness, particularly when he sang ghazals. I haven't sung many duets with him though. In fact, Talat saab recorded very few film songs. I think his voice suited Dilip Kumar's personality best. Somehow

Talat's songs for Dilip Kumar are my favourites. However, there came a time when Dilip saab himself would prefer Rafi to sing his songs instead of Talat. Many songs meant to be sung by Talat came to be recorded in Rafi's voice. Probably because his voice did not have the commanding presence that Rafi saab's voice had. This is my opinion, and I could be wrong.

Kishore Kumar is the best male playback singer we have ever had in the industry. I am saying this because he, and only he, had the ability to sing all types of songs with just the right expression. There is no one else who understood the nuances of playback as well as he did. You didn't have to teach him what to emphasize, what not to in a song. He knew it instinctively. And he was a fast learner. He couldn't sing classical songs, but the energy and enthusiasm he brought to the light-hearted songs were amazing. Sometimes I used to feel he wasn't as good in sad songs as Rafi was, but he was better than Rafi in emoting happy songs. Kishore also adapted to the changing trends in music so well, which is why he had such a long career in playback. Most singers have their musical limits. Kishore is one playback singer without any limits. Even now the current generation of singers are influenced most by him.

The playback scene today

Among contemporary singers, I like Sonu Nigam best. He is serious about his music, has learnt classical and sings with confidence. I also like Udit Narayan because he sings in a completely original style. He is probably the only playback singer in Hindi films who never sang like anyone else. I think it's admirable that he has succeeded so much with his own style.

Alka Yagnik is good too. She's come a long way since she began in the 1980s. People say she sings somewhat like me, but I think Alka listened to my music and just took from that whatever she liked, what suited her. The rest is her own talent, her own effort. She would not have been singing successfully for twenty-five years if she did not have originality. Many other singers who came in the 1970s and 1980s were good singers per se, but either sang like me or like Asha. Which is why they faded out sooner or later. As long as the originals are going strong, where was the need for Xeroxes, tell me?

Sunidhi Chauhan has a good, expressive voice, but she's

crafted a particular image for herself as the singer of fast, racy songs. She has the potential to be a complete singer, if she works hard.

I don't think it is a lack of talented singers that's the problem in the industry today. It is just that there's no composer to test a singer's range; work on exploring the voice of the singer the way composers used to do in the 1950s. I had the benefit of so many composers—Ghulam Haider, Khemchand Prakash, Anil Biswas, Shyam Sunder and Naushad—working on my vocals very early in my career, which is why I grew as singer. Unfortunately, today's singers have no composer to mentor them. The emphasis in music today is on instant popularity, not on creating something that is original; that will last. This is true of the whole country. Creative music is not happening anywhere—not in Mumbai, not the south, or even in Bengal. How can you blame the singers alone for it?

If things have to improve, one of two things has to happen. Either a new musical phenomenon must emerge in composing, or some playback singer or the other should get into composing, taking charge of the music they get to sing. I don't know if either of these will happen. For the sake of film music, I wish it did.

Index of Songs

Song	Film	Year	Composer	Lyricist	Singer	Page No.
Aa Chal Ke Tujhe	Door Gagan Ki Chaon Mein	1964	Kishore Kumar	Shailendra	Kishore	189
Aa Jaan-e-Jaan	Inteqam	1969	Laxmikant-Pyarelal	Rajinder Krishan	Lata	12, 71, 156
Aa Jaane Wafa Aa	Anarkali	1953	Basant Prakash	Jan Nisar Akhtar	Geeta Dutt	161
Aadmi Musafir Hain	Apnapan	1978	Laxmikant-Pyarelal	Anand Bakshi	Rafi, Lata, Anuradha Paudwal	126
Aage Bhi Jaane Na Tu	Waqt	1964	Ravi	Sahir	Asha	13, 41, 60, 115, 165
Aaina Mujh Se Meri	Daddy	1990	Rajesh Roshan	Suraj Sanim	Talat Aziz	181
Aaj Gawat Man Mero Jhoomke	Baiju Bawra	1952	Naushad	Shakeel	Ustad Amir Khan, Pt. D.V. Paluskar	32
Aaj Kal Mein Dhal Gayaa	Beti Bete	1964	Shanker-Jaikishan	Shailendra	Rafi and Lata	117
Aaj Kal Paon Zameen Par	Ghar	1978	R.D. Burman	Gulzar	Lata	69, 123
Aaj Ke Insaan Ko Yeh	Amar Rahe Ye Pyar	1961	C. Ramchandra	Pradeep	Pradeep	106
Aaj Main Upar Aasmaan Neeche	Khamoshi	1996	Jatin-Lalit	Majrooh	Kavita Krishnamurthy	107
Aaj Mausam Bada Beimaan Hain	Loafer	1973	Laxmikant-Pyarelal	Anand Bakshi	Rafi	72
Aaj Phir Jeene Ki Tamanna Hain	Guide	1965	S.D. Burman	Shailendra	Lata	117, 155
Aaj Puraani Raahon Se	Aadmi	1968	Naushad	Shakeel	Rafi	33, 112
Aaj Rapat Jaaye Toh	Namak Halaal	1982	Bappi Lahiri	Anjaan	Kishore, Asha	15
Aaj Sajan Mohe Ang Laga Lo	Pyaasa	1957	S.D. Burman	Sahir	Geeta Dutt	44, 160
Aaj Socha Toh Aansoo Bhar Aaye	Hanste Zakhm	1973	Madan Mohan	Kaifi Azmi	Lata	119
Aaja Aaja Main Hoon Pyar Tera	Teesri Manzil	1966	R.D. Burman	Majrooh	Rafi, Asha	12, 66-67, 109, 156, 165, 184

Song	Film	Year	Composer	Lyricist	Singer	Page No.
Aaja Ab Toh Aaja	*Anarkali*	1953	C. Ramchandra	Rajinder Krishan	Lata	36
Aaja Ke Intezaar Mein	*Halaku*	1956	Shanker-Jaikishan	Shailendra	Rafi, Lata	40
Aaja Mere Barbaad Mohabbat	*Anmol Ghadi*	1946	Naushad	Tanvir Naqvi	Noorjehan	145
Aaja Nindiyaa Aaja	*Bhuaona*	1984	Bappi Lahiri	Kaifi Azmi	Lata	79
Aaja Piya Tohe Pyar Doon	*Baharon Ke Sapne*	1967	R.D. Burman	Majrooh	Lata	67
Aaja Re Ab Mera Dil Pukara	*Aah*	1953	Shanker-Jaikishan	Hasrat Jaipuri	Mukesh, Lata	39
Aaja Re Pardesi	*Madhumati*	1958	Salil Choudhury	Shailendra	Lata	56, 117, 153-54
Aaja Teri Yaad Aayi	*Charas*	1976	Laxmikant-Pyarelal	Anand Bakshi	Rafi, Lata	73, 125
Aan Milo Shyam Saanware	*Devdas*	1955	S.D. Burman	Sahir	Geeta Dutt, Manna Dey	160
Aana Hain Toh Aa	*Naya Daur*	1957	O.P. Nayyar	Sahir	Rafi	52
Aana Meri Jaan Sunday Ke Sunday	*Shehnai*	1947	C. Ramchandra	P.L. Santoshi	Shamshad Begum, Chitalkar	7, 9, 36-37, 93
Aanchal Mein Saja Lena Na	*Phir Wohi Dil Laya Hoon*	1963	O.P. Nayyar	Majrooh	Rafi	53
Aanewaala Pal Jaanewaala Hain	*Golmaal*	1979	R.D. Burman	Gulzar	Kishore	124, 192
Aankhon Hi Aankhon Mein Ishaara Ho Gaya	*CID*	1956	O.P. Nayyar	Jan Nisar Akhtar	Rafi, Geeta Dutt	51, 180
Aankhon Mein Masti Sharab Ki	*Chhaya*	1961	Salil Choudhury	Rajinder Krishan	Talat	57, 177
Aankhon Se Jo Utari Hain Dil	*Phir Wohi Dil Laaya Hoon*	1963	O.P. Nayyar	Majrooh	Asha	53, 164
Aansoo Bhari Hain	*Parvarish*	1958	Dattaram	Hasrat Jaipuri	Mukesh	172
Aansoo Samajh Ke Kyon Mujhe	*Chhaya*	1961	Salil Choudhury	Rajinder Krishan	Talat	55, 177
Aao Naa Gale Lagao Naa	*Mere Jeevan Saathi*	1972	R.D. Burman	Majrooh	Asha	166
Aao Twist Karen	*Bhoot Bangla*	1965	R.D. Burman	Hasrat Jaipuri	Manna Dey	67, 204
Aap Jaisa Koi Mere Zindagi Mein	*Qurbani*	1980	Biddu	Indeewar	Nazia Hassan	66
Aap Ke Anurodh Pe	*Anurodh*	1976	Laxmikant-Pyarelal	Anand Bakshi	Kishore	72, 192
Aap Ki Aankhon Mein Kuch	*Ghar*	1978	R.D. Burman	Gulzar	Kishore, Lata	123
Aap Ki Haseen Rukh Pe	*Baharein Phir Bhi Aayengi*	1966	O.P. Nayyar	Anjaan	Rafi	184
Aap Yun Faaslon Se	*Shankar Hussain*	1977	Khayyam	Jan Nisar Akhtar	Lata	76

215

Song	Film	Year	Composer	Lyricist	Singer	Page No.
Aap Yun Hi Agar Humse Milte Rahe	Ek Musafir Ek Haseena	1962	O.P. Nayyar	Raja Mehdi Ali Khan	Rafi	53
Aapke Pehloon Mein Aakar	Mera Saaya	1966	Madan Mohan	Raja Mehdi Ali Khan	Rafi	183
Aapko Pyar Chupaane Ki Buri	Neela Aakash	1965	Madan Mohan	Raja Mehdi Ali Khan	Rafi, Asha	182
Aaye Bahaar Ban Ke Lubha Kar	Raj Hath	1956	Shanker-Jaikishan	Hasrat Jaipuri	Rafi	40, 181
Aaye Ho Mere Zindagi Mein Tum	Raja Hindustani	1996	Nadeem-Shravan	Sameer	Udit Narayan and Alka Yagnik	83, 194
Aayega Aanewala	Mahal	1950	Khemchand Prakash	Nakshab Jarachavi	Lata	8, 25-26, 152, 159
Aayiye Meherbaan	Howrah Bridge	1958	O.P. Nayyar	Qamar Jalalabadi	Asha	52, 164
Aayo Kahan Se Ghanshyam	Budda Mil Gaya	1971	R.D. Burman	Majrooh	Manna Dey	68
Ab Ke Baras Bhejo Bhaiyya	Bandini	1963	S.D. Burman	Shailendra	Asha	45, 164
Ab Ke Sajan Sawan Mein	Chupke Chupke	1975	S.D. Burman	Anand Bakshi	Lata	47
Ab Kya Misaal Doon Main	Aarti	1962	Roshan	Majrooh	Rafi	58, 182
Ab Main Kaah Karoon Kit Jaoon	Dhartimata	1938	Pankaj Mullick	Pt. Sudarshan	K.L. Saigal	24
Ab Raat Guzarne Wali Hain	Awara	1951	Shanker-Jaikishan	Hasrat Jaipuri	Lata	39
Ab Tere Bin Jee Lenge Hum	Aashiqui	1990	Nadeem-Shravan	Sameer, Rani Malik	Kumar Sanu	17, 83
Abhi Abhi Thi Dushmani	Zakhmee	1975	Bappi Lahiri	Gauhar Kanpuri	Lata	79
Abhi Na Jao Chod Kar	Hum Dono	1961	Jaidev	Sahir	Rafi, Asha	61, 166
Accha Toh Hum Chalte Hain	Aan Milo Sajna	1970	Laxmikant-Pyarelal	Anand Bakshi	Kishore, Lata	73, 125
Aeri Aali Piya Bin	Raag Rang	1952	Roshan	Traditional	Lata	58
Aeri Main Toh Prem Diwaani	Jogan	1950	Bulo C. Rani	Meerabai	Geeta Dutt	159
Aeri Main Toh Prem Diwani	Naubahaar	1952	Roshan	Meerabai	Lata	58
Aisa Ho Toh Kaisa Hoga	Ratnadeep	1979	R.D. Burman	Gulzar	Asha	167
Aji Aisa Mauka Phir Kahaan Milega	An Evening In Paris	1967	Shanker-Jaikishan	Hasrat Jaipuri	Rafi	184
Akele Hain Chale Aao	Raaz	1967	Kalyanji-Anandji	Shamim Jaipuri	Rafi and Lata	64
Akele Hain Toh Kya Gham Hain	Qayamat Se Qayamat Tak	1988	Anand-Milind	Majrooh	Udit Narayan, Alka Yagnik	110
Akeli Hoon Main Piya Aa	Sambandh	1969	O.P. Nayyar	Pradeep	Asha	54

Song	Film	Year	Composer	Lyricist	Singer	Page No.
Akhiyan Milaake	Rattan	1944	Naushad	D.N. Madhok	Zohrabai	5, 30, 149, 209
Akhiyon Ki Jharakon Se	Akhiyon Ki Jharakon Se	1978	Ravindra Jain	Ravindra Jain	Hemlata	77
Akhiyon Ko Rahne De	Bobby	1973	Laxmikant-Pyarelal	Anand Bakshi	Lata	72
Allah Tero Naam Ishwar	Hum Dono	1961	Jaidev	Sahir	Lata	60-61, 115, 155
Ambar Ki Ek Paak Suraahi	Kaadambari	1974	Ustaad Vilayat Khan	Amrita Pritam	Asha	166
Angnaa Mein Baba	Aankhen	1993	Bappi Lahiri	Indeewar	Kumar Sanu, Alka Yagnik	79
Angrezi Mein Kehte Hain	Khuddaar	1982	Rajesh Roshan	Majrooh Sultanpuri	Kishore, Lata	80
Apne Aap Raaton Mein	Shankar Hussain	1977	Khayyam	Kaif Bhopali	Lata	76
Apne Jeevan Ke Uljhan Ko	Uljhan	1975	Kalyanji-Anandji	M.G. Hashmat	Lata and Kishore	66
Apni Toh Har Aah Ek Toofan Hain	Kaala Bazaar	1960	S.D. Burman	Shailendra	Rafi	181
Armaan Bhare Dil Ki Lagan	Jaan Pehchan	1950	Khemchand Prakash	Shakeel	Talat, Geeta Dutt	26
Ashqon Se Teri Humne	Dekh Kabira Roya	1957	Madan Mohan	Rajinder Krishan	Asha	163
Aur Kya Ahd-e-Wafa Hote Hain	Sunny	1984	R.D. Burman	Anand Bakshi	Asha and Suresh Wadkar	69, 167
Awaaz De Kahaan Hain	Anmol Ghadi	1946	Naushad	Tanvir Naqvi	Surendra, Noorjehan	5, 30, 145
Awara Hoon	Awara	1951	Shanker-Jaikishan	Shailendra	Mukesh	39, 116, 170
Aye Bhai Zara Dekh Ke Chalo	Mera Naam Joker	1971	Shanker-Jaikishan	Neeraj	Manna Dey	203
Aye Chand Chup Naa Jaana	Jawaab	1942	Kamal Das Gupta	Pt. Madhur	Kanan Devi	3
Aye Dil Aye Deewaane	Baaz	1953	O.P. Nayyar	Majrooh	Geeta Dutt	159
Aye Dil Hain Mushkil	CID	1956	O.P. Nayyar	Majrooh	Rafi, Geeta Dutt	108
Aye Dil Mujhe Aisi Jagah Le Chal	Aarzoo	1950	Anil Biswas	Majrooh	Talat	28, 108, 125
Aye Dil Mujhe Bata De	Bhai Bhai	1956	Madan Mohan	Rajinder Krishan	Geeta Dutt	48
Aye Dil-e-Naadan	Razia Sultan	1983	Khayyam	Jan Nisar Akhtar	Lata	15, 76
Aye Dil-e-Bekaraar Jhoom	Shahjehan	1946	Naushad	Majrooh	K.L. Saigal	31, 143
Aye Ghame-Dil Kya Karoon	Thokar	1954	Sardar Malik	Majaz	Talat and Asha	177
Aye Jaan-e-Jigar	Aaraam	1951	Anil Biswas	Rajinder Krishan	Mukesh	29, 169
Aye Kaatib-e-Taqdeer	My Sister	1944	Pankaj Mullick	Pt. Bhushan	K.L. Saigal	24-25, 144
Aye Khuda Har Faisla Tera	Abdullah	1980	R.D. Burman	Anand Bakshi	Kishore	192

217

Song	Film	Year	Composer	Lyricist	Singer	Page No.
Aye Malik Tere Bande Hum	Do Aankhen Barah Haath	1957	Vasant Desai	Bharat Vyas	Lata	62
Aye Mere Dil Kahin Aur Chal	Daag	1952	Shanker-Jaikishan	Shailendra	Talat and Lata	39, 116, 176
Aye Mere Dil-e-Nadaan	Tower House	1958	Ravi	Asad Bhopali	Lata	60
Aye Mere Humsafar	Qayamat Se Qayamat Tak	1988	Anand-Milind	Majrooh	Udit Narayan, Alka Yagnik	16, 83-84, 199
Aye Mere Humsafar Aye Mere Jaane Jaan	Baazigar	1993	Annu Malik	Gauhar Kanpuri	Vinod Rathod, Alka Yagnik	84
Aye Mere Pyaare Watan	Kaabuliwaala	1961	Salil Choudhury	Prem Dhawan	Manna Dey	57
Aye Meri Zohra Jabeen	Waqt	1965	Ravi	Sahir	Manna Dey	204-05
Aye Phoolon Ki Rani	Aarzoo	1965	Shanker-Jaikishan	Hasrat Jaipuri	Rafi	183
Aye Watan Ke Naujawan	Baaz	1953	O.P. Nayyar	Majrooh	Geeta Dutt	51, 159
Baadal Aaya Jhoom Ke	Shahjehan	1946	Naushad	Majrooh	Shamshad Begum	31, 149
Baadalon Mein Chup Raha Hain	Phir Teri Kahaani Yaad Aayi	1993	Annu Malik	Qateel Shifai	Kumar Sanu, Alka Yagnik	84
Baagh Lagaa Doon Sajani	Tansen	1943	Khemchand Prakash	D.N. Madhok	K.L. Saigal	26, 143
Baagon Mein Bahaar Hain	Aradhana	1969	S.D. Burman	Anand Bakshi	Rafi, Lata	185
Baalam Aaye Baso More Man Mein	Devdas	1935	R.C. Boral	Kidar Sharma	K.L. Saigal	142, 207
Baandhi Re Kaahe Preet	Sankoch	1976	Kalyanji-Anandji	M.G. Hashmat	Sulakshana Pandit	66
Baar Baar Dekho	China Town	1962	Ravi	Majrooh	Rafi	11, 183
Baat Chalat Nayi Chunari	Ladki	1953	Dhani Ram Sudarshanam	Traditional	Geeta Dutt	161
Baatein Bhool Jaati Hai	Yaadein	2001	Annu Malik	Anand Bakshi	Hariharan	127
Baazigar O Baazigar	Baazigar	1993	Annu Malik	Nawab Arzoo	Kumar Sanu, Alka Yagnik	84
Babuji Dheere Chalna	Aar Paar	1954	O.P. Nayyar	Majrooh	Geeta Dutt	51, 108, 160
Babul Mora Naihar Chootho Hi Jaaye	Street Singer	1938	R.C. Boral	Aarzoo Lucknawi	K.L. Saigal	4, 141, 143-44
Bachna Aye Haseeno	Hum Kisi Se Kum Nahin	1977	R.D. Burman	Majrooh	Kishore, Asha	192
Bachpan Ke Din Bhula Na Dena	Deedar	1951	Naushad	Shakeel	Lata, Shamshad Begum	150

218

Song	Film	Year	Composer	Lyricist	Singer	Page No.
Bachpan Ki Mohabbat Ko	Baiju Bawra	1952	Naushad	Shakeel	Lata	32
Bada Natkhat Hain Re	Amar Prem	1971	R.D. Burman	Anand Bakshi	Lata	156
Badi Barbaadiyan Lekar	Dhun	1954	Madan Mohan	Kaif Irfani	Lata	48
Badi Sooni Sooni Hain	Mili	1975	S.D. Burman	Yogesh Gaud	Kishore	191
Badnaam Mohabbat Kaun Kare	Dost	1944	Sajjad Hussain	Shams Lucknavi	Noorjehan	145
Bahaaron Phool Barsaao	Suraj	1966	Shanker-Jaikishan	Hasrat Jaipuri	Rafi	183
Baharein Phir Bhi Aayengi Magar Hum Tum Judaa Honge	Lahore	1950	Shyam Sunder	Rajinder Krishan	Lata	152
Baharon Mera Jeevan Bhi Sawaaron	Aakhri Khat	1966	Khayyam	Kaifi Azmi	Lata	76
Bairan Ho Gayee Rain	Dekh Kabira Roya	1957	Madan Mohan	Rajinder Krishan	Manna Dey	48
Baiyan Na Dharo	Dastak	1970	Madan Mohan	Majrooh	Lata	50
Bairan Neend Na Aaye	Chacha Zindabad	1959	Madan Mohan	Rajinder Krishan	Lata	48
Balma Anari Man Bhaaye	Bahurani	1963	C. Ramchandra	Sahir	Lata	37
Balma Khuli Hawa Mein	Kashmir Ki Kali	1964	O.P. Nayyar	Majrooh	Asha	54
Bandhan Toote Naa Saanwariya	Mome Ki Gudiya	1972	Laxmikant-Pyarelal	Anand Bakshi	Lata	72
Bane Ho Ek Khaak Se	Aarti	1962	Roshan	Majrooh	Lata	108-09
Barbaad-e-Mohabbat Ki Duaa Saath	Laila Majnu	1976	Madan Mohan	Sahir	Rafi	49, 186
Barsaat Mein Hum Se Mile	Barsaat	1949	Shanker-Jaikishan	Shailendra	Lata	38-39, 116, 150
Bechain Nazar Betaab Jigar	Yasmeen	1956	C. Ramchandra	Jan Nisar Akhtar	Talat	37
Beech Bhanwar Mein	Dard	1947	Naushad	Shakeel	Suraiya	111, 147
Beeti Na Bitayee Raina	Parichay	1972	R.D. Burman	Gulzar	Lata, Bhupinder	68, 123
Bekas Pe Karam Kijiye	Mughal-e-Azam	1960	Naushad	Shakeel	Lata	33, 112
Bekasi Hadh Se Jab Guzar Jaaye	Kalpana	1960	O.P. Nayyar	Jan Nisar Akhtar	Asha	53, 164
Bhai Battoor	Padosan	1968	R.D. Burman	Rajinder Krishan	Lata	155
Bhay Banjana	Basant Bahaar	1956	Shanker-Jaikishan	Shailendra	Manna Dey	202
Bheeni Bheeni	1947- Earth	1999	A.R. Rahman	Javed Akhtar	Hariharan	282

Song	Film	Year	Composer	Lyricist	Singer	Page No.
Bholi Soorat Dil Ke Khote	Albela	1950	C. Ramchandra	Rajinder Krishan	Lata, Chitalkar	37
Bhool Gaya Sab Kuch	Julie	1975	Rajesh Roshan	Anand Bakshi	Kishore, Lata	80
Bhooli Huyi Yaadon	Sanjog	1961	Madan Mohan	Rajinder Krishan	Mukesh	173
Bhoolne Waale Yaad Na Aa	Anokhi Ada	1948	Naushad	Shakeel	Mukesh	170
Bhor Bhaye Panghat Pe	Satyam Shivam Sundaram	1978	Laxmikant-Pyarelal	Anand Bakshi	Lata	72
Bhuja Diye Hain Khud Apne	Shagun	1965	Khayyam	Sahir	Suman Kalyanpur	75
Bichde Huye Pardesi	Barsaat	1949	Shanker-Jaikishan	Hasrat Jaipuri	Lata	38
Bichde Sabi Baari Baari	Kaagaz Ke Phool	1959	S.D. Burman	Kaifi Azmi	Rafi	10
Bin Tere Sanam	Yaara Dildaara	1990	Jatin-Lalit	Majrooh	Udit Naravan, Kavita Krishnamurthy	84, 110
Bindiya Chamkegi	Do Raaste	1969	Laxmikant-Pyarelal	Anand Bakshi	Lata	71
Bole Re Papihara	Guddi	1971	Vasant Desai	Gulzar	Vani Jairam	62
Booji Mera Kya Naam Re	CID	1956	O.P. Nayyar	Majrooh	Shamshad Begum	150
Bulbul Mere Chaman Ke	Heer	1956	Anil Biswas	Majrooh	Geeta Dutt	161
Bulbulon Mar Ro Yahaan	Zeenat	1945	Hafiz khan	Unknown	Noorjehan	145
Chaah Barbaad Karegi	Shahjehan	1946	Naushad	Majrooh	K.L. Saigal	31
Chaand Madham Hain	Railway Platform	1955	Madan Mohan	Sahir	Lata	48
Chaand Phir Nikla	Paying Guest	1957	S.D. Burman	Majrooh	Lata	44
Chaand Taare Tod Laoon	Yes Boss	1997	Jatin-Lalit	Javed Akhtar	Abhijeet	18
Chad Gayo Paapi Bicchua	Madhumati	1958	Salil Choudhury	Shailendra	Lata, Manna Dey	56, 117
Chahe Koi Mujhe Junglee Kahe	Junglee	1962	Shanker-Jaikishan	Shailendra	Rafi	12, 41, 117, 183
Chahoonga Main Tujhe Sanjh Savere	Dosti	1964	Laxmikant-Pyarelal	Majrooh	Rafi	72, 184
Chain Se Humko Kabhi Aapne Na Jaaye	Pran Jaaye Par Vachan Na Jaaye	1973	O.P. Nayyar	S.H. Bihari	Asha	54, 164
Chhaiyan Chhaiyan	Dil Se	1998	A.R. Rahman	Gulzar	Sukhwinder Singh, Sapna Awasti	82, 124

Song	Film	Year	Composer	Lyricist	Singer	Page No.
Chakke Pe Chakka	Brambachari	1969	Shanker-Jaikishan	Hasrat Jaipuri	Rafi	184
Chal Akela Chal Akela Chal	Sambandh	1969	O.P. Nayyar	Pradeep	Mukesh	106
Chal Diyaa Kaarwaan	Laila Majnu	1953	Ghulam Mohammed	Shakeel	Talat	177
Chal Ri Sajni Ab Kya Soche	Bambai Ka Babu	1960	S.D. Burman	Majrooh	Mukesh	172
Chal Ud Jaa Re Panchi	Bhabhi	1957	Chitragupta	Rajinder Krishan	Rafi	182
Chale Chalo	Lagaan	2001	A.R. Rahman	Javed Akhtar	Udit Narayan	82
Chale Pawan Ki Chaal	Doctor	1941	Pankaj Mullick	A.H. Shor	Pankaj Mullick	24
Chhalia Mera Naam	Chhalia	1960	Kalyanji-Anandji	Qamar Jalalabadi	Mukesh	64
Chalkaaye Jaam	Mere Humdum Mere Dost	1968	Laxmikant-Pyarelal	Majrooh	Rafi	109
Chalo Ek Baar Phir Se	Gumraah	1963	Ravi	Sahir	Mahendra Kapoor	60, 115
Chalte Chalte Mere Yeh Geet	Chalte Chalte	1976	Bappi Lahiri	Amit Khanna	Kishore	79
Chham Chham Baaje Re Paayaliya	Jaane Anjaane	1971	Shanker-Jaikishan	S.H. Bihari	Manna Dey	203
Chanchal Sheetal Nirmal Komal	Satyam Shivam Sundaram	1978	Laxmikant-Pyarelal	Anand Bakshi	Mukesh	174
Chand Chupa Baadal Mein	Hum Dil De Chuke Sanam	1999	Ismail Durbar	Mehboob Khan	Udit Narayan	194
Chand Hain Wohi	Parineeta	1953	Aroon Kumar	Bharat Vyas	Geeta Dutt	161
Chand Ko Kya Maaloom	Lal Bangla	1966	Usha Khanna	Indeewar	Mukesh	174
Chand Si Mehbooba Ho Meri	Himalay Ki Godh Mein	1965	Kalyanji-Anandji	Indeewar	Mukesh	64
Chanda Des Piya Ke Jaa	Bhartruhari	1944	Khemchand Prakash	Pt. Indra Chandra	Ameerbai	26
Chanda O Chanda	Lakhon Mein Ek	1972	R.D. Burman	Anand Bakshi	Kishore, Lata	68
Chanda Re Jaa Re Jaa Re	Ziddi	1948	Khemchand Prakash	Prem Dhawan	Lata	25-26, 152
Chandan Sa Badan	Saraswatichandra	1968	Kalyanji-Anandji	Indeewar	Mukesh and Lata	65, 173
Chandni Aayi Banke Pyar	Dulaari	1949	Naushad	Shakeel	Shamshad Begum	149
Chaudhvin Ka Chand Ho	Chaudhvin Ka Chand	1960	Ravi	Shakeel	Rafi	60
Ched Diye Mere Dil Ke Taar Kyon	Raagini	1958	O.P. Nayyar	Jan Nisar Akhtar	Salaamat and Amaanat Ali	53
Chehera Hain Ya Chaand	Saagar	1985	R.D. Burman	Javed Akhtar	Kishore	193
Chingaari Koi Bhadke	Amar Prem	1971	R.D. Burman	Anand Bakshi	Kishore	68, 126, 191
Chin-o-Arab Hamaara	Phir Subah Hogi	1958	S.D. Burman	Sahir	Mukesh	113

221

Song	Film	Year	Composer	Lyricist	Singer	Page No.
Chitthi Aayi Hain	Naam	1986	Laxmikant-Pyarelal	Anand Bakshi	Pankaj Udhas	73
Chhod Aakash Ko Sitaare	Maya Machindra	1932	Govindrao Tembe	Unknown	Govindrao Tembe	2
Chhod Aaye Hum Woh Galiyaan	Maachis	1996	Vishal Bharadwaj	Gulzar	Suresh Wadkar, Hariharan	124
Chhod De Saari Duniya Kisi Ke Liye	Saraswatichandra	1968	Kalyanji-Anandji	Indeewar	Lata	65
Chhod Do Aanchal Zamaana	Paying Guest	1957	S.D. Burman	Majrooh	Asha, Kishore	44, 108, 188
Chhod Gaye Baalam	Barsaat	1949	Shanker-Jaikishan	Hasrat Jaipuri	Mukesh	38, 170
Choli Ke Peeche Kya Hain	Khalnayak	1993	Laxmikant-Pyarelal	Anand Bakshi	Ila Arun,	17, 74, 127, 199
Chhookar Mere Man Ko	Yaarana	1981	Rajesh Roshan	Amit Khanna	Alka Yagnik	80
Chori Chori Koyi Aaye	Noorie	1979	Khayyam	Jan Nisar Akhtar	Kishore	76
Chori Chori Sola Singaar Karoongi	Manoranjan	1974	R.D. Burman	Anand Bakshi	Lata	166
Chota Sa Baalma	Raagini	1958	O.P. Nayyar	Qamar Jalalabadi	Asha	52, 163
Chota Sa Ghar Hoga	Naukri	1954	Salil Choudhury	Shailendra	Asha	187
Chun Chun Ghoongarwa	Mahal	1950	Khemchand Prakash	Nakshab Jarachavi	Kishore, Usha Mangeshkar	26
Chhun Chhun Ghungroo Bole	Phagun	1958	Hemant Kumar	Qamar Jalalabadi	Zohrabai, Rajkumari	52
Chhup Gaya Koi Re Door Se	Champakali	1958	Hemant Kumar	Rajinder Krishan	Asha	59
Chhupnewale Saamne Aa	Tumsa Nahin Dekha	1957	O.P. Nayyar	Majrooh	Lata	52, 108, 183
Chura Liya Hain Tumne Jo Dilko	Yaadon Ki Baaraat	1973	R.D. Burman	Majrooh	Rafi	68
Dafliwaale Dafli Bajaa	Sargam	1979	Laxmikant-Pyarelal	Anand Bakshi	Asha, Rafi	73, 126, 186
Dard Jagake Thes Lagake	Sipahiya	1949	C. Ramchandra	Ram Murthy Chaturvedi	Lata, Rafi	35
Dard Ki Raagini Muskura Ke	Pyaas	1984	Bappi Lahiri	Naqsh Lyallpuri	Lata	79
Dard Mandon Ka Jahaan Mein	Veena	1948	Anil Biswas	Swami Ramanand	Ameerbai	27
Dard-e-Dil	Karz	1980	Laxmikant-Pyarelal	Anand Bakshi	Rafi	72, 74, 126, 186
Darshan Pyaasi Aayi Daasi	Sangdil	1952	Sajjad Hussain	Rajinder Krishan	Geeta Dutt	161
De De Khuda Ke Naam Pe Pyaare	Alam Ara	1931	Phirozshah Mistry and Behram Irani	Unknown	Wazir Mohammed Khan	2

222

Song	Film	Year	Composer	Lyricist	Singer	Page No.
Deewana Leke Aaya Hain	Mere Jeevan Saathi	1972	R.D. Burman	Majrooh	Kishore	13
Dekho Kasam Se	Tumsa Nahin Dekha	1957	O.P. Nayyar	Majrooh	Asha, Rafi	52
Dekh Li Teri Khudai	Kinaare Kinaare	1963	Jaidev	Nyaya Sharma	Talat	61
Dekh Liya Maine	Deedar	1951	Naushad	Shakeel	Rafi, Lata	31, 179
Dekh Lo Aaj Humko Jee Bhar Ke	Bazaar	1982	Khayyam	Mirza Shauq	Jagjit Kaur	76
Dekh Sakta Hoon Main Kuch Bhi	Majboor	1974	Laxmikant-Pyarelal	Anand Bakshi	Kishore	72, 125
Dekha Hain Pehli Baar	Saajan	1991	Nadeem-Shravan	Sameer	Alka Yagnik, S.P. Balasubramaniam	199
Dekha Na Haaye Re Socha Na	Bombay To Goa	1972	R.D. Burman	Rajinder Krishan	Kishore	68, 192
Dekho Jaadu Bhare More Nain	Aasmaan	1952	O.P. Nayyar	Prem Dhawan	Geeta Dutt	51, 159
Dhadakte Dil Ki Tamanna	Shama	1961	Ghulam Mohammed	Kaifi Azmi	Suraiya	148
Dhak Dhak Karne Laga	Beta	1991	Anand-Milind	Sameer	Anuradha Paudwal, Udit Narayan	83, 196
Dharti Kahe Pukaar Ke	Do Bighaa Zameen	1953	Salil Choudhury	Shailendra	Manna Dey, Lata	55
Dharti Ko Aakaash Pukaare	Mela	1948	Naushad	Shakeel	Shamshad Begum	31, 149
Dheere Dheere Aare Badal	Kismet	1943	Anil Biswas	Pradeep	Ameerbai, Aroon Kumar	4
Dheere Jalna	Paheli	2005	M.M. Kreem	Gulzar	Sonu Nigam, Shreya Ghoshal	85
Dheere Se Aaja Ri Akhiyan Mein	Albela	1950	C. Ramchandra	Rajinder Krishan	Lata	36, 93
Dikhayee Diye Yun	Bazaar	1982	Khayyam	Mir Taqi Mir	Lata	15, 76, 157
Dil Aaj Shayar Hain	Gambler	1971	S.D. Burman	Neeraj	Kishore	46, 185, 191
Dil Cheez kya Hain	Umrao Jaan	1981	Khayyam	Shahryar	Asha	15, 76, 167
Dil Deewana Bin Sajna Ke	Maine Pyar Kiya	1989	Ram Laxman	Asad Bhopali	Lata and S.P. Balasubramaniam (solos)	16
Dil Deke Dekho	Dil Deke Dekho	1959	Usha Khanna	Majrooh	Rafi	108
Dil Dhoondta Hain	Mausam	1975	Madan Mohan	Gulzar	Bhupinder (solo), Bhupinder, Lata	47, 50, 122

223

Song	Film	Year	Composer	Lyricist	Singer	Page No.
Dil Hain Chhota Sa	Roja	1993	A.R. Rahman	P.K. Mishra	Minmini	18, 81
Dil Hain Deewana	Aasmaan	1952	O.P. Nayyar	Prem Dhawan	Geeta Dutt	50, 159
Dil Hain Ki Maanta Nahin	Dil Hain Ki Maanta Nahin	1991	Nadeem-Shravan	Sameer	Kumar Sanu and Anuradha Paudwal	83, 195-96
Dil Jalta Hain Toh Jalne De	Pehli Nazar	1945	Anil Biswas	Aah Sitapuri	Mukesh	5, 28, 169, 175
Dil Jo Na Keh Saka	Bheegi Raat	1965	Roshan	Majrooh	Rafi	58, 82
Dil Ka Haal Sune Dilwaala	Shri 420	1955	Shanker-Jaikishan	Shailendra	Manna Dey	132, 203
Dil Ka Khilona Haaye Toot Gaya	Goonj Uthi Shehnai	1959	Vasant Desai	Bharat Vyas	Lata	62
Dil Ki Aawaaz Bhi Sun	Humsaaya	1968	O.P. Nayyar	Shewan Rizvi	Rafi	184
Dil Ki Kashti Bhanwar Mein	Palki	1967	Naushad	Shakeel	Lata	112
Dil Ki Pareshaaniyan	Humlog	1951	Roshan	Anil & Udhav	Mukesh	171
Dil Ki Umangen Hain Jawaan	Munimji	1955	S.D. Burman	Sahir	Hemant Kumar, Geeta Dutt	44
Dil Ki Yeh Aarzoo Thi Koi	Nikaah	1981	Ravi	Hasan Kamaal	Mahendra Kapoor, Salma Agha	60
Dil Kya Kare Jab Kisiko	Julie	1975	Rajesh Roshan	Anand Bakshi	Kishore	80
Dil Laga Kar Hum Yeh Samjhe	Zindagi Aur Maut	1964	C. Ramchandra	Shakeel	Asha	37
Dil Par Huaa Aisa Jaadoo	Mr. & Mrs. 55	1955	O.P. Nayyar	Majrooh	Rafi	180
Dil Shaam Se Dooba Jaata Hain	Sanskaar	1958	Anil Biswas	Sarshar Sailani	Asha	163
Dil Toh Paagal Hain	Dil Toh Paagal Hain	1997	Uttam Singh	Anand Bakshi	Lata, Udit Narayan	127
Dil-e-Naadan Tujhe Hua Kya Hain	Mirza Ghalib	1954	Ghulam Mohammed	Ghalib	Talat, Suraiya	9, 148
Din Dhal Jaaye Raat Na Jaaye	Guide	1965	S.D. Burman	Shailendra	Rafi	46, 117, 181
Disco Station Disco	Hathkadi	1982	Bappi Lahiri	Majrooh	Asha	79
Diwana Huaa Baadal	Kashmir Ki Kali	1964	O.P. Nayyar	Majrooh	Rafi, Asha	53
Diya Jalao	Tansen	1943	Khemchand Prakash	D.N. Madhok	K.L. Saigal	26, 143
Diye Jalte Hain	Namak Haraam	1973	R.D. Burman	Anand Bakshi	Kishore	69, 126
Do Deewane Shehar Mein	Gharonda	1977	Jaidev	Gulzar	Bhupinder, Runa Laila	123
Do Dil Toote Do Dil Haare	Heer Ranjha	1970	Madan Mohan	Kaifi Azmi	Lata	49
Do Hanson Ka Joda	Ganga Jumna	1961	Naushad	Shakeel	Lata	33

Song	Film	Year	Composer	Lyricist	Singer	Page No.
Do Naina Aur Ek Kahani	Masoom	1982	R.D. Burman	Gulzar	Arati Mukherjee	15, 124
Do Naina Matwaare Tihaare	My Sister	1944	Pankaj Mullick	Pt. Bhushan	K.L. Saigal	25
Door Hato Aye Duniyawalon	Kismet	1943	Anil Biswas	Pradeep	Ameerbai	4, 27, 105, 131
Door Rehkar Na Karo Baat	Amaanat	1970	Ravi	Sahir	Rafi	185
Dost Dost Naa Rahaa	Sangam	1964	Shanker-Jaikishan	Shailendra	Mukesh	117, 173
Dukh Ke Ab Din	Devdas	1935	R.C. Boral	Kidar Sharma	K.L. Saigal	4, 24, 101, 141-42, 144
Dukhi Man Mere	Funtoosh	1956	S.D. Burman	Sahir	Kishore	188
Dum Dum Diga Diga	Chhalia	1960	Kalyanji-Anandji	Qamar Jalalabadi	Mukesh	64
Dum Maaro Dum	Hare Rama Hare Krishna	1971	R.D. Burman	Anand Bakshi	Asha, Usha Uthup	66-67, 126, 165-66
Duniya Badal Gayee Meri Duniya	Babul	1950	Naushad	Shakeel	Shamshad Begum, Talat	149
Duniya Banaanewaale	Teesri Kasam	1966	Shanker-Jaikishan	Hasrat Jaipuri	Mukesh	173
Duniya Karen Sawaal Toh Hum	Bahu Begum	1967	Roshan	Sahir	Lata	114
Duniya Mein Logon Ko	Apna Desh	1972	R.D. Burman	Anand Bakshi	Asha, R.D. Burman	68
Duniya Na Bhaaye Mohe	Basant Bahaar	1956	Shanker-Jaikishan	Shailendra	Rafi	40, 116, 181
Eena Meena Deeka	Aasha	1957	C. Ramchandra	Rajendra Krishan	Kishore and Asha (solos)	37, 93
Ehsaan Tera Hoga Mujh Par	Junglee	1962	Shanker-Jaikishan	Hasrat Jaipuri	Rafi	184
Ek Akela Is Shaher Mein	Gharonda	1977	Jaidev	Gulzar	Bhupinder	123
Ek Bangla Bane Nyaara	President	1937	Pankaj Mullick	Kidar Sharma	K.L. Saigal	141
Ek Chatura Naar	Padosan	1968	R.D. Burman	Rajinder Krishan	Kishore, Manna Dey	67
Ek Do Teen	Tezaab	1988	Laxmikant-Pyarelal	Javed Akhtar	Alka Yagnik	15, 74, 128, 199
Ek Dukhiyaari Kahe	Ram Teri Ganga Maili	1985	Ravindra Jain	Ravindra Jain	Lata	77
Ek Haseen Sham Ko Dil Mera	Dulhan Ek Raat Ki	1966	Madan Mohan	Raja Mehdi Ali Khan	Rafi	183
Ek Jhooti Si Tasalli Woh Mujhe	Shisham	1952	Roshan	Zia Sarhadi	Mukesh	171
Ek Kali Naazon Se Pali	Khazanchi	1941	Ghulam Haider	D.N. Madhok	Shamshad Begum	4, 149
Ek Ladki Bheegi Bhaagi Si	Chalti Ka Naam Gaadi	1958	S.D. Burman	Majrooh	Kishore	188
Ek Ladki Ko Dekha Toh Aisa Laga	1942- A Love Story	1994	R.D. Burman	Javed Akhtar	Kumar Sanu	17, 70, 195

Song	Film	Year	Composer	Lyricist	Singer	Page No.
Ek Main Aur Ek Tu	Khel Khel Mein	1975	R.D. Burman	Gulshan Baawra	Asha, Kishore	168, 192
Ek Naya Sansar Basaa Lein	Naya Sansar	1941	Saraswati Devi & Ramachandra Pal	Pradeep	Ashok Kumar, Renuka Devi	105
Ek Raasta Hain Zindagi	Kaala Pathhar	1979	Rajesh Roshan	Sahir	Kishore, Lata	80
Ek Radha Ek Meera	Ram Teri Ganga Maili	1985	Ravindra Jain	Ravindra Jain	Lata	70, 157
Ek Ritu Aaye Ek Ritu Jaave	Sau Saal Baad	1966	Laxmikant-Pyarelal	Anand Bakshi	Manna Dey, Lata	73
Ek Tha Bachpan	Aashirwaad	1968	Vasant Desai	Gulzar	Lata	62
Ek Tu Na Mila Saari Duniya	Himalay Ki Godh Mein	1965	Kalyanji-Anandji	Indeewar	Lata	64
Gaa Mere Man Gaa	Laajwanti	1959	S.D. Burman	Majrooh	Asha	164
Gaadi Bulaa Rahi Hain	Dost	1974	Laxmikant-Pyarelal	Anand Bakshi	Kishore	125
Gaata Rahe Mera Dil	Guide	1965	S.D. Burman	Shailendra	Kishore, Lata	46, 87, 189
Gaaye Jaa Geet Milan Ke	Mela	1948	Naushad	Shakeel	Mukesh	170
Ganga Aaye Kahaan Se	Kaabuliwala	1961	Salil Choudhury	Prem Dhawan	Hemant Kumar	122
Gayi Tu Gayi Seeta Sati	Ram Rajya	1943	Shankar Rao Vyas	Ramesh Gupta	Manna Dey	202
Ghabra Ke Jo Hum Sar Ko	Mahal	1950	Khemchand Prakash	Nakshab Jarachavi	Rajkumari	26
Ghanan Ghanan	Lagaan	2001	A.R. Rahman	Javed Akhtar	Udit Narayan, Alka Yagnik	82
Chapla Hain	Hu Tu Tu	1999	Vishal Bharadwaj	Gulzar	Roop Kumar Rathod	135
Ghar Aaja Ghir Aayee Badra	Chote Nawaab	1961	R.D. Burman	Shailendra	Lata	67
Ghar Ghar Mein Diwaali Hain	Kismet	1943	Anil Biswas	Pradeep	Ameerbai	105
Ghar Se Nikalte Hi	Papa Kehte Hain	1996	Rajesh Roshan	Javed Akhtar	Udit Narayan	81
Ghazab Ka Hain Din Socho Zara	Qayamat Se Qayamat Tak	1988	Anand-Milind	Majrooh	Udit Narayan, Alka Yagnik	83
Goli Maar Bheje Mein	Satya	1999	Vishal Bharadwaj	Gulzar	Mano	135
Gore Gore O Baanke Chore	Samadhi	1949	C. Ramchandra	Rajinder Krishan	Lata, Ameerbai	9, 37
Gum Hain Kisi Ke Pyar Mein	Rampur Ka Laxman	1972	R.D. Burman	Majrooh	Kishore, Lata	68
Gunguna Rahen Hain Bhawre	Aradhana	1969	S.D. Burman	Anand Bakshi	Rafi, Asha	185
Guzar Gaya Woh Zamana Kaisa	Doctor	1941	Pankaj Mullick	A.H. Shore	Pankaj Mullick	25
Guzren Hain Aaj Ishq Mein	Dil Diya Dard Liya	1966	Naushad	Shakeel	Rafi	112

Song	Film	Year	Composer	Lyricist	Singer	Page No.
Haay Haay Yeh Majboori	Roti Kapda Aur Makaan	1974	Laxmikant-Pyarelal	Verma Malik	Lata	72
Haale-Dil Unko Sunana Tha	Fariyaad	1964	Snehal Bhatkar	Kidar Sharma	Suman Kalyanpur	102
Haathon Ki Chand Lakeeron Ka	Vidhaata	1982	Kalyanji-Anandji	Anand Bakshi	Suresh Wadkar, Anwar	66
Haaye Rama Yeh Kya Ho Gaya	Rangeela	1995	A.R. Rahman	Mehboob Khan	Hariharan	81-82
Hain Agar Dushman	Hum Kisi Se Kam Nahin	1977	R.D. Burman	Majrooh	Rafi, Asha	166, 186
Hain Isi Mein Pyaar Ki Aabroo	Anpadh	1962	Madan Mohan	Raja Mehdi Ali Khan	Lata	49
Hain Sab Se Madhur Woh Geet	Patita	1953	Shanker-Jaikishan	Shailendra	Talat	39, 116, 176
Hamaare Baad Ab Mehfil Mein	Bhaagi	1953	Madan Mohan	Majrooh	Lata	47
Hamaare Dil Se Na Jaana	Udan Khatola	1955	Naushad	Shakeel	Lata	32
Hamen Aur Jeene Ki Chahat Na Hoti	Agar Tum Na Hote	1984	R.D. Burman	Gulshan Baawra	Kishore and Lata	193
Hamen Toh Shaam-e-Gham Mein	Jugnu	1947	Firoze Nizami	Asghar Sarhady	Noorjehan	6, 146
Hamen Raaston Ki Zaroorat	Naram Garam	1982	R.D. Burman	Gulzar	Asha	167
Hamen Tumse Pyar Kitna	Kudrat	1981	R.D. Burman	Majrooh	Begum Parveen Sultana and Kishore (solos)	70, 109-10, 193
Hamne Dekhi Hain Un Aankhon	Khamoshi	1969	Hemant Kumar	Gulzar	Lata	59, 122
Har Kisi Ko Nahin Milta Yahaan	Jaanbaaz	1986	Kalyanji-Anandji	Indeewar	Manhar, Sadhna Sargam	66
Har Taraf Ab Yahin Afsaane Hain	Hindustan Ki Kasam	1973	Madan Mohan	Kaifi Azmi	Manna Dey	203
Hari Om Hari	Pyaara Dushman	1980	Bappi Lahiri	Anjaan	Usha Uthup	79
Hasne Ki Chaah Ne Itna Mujhe	Aavishkaar	1974	Kanu Roy	Kapil Kumar	Manna Dey	123
Hawa Hawaai	Mr. India	1987	Laxmikant-Pyarelal	Javed Akhtar	Kavita Krishnamurthy	15, 128, 197
Hawa Ke Saath Saath	Seeta Aur Geeta	1972	R.D. Burman	Anand Bakshi	Kishore, Asha	68
Hindustan Ke Hum Hain	Pehle Aap	1944	Naushad	D.N. Madhok	Rafi	5
Ho Raamji Bada Dukh Deena	Ram Lakhan	1989	Laxmikant-Pyarelal	Anand Bakshi	Lata	72
Hoke Majboor Usne Mujhe	Haqeeqat	1964	Madan Mohan	Kaifi Azmi	Talat, Rafi, Bhupinder	129
Hoton Pe Beeti Baat Aayi Hain	Angoor	1982	R.D. Burman	Gulzar	Asha	168
Hoton Pe Sachchayi Rehti Hain	Jis Desh Mein Ganga Behti Hain	1961	Shanker-Jaikishan	Shailendra	Mukesh	116, 173

227

Song	Film	Year	Composer	Lyricist	Singer	Page No.
Hum Aapki Aankhon Mein	Pyaasa	1957	S.D. Burman	Sahir	Rafi, Geeta Dutt	180
Hum Aur Tum Aur Yeh Khushi	Alibaba	1940	Anil Biswas	Dr. Safdar 'Aah'	Surendra, Wahidan Bai	28
Hum Bane Tum Bane Ek Duje	Ek Duje Ke Liye	1981	Laxmikant-Pyarelal	Anand Bakshi	Lata, S.P. Balasubramaniam	73
Hum Bekhudi Mein	Kaala Paani	1958	S.D. Burman	Majrooh	Rafi	181
Hum Dard Ka Afsana	Dard	1947	Naushad	Shakeel	Shamshad Begum	149
Hum Dil De Chuke Sanam	Hum Dil De Chuke Sanam	1999	Ismail Durbar	Mehboob Khan	Kavita Krishnamurthy	197
Hum Hain Mataare-Koocha	Dastak	1970	Madan Mohan	Majrooh	Lata	50, 109
Hum Hain Raahi Pyaar Ke	Nau Do Gyarah	1957	S.D. Burman	Majrooh	Kishore	10, 108, 188
Hum Ishq Ke Maron Ko	Bhuumangal	1954	Bulo C. Rani	D.N. Madhok	Suraiya	104
Hum Ko Man Ki Shakti Dena	Guddi	1971	Vasant Desai	Gulzar	Vani Jairam	62
Hum Laaye Hain Toofan Se	Jaagriti	1954	Hemant Kumar	Pradeep	Rafi	106
Hum The Jinke Sahaare	Safar	1970	Kalyanji-Anandji	Indeewar	Lata	65
Hum Tujh Se Mohabbat	Awara	1951	Shanker-Jaikishan	Hasrat Jaipuri	Mukesh	39
Hum Tum Ik Kamre Mein	Bobby	1973	Laxmikant-Pyarelal	Anand Bakshi	Lata, Shailendra Singh	73, 125
Humko Hamin Se Churaa Lo	Mohabbatein	2000	Jatin-Lalit	Anand Bakshi	Lata, Udit Narayan	127
Humko Tumhaare Ishq Ne Kya	Ek Musafir Ek Haseena	1962	O.P. Nayyar	Shewan Rizvi	Rafi	53, 184
Humko Tumse Ho Gayaa Hain	Amar, Akbar, Anthony	1977	Laxmikant-Pyarelal	Anand Bakshi	Lata, Rafi, Mukesh, Kishore	125-26
Humne Jafaa Na Seekhi	Zindagi	1964	Shanker-Jaikishan	Hasrat Jaipuri	Rafi	117
Humne Tujhko Pyaar Kiya	Dulha Dulhan	1958	Madan Mohan	Indeewar	Mukesh and Lata (solos)	64, 173
Humsafar Saath Apna Chod Chale	Aakhri Dao	1957	Madan Mohan	Majrooh	Rafi, Asha	182
Humse Aaya Na Gaya	Dekh Kabira Roya	1985	Ravindra Jain	Rajinder Krishan	Talat	9, 48, 177
Husn Pahaadon Ka	Ram Teri Ganga Maili	1985	Ravindra Jain	Ravindra Jain	Lata, Suresh Wadkar	77
Huye Hum Jinke Liye Barbaad	Deedar	1951	Naushad	Shakeel	Rafi	31, 179
Huyi Shaam Unka Khayal Aa Gaya	Mere Humdum Mere Dost	1968	Laxmikant-Pyarelal	Majrooh	Rafi	72
I Am a Disco Dancer	Disco Dancer	1981	Bappi Lahiri	Anjaan	Vijay Benedict	15, 79
Ik Pyaar Ka Naghma Hain	Shor	1972	Laxmikant-Pyarelal	Santosh Anand	Lata, Mukesh	73-74
Ik Shahenshah Ne Banwa Ke Haseen Taj Mahal	Leader	1964	Naushad	Shakeel	Rafi, Lata	33, 112

Song	Film	Year	Composer	Lyricist	Singer	Page No.
Ik Tu Jo Mila Saari Duniya Mili	Himalay Ki Godh Mein	1965	Kalyanji-Anandji	Indeewar	Lata	64
Insaaf Ka Mandir Hain Yeh	Amar	1954	Naushad	Shakeel	Rafi	32
Insaan Bano	Baiju Bawra	1952	Naushad	Shakeel	Rafi	32, 180
Inteha Ho Gayi Intezaar Ki	Sharaabi	1984	Bappi Lahiri	Anjaan	Kishore, Asha	79
Intezaar Aur Abhi Aur Abhi	Char Dil Char Raahein	1959	Anil Biswas	Sahir	Lata	28
Is Mod Se Jaate Hain	Aandhi	1975	R.D. Burman	Gulzar	Lata, Kishore	69, 123, 192
Ishq Bina Kya Jeena Yaaron	Taal	1999	A.R. Rahman	Anand Bakshi	Udit Narayan, Alka Yagnik	82, 127
Itna Na Mujh Se Tu Pyaar Badha	Chhaya	1961	Salil Choudhury	Rajinder Krishan	Lata, Talat	55, 177
Itne Kareeb Aake Bhi	Shagun	1965	Khayyam	Sahir	Talat, Mubarak Begum	75
Ja Ja Ja Bewafa	Aar Paar	1954	O.P. Nayyar	Majrooh	Geeta Dutt	51, 160
Ja Re Ja Re Ud Ja Re Panchi	Maya	1961	Salil Choudhury	Majrooh	Lata	56
Jaane Jaan Dhoondta Phir Raha	Jawaani Diwani	1972	R.D. Burman	Anand Bakshi	Kishore, Asha	68, 166
Jaane Kahaan Gaye Woh Din	Mera Naam Joker	1971	Shanker-Jaikishan	Hasrat Jaipuri	Mukesh	173
Jaane Kya Baat Hain	Sunny	1984	R.D. Burman	Anand Bakshi	Lata	15, 69
Jaane Kya Dhoondti Rehti Hain Yeh	Shola Aur Shabnam	1961	Khayyam	Kaifi Azmi	Rafi	75, 119
Jaane Kya Tune Kahi	Pyaasa	1957	S.D. Burman	Sahir	Geeta Dutt	160, 204
Jaane Kyon Log Pyar Karte Hain	Dil Chahta Hain	2001	Shankar-Ehsaan-Loy	Javed Akhtar	Alka Yagnik, Udit Narayan	199
Jaane Na Nazar Pehchane Jigar	Aah	1953	Shanker-Jaikishan	Hasrat Jaipuri	Mukesh, Lata	39
Jaane Woh Kaise Log The	Pyaasa	1957	S.D. Burman	Sahir	Hemant Kumar	44
Jaanewaalo Zara	Dosti	1964	Laxmikant-Pyarelal	Majrooh	Rafi	72, 184
Jaayiye Aap Kahaan Jaayenge	Mere Sanam	1965	O.P. Nayyar	Majrooh	Asha	12, 53, 164
Jab Chali Thandi Hawa	Do Badan	1966	Ravi	Shakeel	Asha	165
Jab Dil Hi Toot Gaya	Shahjehan	1946	Naushad	Majrooh	K.L. Saigal	6, 24, 31, 107-08, 143-44
Jab Dil Ko Satave Gham	Sargam	1950	C. Ramchandra	P.L. Santoshi	Lata	36
Jab Dweep Jale Aana	Chitchor	1976	Ravindra Jain	Ravindra Jain	Yesudas, Hemlata	77
Jab Hum Jawaan Honge	Betaab	1983	R.D. Burman	Anand Bakshi	Lata, Shabbir Kumar	126
Jadoo Hain Nasha Hain	Jism	2003	M.M. Kreem	Sayeed Quadri, Neelesh Mishra	Shreya Ghoshal	85

Song	Film	Year	Composer	Lyricist	Singer	Page No.
Jahaan Mein Aisa Kaun Hain	Hum Dono	1961	Jaidev	Sahir	Asha	61, 166
Jai Jagdish Hare	Anandmath	1952	Hemant Kumar	Traditional	Hemant Kumar, Geeta Dutt	59
Jaise Radha Ne Maala Japi	Tere Mere Sapne	1971	S.D. Burman	Neeraj	Lata	46
Jalte Hain Jiske Liye	Sujata	1959	S.D. Burman	Majrooh	Talat	45, 108, 177, 204
Jao Jao Nand Ke Lala	Rangoli	1962	Shanker-Jaikishan	Shailendra	Lata	41
Jawan Hain Mohabbat	Anmol Ghadi	1946	Naushad	Tanvir Naqvi	Noorjehan	5, 30, 145
Jawaan-e-Jaaneman	Namak Halaal	1982	Bappi Lahiri	Anjaan	Asha	79
Jayen To Jayen Kahaan	Taxi Driver	1954	S.D. Burman	Sahir	Talat and Lata (solos)	47
Jeet Hi Lenge Baazi Hum	Shola Aur Shabnam	1961	Khayyam	Kaifi Azmi	Rafi, Lata	75
Jeevan Dor Tumhi Sang Baandhi	Sati Savitri	1964	Laxmikant-Pyarelal	Bharat Vyas	Lata	71
Jeevan Hain Madhuban	Jasoos	1955	Anil Biswas	Indeewar	Talat	29
Jeevan Ke Din Chote Sahi	Bade Dilwaala	1983	R.D. Burman	Majrooh	Kishore	110
Jeevan Ke Safar Mein Raahi	Munimji	1955	S.D. Burman	Sahir	Kishore and Lata	44, 113, 188
Jeevan Ki Bagiyan Mehkegi	Tere Mere Sapne	1971	S.D. Burman	Neeraj	Kishore, Lata	191
Jeevan Mein Piya Tera Saath Rahen	Goonj Uthi Shehnai	1959	Vasant Desai	Bharat Vyas	Rafi, Lata	183
Jeevan Sapna Toot Gaya	Anokha Pyar	1948	Anil Biswas	Behzad Lucknawi	Lata and Mukesh	28, 169
Jeevan Se Bhari Teri Aankhen	Safar	1970	Kalyanji-Anandji	Indeewar	Kishore	65
Jhan Jhan Jhan Jhan Paayal Baaje	Buzdil	1951	S.D. Burman	Sahir	Lata	43
Jhoom Jhoom Ke Naacho Aaj	Andaaz	1949	Naushad	Majrooh	Mukesh	170
Jhoomti Chali Hawa	Sangeet Samraat Tansen	1962	S.N. Tripathi	Shailendra	Mukesh	174
Jhopdi Mein Charpayee	Mawaali	1983	Bappi Lahiri	Indeewar	Kishore, Asha	79, 127
Jhuki Jhuki Si Nazar	Arth	1982	Jagjit and Chitra Singh	Kaifi Azmi	Jagjit Singh	15, 120
Jin Raaton Ki Bhor Nahin	Door Gagan Ki Chaon Mein	1964	Kishore Kumar	Shailendra	Kishore	189
Jinhe Naaz Hain Hind Par	Pyaasa	1957	S.D. Burman	Sahir	Rafi	11, 113, 180
Jis Dil Mein Basaa Tha Pyar Tera	Saheli	1965	Kalyanji-Anandji	Indeewar	Mukesh	173
Jis Gali Mein Tera Ghar Na	Kati Patang	1970	R.D. Burman	Anand Bakshi	Mukesh	126
Jise Tu Qabool Karle	Devdas	1955	S.D. Burman	Sahir	Lata	44

Song	Film	Year	Composer	Lyricist	Singer	Page No.
Jiya Jale	Dil Se	1998	A.R. Rahman	Gulzar	Lata	82, 158
Jiya Na Laage Mora	Budda Mil Gaya	1971	R.D. Burman	Majrooh	Lata	68
Jo Baar Tujh Mein Hain	Taj Mahal	1963	Roshan	Sahir	Rafi	58, 182
Jo Humne Daastan Apni Sunayi	Woh Kaun Thi	1964	Madan Mohan	Raja Mehdi Ali Khan	Lata	49
Jo Tum Todo Piya	Jhanak Jhanak Paayal Baaje	1955	Vasant Desai	Meerabai	Lata	62, 153
Jogi Jab Se Tu Aaya Mere Dwaare	Bandini	1963	S.D. Burman	Shailendra	Lata	45
Jogia Mere Ghar Aaye	Raagini	1958	O.P. Nayyar	Jan Nisar Akhtar	Ustaad Amir Khan	53
Jumma Chumma De De	Hum	1991	Laxmikant-Pyarelal	Anand Bakshi	Sudesh Bhosle and Kavita Krishnamurthy	17, 74, 127
Jurm-e-Ulfat Pe Hamen Log Sazaa Dete Hain	Taj Mahal	1963	Roshan	Sahir	Lata	58
Just Chill	Maine Pyar Kyon Kiya	2005	Himesh Reshammiya	Sameer	Jayesh Gandhi, Sonu Nigam, Amrita Kak	85
Justuju Jiski Thi	Umrao Jaan	1981	Khayyam	Shahryar	Asha	76, 167
Jyot Se Jyot Jagaate Chalo	Sant Gyaneshwar	1964	Laxmikant-Pyarelal	Bharat Vyas	Lata and Mukesh (solos)	71
Ka Karoon Sajni	Swami	1977	Rajesh Roshan	Amit Khanna	Yesudas	80
Kaahe Gumaan Kare	Tansen	1943	Khemchand Prakash	D.N. Madhok	K.L. Saigal	26, 143
Kaahe Koyal Shor Machaaye Re	Aag	1948	Ram Ganguly	Behzad Lucknawi	Shamshad Begum	149
Kaahe Sataaye	Qeyamat Se Qeyamat Tak	1988	Anand-Milind	Majrooh	Alka Yagnik	199
Kaali Ghata Chhaye Mora	Sujata	1959	S.D. Burman	Majrooh	Asha	45, 164
Kabhi Aar Kabhi Paar	Aar Paar	1954	O.P. Nayyar	Majrooh	Shamshad Begum	150
Kabhi Dil Se Takrata To Hoga	Anmol Ghadi	1946	Naushad	Tanvir Naqvi	Mukesh	169
Kabhi Khud Pe Kabhi Haalaat Pe Rona Aaya	Hum Dono	1961	Jaidev	Sahir	Rafi	11, 61
Kabhi Na Kabhi Kahin Na Kahin	Sharaabi	1964	Madan Mohan	Rajinder Krishan	Rafi	182
Kabhi Tanhaiyon Mein Yun	Hamari Yaad Aayegi	1961	Snehal Bhatkar	Kidar Sharma	Mubarak Begum	102
Kabhi Kabhie Mere Dil Mein	Kabhie Kabhie	1975	Khayyam	Sahir	Mukesh and Lata	76

231

Song	Film	Year	Composer	Lyricist	Singer	Page No.
Kahan Jaa Raha Hain	Seema	1955	Shanker-Jaikishan	Shailendra	Rafi	40
Kahin Deep Jale Kahin Dil	Bees Saal Baad	1962	Hemant Kumar	Shakeel	Lata	59
Kahin Door Jab Din	Anand	1970	Salil Choudhury	Yogesh	Mukesh	57, 174
Kajra Mohabbatwaala	Kismet	1968	O.P. Nayyar	S.H. Bihari	Sahmshad Begum, Asha	150
Kajra Re	Bunty Aur Babli	2005	Shankar-Ehsaan-Loy	Gulzar	Alisha Chinai, Shankar Mahadevan, Javed Ali	85, 124, 135
Kal Ho Na Ho	Kal Ho Na Ho	2003	Shankar-Ehsaan-Loy	Javed Akhtar	Sonu Nigam	129, 198
Kamsini Mein Dil Pe Gham Ka	Amritmanthan	1934	Keshavrao Bhole	Veer Mohammedpuri	Shanta Apte	3
Kar Chale Hum Fidaa	Haqeeqat	1964	Madan Mohan	Kaifi Azmi	Rafi	119, 182
Kareeb Aayi Nazar	Anita	1967	Laxmikant-Pyarelal	Raja Mehdi Ali Khan	Lata	71
Karoon Kya Aas Niras Bhayee	Dushman	1939	Pankaj Mullick	Aarzoo Lucknawi	K.L. Saigal	24
Kasme Waade Pyar Wafa	Upkaar	1967	Kalyanji-Anandji	Indeewar	Manna Dey	64, 204
Kathe Hain Dukh Mein Yeh Din	Parchayin	1952	C. Ramchandra	Noor Lucknawi	Lata	36
Kathti Hain Ab Toh Zindagi	Naaz	1954	Anil Biswas	Prem Dhawan	Lata	28
Katra Katra Milti Hain	Ijaazat	1987	R.D. Burman	Gulzar	Asha	69, 124, 167
Kaun Aaya Mere Man Ke Dwaare	Dekh Kabira Roya	1957	Madan Mohan	Rajinder Krishan	Manna Dey	48, 203
Kay Sera Sera	Pukar	1999	A.R. Rahman	Javed Akhtar	Kavita Krishnamurthy	198
Kayin Baar Yun Bhi Dekha Hain	Rajnigandha	1974	Salil Choudhury	Yogesh Gaud	Mukesh	57, 174
Kehdo Koi Na Kare Yahaan Pyaar	Goonj Uthi Shehnai	1959	Vasant Desai	Bharat Vyas	Rafi	62
Kehna Hain Kehna Hain	Padosan	1968	R.D. Burman	Rajinder Krishan	Kishore	67, 189
Kesariya Balma	Lekin	1990	Hridaynath Mangeshkar	Gulzar	Lata	157
Keraki Gulab Juhi Champak	Basant Bahaar	1956	Shanker-Jaikishan	Shailendra	Pt. Bhimsen Joshi, Manna Dey	40, 203
Khaike Paan Banaraswaala	Don	1978	Kalyanji-Anandji	Anjaan	Kishore	65
Khambe Jaisi Khadi Hain	Dil	1990	Anand-Milind	Sameer	Udit Narayan	83
Khayalon Mein Kisi Ke	Baawre Nain	1950	Roshan	Kidar Sharma	Geeta Dutt, Mukesh	58, 102
Khayi Hain Re Humne Kasam	Talash	1969	S.D. Burman	Majrooh	Lata	46

Song	Film	Year	Composer	Lyricist	Singer	Page No.
Khilona Jaan Kar Tum Toh	Khilona	1970	Laxmikant-Pyarelal	Anand Bakshi	Rafi	72
Khilte Hain Gul Yahaan	Sharmilee	1971	S.D. Burman	Neeraj	Kishore and Lata (solos)	191
Khoobsoorat Haseena	Mr. X in Bombay	1964	Laxmikant-Pyarelal	Anand Bakshi	Kishore, Lata	73, 84
Khuda Nigehbaan Ho Tumhara	Mughal-e-Azam	1960	Naushad	Shakeel	Lata	33, 112
Kise Yaad Rakhoon Kise	Anuraag	1956	Mukesh	Kaif Irfani	Mukesh	171
Kisi Baat Par Main Kisi Se	Bemisaal	1982	R.D. Burman	Anand Bakshi	Kishore	193
Kisi Ne Apna Banake Mujhko	Patita	1953	Shanker-Jaikishan	Shailendra	Lata	116
Kiska Rasta Dekhein	Joshilaa	1973	R.D. Burman	Sahir	Kishore	69
Kisko Pyar Karoon	Tumse Achcha Kaun Hain	1967	Shanker-Jaikishan	Rajinder Krishan	Rafi	12, 184
Kitna Haseen Hain Mausam	Azaad	1955	C. Ramchandra	Rajinder Krishan	Lata, Chitalkar	37
Koi Chupke Se Aake	Anubhav	1971	Kanu Roy	Gulzar	Geeta Dutt	162
Koi Door Se Aawaaz De Chale Aao	Sahib Bibi Aur Ghulam	1962	Hemant Kumar	Shakeel	Geeta Dutt	59, 162
Koi Gaata Main So Jaata	Aalaap	1977	Jaidev	Rahi Masoom Raza	Yesudas	61
Koi Hota Jisko Apna	Mere Apne	1971	Salil Choudhury	Gulzar	Kishore	57, 122
Koi Humdum Na Rahaa	Jhumroo	1961	Kishore Kumar	J.S. Kashyap 'Natwan	Kishore	189, 191
Koi Jab Tumhaara Hriday Tod De	Purab Aur Paschim	1970	Kalyanji-Anandji	Indeewar	Mukesh	65, 173
Koi Lauta De Mere Beete Huye Din	Door Gagan Ki Chaon Mein	1964	Kishore Kumar	Shailendra	Kishore	189
Koi Matwala Aaya Mere Dwaare	Love In Tokyo	1966	Shanker-Jaikishan	Shailendra	Lata	41
Koi Saagar Dil Ko Behlata Nahin	Dil Diya Dard Liya	1966	Naushad	Shakeel	Rafi	33
Kuch Aur Zamana Kehta Hain	Chhoti Chhoti Baatein	1965	Anil Biswas	Shailendra	Meena Kapoor	26, 117
Kuch Dil Ne Kahaa	Anupama	1966	Hemant Kumar	Kaifi Azmi	Lata	59, 119
Kuch Na Kaho	1942-A Love Story	1994	R.D. Burman	Javed Akhtar	Kumar Sanu and Lata (solos)	17, 70
Kuch Toh Huaa Hain	Kal Ho Na Ho	2003	Shankar-Ehsaan-Loy	Javed Akhtar	Alka Yagnik, Shaan	199
Kuch Toh Log Kahenge	Amar Prem	1971	R.D. Burman	Anand Bakshi	Kishore	13, 68, 191
Hum Kisi Se Kum Nahin	Hum Kisi Se Kum Nahin	1977	R.D. Burman	Majrooh	Rafi	186
Kya Huaa Tera Waada	Lal Dupatta Malmal Ka	1989	Anand-Milind	Majrooh	Anuradha Paudwal, Anwar	110
Kya Karte The Sajna						
Kya Mausam Hain	Doosra Aadmi	1977	Rajesh Roshan	Majrooh	Rafi, Lata, Kishore	80

233

Song	Film	Year	Composer	Lyricist	Singer	Page No.
Kya Se Kya Ho Gaya	Guide	1965	S.D. Burman	Shailendra	Rafi	46, 117, 181
Kya Yahi Pyaar Hain	Rocky	1981	R.D. Burman	Anand Bakshi	Lata, Kishore	126
Kyon Zindagi Ki Raah Mein	Saath Saath	1982	Kuldeep Singh	Javed Akhtar	Chitra Singh	128
Laaga Chunri Mein Daag	Dil Hi To Hain	1963	Roshan	Sahir	Manna Dey	58, 202, 205
Lag Jaa Gale	Woh Kaun Thi	1964	Madan Mohan	Raja Mehdi Ali Khan	Lata	11, 155
Laila O Laila	Qurbani	1980	Kalyanji-Anandji	Indeewar	Amit Kumar, Kanchan	66
Lakdi Ki Kathi	Masoom	1982	R.D. Burman	Gulzar	Vanita Mishra, Gauri Bapat, Gurpreet Kaur	135
Lal Chadi Maidan Khadi	Jaanwar	1965	Shanker-Jaikishan	Shailendra	Rafi	184
Lambi Judaai	Hero	1983	Laxmikant-Pyarelal	Anand Bakshi	Reshma	74
Lekar Hum Deewana Dil	Yaadon Ki Baarraat	1973	R.D. Burman	Majrooh	Asha, Kishore	68, 109, 192
Leke Pehla Pehla Pyar	CID	1956	O.P. Nayyar	Majrooh	Rafi, Shamshad Begum, Asha	150
Liye Sapne Nigahon Mein	Mashaal	1984	Hridaynath Mangeshkar	Javed Akhtar	Kishore	193
Maana Ho Tum Behad Haseen	Toote Khilone	1978	Bappi Lahiri	Kaifi Azmi	Yesudas	79
Maana Janab Ne Pukaara Nahin	Paying Guest	1957	S.D. Burman	Majrooh	Kishore	44, 188
Maang Ke Saath Tumhaara	Naya Daur	1957	O.P. Nayyar	Sahir	Asha, Rafi	51, 180
Machalti Aarzoo Khadi Hain	Usne Kahaa Tha	1961	Salil Choudhury	Shailendra	Lata	56
M-A-D Mad, Mad Maane Paagal	Dilli Ka Thug	1958	Ravi	Majrooh	Kishore, Asha	60
Madhbari Rut Jawan Hain	Nartaki	1940	Pankaj Mullick	Munshi Aarzoo	Pankaj Mullick	24
Madhuban Mein Radhika	Kohinoor	1960	Naushad	Shakeel	Rafi	32, 211
Madhukar Shyam Hamaare Chor	Bhakt Surdas	1942	Gyan Dutt	D.N. Madhok	K.L. Saigal	104, 143
Main Ban Ki Chidiya	Achyut Kanya	1936	Saraswati Devi	J.S. Kashyap 'Natwan'	Ashok Kumar, Devika Rani	2
Main Bhawara Tu Hain Phool	Mela	1948	Naushad	Shakeel	Shamshad Begum, Mukesh	31
Main Dil Hoon Ek Armaan Bhara	Anhonee	1952	Roshan	Sathyendra Athaiyya	Talat	58, 176
Main Duniya Bhula Doonga	Aashiqui	1990	Nadeem-Shravan	Sameer	Kumar Sanu, Anuradha Paudwal	17
Main Kaa Karun Ram Mujhe	Sangam	1964	Shanker-Jaikishan	Hasrat Jaipuri	Lata	12

234

Song	Film	Year	Composer	Lyricist	Singer	Page No.
Main Kya Janoon Kya Jaadoo Hain	Zindagi	1940	Pankaj Mullick	Kidar Sharma	K.L. Saigal	24, 143, 207
Main Na Bhooloonga	Roti Kapda aur Makaan	1974	Laxmikant-Pyarelal	Santosh Anand	Mukesh, Lata	73
Main Paagal Mera Manwa Paagal	Aashiana	1952	Madan Mohan	Rajinder Krishan	Talat	48, 176
Main Pal Do Pal Ka Shaayar Hoon	Kabhie Kabhie	1975	Khayyam	Sahir	Mukesh	76, 115, 174
Main Piya Teri Tu Maane	Basant Bahaar	1956	Shanker-Jaikishan	Hasrat Jaipuri	Lata	40
Main Shaayar Badnaam	Namak Haram	1973	R.D. Burman	Anand Bakshi	Kishore	126, 192
Main Shaayar Toh Nahin	Bobby	1973	Laxmikant-Pyarelal	Anand Bakshi	Shailendra Singh	73
Main Soya Akhiyan Meeche	Phagun	1958	O.P. Nayyar	Qamar Jalalabadi	Rafi, Asha	52
Main Toh Bhool Chali Babul Ka Des	Saraswatichandra	1968	Kalyanji-Anandji	Indeewar	Lata	65
Main Toh Ek Khwaab Hoon	Himalay Ki Godh Mein	1965	Kalyanji-Anandji	Indeewar	Mukesh	64, 173
Main Toh Giridhar Ke Ghar Jaaoon	Jogan	1950	Bulo C. Rani	Meerabai	Geeta Dutt	159
Main Tulsi Tere Aangan Ki	Main Tulsi Tere Aangan Ki	1978	Laxmikant-Pyarelal	Anand Bakshi	Lata	72, 125
Main Zindagi Ka Saath Nibhata Chala Gaya	Hum Dono	1961	Jaidev	Sahir	Rafi	61, 88
Maine Poocha Chand Se	Abdullah	1980	R.D. Burman	Anand Bakshi	Rafi	186
Maine Tere Liye Hi Saath Rang Ke	Anand	1971	Salil Choudhury	Gulzar	Mukesh	122
Mama Mia, Pom Pom	Justice Chaudhury	1983	Bappi Lahiri	Indeewar	Asha, Kishore	79
Mammaiyya Kero Kero Kero Mamma	Arjun	1985	R.D. Burman	Javed Akhtar	Shailendra Singh	128
Man Dole Mera Tan Dole	Naagin	1954	Hemant Kumar	Rajinder Krishan	Lata	59, 64
Man Ki Been Matwari Baaje	Shabab	1954	Naushad	Shakeel	Rafi, Lata	32
Man Kyon Behkaa	Utsav	1984	Laxmikant-Pyarelal	Vasant Dev	Lata, Asha	73
Man Mohana Bade Jhoote	Seema	1955	Shanker-Jaikishan	Shailendra	Lata	39, 153
Man Moorakh Kehna Maan	Meenakshi	1943	Pankaj Mullick	Pt. Bhushan	K.C. Dey	24
Man Mora Baawra	Raagini	1958	O.P. Nayyar	Jan Nisar Akhtar	Rafi	53
Man Re Tu Kaahe Na Dheer Dhare	Chitralekha	1964	Roshan	Sahir	Rafi	58, 114
Man Tarpat Hari Darshan Ko	Baiju Bawra	1952	Naushad	Shakeel	Rafi	32, 111, 179
Manzil Ki Chaah Mein	Devdas	1955	S.D. Burman	Sahir	Rafi	44

235

Song	Film	Year	Composer	Lyricist	Singer	Page No.
Marne Ki Duayen Kyon Mangoon	Ziddi	1948	Khemchand Prakash	Prem Dhawan	Kishore	25, 187
Mast Bahaaron Ka Main Aashiq	Farz	1967	Laxmikant-Pyarelal	Anand Bakshi	Rafi	72
Mat Jaa Jogi	Jogan	1950	Bulo C. Rani	Meerabai	Geeta Dutt	159
Mayee Ri Main Kaase Kahoon	Dastak	1970	Madan Mohan	Majrooh	Lata	50
Meet Na Mila Re Man Ka	Abhimaan	1972	S.D. Burman	Majrooh	Kishore	43, 46, 191
Megha Chaaye Aadhi Raat	Sharmilee	1971	S.D. Burman	Neeraj	Lata	43, 46
Mehbooba Mehbooba	Sholay	1975	R.D. Burman	Anand Bakshi	R.D. Burman	126
Mehendi Hain Rachne Waali	Zubeida	2000	A.R. Rahman	Javed Akhtar	Alka Yagnik	199
Mehfil Mein Jal Uthi Shama	Nirala	1950	C. Ramchandra	P.L. Santoshi	Lata	36
Mein Zindagi Mein Hardam Rota	Barsaat	1949	Shanker-Jaikishan	Hasrat Jaipuri	Rafi	38, 181
Mera Dil Bhi Kitna Paagal Hain	Saajan	1991	Nadeem-Shravan	Sameer	Kumar Sanu, Alka Yagnik	83, 195
Mera Dil Jo Mera Hota	Anubhav	1971	Kanu Roy	Gulzar	Geeta Dutt	162
Mera Dil Todnewaale	Mela	1948	Husnlal-Bhagatram	Shakeel	Shamshad Begum, Mukesh	31, 170
Mera Dildaar Na Milaaya	Shama Parwaana	1954	Naushad	Majrooh	Suraiya	148
Mera Jeevan Kora Kagaz	Kora Kaagaz	1974	Kalyanji-Anandji	M.G. Hashmat	Kishore	66
Mera Jeevan Saathi Bichad Gaya	Babul	1950	Naushad	Shakeel	Talat	176
Mera Joota Hain Japani	Shri 420	1955	Shanker-Jaikishan	Shailendra	Mukesh	10, 39, 116, 132, 170-71
Mera Karma Tu	Karma	1986	Laxmikant-Pyarelal	Anand Bakshi	Anuradha Paudwal, Mohammed Aziz	15
Mera Kuch Saamaan	Ijaazat	1987	R.D. Burman	Gulzar	Asha	69, 124, 167
Mera Man Tera Pyaasa	Gambler	1971	S.D. Burman	Neeraj	Rafi	185
Mera Naam Chin Chin Choo	Howrah Bridge	1958	O.P. Nayyar	Qamar Jalalabadi	Geeta Dutt	9, 52
Mera Naam Hain Shabnam	Kati Patang	1970	R.D. Burman	Anand Bakshi	Asha	13, 69, 126, 165
Mera Piya Ghar Aaya	Yaarana	1996	Annu Malik	Unknown	Kavita Krishnamurthy	84, 197
Mera Sunder Sapna Beet Gaya	Do Bhai	1947	S.D. Burman	Raja Mehdi Ali Khan	Geeta Roy (Dutt)	158
Mere Angne Mein	Laawaris	1982	Kalyanji-Anandji	Anjaan	Amitabh Bachchan and Alka Yagnik (solos)	66, 199

236

Song	Film	Year	Composer	Lyricist	Singer	Page No.
Mere Aye Dil Bata	Jhanak Jhanak Paayal Baaje	1955	Vasant Desai	Hasrat Jaipuri	Lata	62
Mere Desh Ki Dharti	Upkaar	1967	Kalyanji-Anandji	Indeewar	Mahendra Kapoor	64
Mere Dil Mein Aaj Kya Hain	Daag	1973	Laxmikant-Pyarelal	Sahir	Kishore	72, 192
Mere Dost Kissa Yeh Kya Ho Gaya	Dostaana	1979	Laxmikant-Pyarelal	Anand Bakshi	Rafi	186
Mere Labon Mein Chhipe	Baazi	1951	S.D. Burman	Sahir	Kishore	188
Mere Liye Woh Gham-e-Intezaar Chhod Gaye	Anokha Pyar	1948	Anil Biswas	Behzad Lucknawi	Lata and Meena Kapoor	28
Mere Mehboob Qayamat Hogi	Mr. X in Bombay	1964	Laxmikant-Pyarelal	Anand Bakshi	Kishore	72, 95, 125
Mere Mehboob Tujhe Meri Mohabbat Ki Kasam	Mere Mehboob	1963	Naushad	Shakeel	Rafi and Lata	33, 112, 183
Mere Naina Saawan Bhadon	Mehbooba	1976	R.D. Burman	Anand Bakshi	Kishore and Lata	192
Mere Naseeb Mein Aye Dost	Do Raaste	1969	Laxmikant-Pyarelal	Anand Bakshi	Kishore	72, 190-91
Mere Paas Aao Mere Doston	Mr. Natwarlal	1978	Rajesh Roshan	Anand Bakshi	Amitabh Bachchan	80
Mere Piya Gaye Rangoon	Patanga	1949	C. Ramchandra	Rajinder Krishan	Shamshad Begum, Chitalkar	7, 37
Mere Qismat Mein Tu Nahin Shaayad	Prem Rog	1982	Laxmikant-Pyarelal	Anand Bakshi	Suresh Wadkar	73
Mere Roothe Huye Chanda	Baawre Nain	1950	Roshan	Kidar Sharma	Rajkumari	131
O Mere Sanam O Mere Sanam	Sangam	1964	Shanker-Jaikishan	Shailendra	Mukesh, Lata	41
Mere Sapnon Ki Rani	Aradhana	1969	S.D. Burman	Anand Bakshi	Kishore	13, 185, 190
Mere Toote Hue Dil Se	Chalia	1960	Kalyanji-Anandji	Qamar Jalalabadi	Mukesh	64, 173
Meri Aawaaz Suno	Naunihal	1967	Madan Mohan	Kaifi Azmi	Rafi	120
Meri Dosti Mera Pyar	Dosti	1964	Laxmikant-Pyarelal	Majrooh	Rafi	72
Meri Veena Tum Bin Roye	Dekh Kabira Roya	1957	Madan Mohan	Rajinder Krishan	Lata, Rafi	48
Meri Yaad Mein Tum Na	Madhosh	1951	Madan Mohan	Raja Mehdi Ali Khan	Talat	48, 178
Mil Gayo Humko Saathi	Hum Kisi Se Kum Nahin	1977	R.D. Burman	Majrooh	Kishore, Asha	166, 192
Mile Na Phool Toh Kaanton	Anokhi Raat	1967	Roshan	Kaifi Azmi	Rafi	174, 182
Milke Bicchad Gayee Akhiyan	Rattan	1944	Naushad	D.N. Madhok	Ameerbai	30

Song	Film	Year	Composer	Lyricist	Singer	Page No.
Milo Na Tum Toh Hum Ghabraye	Heer Ranjha	1970	Madan Mohan	Kaifi Azmi	Lata	49
Mitwa Lagi Re Yeh Kaisi	Devdas	1955	S.D. Burman	Sahir	Talat	44, 176
Mitwaa O Mitwaa	Lagaan	2001	A.R. Rahman	Javed Akhtar	Udit Narayan, Alka Yagnik	82, 199
Mohabbat Aisi Dhadkan Hain	Anarkali	1953	C. Ramchandra	Rajinder Krishan	Lata	36
Mohabbat Hain Kya Cheez	Prem Rog	1982	Laxmikant-Pyarelal	Anand Bakshi	Lata, Suresh Wadkar	73
Mohabbat Hi Na Jo Samjhe Woh	Parchayin	1952	C. Ramchandra	Noor Lucknawi	Talat	37
Mohabbat Ki Jhooti Kahaani	Mughal-e-Azam	1960	Naushad	Shakeel	Lata	33
Mohabbat Turk Ki Maine	Do Raha	1952	Anil Biswas	Sahir	Talat	28
Mohan Ki Muraliya Baaje	Mela	1948	Naushad	Shakeel	Shamshad Begum	31
Mohe Bhool Gaye Sanwariya	Baiju Bawra	1952	Naushad	Shakeel	Lata	8, 32, 152
Mora Dheere Se Ghoonghat Uthaye Piya	Bhartruhari	1944	Khemchand Prakash	Pt. Indra Chandra	Ameerbai	26
Mora Gora Ang Lai Lai	Bandini	1963	S.D. Burman	Gulzar	Lata	45, 121
More Saajan Hain Us Paar	Bandini	1963	S.D. Burman	Shailendra	S.D. Burman	45, 172
Mori Chham Chham Baaje Paayaliya	Ghungat	1960	Ravi	Shakeel	Lata	60
Mose Chal Kiye Jaaye	Guide	1965	S.D. Burman	Shailendra	Lata	46
Mudh Mudh Ke Na Dekh	Shri 420	1955	Shanker-Jaikishan	Shailendra	Manna Dey, Asha	39
Mujh Se Mat Pooch Mere Ishq	Anarkali	1953	C. Ramchandra	Rajinder Krishan	Lata	36, 153
Mujhe Naaraaz Ho Toh Ho Jaao	Papa Kehte Hain	1996	Rajesh Roshan	Javed Akhtar	Sonu Nigam	198
Mujhe Ja Na Kaho Meri Jaan	Anubhav	1971	Kanu Roy	Gulzar	Geeta Dutt	123, 162
Mujhe Neend Na Aaye	Dil	1990	Anand-Milind	Sameer	Udit Narayan, Anuradha Paudwal	83
Mujhe Rang De Rang De	Takshak	1999	A.R. Rahman	Mehboob Khan	Asha	168
Mujhe Sach Sach Bata Do	Baawre Nain	1950	Roshan	Kidar Sharma	Mukesh, Rajkumari	102
Mujhko Is Raat Ki Tanhayi Mein	Dil Bhi Tera Hum Bhi Tere	1960	Kalyanji-Anandji	Shamim Jaipuri	Mukesh and Lata (solos)	173
Musafir Hoon Yaaron	Parichay	1972	R.D. Burman	Gulzar	Kishore	192
My Heart Is Beating	Julie	1975	Rajesh Roshan	Harindranath Chattopadhyay	Preeti Sagar	80

Song	Film	Year	Composer	Lyricist	Singer	Page No.
My Name Is Anthony Gonsalves	Amar Akbar Anthony	1977	Laxmikant-Pyarelal	Anand Bakshi	Kishore	72
Na Jaane Kyon	Chhoti Si Baat	1975	Salil Choudhury	Yogesh Gaud	Lata	56
Na Jao Saiyan Chuda Ke Baiyan	Sahib Bibi Aur Ghulam	1962	Hemant Kumar	Shakeel	Geeta Dutt	59, 162
Na Milta Gham Toh Barbaadi	Amar	1954	Naushad	Shakeel	Lata	111
Na Mooh Chhupa Ke Jiyo	Humraaz	1967	Ravi	Sahir	Mahendra Kapoor	115
Na Toh Karwaan Ki Talaash Hain	Barsaat Ki Raat	1960	Roshan	Sahir	Rafi, Manna Dey, Asha	58
Na Tu Zameen Ke Liye	Dastaan	1972	Laxmikant-Pyarelal	Sahir	Rafi	185
Na Yeh Chaand Hoga	Shart	1954	Hemant Kumar	S.H. Bihari	Geeta Dutt and Hemant Kumar (solos)	161
Naa Jiya Laage Naa	Anand	1970	Salil Choudhury	Gulzar	Lata	56, 122
Naache Man Mora Magan	Meri Soorat Teri Aankhen	1963	S.D. Burman	Shailendra	Rafi	45
Naam Gum Jaayega	Kinaara	1977	R.D. Burman	Gulzar	Lata, Bhupinder	69, 123
Nadi Naare Na Jao Shyam	Mujhe Jeene Do	1963	Jaidev	Sahir	Asha	61
Nafrat Karnewalon Ki Seene Mein	Johny Mera Naam	1970	Kalyanji-Anandji	Indeewar	Kishore	65
Nagma-o-Sher Ki Saughaat	Ghazal	1964	Madan Mohan	Sahir	Lata	11, 49
Naina Barse Rimjhim Rimjhim	Woh Kaun Thi	1964	Madan Mohan	Raja Mehdi Ali Khan	Lata	49
Nainon Mein Sapna	Himmatwala	1981	Bappi Lahiri	Indeewar	Asha, Kishore	15, 79
Nakhrewaali	Shararat	1959	Shanker-Jaikishan	Shailendra	Kishore	41
Nanhi Kali Sone Chali	Sujata	1959	S.D. Burman	Majrooh	Geeta Dutt	45, 160
Nainon Mein Badra Chaaye	Mera Saaya	1966	Madan Mohan	Raja Mehdi Ali Khan	Lata	49
Nazar Aati Nahin Manzil	Kaanch Aur Heera	1972	Ravindra Jain	Ravindra Jain	Rafi and Chandrani Mukherjee	185
Nazar Ke Saamne	Aashiqui	1990	Nadeem-Shravan	Sameer	Anuradha Paudwal, Kumar Sanu	196
Nazar Laagi Raaja Tore Bangle Par	Kala Paani	1958	S.D. Burman	Majrooh	Asha	164
Neele Aasmaane	Mr. & Mrs. 55	1955	O.P. Nayyar	Majrooh	Geeta Dutt	160
Neend Churaake Raaton Mein	Shareef Badmaash	1973	R.D. Burman	Anand Bakshi	Asha, Kishore	166
Nimbuda Nimbuda	Hum Dil De Chuke Sanam	1999	Ismail Durbar	Mehboob Khan	Kavita Krishnamurthy, Karsan Sargathia	197

239

Song	Film	Year	Composer	Lyricist	Singer	Page No.
Nukta Cheen Hain	Yahudi ki Ladki	1933	Pankaj Mullick	Ghalib	K.L. Saigal	23-24
Nukta Cheen Hain	Mirza Ghalib	1954	Ghulam Mohammed	Ghalib	Suraiya	142, 147
O Door Jaane Waale	Pyar Ki Jeet	1948	Husnlal-Bhagatram	D.N. Madhok	Suraiya	147
O Duniya Ke Rakhwale	Baiju Bawra	1952	Naushad	Shakeel	Rafi	40, 111, 179
O Ganga Maiyya	Chandan Ka Palna	1967	R.D. Burman	Anand Bakshi	Lata	67
O Ghata Saanwari	Abhinetri	1970	Laxmikant-Pyarelal	Majrooh	Lata	71
O Haseena Zulfonwaali	Teesri Manzil	1966	R.D. Burman	Majrooh	Asha, Rafi	109, 165
O Jaane Waale Ho Sake Toh	Bandini	1963	S.D. Burman	Shailendra	Mukesh	117, 172
O Jaanewale Mudh Ke Zara	Shri 420	1955	Shanker-Jaikishan	Hasrat Jaipuri	Lata	39
O Maria	Saagar	1985	R.D. Burman	Javed Akhtar	S.P. Balasubramaniam, Asha	70
O Mere Dil Ke Chain	Mere Jeewan Saathi	1972	R.D. Burman	Majrooh	Kishore	68
O Mere Pyar Aaja	Bhoot Bangla	1965	R.D. Burman	Hasrat Jaipuri	Manna Dey	67
O Mere Raaja	Johny Mera Naam	1970	Kalyanji-Anandji	Indeewar	Kishore, Asha	65
O Mere Sharmilee	Sharmilee	1971	S.D. Burman	Neeraj	Kishore and Lata	191
O Mere Sona Re	Teesri Manzil	1966	R.D. Burman	Majrooh	Rafi, Asha	69, 165
O Meri Pyari Bindu	Padosan	1968	R.D. Burman	Rajinder Krishan	Kishore	67
O Mitwaa	Jal Bin Machli Nritya Bin Bijli	1971	Laxmikant-Pyarelal	Majrooh	Lata	72
O More Sajna O More Balma	Baharon Ke Sapne	1967	R.D. Burman	Majrooh	Lata	67
O Mujhe Kisi Se Pyar Ho Gaya	Barsaat	1949	Shanker-Jaikishan	Jalal Malihabadi	Lata	38
O Neend Na Mujhko Aaye	Post Box No. 999	1958	Kalyanji Virji Shah	P.L. Santoshi	Hemant Kumar, Lata	64
O Nindayee Preetam	Stree	1963	C. Ramchandra	Bharat Vyas	Lata	37
O Priya Priya	Dil	1990	Anand-Milind	Sameer	Suresh Wadkar, Anuradha Paudwal	83, 196
O Saathi Re	Muqaddar Ka Sikander	1979	Kalyanji-Anandji	Prakash Mehra	Kishore and Asha (solos)	65
O Sajna Barkha Bahaar Aayee	Parakh	1960	Salil Choudhury	Shailendra	Lata	55-56
Oh Re Taal Mile Nadi Ke Jal Mein	Anokhi Raat	1967	Roshan	Indeewar	Mukesh	58

Song	Film	Year	Composer	Lyricist	Singer	Page No.
Om Shanti Om	Karz	1980	Laxmikant-Pyarelal	Anand Bakshi	Kishore	72-73
One Two Ka Four	Ram Lakhan	1989	Laxmikant-Pyarelal	Anand Bakshi	Mohammed Aziz, Anuradha Paudwal, Nitin Mukesh	15, 74, 127
Oopar Gagan Vishaal	Mashaal	1950	S.D. Burman	Pradeep	Manna Dey	202
Pal Bhar Mein Yeh Kya Ho Gaya	Swami	1977	Rajesh Roshan	Amit Khanna	Lata	157
Pal Do Pal Ka Saath Hamaara	The Burning Train	1980	R.D. Burman	Sahir	Rafi, Asha	115
Pal Pal Dil Ke Paas	Blackmail	1973	Kalyanji-Anandji	Rajinder Krishan	Kishore Kumar	66
Palbhar Ke Liye Koi Hamen	Johny Mera Naam	1970	Kalyanji-Anandji	Indeewar	Kishore, Usha Khanna	65
Panchi Baawra	Bhakt Surdas	1942	Gyan Dutt	D.N. Madhok	Khursheed	104
Panchi Jaa Peeche Raha Hain	Sharda	1941	Naushad	D.N. Madhok	Suraiya	103, 146
Panchi Nadiyaan Pawan Ke Jhoke	Refugee	2000	Annu Malik	Javed Akhtar	Sonu Nigam, Alka Yagnik	129, 198
Panna Ki Tamanna Hain	Heera Panna	1973	R.D. Burman	Anand Bakshi	Lata, Kishore	69
Papa Kehte Hain Bada Kaam Karega	Qayamat Se Qayamat Tak	1988	Anand-Milind	Majrooh	Udit Narayan	16, 83, 110, 194
Parbat Ke Us Paar	Sargam	1979	Laxmikant-Pyarelal	Anand Bakshi	Lata	72
Parbaton Ke Pedon Par	Shagun	1965	Khayyam	Sahir	Rafi, Suman Kalyanpur	75
Pardah Hain Pardah	Amar Akbar Anthony	1977	Laxmikant-Pyarelal	Anand Bakshi	Rafi	72, 186
Pardesion Se Na Akhiyan Milana	Jab Jab Phool Khile	1965	Kalyanji-Anandji	Anand Bakshi	Rafi	64, 125
Paththar Ke Sanam	Paththar Ke Sanam	1967	Laxmikant-Pyarelal	Majrooh	Rafi	109
Pehchaan Toh Thi Pehchaana Nahin	Grihapravesh	1979	Kanu Roy	Gulzar	Chandrani Mukherjee	123
Pehla Nasha Pehla Khumaar	Jo Jeeta Wohi Sikandar	1992	Jatin-Lalit	Majrooh	Udit Narayan, Sadhna Sargam	84, 107, 110
Pehle Jo Mohabbat Se Inkaar Kiya	Pardesi	1941	Khemchand Prakash	D.N. Madhok	Khursheed	103-04
Phir Chidi Raat Baat Phoolon Ki	Bazaar	1982	Khayyam	Maqdoom Mohiuddin	Talat Aziz, Lata	76
Phir Janam Lenge Hum	Phir Janam Lenge Hum	1977	Bappi Lahiri	Gauhar Kanpuri	Kishore, Lata	79
Phir Mujhe Deedar-e-Tar Yaad Aaya	Mirza Ghalib	1954	Ghulam Mohammed	Ghalib	Talat	176
Phir Tumhari Yaad Aayi Aye Sanam	Rustom Sohrab	1961	Sajjad Hussain	Jan Nisar Akhtar	Manna Dey, Rafi	91
Phir Wohi Raat Hain	Ghar	1978	R.D. Burman	Gulzar	Kishore	192

241

Song	Film	Year	Composer	Lyricist	Singer	Page No.
Phir Wohi Shaam Wohi Gham	Jahan Ara	1964	Madan Mohan	Rajinder Krishan	Talat	11, 49, 178
Piya Baawri Piya Baawri	Khubsoorat	1980	R.D. Burman	Gulzar	Asha	69, 167
Piya Bina Piya Bina	Abhimaan	1972	S.D. Burman	Majrooh	Lata	46, 109
Piya Milan Ko Jaana	Kapalkundala	1939	Pankaj Mullick	Pankaj Mullick	Pankaj Mullick	23-24
Piya Piya Na Laage Mora Jiya	Phagun	1958	O.P. Nayyar	Qamar Jalalabadi	Asha	52, 164
Piya Tose Naina Laage Re	Guide	1965	S.D. Burman	Shailendra	Lata	46, 117
Piya Tu Ab Toh Aaja	Caravan	1971	R.D. Burman	Majrooh	Asha, R.D. Burman	66, 67
Piyu Bole	Parineeta	2005	Shantanu Moitra	Swanand Kirkire	Shreya Ghoshal, Sonu Nigam	85
Poocho Na Hamein Hum Unke Liye	Mitti Mein Sona	1960	O.P. Nayyar	Raja Mehdi Ali Khan	Asha	54, 164
Poocho Na Kaise Main Ne	Meri Soorat Teri Aankhen	1963	S.D. Burman	Shailendra	Manna Dey	45, 117, 204-05
Poocho Na Yaar Kya Huaa	Zamaane Ko Dikhaana Hain	1981	R.D. Burman	Majrooh	Asha and Rafi	109
Preetam Aan Milo	Mr. & Mrs. 55	1955	O.P. Nayyar	Saroj Mohini Nayyar	Geeta Dutt	160
Preetam Daras Dikhaao	Chacha Zindabad	1959	Madan Mohan	Rajinder Krishan	Manna Dey, Lata	48, 53, 203
Preetam Meri Duniya Mein	Ada	1951	Madan Mohan	Prem Dhawan	Lata	47
Pukarta Chala Hoon Main	Mere Sanam	1965	O.P. Nayyar	Majrooh	Rafi	53, 184
Pyaar Par Bas Toh Nahin Hain	Sone Ki Chidiya	1958	O.P. Nayyar	Sahir	Talat and Asha (solos)	52, 163, 177
Pyaare Darshan Deejo Aaj	Jogan	1950	Bulo C. Rani	Meerabai	Geeta Dutt	159
Pyaar Ki Kashti Mein	Kaho Naa Pyaar Hain	1999	Rajesh Roshan	Saawan Kumar	Udit Narayan, Alka Yagnik	80, 199
Pyar Deewaana Hota Hain	Kati Patang	1970	R.D. Burman	Anand Bakshi	Kishore	190
Pyar Do Pyar Lo	Jaanbaaz	1986	Kalyanji-Anandji	Indeewar	Sapna Mukherjee	66
Pyar Hua Ikraar Hua	Shri 420	1955	Shanker-Jaikishan	Shailendra	Manna Dey, Lata	39, 203
Pyar Huaa Chupke Se	1942-A love Story	1994	R.D. Burman	Javed Akhtar	Kavita Krishnamurthy	70, 128, 197
Pyar Ka Tohfa Tera	Tohfa	1984	Bappi Lahiri	Indeewar	Asha, Kishore	79
Pyar Ke Is Khel Mein	Jugnu	1972	S.D. Burman	Anand Bakshi	Kishore	191
Pyar Kiya Toh Darna Kya	Mughal-e-Azam	1960	Naushad	Shakeel	Lata	33, 111, 154
Qadar Jaane Na	Bhai Bhai	1956	Madan Mohan	Rajinder Krishan	Lata	48
Raat Bhar Ka Hain Mehmaan	Sone Ki Chidiya	1958	O.P. Nayyar	Sahir	Rafi	52

Song	Film	Year	Composer	Lyricist	Singer	Page No.
Raat Kali Ik Khwaab Mein Aayi	Buddha Mil Gaya	1971	R.D. Burman	Majrooh	Kishore	109
Raat Ne Kya Kya Khwaab Dikhaaye	Ek Gaon Ki Kahaani	1957	Salil Choudhury	Shailendra	Talat	56
Raaton Ke Saaye Ghane	Annadaata	1972	Salil Choudhury	Yogesh Gaud	Lata	56
Radha Kaise Na Jale	Lagaan	2001	A.R. Rahman	Javed Akhtar	Asha, Udit Narayan	82
Radha Na Bole Na Bole Na Bole Re	Azaad	1955	C. Ramchandra	Rajinder Krishan	Lata	37
Raha Gardishon Mein Har Dam	Do Badan	1964	Ravi	Shakeel	Rafi	60
Rail Gaadi Chuk Chuk Chuk Chuk	Aashirwaad	1968	Vasant Desai	Harindranath Chattopadhyay	Ashok Kumar	62
Raina Beeti Jaaye	Amar Prem	1971	R.D. Burman	Anand Bakshi	Lata	13, 43, 68, 156
Raja Ki Aayegi Baraat	Aah	1953	Shanker-Jaikishan	Shailendra	Lata	39
Rajnigandha Phool Tumhaare	Rajnigandha	1974	Salil Choudhury	Yogesh Gaud	Lata	56
Ram Kare Aisa Ho Jaaye	Milan	1967	Laxmikant-Pyarelal	Anand Bakshi	Mukesh	125
Ramaiyya Vastavaiyya	Shri 420	1955	Shanker-Jaikishan	Shailendra	Rafi, Lata, Mukesh	39
Ramba Ho	Armaan	1981	Bappi Lahiri	Indeewar	Usha Uthup, Bappi	79
Rang Aur Noor Ki Baaraat Kise	Ghazal	1964	Madan Mohan	Sahir	Rafi	182
Rasik Balma	Chori Chori	1956	Shanker-Jaikishan	Hasrat Jaipuri	Lata	40
Rasiya Re Man Basiya Re	Pardesi	1957	Anil Biswas	Prem Dhawan	Meena Kapoor	29
Re Man Sur Mein Gaa	Lal Paththar	1971	Shanker-Jaikishan	Neeraj	Asha, Manna Dey	166, 203
Rehte The Kabhi Jinke Dil Mein	Mamta	1966	Roshan	Majrooh	Lata	58, 109, 155
Ritu Aaye Ritu Jaaye Sakhi	Humdard	1953	Anil Biswas	Prem Dhawan	Manna Dey, Lata	202
Roop Tera Mastana	Aradhana	1969	S.D. Burman	Anand Bakshi	Kishore	13, 185, 188, 190
Rote Rote Guzar Gayi Raat Re	Buzdil	1951	S.D. Burman	Sahir	Lata	43
Roz Roz Daali Daali Kya Likh Jaaye	Angoor	1982	R.D. Burman	Gulzar	Asha	69, 124, 167
Saagar Kinare	Saagar	1985	R.D. Burman	Javed Akhtar	Kishore, Lata	15, 70, 128, 167
Saanjh Dhale Gagan Tale	Utsav	1984	Laxmikant-Pyarelal	Vasant Dev	Suresh Wadkar	74
Saari Saari Raat Teri Yaad Sataaye	Aji Bas Shukriya	1958	Roshan	Farooq Kaiser	Lata	58
Saason Ki Zaroorat Hain Jaise	Aashiqui	1990	Nadeem-Shravan	Rani Malik, Sameer	Kumar Sanu and Anuradha Paudwal	16, 83

243

Song	Film	Year	Composer	Lyricist	Singer	Page No.
Saar Saheliyan Khadi Khadi	Vidhaata	1982	Kalyanji-Anandji	Anand Bakshi	Kishore, Anuradha and Alka Yagnik	15, 66
Saathi Haath Badhaana	Naya Daur	1957	O.P. Nayyar	Sahir	Rafi, Asha	52, 114
Saathi Na Koyi Manzil	Bambai Ka Babu	1960	S.D. Burman	Majrooh	Rafi	172, 181
Saathi Re Bhool Na Jaana	Kotwaal Saab	1977	Ravindra Jain	Ravindra Jain	Asha	77
Saathi Re Tujh Bin Jiya Udaas Re	Poonam Ki Raat	1965	Salil Choudhury	Shailendra	Lata	56
Saathiya Tune Kya Kiya	Love	1991	Anand-Milind	Majrooh	Chitra, S.P. Balasubramaniam	110
Saawan Ke Jhoole Pade	Jurmaana	1979	R.D. Burman	Anand Bakshi	Lata	126
Saawan Ke Nazaaren Hain	Khazanchi	1941	Ghulam Haider	D.N. Madhok	Ghulam Haider, Shamshad Begum	149
Sab Kuch Lutaa Ke Hosh Mein	Ek Saal	1957	Ravi	Prem Dhawan	Talat	60
Sab Kuch Seekha Humne Na	Anari	1959	Shanker-Jaikishan	Shailendra	Mukesh	41, 116, 172
Sach Bata Tu Mujh Pe Fida	Sone Ki Chidya	1958	O.P. Nayyar	Sahir	Asha, Talat	52
Saiyan Bina Ghar Soona	Aangan Ki Kali	1979	Bappi Lahiri	Shaili Shailendra	Lata, Bhupinder	79
Saiyan Jhooton Ka Bada Sartaj Nikla	Do Aankhen Barah Haath	1957	Vasant Desai	Bharat Vyas	Lata	62
Sajan Re Jhoot Mat Bolo	Teesri Kasam	1966	Shanker-Jaikishan	Shailendra	Mukesh	42
Sajan Sang Kaahe Neha Lagaye	Main Nashe Mein Hoon	1959	Shanker-Jaikishan	Hasrat Jaipuri	Lata	40
Sajanwa Bairi Ho Gaye Hamaar	Teesri Kasam	1966	Shanker-Jaikishan	Shailendra	Mukesh	42
Sajti Hain Yun Hi Mehfil	Kudrat	1981	R.D. Burman	Majrooh	Asha	167
Sandese Aate Hain	Border	1997	Annu Malik	Javed Akhtar	Roopkumar Rathod, Sonu Nigam	18, 84, 128-29, 198
Sansaar Se Bhaage Phirte Ho	Chitralekha	1964	Roshan	Sahir	Lata	102
Sapna Mera Toot Gaya	Khel Khel Mein	1975	R.D. Burman	Gulshan Baawra	Asha, R.D. Burman	69, 166
Sapnon Ki Suhaani Duniya Ko	Shikast	1953	Shanker-Jaikishan	Shailendra	Talat	176
Sar Jo Tera Chakraaye	Pyaasa	1957	S.D. Burman	Sahir	Rafi	181
Saranga Teri Yaad Mein	Saranga	1960	Sardar Malik	Bharat Vyas	Mukesh	84, 172
Sawan Ka Mahina Pawan Kare Sor	Milan	1967	Laxmikant-Pyarelal	Anand Bakshi	Mukesh, Lata	73, 125

244

Song	Film	Year	Composer	Lyricist	Singer	Page No.
Seene Mein Jalan	Gaman	1978	Jaidev	Shahryar	Suresh Wadkar	61
Seene Mein Sulagte Hain Armaan	Tarana	1951	Anil Biswas	D.N. Madhok	Talat, Lata	29, 176
Shaayaraana Si Hain	Phir Teri Kahaani Yaad Aayi	1993	Annu Malik	Qateel Shifai	Alka Yagnik	84, 199
Sham-e-Gham Ki Kasam	Footpath	1953	Khayyam	Ali Sardar Jafri	Talat	75, 176
Sharm Aati Hain Magar Aaj Yeh	Padosan	1968	R.D. Burman	Rajinder Krishan	Lata	67
Sheesha Ho Ya Dil Ho	Aasha	1980	Laxmikant-Pyarelal	Anand Bakshi	Lata	72
Shola Jo Bhadke	Albela	1951	C. Ramchandra	Rajendra Krishan	Lata, C. Ramchandra	9
Shyam Teri Bansi Pukare	Geet Gaata Chal	1975	Ravindra Jain	Ravindra Jain	Aarti Mukherjee, Jaspal Singh	77
Soch Ke Yeh Gagan Jhoome	Jyoti	1969	S.D. Burman	Anand Bakshi	Lata, Manna Dey	46
Soch Samajh Kar Dil Ko Lagaana	Jaal	1952	S.D. Burman	Sahir	Geeta Dutt	159
Socha Tha Kya Kya Ho Gaya	Anmol Ghadi	1946	Naushad	Tanvir Naqvi	Suraiya	146
Sochenge Tumhe Pyar Karen	Deewana	1992	Nadeem-Shravan	Sameer	Kumar Sanu	83, 195
Solah Baras Ki Baali Umar	Ek Duje Ke Liye	1981	Laxmikant-Pyarelal	Anand Bakshi	Lata	72, 126
Subah Ka Intezaar Kaun Kare	Jonu Ka Bhai	1955	Jaidev	Sahir	Lata and Talat	61
Suhaani Raat Dhal Chuki	Dulaari	1949	Naushad	Shakeel	Rafi	7, 31, 90, 179
Sun Bairi Balam Sach Bol Re	Baawre Nain	1950	Roshan	Kidar Sharma	Rajkumari	58, 102
Sun Ja Pukar	Phagun	1958	O.P. Nayyar	Qamar Jalalabadi	Asha	52
Sun Ri Pawan Pawan Puruvaiyya	Anuraag	1975	S.D. Burman	Anand Bakshi	Lata	47
Sun Sun Sun Sun Zaalima	Aar Paar	1954	O.P. Nayyar	Majrooh	Rafi, Geeta Dutt	51, 180
Suno Choti Si Gudiya Ki	Seema	1955	Shanker-Jaikishan	Hasrat Jaipuri	Lata	40
Suno Gajar Kya Gaaye	Baazi	1951	S.D. Burman	Sahir	Geeta Dutt	43
Suno Sajna Papihe Ne	Aaye Din Bahaar Ke	1966	Laxmikant-Pyarelal	Anand Bakshi	Lata	71
Suno Suno Ban Ke Prani	Amar Jyoti	1936	Keshavrao Bhole	Pt. Narottam Vyas	Shanta Apte	3
Sur Na Saje Kya Gaoon Main	Basant Bahaar	1956	Shanker-Jaikishan	Shailendra	Manna Dey	40, 181, 202, 205
Taaki, Taaki O Taaki	Himmatwaala	1981	Bappi Lahiri	Indeewar	Asha, Kishore	79
Taal Se Taal Mila	Taal	1999	A.R. Rahman	Anand Bakshi	Udit Narayan, Alka Yagnik	82
Taara Toote Duniya Dekhe	Malhaar	1951	Roshan	Indeewar	Mukesh	171

245

Song	Film	Year	Composer	Lyricist	Singer	Page No.
Taare Chaandni Afsaane	Baaz	1953	O.P. Nayyar	Majrooh	Geeta Dutt	51, 159
Tadap Yeh Din Raat Ki	Amrapali	1966	Shanker-Jaikishan	Shailendra	Lata	41
Tadbeer Se Bigdi Hui Taqdeer	Baazi	1951	S.D. Burman	Sahir	Geeta Dutt	9, 43, 87, 113, 159
Tang Aa Chuke Hain	Pyaasa	1957	S.D. Burman	Sahir	Rafi	44, 53, 180
Kashmakash-e-Zindagi Se Hum						
Tanha Tanha	Rangeela	1995	A.R. Rahman	Mehboob Khan	Asha	81, 168
Taqdeer Bani Bankar Bigdi	Mela	1948	Naushad	Shakeel	Shamshad Begum	31, 149
Tara Ri Yara Ri	Dastaan	1950	Naushad	Shakeel	Suraiya, Rafi	147, 179
Tareef Karoon Kya Uski	Kashmir Ki Kali	1964	O.P. Nayyar	Majrooh	Rafi	53, 183
Tehero Zarasi Der Toh	Savera	1958	Sailesh Mukherjee	Prem Dhawan	Geeta Dutt	161
Tere Bin Soone Nain Hamaare	Meri Soorat Teri Aankhen	1963	S.D. Burman	Shailendra	Rafi, Lata	45
Tere Bina Zindagi Se Koi	Aandhi	1975	R.D. Burman	Gulzar	Kishore, Lata	123
Tere Mere Milan Ki Yeh Raina	Abhimaan	1972	S.D. Burman	Majrooh	Kishore, Lata	191
Tere Mere Sapne Ab Ek Rang Hain	Guide	1965	S.D. Burman	Shailendra	Rafi	46, 117, 181
Tere Naina Talaash Karen	Talaash	1969	S.D. Burman	Majrooh	Manna Dey	204
Tere Nainon Ne Chori Kiya	Pyar Ki Jeet	1948	Husnlal-Bhagatram	D.N. Madhok	Suraiya	147
Tere Sur Aur Mere Geet	Goonj Uthi Shehnai	1959	Vasant Desai	Bharat Vyas	Lata	62
Teri Aankh Ke Aansoo Pee Jaaoon	Jahan Ara	1963	Madan Mohan	Rajinder Krishan	Talat	178
Teri Aankhon Ke Siva	Chirag	1969	Madan Mohan	Majrooh	Rafi and Lata	12, 109, 183
Teri Duniya Mein Dil Lagraa Nahin	Baawre Nain	1950	Roshan	Kidar Sharma	Mukesh	170
Teri Duniya Mein Jeene Se	House No. 44	1955	S.D. Burman	Sahir	Hemant Kumar	113
Teri Galiyon Mein Na	Hawas	1974	Usha Khanna	Saawan Kumar	Rafi	185
Teri Mehfil Mein Qismat Aazmakar	Mughal-e-Azam	1960	Naushad	Shakeel	Shamshad Begum, Lata	150
Teri Pyari Pyari Soorat Ko	Sasuraal	1961	Shanker-Jaikishan	Hasrat Jaipuri	Rafi	183
Teri Yaad Dil Se Bhula Ne	Hariyaali Aur Raasta	1962	Shanker-Jaikishan	Shailendra	Mukesh	173
Thandi Hawa Kaali Ghata	Mr. & Mrs. 55	1955	O.P. Nayyar	Majrooh	Geeta Dutt	139, 160
Thandi Hawa Yeh Channdni	Jhumroo	1961	Kishore Kumar	Majrooh	Kishore	189

246

Song	Film	Year	Composer	Lyricist	Singer	Page No.
Thandi Hawaayen Leheraake Aayen	Naujawaan	1951	S.D. Burman	Sahir	Lata	113
Thoda Hain Thode Ki Zaroorat Hain	Khatta Meetha	1977	Rajesh Roshan	Gulzar	Kishore, Lata	80
Toofan Mail	Jawaab	1942	Kamal Das Gupta	Pt. Madhur	Kanan Devi	3
Toote Huye Khwabon Ne	Madhumati	1958	Salil Choudhury	Shailendra	Rafi	31, 56, 117
Toote Naa Dil Toote Naa	Andaaz	1949	Naushad	Majrooh	Mukesh	170
Tora Mann Darpan Kehlaaye	Kaajal	1965	Ravi	Sahir	Asha	60, 165
Tori Jai Jai Kar	Baiju Bawra	1952	Naushad	Shakeel	Ustaad Amir Khan	32
Tu Chanda Main Chandni	Reshma Aur Shera	1972	Jaidev	Balkavi Bairaagi	Lata	61
Tu Cheez Badi Hain Mast Mast	Mohraa	1994	Viju Shah	Anand Bakshi	Udit Narayan, Kavita Krishnamurthy	127, 197
Tu Ganga Ki Mauj	Baiju Bawra	1952	Naushad	Shakeel	Rafi, Lata	31-32
Tu Hain Mera Prem Devta	Kalpana	1960	O.P. Nayyar	Qamar Jalalabadi	Rafi, Manna Dey	53, 205
Tu Hi Re	Bombay	1993	A.R. Rahman	Mehboob Khan	Hariharan, Kavita Krishnamurthy	197
Tu Hi Saagar Tu Hain Kinara	Sankalp	1974	Khayyam	Kaifi Azmi	Sulakshana Pandit, Vinod Sharma	76
Tu Hindu Banegaa Na Mussalman Banegaa	Dhool Ka Phool	1959	N. Dutta	Sahir	Rafi	114
Tu Jahaan Jahaan Chalega	Mera Saaya	1966	Madan Mohan	Raja Mehdi Ali Khan	Lata	11, 49, 155
Tu Jo Mere Sur Mein	Chitchor	1976	Ravindra Jain	Ravindra Jain	Yesudas, Hemlata	77
Tu Kaun Si Badli Mein Mere	Khandaan	1942	Ghulam Haider	D.N. Madhok	Noorjehan	104, 145
Tu Mera Chaand Main	Dillagi	1949	Naushad	Shakeel	Suraiya, Shyam	147
Tu Mera Jaanu Hain	Hero	1983	Laxmikant-Pyarelal	Anand Bakshi	Anuradha Paudwal, Manhar	15, 73, 126
Tu Mere Saamne Hain	Suhaagan	1964	Madan Mohan	Hasrat Jaipuri	Rafi	182
Tu Meri Zindagi Hain	Aashiqui	1990	Nadeem-Shravan	Sameer, Rani Malik	Kumar Sanu, Anuradha Paudwal	196

247

Song	Film	Year	Composer	Lyricist	Singer	Page No.
Tu Mile Dil Khile	Criminal	1995	M.M. Kreem	Indeewar	Kumar Sanu	85
Tu Pee Aur Jee	Des Pardes	1978	Rajesh Roshan	Amit Khanna	Kishore	80
Tu Pyaar Ka Sagar Hain	Seema	1955	Shanker-Jaikishan	Shailendra	Manna Dey	40, 116, 204
Tu Pyar Kare Ya Thukraaye	Dekh Kabira Roya	1957	Madan Mohan	Rajinder Krishan	Lata	48
Tu Tu Tu Tu Taara	Bol Radha Bol	1992	Anand-Milind	Sameer	Kumar Sanu, Sushma Shreshta	83
Tujh Sang Preet Lagaayi Sajna	Kaamchor	1982	Rajesh Roshan	Indeewar	Kishore, Lata	81
Tujhe Dekha Toh Ye Jaana Sanam	Dilwale Dulhaniya Le Jaayenge	1995	Jatin-Lalit	Anand Bakshi	Kumar Sanu, Lata	17, 84, 127
Tujhe Jeevan Ki Dor Se	Asli Naqli	1961	Shanker-Jaikishan	Hasrat Jaipuri	Rafi, Lata	41
Tujhe Kya Sunaoon Main Dilruba	Aakhri Dao	1958	Madan Mohan	Majrooh	Rafi	49
Tum Apna Ranjh-o-Gham	Shagun	1965	Khayyam	Sahir	Jagjit Kaur	75
Tum Bin Jaoon Kahaan	Pyar Ka Mausam	1969	R.D. Burman	Majrooh	Kishore and Rafi (solos)	190
Tum Bin Jeevan Kaise Beeta	Anita	1967	Laxmikant-Pyarelal	Raja Mehdi Ali Khan	Mukesh	173
Tum Dil Ki Dhadkan Mein	Dhadkan	2000	Nadeem-Shravan	Sameer	Kumar Sanu and Abhijeet (solos)	84, 196
Tum Gagan Ke Chandrama	Sati Savitri	1964	Laxmikant-Pyarelal	Bharat Vyas	Lata, Manna Dey	73, 204
Tum Itna Jo Muskura Rahe Ho	Arth	1982	Jagjit and Chitra Singh	Kaifi Azmi	Jagjit Singh	15, 120
Tum Jaao Jaao Bhagwan Bane	Chitralekha	1941	Jhande Khan	Kidar Sharma	Ram Dulaari	101-02
Tum Jo Mil Gaye Ho	Hanste Zakhm	1973	Madan Mohan	Kaifi Azmi	Rafi	49, 183
Tum Kamsin Ho Nadaan Ho	Aayee Milan Ki Bela	1964	Shanker-Jaikishan	Hasrat Jaipuri	Rafi	183
Tum Kya Jaano Tumhaari Yaad Mein	Shin Shinaki Babla Boo	1952	C. Ramchandra	P.L. Santoshi	Lata	36
Tum Mujhe Bhool Bhi Jaao	Didi	1959	Sudha Malhotra	Sahir	Sudha Malhotra, Mukesh	114
Tum Pukar Lo	Khamoshi	1967	Hemant Kumar	Gulzar	Hemant Kumar	59
Tumhaare Bulaane Ko Jee	Laadli	1949	Anil Biswas	Behzad Lucknawi	Lata	28, 152
Tumhaari Zulf Ke Saaye Mein	Naunihal	1967	Madan Mohan	Kaifi Azmi	Rafi	49, 183
Tumhe Apna Banaa Ne Ki Kasam	Sadak	1993	Nadeem-Shravan	Sameer	Anuradha Paudwal and Kumar Sanu (solos)	196

Song	Film	Year	Composer	Lyricist	Singer	Page No.
Tumhe Ho Na Ho	Gharonda	1977	Jaidev	Naqsh Lyallpuri	Runa Laila	61
Tumhen Yaad Hoga Kabhi Hum Mile The	Satta Bazaar	1959	Kalyanji-Anandji	Gulshan Baawra	Hemant Kumar, Lata	64
Tumko Dekha Toh Yeh Khayal Aaya	Saath Saath	1982	Kuldeep Singh	Javed Akhtar	Jagjit and Chitra Singh	15, 128
Tumne Mujhe Dekha Hokar	Teesri Manzil	1966	R.D. Burman	Majrooh	Rafi	185
Tumsa Nahin Dekha	Tumsa Nahin Dekha	1957	O.P. Nayyar	Majrooh	Rafi	52
Tumse Milkar Na Jaane Kyon	Pyar Jhukta Nahin	1984	Laxmikant-Pyarelal	S.H. Bihari	Kavita Krishnamurthy, Shabbir Kumar	73
Tumse Milke Hain Jo Dilka	Main Hoon Na	2004	Annu Malik	Javed Akhtar	Sonu Nigam, Sabri Brothers	198
Ud Jaa Panchi Ud Jaa	Khandaan	1942	Ghulam Haider	D.N. Madhok	Noorjehan	145
Udan Khatole Pe Ud Jaaoon	Anmol Ghadi	1946	Naushad	Tanvir Naqvi	Shamshad Begum, Zohrabai	149
Ude Jab Jab Zulfein Teri	Naya Daur	1957	O.P. Nayyar	Sahir	Rafi, Asha	51
Udhar Tum Haseen Ho	Mr. & Mrs. 55	1955	O.P. Nayyar	Majrooh	Rafi, Geeta Dutt	51
Udi Baba Udi Baba	Vidhaata	1982	Kalyanji-Anandji	Anand Bakshi	Asha	15
Umad Ghumad Kar Aayee Re Ghata	Do Aankhen Barah Haath	1957	Vasant Desai	Bharat Vyas	Chorus	62
Unke Khayal Aaye Toh	Lal Pathhar	1970	Shanker-Jaikishan	Hasrat Jaipuri	Rafi	185
Unko Yeh Shikayat Hain	Adalat	1958	Madan Mohan	Rajinder Krishan	Lata	9, 48, 154
Uthaye Jaa Unke Sitam	Andaaz	1949	Naushad	Majrooh	Lata	31, 107, 149, 152, 170
Uthe Sabke Kadam Dekho Rum Pum Pum	Baaton Baaton Mein	1979	Rajesh Roshan	Rajkavi Indrajeet Singh Tulsi	Lata, Amit Kumar	80
Waada Rahaa Sanam	Khilaadi	1994	Jatin-Lalit	Anwar Sagar	Abhijeet, Alka Yagnik	84
Wada Karo Nahin Chodoge	Aa Gale Lag Jaa	1973	R.D. Burman	Sahir	Kishore, Lata	68
Wah Wah Wah Khel Shuroo	Himmatwaala	1981	Bappi Lahiri	Indeewar	Asha, Kishore	79
Waqt Karta Jo Wafa	Dil Ne Pukara	1967	Kalyanji-Anandji	Indeewar	Mukesh	173
Waqt Ne Kiya	Kaagaz Ke Phool	1959	S.D. Burman	Kaifi Azmi	Geeta Dutt	45, 118, 160-61
Woh Din Kahaan Gaye Bataa	Taraana	1951	Anil Biswas	D.N. Madhok	Lata	104
Woh Hanske Mile Humse	Baharein Phir Bhi Aayengi	1966	O.P. Nayyar	Anjaan	Asha	54, 164

Song	Film	Year	Composer	Lyricist	Singer	Page No.
Woh Haseen Dard De Do	Humsaaya	1968	O.P. Nayyar	Shewan Rizvi	Asha	54, 164
Woh Jab Yaad Aaye	Parasmani	1963	Laxmikant-Pyarelal	Asad Bhopali	Rafi, Lata	73
Woh Paas Rahen Ya Door Rahen	Badi Behen	1949	Husnlal-Bhagatram	Qamar Jalalabadi	Suraiya	147
Woh Shaam Kuch Ajeeb Thi	Khamoshi	1969	Hemant Kumar	Gulzar	Kishore	59, 190
Woh Subah Kabhi Toh Aayegi	Phir Subah Hogi	1958	Khayyam	Sahir	Mukesh, Asha	11, 75, 172
Woh Toh Hain Albela	Kabhi Haan Kabhi Naa	1992	Jatin-Lalit	Majrooh	Kumar Sanu, Sadhna Sargam	110
Ya Dil Ki Suno Duniyawalon	Anupama	1966	Hemant Kumar	Kaifi Azmi	Hemant Kumar	59
Yaad Aa Rahi Hain	Love Story	1981	R.D. Burman	Majrooh	Lata, Amit Kumar	14, 126
Yaad Na Jaaye Beete Dinon Ki	Dil Ek Mandir	1963	Shanker-Jaikishan	Shailendra	Rafi	41, 117, 183
Yaara Seeli Seeli	Lekin	1990	Hridaynath Mangeshkar	Gulzar	Lata	124
Yaari Hain Imaan Mera	Zanjeer	1973	Kalyanji-Anandji	Indeewar	Manna Dey	65
Yaayi Re Yaayi Re	Rangeela	1995	A.R. Rahman	Mehboob Khan	Asha	81
Yahan Badla Wafa Ka	Jugnu	1947	Firoze Nizami	Asghar Sarhady	Noorjehan, Rafi	6
Ye Lo Main Haari Piya	Aar Paar	1954	O.P. Nayyar	Majrooh	Geeta Dutt	51, 160
Yeh Dil Aur Unki Nigahon Ke Saaye	Prem Parbat	1973	Jaidev	Padma Sachdev	Lata	61
Yeh Dil Deewaana	Pardes	1997	Nadeem-Shravan	Anand Bakshi	Sonu Nigam	83, 127
Yeh Dil Na Hota Bechara	Jewel Thief	1967	S.D. Burman	Majrooh	Kishore	189
Yeh Dil Tum Bin Kahin Lagta Nahin	Izzat	1969	Laxmikant-Pyarelal	Sahir	Rafi, Lata	73
Yeh Din Kya Aaye	Chhoti Si Baat	1975	Salil Choudhury	Yogesh	Mukesh	174
Yeh Dosti, Hum Nahin Todenge	Sholay	1975	R.D. Burman	Anand Bakshi	Manna Dey, Kishore	205
Yeh Duniya Agar Mil Bhi Jaaye	Pyaasa	1957	S.D. Burman	Sahir	Rafi	10, 44, 113, 180
Yeh Duniya Yeh Mehfil Mere Kaam Ki Nahin	Heer Ranjha	1970	Madan Mohan	Kaifi Azmi	Rafi	50, 119
Yeh Hariyali Aur Yeh Raasta	Hariyali Aur Raasta	1962	Shanker-Jaikishan	Hasrat Jaipuri	Lata	41
Yeh Hawa Yeh Raat Yeh Chaandni	Sangdil	1952	Sajjad Hussain	Rajinder Krishan	Talat	49, 176
Yeh Jawaani Hain Diwaani	Jawaani Diwaani	1972	R.D. Burman	Anand Bakshi	Kishore	192
Yeh Jeevan Hain	Piya Ka Ghar	1972	Laxmikant-Pyarelal	Anand Bakshi	Kishore	72, 125, 192

Song	Film	Year	Composer	Lyricist	Singer	Page No.
Yeh Jo Des Hain Tera	Swades	2004	A.R. Rahman	Javed Akhtar	A.R. Rahman	82
Yeh Jo Mohabbat Hain	Kati Patang	1970	R.D. Burman	Anand Bakshi	Kishore	13, 190
Yeh Kahan Aa Gaye Hum	Silsila	1981	Shiv-Hari	Javed Akhtar	Lata	15
Yeh Kaisa Sur Mandir Hain	Prem Nagar	1974	S.D. Burman	Anand Bakshi	Lata	47
Yeh Kaisi Ajab Daastan	Rustom Sohrab	1963	Sajjad Hussain	Kaifi Azmi	Suraiya	148
Yeh Kali Kali Akhen	Baazigar	1993	Annu Malik	Dev Kohli	Kumar Sanu	84
Yeh Kaun Aaj Aaya Savere Savere	Nartaki	1940	Pankaj Mullick	Munshi Aarzoo	Pankaj Mullick	24
Yeh Kya Huaa	Amar Prem	1971	R.D. Burman	Anand Bakshi	Kishore	68
Yeh Kya Jageh Hain Doston	Umrao Jaan	1981	Khayyam	Shahryar	Asha	76, 167
Yeh Ladka Haaye Allah	Hum Kisise Kam Nahin	1977	R.D. Burman	Majrooh	Asha, Rafi	109
Yeh Mera Deewanapan Hain	Yahudi	1958	Shanker-Jaikishan	Shailendra	Mukesh	172, 177
Yeh Mera Prem Patra Padhkar	Sangam	1964	Shanker-Jaikishan	Hasrat Jaipuri	Rafi	183
Yeh Mulaaqat Ik Bahaana Hain	Khaandaan	1979	Khayyam	Naqsh Lyallpuri	Lata	76
Yeh Na Thi Hamaari Kismet	Mirza Ghalib	1954	Ghulam Mohammed	Ghalib	Suraiya	147
Yeh Nayan Dare Dare	Kohraa	1963	Hemant Kumar	Kaifi Azmi	Hemant Kumar	59
Yeh Raaste Hain Pyaar Ke	Yeh Raaste Hain Pyaar Ke	1963	Ravi	Rajinder Krishan	Asha	165
Yeh Raat Yeh Chandni Phir Kahaan	Jaal	1952	S.D. Burman	Sahir	Hemant Kumar, Lata	111
Yeh Saayen Hain Yeh Duniya Hain	Sitaara	1980	R.D. Burman	Gulzar	Asha	167
Yeh Shaam Ki Tanhayiyan	Aah	1953	Shanker-Jaikishan	Shailendra	Lata	39
Yeh Shaam Mastaani	Kati Patang	1970	R.D. Burman	Anand Bakshi	Kishore	190
Yeh Taara Woh Taara	Swades	2004	A.R. Rahman	Javed Akhtar	Udit Narayan	194
Yeh Zindagi Ke Mele	Mela	1948	Naushad	Shakeel	Rafi	31, 179
Yeh Zindagi Usi Ki Hain	Anarkali	1953	C. Ramchandra	Rajinder Krishan	Lata	36
Yehi Woh Jagah Hain	Yeh Raat Phir Na Aayegi	1965	O.P. Nayyar	S.H. Bihari	Asha	164
Yun Hasraton Ke Daagh	Adalat	1958	Madan Mohan	Rajinder Krishan	Lata	48
Zamaane Ka Dastoor Hain	Laajwab	1951	Anil Biswas	Prem Dhawan	Lata, Mukesh	29, 169
Zara Haule Haule Chalo	Saawan Ki Ghata	1966	O.P. Nayyar	Majrooh	Asha	164

251

Song	Film	Year	Composer	Lyricist	Singer	Page No.
Zara Si Aahat Hoti Hain	Haqeeqat	1964	Madan Mohan	Kaifi Azmi	Lata	49
Zehar Detaa Hain Mujhe Koi	Wohi Baat	1977	Jaidev	Naqsh Lyallpuri	Asha	166
Zid Naa Karo Ab Toh Ruko	Lahu Ke Do Rang	1979	Bappi Lahiri	Farooq Kaiser	Yesudas and Lata (solos)	79
Zinda Hoon Is Tarah Ke	Aag	1948	Ram Ganguly	Behzad Lucknawi	Mukesh	170
Zindagi Aaj Mere Naam Se	Son Of India	1962	Naushad	Shakeel	Rafi	33, 184
Zindagi Bhar Nahin Bhoolegi	Barsaat Ki Raat	1960	Roshan	Sahir	Rafi and Lata (solos)	10, 58, 114, 182
Zindagi Denewaale Sun	Dil-e-Naadaan	1953	Ghulam Mohammed	Shakeel	Talat	177
Zindagi Ek Safar Hain Suhana	Andaaz	1971	Shanker-Jaikishan	Hasrat Jaipuri	Kishore	42
Zindagi Har Kadam	Meri Jung	1985	Laxmikant-Pyarelal	Anand Bakshi	Lata, Nitin Mukesh, Shabbir Kumar	127
Zindagi Jab Bhi Teri Bazm Mein	Umrao Jaan	1981	Khayyam	Shahryar	Talat Aziz	76
Zindagi Ka Ajab Fasaana Hain	Chhoti Chhoti Baatein	1965	Anil Biswas	Shailendra	Lata, Mukesh	29, 174
Zindagi Kaisi Hain	Anand	1970	Salil Choudhury	Yogesh	Manna Dey	57
Zindagi Ka Safar	Safar	1970	Kalyanji-Anandji	Indeewar	Kishore	65, 191
Zindagi Ke Safar Mein Guzar Jaate Hain	Aap Ki Kasam	1974	R.D. Burman	Anand Bakshi	Kishore	126, 192
Zindagi Khwaab Hain	Jaagte Raho	1956	Salil Choudhury	Shailendra	Mukesh	56, 171
Zindagi Ki Na Toote Ladi	Kranti	1981	Laxmikant-Pyarelal	Santosh Anand	Lata, Nitin Mukesh	73
Zindagi Ki Yahi Reet Hain	Mr. India	1987	Laxmikant-Pyarelal	Javed Akhtar	Kishore	95
Zindagi Maut Na Ban Jaaye	Sarfarosh	1999	Jatin-Lalit	Israar Ansari	Roopkumar Rathod, Sonu Nigam	84, 198
Zindagi Mein Jab Tumhaare	Dooriyan	1979	Jaidev	Sudarshan Fakir	Anuradha Paudwal, Bhupinder	196
Zindagi Mere Ghar Aana	Dooriyan	1979	Jaidev	Sudarshan Fakir	Anuradha Paudwal, Bhupinder	61, 196

General Index

Aadmi (1968), 30, 33, 112, 178
Aag (1948), 38, 92, 170
Aakhri Khat (1966), 75–76
Aan Milo Sajna (1970), 125
Aanchal (1960), 37
Aandhi (1975), 14, 69, 122–23, 192
Aandhiyan, 87, 88
Aap Ke Deewane (1980), 80–81
Aap Ki Kasam (1974), 126, 192
Aar Paar (1954), 51, 108, 150, 159, 180
Aarti (1962), 58, 108, 182
Aarzoo (1950), 28, 108, 183
Aasha (1957), 37
Aasha (1980), 72
Aashiana (1952), 48, 176
Aashiqui (1990), 16, 17, 83, 128, 195, 196
Aasmaan (1952), 51, 159
Aavishkar (1974), 123
Aaye Din Bahaar Ke (1966), 71
Abdullah (1980), 186, 192
Abhijeet, 84
Abhimaan (1973), 16, 46–47, 83, 109, 185, 196
Abhogi Kaanada Raag, 79
Achhut Kanya (1936), 2
Adalat (1958), 9, 48, 154
Afsar, 86, 87
Agha, Salma, 60
Ahir Bhairav Raag, 45, 48, 76
Akhiyon Ke Jharokhon Se (1978), 77
Akhtar, Begum, 48
Akhtar, Javed, 18, 82, 100, 110, 121, 127–29, 134, 193

Akhtar, Jan Nisar, 128
Alam Ara (1931), 2
Albela (1951), 9, 35, 37, 36, 37, 93
All India Radio (AIR), 51, 133
Amar (1954), 32, 111
Amar Akbar Anthony (1977), 72, 126, 186
Amar Jyoti (1936), 2, 3
Amar Prem (1971), 13, 43, 68, 126, 156, 185, 191
Ameerbai Karnataki, 4, 5, 7, 26, 27, 30, 103, 105, 148, 149
Amit Kumar, 14, 66
Amritmanthan (1934), 2, 3
Anand (1970), 56, 57
Anand–Milind, 16, 17, 71, 74, 78, 82–83, 95, 110
Anand, Chetan, 49, 75, 87, 119
Anand, Dev, 10, 21, 39, 44–46, 61, 67, 86–88, 95, 165, 176, 177, 181, 187–89
Anari (1959), 41, 116, 173
Anarkali (1953), 8, 33, 35–36, 38, 51, 93, 111–12, 153, 161
Andaaz (1949), 7, 31–32, 38, 42, 108, 149, 170
Angoor (1981), 69, 124, 167–68
Anhonee (1952), 58, 176
Anita (1967), 71, 173
Anjaan, 79
Anmol Ghadi (1946), 5, 30, 144, 145–46, 149, 169
Anokha Pyar (1948), 28, 169
Anokhi Ada (1948), 169, 170

General Index

Anokhi Raat (1967), 58, 174, 182
Anubhav (1971), 123, 162
Anupama (1966), 59, 119
Anuradha (1960), 154
Anurodh (1976), 72, 192
Apte, Shanta, 3
Aradhana (1969), 13, 46, 174, 185, 188, 190
Armaan (1981), 79
Arth (1982), 15, 120, 128
Asif, K., 111
Atma, C.H., 142, 160
Awara (1951), 10, 38–39, 116, 176
Awasthi, Sapna, 82
Aziz, Mohammed, 74
Aziz, Talat, 16, 76, 81
Azmi, Kaifi, 45, 75, 107, 118–20, 129, 133, 160

B.R. Films, 60
Baaton Baaton Mein (1979), 80
Baawre Nain (1950), 58, 102, 170
Baaz (1953), 51, 159
Baazi (1951), 9, 28, 43, 87 113, 159, 188
Baazigar, 84
Babul (1950), 149, 176
Bachchan, Amitabh, 14, 15, 41, 63, 80, 127, 174, 186
Bageshri Raag, 31, 37, 41, 48
Baharein Phir Bhi Ayengi (1966), 54, 164, 184
Baharon Ke Sapne (1967), 67
Bahu Begum (1967), 114, 182
Baiju Bawra (1952), 6, 8, 9, 29, 31–33, 51, 91, 92, 111, 135, 152–53, 179, 180
Bakshi, Anand, 14, 109, 121, 124–27, 133, 134
Balasubramaniam, S.P., 110
Bali, Geeta, 58, 87, 102, 159
Bambai Ka Babu (1960), 172, 181
Bandini (1963), 45, 117, 121, 164
Baran, Timir, 3
Barsaat (1949), 7, 38, 39, 42, 149, 150, 181
Barsaat Ki Raat (1960), 10, 58, 114, 182
Basant Bahar (1956), 8, 33, 40, 91, 116, 181, 202
Bazaar (1982), 15, 76, 157

Bees Saal Baad (1962), 59, 112
Behag Raag, 31, 32, 41, 51, 62, 69
Benedict, Vijay, 79
Beta (1991), 83, 196
Betaab (1983), 69, 126
Bhairavi (1995), 74, 197
Bhairavi Raag, 4, 8, 24, 31, 32, 36, 38, 40, 41, 45, 48, 49, 55, 58, 62, 68, 70, 75, 102, 143, 144, 146, 152, 153, 157, 161, 166
Bhakt Prahlad, 158
Bhakt Surdas (1942), 103, 104, 143
Bharat Bhushan, 176, 180
Bhatkar, Snehal, 102–03
Bhatkhande, Pandit Vishnu Narayan, 2
Bhatt, Mahesh, 81, 84, 120
Bhatt, Vijay, 32, 91, 201–02
Bhattacharya, Basu, 117, 123
Bheegi Raat (1965), 58, 182
Bhimpalasi Raag, 24, 41, 49, 58
Bhole, Keshavrao, 2
Bhonsle, Asha, 9, 13, 35, 37, 39, 44, 45, 51, 52, 54, 60, 61, 68, 69, 70, 75, 76–77, 79, 81, 107, 109, 124, 126, 139–40, 150, 159, 161, 162–68, 172, 180, 182, 184–85, 188, 192, 196, 204, 210, 212
Bhonsle, Sudesh, 74
Bhoot Bangla (1964), 67, 204
Biddu, 66
big banners and music, 10
Binaca Geetmala, 42
Bismillah Khan, Ustad, 8, 62
Biswas, Anil, 4–5, 7, 8, 9, 21, 23, 26–29, 37, 40, 104–05, 108, 152, 161, 163, 166, 169, 171, 174–76, 202, 209, 213
Bobby (1973), 42, 72, 125, 156
Bombay (1993), 96, 197
Bombay Talkies, 2, 4
Bombay To Goa (1972), 68, 192
Boral, R.C., 3, 4, 22, 24, 93, 101, 143
Border (1997), 18, 129, 198
Bose, Debaki, 101
Brahmachari (184), 41, 184
Buddha Mil Gaya (1971), 68, 109
Bunty Aur Babli (2005), 85, 124, 135
Burman, R.D., 13, 14, 17, 21, 37–38, 43, 46, 50, 57, 63, 66–70, 71,

General Index 255

78–81, 84, 87, 94–95, 109, 123, 126, 155–56, 165–68, 184–85, 189, 191–93, 195, 204
Burman, S.D., 7–9, 16, 42–47, 50, 53, 61, 66, 83, 86–88, 91, 93, 108–09, 113–14, 117–18, 121, 134, 139, 155–56, 158–61, 163–65, 172, 176–77, 180–82, 188–91, 196, 201–02, 204
Buzdil (1951), 43–44

Caravan (1971), 67
Chacha Zindabad (1959), 48
Chalti Ka Naam Gaadi (1958), 48, 188
Chandan Ka Palna (1967), 67
Chandidas (1934), 3
Charukeshi Raag, 49, 64
Chaudhvin Ka Chand (1960), 60, 112
Chauhan, Sunidhi, 212–13
Chemmeen (1965), 57
Chhalia (1960), 64, 173
Chhaya (1961), 55, 57, 177
Chhoti Chhoti Baatein (1965), 29, 117, 174
Chhoti Si Baat (1975), 14, 56, 174
China Town (1962), 183
Chinai, Alisha, 85
Chirag (1969), 109, 183
Chitchor (1976), 14, 77
Chitragupt, 82
Chitralekha (1941), 101
Chitralekha (1964), 58, 102, 114
Chopra, B.R., 51, 115
Chopra, Yash, 76, 95, 115, 127
Chori Chori (1956), 40, 203
Choudhury, Salil, 35, 54-57, 117, 122, 153, 171, 174, 177, 187
Chupke Chupke (1975), 47
CID (1956), 51, 108, 150, 180
Criminal (1995), 85

Daag (1952), 39, 116, 176, 181
Daag (1973), 72, 192
Daddy (1990), 81
Darbar, Ismail, 85
Darbari Raag, 32–33, 41, 111
Dard (1947), 5, 6, 110–11, 146, 149
Dastaan (1950), 6, 92, 147, 179
Dastak (1970), 50, 109
Dattaram, 172
Deedar (1951), 31–32, 150, 176, 179

Deepak Raag, 26, 143
Deewana (1992), 83, 128, 195
Dekh Kabira Roya (1957), 9, 48, 163, 177, 203
Des Pardes (1978), 80
Des Raag, 4, 142, 148, 164, 216
Desai, Vasant, 8, 40, 62, 153
Devdas (1935), 3, 24, 100, 101, 142
Devdas (1955), 44, 51, 160, 176
Devdas (2004), 85, 197
Dey, K.C., 3, 24, 201, 202
Dey, Manna, 10, 13, 29, 33, 37, 40, 45–46, 48, 56, 58, 64–65, 67–68, 73, 116, 123, 160, 166, 179, 181–82, 186, 200–05, 211
Dhadkan (2001), 84, 196
Dhoop Chaon (1935), 2, 4
Didi (1959) 71, 114
Dil (1991), 16, 83, 128, 196
Dil Chahta Hai (2001), 18, 85, 199
Dil Deke Dekho (1959), 108, 183
Dil Diya Dard Liya (1966), 33, 112
Dil Ek Mandir (1963), 41, 117, 183
Dil Hain Ki Maanta Nahin (1991), 16, 17, 83, 195, 196
Dil Hi To Hain (1963), 58, 202
Dil Se (1998), 18, 82, 124 158
Dilip Kumar, 33, 39, 51, 56, 75, 91, 104, 128, 146, 153, 159, 170–72, 176–77, 179, 183–84, 211–12
Dillagi (1949), 5, 147
Dilli Ka Thug (1958), 60, 108
Dilwale Dulhaniya Le Jaayenge (1995), 17, 84, 127
Disco Dancer (1982), 15, 79
Do Ankhen Barah Haath (1957), 62
Do Badan (1966), 60, 112, 165
Do Bhai (1947), 6, 158–59, 209
Do Bigha Zameen (1953), 55
Do Raaste (1969), 71, 72, 191
Don (1978), 192
Door Gagan Ki Chaon Mein (1964), 189
Dooriyan (1979), 61, 196
Doosra Aadmi (1977), 80, 192
Dosti (1964), 72, 92, 95 184, 186
Dulaari (1949), 7, 31, 149, 179
Dulha Dulhan (1964), 64, 173
Durrani, G.M., 142
Dutt, Geeta (nee Roy), 6–9, 10, 23, 26, 27–29, 36, 43–45, 48, 51–52,

54, 58, 102, 108, 113, 118, 123, 139, 156, 158–62, 163, 180–81, 209–10
Dutt, Guru, 10, 44–45, 51, 59, 113, 118, 133, 159–162, 180
Dutt, Gyan, 143

Ek Duje Ke Liye (1981), 72, 126
Evening In Paris (1967), An, 184

Fazli, Nida, 134
folk music, 4–5, 23, 30, 32, 55, 93
Footpath (1953), 75, 176
Funtoosh (1956), 87, 188

Gaara Raag, 26, 33
Gaman (1979), 61
Gambler (1971), 46, 185, 191
Gandharva, Bal, 2
Ganga Jumna (1961), 33
Ganguly, Ram, 38, 92
Gentleman (1993), 81, 84
Ghai, Subhash, 70, 71, 95, 96, 127
Ghalib, Mirza, 23, 142
Ghar (1978), 14, 69, 123, 192
Gharonda (1977), 61, 123
Ghazal (1964), 49, 182
ghazal, 10–11, 21, 36, 37, 49, 50, 58, 73
Ghoshal, Shreya, 85, 89
Ghulam Mohammed, 8, 91, 147, 148, 177
Golmaal (1979), 124, 192
Goonj Uthi Shehnai (1959), 8, 62, 183
Gramophone Singer (1938), 28
Grihapravesh (1979), 123
Guddi (1971), 62
Guide (1965), 8, 16, 45–46, 64, 83, 87, 117, 155, 181, 189
Gulzar, 14, 16, 50, 59, 69, 70, 82, 100, 113, 121–24, 154, 167–68; on the poets of Hindi film music, 130ff
Gumrah (1963), 60, 115

Haider, Ghulam, 4, 5, 6, 21, 30, 104, 144, 145, 149, 213
Hameer Raag, 33, 49
Hanste Zakhm (1973), 49, 119, 183
Haqeeqat (1964), 49, 119, 129, 182
Hare Rama Hare Krishna (1971), 67–68, 88, 126, 165

Hariharan, 82, 127
Hariyali Aur Raasta (1962), 41, 173
Hasrat Jaipuri, 38, 116, 125
Heer Ranjha (1970), 49–50, 119, 183
Heera Panna (1973), 69, 88
Hema Malini, 14, 156
Hemant Raag, 26, 44
Hemlata, 77, 157
Hero (1982), 126, 196
Himalay Ki Godh Mein (1965), 64, 173
Himmatwala (1981), 15, 79
Hindustan Ki Kasam, 203
Hindustani classical music, 7–9, 21, 31, 34
HMV (His Master's Voice), 16, 17, 35, 77, 175
Howrah Bridge (1958), 9, 52, 164
Hu Tu Tu (1999), 124, 135
Hum (1991), 17, 74, 127
Hum Dil De Chuke Sanam (1999), 85, 194, 197
Hum Dono (1961), 45, 60–61, 88, 91, 115, 154–55, 166
Hum Kisi Se Kum Nahin (1977), 13, 14, 69, 94, 109, 166, 186, 192
Humsaaya (1968), 54, 164
Husnlal–Bhagatram, 5, 147
Hussain, Sajjad, 5, 49, 91, 93, 145, 148, 161 176

Ijaazat (1987), 69, 70, 124, 167–68
Ila Arun, 74, 199
Indeewar, 65, 79, 127
Indian Peoples' Theatre Association (IPTA), 55, 131–32, 133
Indrasabha (1932), 2
Inteqam (1969), 71, 156
Irani, Ardheshir, 2

Jaagriti (1954), 105
Jaagte Raho (1956), 56, 171
Jaal (1952), 113, 133, 159
Jaanwar (1965), 41, 184
Jab Jab Phool Khile (1965), 64, 125
Jahan Ara (1964), 49, 178, 182, 198
Jaidev, 45, 60–61, 87–88, 91, 115, 154–55, 166, 196
Jaijaiwanti Raag, 40, 48, 152, 203
Jain, Ravindra, 15, 63, 77, 157 185
Jal Bin Machli Nritya Bin Bijli (1971), 72

General Index

Jashn of Kashmir, 1
Jatin–Lalit, 17, 78, 84, 95, 110, 127, 168
Jatra in Bengali theatre, 1
Jaunpuri Raag, 24, 36, 47, 48, 142
Jawani Diwani (1972), 68, 166, 192
Jewel Thief (1967), 46, 109, 189
Jhanak Jhanak Payal Baje (1955), 8, 40, 62, 153
Jhumroo (1961), 189
Jis Desh Mein Ganga Behti Hai (1961), 116, 172–73
Jo Jeeta Wohi Sikandar (1992), 84, 107, 110
Jogiya Raag, 62, 67
Johny Mera Naam (1970), 65
Joshi, Bhimsen, 40 152, 203
Jugnu (1947), 6, 146
Julie (1975), 80, 192
Junglee (1963), 41, 183

Kaabuliwala (1961), 57, 122
Kaagaz Ke Phool (1959), 10, 45, 118, 133, 160
Kaajal (1965), 60, 165
Kaala Bazaar (1960), 87, 181
Kaala Paani (1958), 87, 164, 181, 188
Kaamchor (1982), 81
Kabhi Kabhie (1975), 76, 115, 174–75
Kabhi Khushi Kabhi Gham (2002), 18, 84
Kaho Naa Pyaar Hain (1999), 18, 80, 81, 199
Kal Ho Na Ho (2003), 18, 85, 129, 198, 199
Kalpana (1960), 48, 205
Kalyan Raag, 24, 69
Kalyanji–Anandji, 14, 15, 42, 63–66, 71, 80, 91, 94, 173, 191, 192, 204
Kalyanpur, Suman, 75, 102
Kanan Devi, 3, 209
Kapoor, Mahendra, 37, 60, 64, 178
Kapoor, Meena, 27, 28, 29, 117
Kapoor, Raj, 7, 10, 15, 38, 39, 41, 55, 64, 71, 75, 77, 92, 95, 96, 102, 115–16, 118, 132, 149, 157, 170–75, 179, 181, 203
Kapoor, Rishi, 14, 186

Kapoor, Shammi, 33, 41, 42, 52, 108, 177, 183–84
Kardar, A.R., 107, 110
Kareem, M.M., 85
Karz (1980), 72, 73, 126, 186
Kashmir Ki Kali (1963), 54, 183
Kathakali of Kerala, 1
Kati Patang (1970), 13, 69, 94, 126, 165, 174, 185, 190
Kaur, Jagjit, 75–76
Kedar Raag, 31, 33, 48, 62, 75, 112
Khalnayak (1993), 17, 74, 127
Khamaj Raag, 45, 68
Khamoshi (1969), 190
Khamoshi (1996), 59, 107, 122, 198
Khan, Ali Akbar, 87–88
Khan, Bade Ghulam Ali, 37, 80, 153
Khan, Ustad Amir, 32, 153
Khan, Wazir Mohammed, 2
Khandaan (1942), 4, 104, 144–45, 208
Khanna, Rajesh, 13, 14, 72, 94, 174, 185, 190–91
Khanna, Usha, 139, 174, 183, 185
Khayyam, 15, 63, 75–76, 93, 115, 118, 157, 167, 176
Khazanchi (1941), 4, 148, 209
Khel Khel Mein (1975), 69, 166, 186, 192
Khubsoorat (1980), 69, 167
Khosla, Raj, 49, 125
Khursheed Anwar, 103, 104, 147, 209
Kinara (1977), 14, 69, 123
Kismet (1943), 4, 27, 105
Kohinoor (1960), 32, 33
Kohraa (1963), 59
Kora Kagaz (1974), 65–66
Krishnamurthy, Kavita, 70, 84, 110, 168, 196–98
Kudrat (1981), 70, 110, 167,193
Kumar, Aroon, 4, 161
Kumar, Ashok, 2, 62, 105, 188
Kumar, Gulshan, 17, 83, 157, 196–97
Kumar, Hemant, 10, 13, 58–60, 64, 105, 112, 113, 119, 161, 181, 190
Kumar, Kishore, 9, 13–14, 16, 25, 37, 41, 42, 44, 46, 53, 56–57, 59–60, 65–70, 72–73, 79–80, 83, 87, 94–95, 108–10, 113, 123–26, 128,

139, 142, 165–67, 176, 179, 181, 185, 187–93, 194, 202, 204–05, 208, 212
Kumar, Manoj, 64, 71, 95, 96, 178

Laawaris (1982), 66, 199
Ladki (1953), 161
Lagaan (2001), 18, 82, 199
Lahiri, Bappi, 15, 63, 70, 77, 78–79, 157, 167, 192, 193
Laila Majnu (1976), 49, 177, 186
Laila, Runa, 61, 123, 156
Lajwanti (1959), 164
Lal Paththar (1971), 166 185, 203
Lavani, 2, 8
Laxmikant–Pyarelal, 14, 15, 17, 22, 28, 42, 57, 63, 70, 71, 80, 84, 89–96, 109, 124, 156, 173, 175, 184–86, 190, 192, 196–97, 204
Leader (1964), 33, 112
Lekin (1990), 16, 124, 157
Love Story (1980), 14, 69, 126

Maachis (1996), 124
Maand Raag, 32, 49
Madan Mohan, 8–10, 21, 36, 43, 47–50, 57–58, 60, 91, 93, 109, 119, 122, 139, 150, 152, 154–55, 163, 173, 175–78, 182–83, 186, 193, 198, 203
Madhok, D.N., 30, 101, 103–04, 130–32
Madhubala, 32, 36, 102, 104, 147
Madhumati (1958), 56–57, 117, 171, 177
Mahal (1950), 8, 25, 26, 152, 159
Main Tulsi Tere Aangan Ki (1978), 72, 125
Maine Pyar Kiya, (1989), 16, 79, 168
Majboor (1948), 4, 6
Majboor (1974), 72, 125
Majrooh Sultanpuri, 7, 10, 50, 99, 104, 107–11, 125, 130, 132
Malik, Annu, 17, 81, 84, 90, 95
Malik, Sardar, 84, 172
Malkauns Raag, 8, 32
Mamta (1966), 58, 109, 155
Mangeshkar, Hridaynath, 16, 90, 128, 154, 157, 193
Mangeshkar, Lata, 4, 6–10, 13–16, 23, 25–26, 28–29, 31–33, 35–37, 38–50, 53–56, 58–62, 64–77, 79–80, 82, 84, 88, 90, 95, 102, 104, 109, 111–15, 119, 122–26, 139, 140–41, 144–45, 148–61, 163–64, 166–70, 179, 183, 185, 195–199, 202–04; on other playback singers, 206–13
Marathi Bhavgeet, 1, 2, 5, 8, 36
Marwa Raag, 32
Mashaal (1950), 201
Mashaal (1984), 128, 193
Masoom (1982), 15, 70, 124, 135
Mausam (1975), 47, 50, 122
Mawaali (1982), 15, 79, 127
Megh Malhar Raag, 26, 143
Mehbooba (1976), 94, 192
Mehdi Hassan, 175
Mehmood, Talat, 9–10, 13, 21, 23, 26, 28–29, 37, 39, 44, 47–49, 52, 55–58, 60, 61, 75, 108, 113, 116, 142, 149, 171, 175–78, 179, 182, 185, 187, 202, 211–12
Mela (1948), 31, 149, 170, 179
Mera Naam Joker (1971), 42, 65, 173, 203
Mera Saaya (1966), 49 155, 183
Mere Apne (1971), 57, 122
Mere Humdum Mere Dost (1968), 72, 109
Mere Jeevan Saathi (1972), 13, 68, 166
Mere Mehboob (1963), 33, 34, 112, 183
Mere Sanam (1964), 13, 64, 164
Meri Soorat Teri Ankhen (1963), 45, 117, 182, 204
Mirza Ghalib (1954), 9, 147, 176
Mohra (1994), 127, 197
Mr. & Mrs. 55 (1955), 51, 139, 160, 180
Mr. India (1987), 95, 128, 197
Mr. Natwarlal (1979), 80
Mr. X in Bombay (1964), 72, 84, 95, 125
Mughal-e-Azam (1960), 6, 26, 29, 33, 91, 111–12, 150, 154
Mukesh, 5, 7, 10, 23, 28–29, 31, 41–42, 56–58, 63–65, 75–76, 102, 114, 116, 122, 125–26, 139, 142, 168–75, 181, 185, 202–03, 208, 210–12
Mullick, Pankaj, 3, 9, 21, 23–25, 93, 143–44

Munimji (1955), 44, 113, 188
Muqaddar Ka Sikander (1979), 65, 192
My Sister (1944), 24, 25, 144

Nadeem-Shravan, 16, 17, 71, 74, 78, 83-84, 95, 127, 168, 195-97
Nagin (1954), 59, 64
Namak Halal (1982), 15, 79
Namak Haram (1973), 13, 69, 126, 192
Nand Raag, 49, 67
Narayan, Udit, 16, 83, 110, 194-95, 199, 212
Nargis, 39, 107, 147, 159
Nau Do Gyarah (1957), 108, 163 188
Naunihal (1967), 49, 120, 183
Naushad, 4-10, 21, 23-24, 26, 27, 29-36, 38-40, 43, 49, 52, 59, 62, 70-71, 78, 90, 91-92, 103, 110-12, 116, 125, 139, 143-47, 149-50, 152, 158, 169-70, 175-76, 179-81, 184-85
Navketan Films, 21, 43, 45, 44-45, 61, 86-88, 154, 181, 188
Naya Daur (1957), 51, 52, 114, 163, 180
Nayyar, O.P., 7, 9, 24, 27, 35, 37, 44, 47-48, 50-54, 69, 108, 128, 150, 159-61, 163-66, 177, 180, 183, 193, 205
New Theatres, 2-3, 24, 101, 142-43, 175
Nigam, Sonu, 84, 85, 89, 139, 186, 194, 198, 212
1942-A Love Story, 17, 18, 70, 95, 127-28, 168, 193, 195, 197
Noorjehan, 4-6, 30, 104, 140-41, 144-46, 149, 152, 208

Padosan (1968), 67, 94, 155, 156, 189
Pahadi Raag, 30-31, 75, 77, 179
Pakeezah, 91
Pandit, Sulakshana, 66, 76
Papa Kehte Hain (1996), 81, 198
Pardesi (1957), 29, 103
Parichay (1972), 14, 68, 69, 123, 192
Parveen Sultana, Begum, 70, 110
Patita (1953), 39, 116, 176, 181

Paudwal, Anuradha, 17, 61, 66, 83, 110, 126, 158, 168, 196-97
Paying Guest (1957), 44, 108, 163, 188, 191
Pehli Nazar (1945), 5, 28, 169
Phagun, 52, 164
Phir Subah Hogi (1958), 75, 113, 172
Pilu Raag, 52, 143
Piya Ka Ghar (1972), 72, 125, 192
pop and jazz, 13, 21, 37, 73
Prabhat Film Company, 2, 3
Pradeep, 101, 104-07, 131, 201
Prakash, Khemchand, 5, 23, 25-26, 29-30, 50, 103, 143, 149, 152, 187, 201, 213
Pran Jaaye Par Vachan a Jaaye (1973), 54, 164
Prem Nagar (1940), 5, 30, 103
Prem Nagar (1974), 47
Prem Pujari, 88
Pukar (2001), 197-98
Punjabi folk, 5, 7, 51
Purab Aur Pashchim (1970), 65, 173
Pyaara Dushman (1980), 79
Pyaasa (1957), 10, 44-45, 113, 160, 180-81, 204

Qayamat Se Qayamat Tak (1988), 16, 82, 110, 194, 199
Qurbani (1980), 66

Raageshri Raag, 48, 56
Raagini (1958), 53, 163
Rabindra Sangeet, 1, 3, 5, 21, 23-25, 55, 59, 86, 94
Rafi, Mohammed, 5-8, 10, 13-14, 23, 31-34, 37, 40-41, 44-46, 49-52, 56-58, 60-61, 64, 68, 72, 75, 80, 87, 105, 108-09, 111, 114, 118-19, 125-26, 139, 142, 147, 150, 152, 163, 165-66, 171-74, 176, 178-86, 188-91, 198, 202-05, 211-12
Raja Hindustani (1996), 83, 194, 199
Raj Hath (1956), 40, 181
Rajkumari, 7, 26, 102
Rajnigandha (1974), 56-57, 174
Ram Lakhan (1989), 15, 70, 72, 74, 127, 196
Ram Teri Ganga Maili (1985), 15, 77, 157

Ramchandra, C., 7–9, 33, 35–38, 40, 54, 56, 71, 90–91, 93, 150, 153, 155, 161
Rangeela (1995), 81, 168
Rani, Bulo C, 104
Ranjit Movietone, 101, 143
Rathod, Roopkumar, 84, 198
Ratnadeep (1979), 167
Ratnam, Mani, 18, 81, 82
Rattan (1944), 5, 30, 91, 103
Ravi, 60, 112, 115, 165, 183, 185, 204
Razia Sultan (1983), 15, 76
Refugee (2000), 129, 198
Rahman, A.R., 18, 78, 81–82, 95–96, 127, 139, 158, 168, 199
Rehman, Waheeda, 118, 161
Rekha, 14, 156–67
Renuka Devi, 105
Reshammiya, Himesh, 85
RK Films, 77, 93, 157, 170
Roja (1993), 18, 81, 96
Roshan, 8, 10, 58, 80, 93, 102, 114, 182, 202
Roshan, Rajesh, 78, 80–81, 88, 157, 192, 198
Roy, Bimal, 44, 55, 117, 177
Rustom Sohrab (1961), 91, 148

Saagar (1985), 15, 70, 128, 193
Saajan (1991), 18, 83, 128, 195, 199
Saath Saath (1982), 15, 128
Safar (1970), 65, 191
Sahib, Bibi Aur Ghulam (1963), 59, 112, 161
Sahir Ludhianvi, 6, 9–10, 21, 28, 52, 75–76, 99, 102, 104, 107, 111–15, 118–19, 125, 130, 132–33, 180
Saigal, Kundan Lal, 3–5, 10, 23–26, 29–31, 100–01, 104, 107, 131, 139–45, 147, 168–69, 175, 178, 186–87, 207–08
Sambandh (1969), 54, 106
Sameer, 17, 110, 128
Sanam Teri Kasam (1983), 70
Sangam (1964), 41, 92, 117, 173, 183
Sangdil (1953), 49, 161, 176
Sant Gyaneshwar (1964), 71, 173
Sanu, Kumar, 16–17, 70, 79, 83–84, 193, 195–96, 198

Saranga (1960), 84, 172
Saraswati Devi, 2, 139
Saraswatichandra (1968), 65, 173
Sargam (1950), 36, 38
Sargam (1979), 72, 126, 186
Sargam, Sadhna, 66, 84, 110
Sati Savitri (1964), 71 204
Satyam Shivam Sudaram (1978), 72, 175
Savera (1958), 161
Seema (1955), 39–40, 152, 204
Shahjehan (1946), 5–6, 30–31, 107, 143, 144, 149, 207
Shahryar, 134
Shailendra, 7, 10, 42, 99, 107, 111, 115–18, 121, 125, 130, 132, 134
Shakeel Badayuni, 10, 32, 91, 104, 107, 110–12, 125, 132
Shamshad Begum, 4–5, 7–8, 27, 31, 54, 140–41, 148–50, 158, 209
Shankar Hussain (1977), 76
Shankar, Pandit Ravi, 154
Shankarabharanam (1980), 74
Shankar-Ehsaan-Loy, 85, 96, 139
Shanker–Jaikishan, 7–8, 27, 33, 38–42, 46–47, 52, 56, 58, 63–65, 71–72, 92–93, 116–17, 125, 149, 153, 166, 170, 173, 176, 180–81, 183, 202–03
Shantaram, V., 3, 62
Sharaabi (1984), 15, 79, 182, 192
Sharda (1942), 103, 146
Sharma, Kidar, 100–03, 130–31
Sharmilee (1971), 43, 46, 185, 191
Shehnai (1947), 7, 37, 93
Shiv-Hari, 14
Shola Aur Shabnam (1961), 75, 119
Sholay (1975), 14, 126, 205
Shreshta, Sushma, 83
Shri 420 (1955), 10, 39, 116, 170, 203
Shyam Sunder, 5, 147, 149, 152, 179, 213
Silsila (1981) 14, 127–28
Singh, Bhupinder, 50, 61, 68–69, 79, 123, 196
Singh, Chitra, 15–16, 128
Singh, Jagjit, 15–16, 84, 120, 128, 175
Singh, Kuldeep, 15
Singh, Shailendra, 125

Singh, Sukhwinder, 82
Sone Ki Chidiya (1958), 52, 163, 177
Street Singer (1938), 3, 4, 143
Sujata (1959), 45, 108, 160, 164, 177, 204
Sunny (1984), 15, 69, 167
Sur Sangam (1985), 74
Suraiya, 6–7, 9, 29, 86, 103–04, 140–41, 146–49, 171, 179, 209
Suraj (1966), 46, 64, 183
Surendra, 28, 30, 142, 145, 169
Swades (2004), 82, 194, 199
Swami (1977), 80, 157

Taal (1999), 18, 82, 127
Tagore, Rabindranath 25, 204
Taj Mahal (1963), 8, 58, 114, 182
Talash (1969), 46, 189, 204
Tansen (1943), 26, 32, 103, 143, 207
Tarana (1951), 29, 104, 176
Taxi Driver (1954), 47, 113, 176
Teesri Kasam (1966), 42, 117, 173
Teesri Manzil (1966), 66–67, 69, 109 156, 165, 184
Tembe, Govindrao, 2
Tere Ghar Ke Saamne, 87–88
Tezaab (1988), 15, 74, 128, 199
thumri, 35–36, 80
Tilang Raag, 52, 163
Todi Raag, 32, 40, 62, 68
Tridev (1989), 15, 66
Tripathi, S.N., 174
T-Series, 17, 83, 158, 196, 197
Tumsa Nahin Dekha (1957), 52, 108, 183
Tumse Achcha Kaun Hain (1967), 41, 184

Udhas, Manhar, 66, 126
Udhas, Pankaj, 16
Uma Devi (Tuntun), 8
Umrao Jaan (1981), 15, 76, 167

Upkar (1967), 64, 204
Uthup, Usha, 79
Utsav (1982), 73

Vani Jairam, 62, 154, 156
Vidhaata (1982), 15, 66
Vidyapati (1937), 3, 101
Vividh Bharati, 134
Vyas, Shankar Rao, 201
Vyjayanthimala, 51, 56, 163

Wadkar, Suresh, 61, 73, 77, 83
Wahidan Bai, 28
Waqt (1964), 13, 60, 115, 165, 204
Western influence on Hindi film music, 9, 81
Woh Kaun Thi (1964), 49, 155

Yaadein (2001), 127
Yaadon Ki Baaraat (1973), 13, 14, 68–69, 166, 192
Yaara Dildara (1991), 110
Yagnik, Alka, 16, 66, 74, 79, 83–85, 168, 194–96, 198–99, 212
Yahudi (1958), 172
Yahudi Ki Ladki (1933), 23, 142
Yaman Raag, 33, 39, 58, 65, 112, 147, 166, 172
Yaraana (1981), 80
Yeh Raaste Hain Pyaar Ke (1963), 165
Yeh Raat Phir Na Aayegi (1965), 164
Yes Boss (1997), 18
Yesudas, 61, 77, 79, 80

Zakhmee (1975), 79
Zamane Ko Dikhana Hain (1981), 109
Zanzeer (1973), 14, 65
Ziddi (1948), 25, 152, 187
Zohrabai Ambalewali, 5, 7, 26, 28, 30–31, 103, 148, 149, 209
Zubeida (2000), 199